HOLLAND

Antwerp

BELGIUM

BRUSSELS

Liége

Cologne

unkirk

Calais

Boulogne   Lille

Abbeville

Amiens   Chaulnes

Somme   Péronne   Oise

reste

Roye   MASSIF OF
ST. GOBAIN

Compiègne   Coucy   Sedan   Montmédy   LUXEMBOURG

Beauvais   Aisne   Rethel   Longuyon

Soissons   Reims

Marne   Verdun   Metz   Bitche   Haguenau

Vincennes   Châlons   Nancy   Strasbourg

Ver-   PARIS

sailles   Vitry le   Séléstat

Melun   François

Seine   Troyes   Attigny

Orleans   Mulhouse
Belfort   Basle

Loire   Briare   Dijon   Neuchâtel
BERNE

La Charité
sur Loire   SWITZERLAND

Nevers

FRANCE

Cher   Geneva

Vichy   Lyons

PLATEAU   St.Etienne   ITALY

CENTRAL   Rhône

Nice

oulouse   Marseilles

120   160 MLS.

ARDENNES

Rhine

Moselle

ARGONNE HILLS

Meuse

Saar

ALSACE

BLACK
FOREST

GERMANY

ASSIGNMENT TO CATASTROPHE

Volume II

THE FALL OF FRANCE

June 1940

Dunkirk

ASSIGNMENT TO CATASTROPHE

Volume II

THE FALL OF FRANCE

June 1940

by

MAJOR-GENERAL

SIR EDWARD SPEARS

A. A. WYN, INC., NEW YORK

DEDICATED, BY PERMISSION, TO
THE RT. HON. SIR WINSTON CHURCHILL
K.G., O.M., C.H., D.C.L., M.P.

Contents

PART II

vii

the secretaries' room—Churchill telephones to Reynaud—We withdraw the two telegrams about the Fleet—An agonising wait for the French Cabinet's decision.

Illustrations

Preface

THE first volume of this book concluded with an account of the meeting of the Supreme War Council held in Paris on May 31st, 1940, which I attended as Mr. Churchill's personal representative with the French Prime Minister and Minister of Defence, M. Paul Reynaud.

I had arrived in Paris on May 24th, 1940, and had immediately been plunged into the catastrophic events in the French political and military sphere which preceded the Dunkirk evacuation.

I take up my narrative on the day following the Paris Conference.

THE invasion terrified the population, but France cast down did not have a tremor of revolt. The metaphysical idea of the violated homeland, which had had in '92, whatever may be said, such a powerful action on a nation young, or rejuvenated by liberty, that idea did not arouse a people aged by war, weary of sacrifices, and avid of rest. The brutal and material fact of foreign occupation with its adjunct of evils, requisitions, pillage and assaults, murder and incendiarism were needed to awaken anger and hatred. The invasion at first, far from raising hearts and giving the Emperor the moral force he was entitled to rely on and of which he stood in such dire need, depressed public opinion still further.

From "1814" by HENRY HOUSSAYE.

CHAPTER I

Saturday, June 1st

*Churchill leaves for London—The fighter escort pilots—
Reynaud gives me Weygand's note demanding increased
British air support—French air losses—Margerie urges the
immediate re-embarkation for France of the British troops
from Dunkirk—Reynaud expects an early German attack
towards Paris—His information about the panzer divisions
—Churchill telephones the news from Dunkirk—A telegram
for Reynaud and Weygand—Reynaud's criticism of Gort—
I complain of Weygand's attitude—My report to Ismay—
A further telegram from Churchill about Dunkirk.*

By 6 a.m. I was on my way to Villacoublay to see Churchill off.
Hundreds of labourers were still working, as they had been since I
arrived in Paris, at widening the road on the far side of the Bois de
Boulogne towards the St. Cloud bridge. There were, I knew,
practically no field fortifications north of Paris, and one of the
difficulties in making minefields south of the Somme was alleged to
be lack of workers. What about these men? Was disorganisation
complete and irremediable?

The Prime Minister, who looked rested and buoyant, referred to
the small enemy air-raids there had been during the night. Did they
occur every night? On most nights, I thought, but not on a scale to
cause inconvenience. They certainly did not keep me awake.

On the aerodrome I saw a picture and received an impression of
beauty unequalled in my life. The nine fighter planes were drawn
up in a wide semicircle round the Prime Minister's Flamingo. Very
slight they seemed on their undercarriages, high and slender as
mosquitoes. Churchill walked towards the machines, grinning,
waving his stick, saying a word or two to each pilot as he went from
one to the other, and, as I watched their faces light up and smile in
answer to his, I thought they looked like the angels of my childhood.

1

As far back as I can remember I have been enthralled by pictures of angels; Michael Angelo's, Giotto's, Botticelli's attempts to depict these divine beings have given me pleasure, though if the truth be told none of these great artists ever evoked the awe and love conjured up by the wide-winged angels of the prints in my nursery, to whom we children lent such serene and protective powers. Here they were, as they had been so long ago, beautiful and smiling. It was wonderful to see. These young men may have been naturally handsome, but that morning they were far more than that, creatures of an essence that was not of our world: their expressions of happy confidence as they got ready to ascend into their element, the sky, left me feeling inspired, awed and earthbound.

On my return to Paris I found a message asking me to call at once on Reynaud. He was nervous and irritable, very unlike his usual self, very different from the man he had been the day before. In the absence of fresh bad news, either his colleagues or Weygand were obviously giving trouble.

It soon became evident that, whatever his colleagues' machinations might be, it was the Commander-in-Chief who was at the root of the difficulty I was asked to deal with. He had sent Reynaud a note stating that the enemy would probably attack shortly on the fronts of the Somme and Meuse, and that if the R.A.F. remained based on England, the French Army would be left to face the weight of the forthcoming attack alone.

It was essential, the note went on, that the maximum number of British fighters and bombers should take part in the forthcoming battle on which hung the fate of Britain as much as that of France. It was therefore necessary that numerous air squadrons, particularly fighters, should have their bases brought over forthwith to France to act in intimate liaison with the French Army against the enemy's front and immediate back areas.

The concluding paragraph was to the effect that the French Army was being destroyed by bombardment and tanks and that this would be the fate of the British Army in its turn if this demand was not complied with.

"Surely," I observed, "that is ground we went over yesterday. The Prime Minister and his advisers must have the opportunity of considering what they can do in the light of yesterday's discussion. They are not even back in England yet.

"In any case," I added, "one thing is clear, and General Weygand must know it as well as anyone else: you cannot suddenly improvise air bases and whisk over ground staffs and all the paraphernalia they need."

But Reynaud was irascible. Weygand must have really upset him.

"Your people," he observed, "do not seem to realise their fate is in the balance, they are acting as if they were merely interested onlookers.

"Now really," I said, "if I were to pass on this conversation to London, they would in the first place feel aggrieved and then think that we here were losing our heads and all sense of reality. They would find it difficult to believe that such a point of view was being put forward today by the same people who were discussing these very points so reasonably yesterday. Nothing whatever has occurred since to justify a change of attitude. It seems to me," I went on, "that Weygand is forgetting that at this very moment our Army as well as yours is fighting its way out of Dunkirk, and that if any get away today it will be thanks to a stupendous effort on the part of the R.A.F., not to mention the Navy. It is not the moment to infer that our Air Force could do more than it is already doing."

I took my leave, rather out of temper, feeling less in sympathy with Reynaud than usual. As I was leaving, he handed me a paper giving the French losses up to June 1st. It ran:

> Total losses: 700 planes made up as follows:
> 300 in air fighting
> 200 destroyed on ground in Army zone
> 200 destroyed by accident.

Hardly had I despatched Weygand's note to London, together with an apology for repeating what had been said over and over again the previous day, when Margerie telephoned asking to see me as soon as possible.

Either Weygand or his staff had been at work on him also. He said he had to ask me as a matter of extreme urgency to arrange that our troops saved from Dunkirk should be sent back to France forthwith, armed only with their rifles, to dig strong positions behind the Somme front.

Would the French provide them with artillery? I asked. No, he said, that would not be possible. "Then," I answered, "I cannot transmit this request. I could have done so had you been prepared to attach adequate artillery to them. There would be some analogy in this to the practice adopted of sending British troops for training without their artillery to the Maginot Line sector, where French guns took the place of British ones, though I really do not believe for a moment it will be possible to re-engage the Dunkirk troops before they have been sorted out, regrouped and taken in hand."

I then left him, but later in the day he reiterated the request, even more strongly. It would have a good effect on morale, he said, that British troops should come straight back to France. This time I was really cross. "You are, in effect, asking us to use our precious troops as navvies," I said. "If you are short of navvies why don't you use the gangs of hale and hearty men I saw this morning working on widening the road to St. Cloud? From all I hear, your depots are full of men. Where are the men from Corap's Army?" And I went on to argue that if the proposal was to employ our men as soldiers, armed only with rifles, to stop the panzer divisions, the idea would be funny if it were not so exasperatingly silly and futile. It was inviting us to have our men massacred. Who, in Heaven's name, would think of giving such an order? The French troops now facing the Germans were perhaps not as well equipped as might be desirable, but they had artillery, anti-tank guns, machine-guns.

Then, more calmly, feeling he was himself essentially intelligent and reasonable, I assured him once more that the only sensible way to act was to regroup our troops in England, then, as soon as may be, send them back to France.

I realised that the French felt it was very important for morale to counteract the impression that the British were leaving France and not returning. It was also possible that there existed, although unavowed, a feeling that the stubborn staunchness it was now generally conceded our troops had displayed on all occasions would tend to steady the new line.

Margerie inferred that Admiral Abrial's reports from Dunkirk were causing great concern, but what they were he did not say.

I had several further meetings with Reynaud in the course of the day.

At the first he told me, for Churchill's immediate information, that he had just received reliable information that the Germans would attack across the Somme between the 3rd and 5th of June in the directions of Amiens–Paris and Reims–Paris.

Also, that at the moment nine German panzer divisions were almost entirely withdrawn from the fighting for overhaul. He said the French Command believed that massive air bombardments on this great mass of armour while it was temporarily immobilised would yield very considerable results. General Georges' headquarters could give precise indications as to where the British aviation should intervene immediately.

Finally he asked me to place before the Prime Minister as a personal request from him an appeal for anti-tank rifles. As many as possible. I wrote in my notes: "Have they then nothing?"*

The message concerning the panzer divisions was extremely interesting. I transmitted it by telephone, and in the course of conversation with Ismay gathered there were great difficulties in dealing with Admiral Abrial and the French commanders at Dunkirk, who, remaining under 30 feet of concrete, were inaccessible and largely unaware of what was going on. In our attempt to give nothing away on the telephone, we sometimes only confused each other. Exasperated, Ismay asked: "Do you speak Urdu?" "No." "A pity, Redman can." "Well, I can't." Out of this incident grew a suggestion that I should have a Welsh speaker who would pass messages in Gael to a fellow-countryman in London. But this would be of little use, I pointed out. The French would tumble to it at once and put on a Breton to listen in, who would understand easily enough.

I also gathered that the situation was working up to a climax at Dunkirk and that the time we could hold on for was now a matter of hours. It was extremely doubtful if it would be possible to carry on beyond that night. Losses to shipping and to the R.A.F. were becoming prohibitive.

Then the Prime Minister called me up. It was simply to give me news. It was none too good. Six transports had been sunk. "The end at Dunkirk is very near," he said. "The decision as to when the harbour is to be blocked and transportation brought to an end must be left to the commanders on the spot." He, like Ismay, referred to the difficulty created by Admiral Abrial's troglodyte habits. The Admiral was no doubt a naturally brave man, but a 30-foot shell of concrete endowed him with the confidence and aggressiveness

---

* A report by General Picquender quoted by Daladier at the Riom Trial stated that, at the Armistice, there were 520 new 20-millimetre anti-tank guns in depots, that is, the armament of 10 divisions at 52 guns per division.

of a rhinoceros, and his vision was as limited. He, at any rate, could not be sunk, whatever happened to the transports outside.

Later came a telegram from the Prime Minister to Reynaud and Weygand. It covered much the same ground as his conversation with me, but contained one or two additional points. Its paraphrase was: "The critical point of the evacuation has now been reached. Five fighter squadrons are practically continuously in action. This is all we can provide. Six ships, several of which were packed with troops, were sunk this morning.

"The only practicable channel is under artillery fire. The enemy's grip is tightening, and the bridgehead is narrowing. By attempting to hold on till tomorrow we may lose everything. If we close down tonight much will certainly be saved, although much may be lost. The situation cannot be assessed as a whole by Admiral Abrial, alone in the depth of his fortress, nor can it be by you, nor by us here. We have therefore ordered General Alexander, commanding the British sector of the bridgehead, to examine with Admiral Abrial the best line to follow. We are relying upon your agreement."

"And, pray, what do you think General Alexander's decision will be?" asked Reynaud when I read him the message. The acidity of his tone made me scrutinise his expression.

He certainly was not himself, pale, almost grey, his face distorted continuously by his *tique*. The friendliness I almost always discerned in the pleats round his eyes had disappeared. "I cannot of course be certain," I said, "but I should not be surprised if General Alexander decided to close the harbour some time during the night."

"I note," said Reynaud icily, "that the decision to have a united command only lasted 24 hours."

"You will remember," I said, "that General Dill pointed out at the conference yesterday that the situation was too difficult to impose a single command. He is being proved right. I have not heard much of what is going on at Dunkirk, but one thing has become clear, and that is that the Admiral seldom emerges from his dug-out." Then, firing a broadside of my own at the recluse Admiral, I concluded: "*C'est l'Amiral Abri*," a poor pun, but it helped to lower the temperature.

The asperities of this difficult interview were, however, not ended. Far worse was to come.

"I have also a most serious complaint against Lord Gort," said Reynaud. "Based on what?" "The report of a French Air Colonel," he answered. "French rights, in spite of Churchill's promise, are being grossly violated, and high-ranking Frenchmen are being insulted. When a French General asked Gort for a permit for himself and his A.D.C. to embark, he was *rudoyé*—man-handled—and told by Gort that two French going meant two less British.

"*Le Général* Gort may perhaps have been a lion in the last war, but in this one he only fights when it suits his force." He spoke in cold anger, but now I was far angrier than he was.

"And who is this General, may I ask? Who is this General Officer clamouring for a passage for himself and his A.D.C.? Was he insisting that room be found for his troops? Not at all. He was demanding a passage for himself. I would not spread that story if I were Weygand, from whom it clearly originates. The picture it evokes in my mind is of an excited little man trying to force his way on board out of turn.

"If he was *rudoyé* that is the explanation. He was probably trying to take the place of a French soldier, or to use his rank to get on board a ship earmarked for British troops. As for the accusation levelled against Gort, it can only be repudiated with contempt. The implication that he was lacking in courage and loyalty is positively funny, especially coming from the quarters which must have made the accusation.

"As a matter of fact, Gort's fault lies entirely the other way," I stormed on. "In my view he has been far too anxious to comply with the orders of a totally inadequate and often non-existing Command. He has been too disciplined, too uncomplaining. He has refrained from reporting on the abysmal collapse of the French Staff and French Generals. His withdrawal has been magnificent."*

* Extract from Diary of Major Miles Reid, M.C., liaison officer to 1st French Army:
"Although the French and Belgians had been allotted a beach further south for their assembly and embarkation . . . every conceivable type of car sought access to the beach. A cordon of Welsh Guards with fixed bayonets blocked the entrance, but still the motors came worming their way round the cordon. Their occupants, mostly French and Belgian officers, were deaf to entreaties or orders to drive (to their own beach). When it was seen that force might have to be used, the cars were deliberately put out of action by their owners. I gave the occupants of one motor instructions to turn round, and the result was the ripping of all the wires from under the dashboard. Every step was taken to interfere with the task of organising the beaches to make full use of the available space and craft. . . . Finally, in desperation we had to call on two Welsh Guardsmen to remove forcibly a French Air Force Colonel, who, obviously the senior, obdurately refused to help us in any way whatever."

My annoyance was spent. What I had said was cruelly true, but Reynaud had no responsibility for our misfortunes. I suddenly saw him as the captain of a sinking ship, the wind of defeat in his hair. Clinging to the rail, he could not cover his ears and be deaf to the high-pitched cackling whine: "It is the fault of the English. . . . Gort ran away . . ."

And I was not only sorry for him, but appreciative of the way he clung on. I was sorry I had been cross, and said so. Then once more I expatiated on the danger of these tales. If they exasperated me, a notorious Francophile, what would their effect be on others in England? I told him that I was certain he really did not believe these stories, but who kept pouring them into his ears?

I felt, I said, that it was Weygand who was trying to escape responsibility by blaming the British, not old Pétain, defeatist though he might be. Then, developing my complaint against the Generalissimo, I said he was proving himself incapable of dealing with the situation; he was constituting no reserves, the depots were obviously not being searched for weapons. I had heard of no attempt to re-equip what was left of Corap's Army. The possibility of holding Brittany was not, as far as I knew, being seriously studied. Weygand's answer to everything was to blame the British.

The whole atmosphere of the conversation had now changed. Reynaud was attentive and more relaxed. Unpleasant though the statements I was making were, he knew they were true. He listened when I said that the only result of Weygand's policy was likely to be that the British would begin to reckon up their grievances against the French and present a terrible bill.

This was exactly what Mr. Churchill wished to avoid. "There must be no recriminations," he had said. But General Weygand had different views. What his purpose was I could not yet discern beyond his obvious desire to cover his own deficiencies.

"He will presently turn on you just as he is baring his teeth at the British today," I said.

Then, returning to Dunkirk, I assured him that I felt certain Churchill completely understood his tragic difficulties. He knew exactly what it meant on moral as well as on military grounds to find so many French troops trapped. Churchill would do everything in the world to help him, and to save all that was possible, but it really was not our fault that the French troops found themselves unfavourably placed from the point of view of the evacuation. They were where they were by the orders of their own commanders.

"Churchill is your friend, and I am your friend. I am only here to help. I should be failing in my duty if I allowed misunderstandings based on lies to develop and fester. If we have the courage to face the facts, and if we are generous and understanding of each other's difficulties, we shall pull through. If we fight each other we certainly shall not."

"I rely on you to remind Churchill of the vital importance of getting every Frenchman out of Dunkirk," said Reynaud as I left. "That I promise," I replied as we shook hands.

I reported the whole conversation in a letter to Ismay as I thought it should be on record. I was happier at the end of the interview than during its course, and felt renewed sympathy for Reynaud, who was bearing a weight of responsibility and sorrow none but he could weigh or assess.

I am quite sure Reynaud never repeated my remarks to Weygand, but he may have mentioned my conclusions without attributing them to me; Weygand certainly knew he had been criticised and had no difficulty in divining where the criticism came from, for from that day he barely concealed his hostility.

Hardly had I got back to the Embassy when a further message from Churchill to Reynaud came through. It was very like the earlier telegram to Reynaud and Weygand. It now seemed possible that the embarkation of the Dunkirk troops could go on throughout the night and might continue for some time the next day (June 2nd). "It is hardly possible that embarkation can be prolonged beyond daylight tomorrow. It is therefore desirable that the operation should come to an end tomorrow.

"Up to date 225,000 men have been embarked. To attempt to prolong the operation beyond tomorrow means running the risk of being unable to embark anyone.

"Nothing like the numbers of effective French troops you mentioned are believed to be in the bridgehead now.

"Six ships have been sunk, several of which were packed with troops.

"Abrial is very anxious to prolong the period of embarkation, but he is perhaps not in a very good position to judge since he is directing operations from the depths of a casemate. The Generals on the spot must be allowed to decide when the embarkations must cease. We may lose all by waiting too long."

"You were too pessimistic," said Reynaud when he read the message. "I am all the more relieved to hear that some hours have been gained," I answered.

CHAPTER II

Sunday, June 2nd

*Darlan on Dunkirk—Meeting of the War Committee—
Renewed appeal for British support—Reynaud's visit to the
front—The Place de la Concorde—General Vuillemin—
Rollin pleads for reinforcements against Italy in Africa—
Pétain's strictures on Weygand—He tells me of Weygand's
attack on Churchill—but supports his demands for British
reinforcements—Pétain on the Battle of the Dunes in 1658—
Weygand's telegram about Dunkirk—Four-fifths of the
B.E.F. safely evacuated.*

DURING the night one of Ismay's officers telephoned concerning the
French appeal that the panzer divisions, now refitting, should be
bombed. Should the Prime Minister be called? I said no, but that
I assumed the Air Ministry and the War Office had been informed.
He seemed astonished that the request had not been made by
General Georges. This led to my sending a message early in the
morning explaining that Weygand was, apparently, taking all
control out of Georges' hands and dealing with everything himself,
and as Weygand was in daily contact with Reynaud, this resulted in
military liaison matters drifting in my direction for lack of other
channels, since Reynaud naturally wanted Churchill informed of
anything Weygand told him.

In the early part of the morning I ran into Darlan at the Ministry
of War. He told me that the latest embarkation figures the French
had received from Dunkirk were 194,000 British and 22,000 French.
His appreciation of the facts was sounder than any I had so far
heard from the French side, for he volunteered the view that there
appeared to have been a fundamental misunderstanding from the
beginning between British and French; the French Command had
believed Dunkirk could be defended, the British had not, and had
therefore laid every stress on the necessity of getting the troops away,

11

whereas the French had made their plans in terms of defending the perimeter.

I told him how glad I was to hear him say this, for we had feared from the outset there would be misunderstanding on this all-important point. This was the reason for our endeavour to ensure that the French and British commanders on the spot received similar orders. We had been successful too late.

As the Admiral walked off I wondered why he had made this obvious criticism of Weygand. I assumed he was anxious to exculpate himself from blame now that it was evident Dunkirk could not have been held and that it might be necessary to close the harbour at any moment. It would then become obvious that if only a comparatively small number of French troops got away the French Admiralty would not be to blame: the responsibility would lie with the French supreme and local military commands for not having moved into the perimeter in time. This was in any case an obvious explanation of why, in spite of Churchill's wishes, the French were forming the rearguard, that is, assuming they were in fact doing so, as Weygand alleged. They were the farthest from the harbour and the beaches.

Before eleven I attended the War Committee.

I saw at once that the Premier was in his normal self-possessed, friendly mood. Although the matters discussed were not pleasant and could easily have led to bitter exchanges, they were dealt with calmly and frankly.

When Weygand snarled and muttered unpleasant asides about the British, Reynaud cut him short with a gesture or a word. I was glad of this, and later wrote to Ismay that, unpleasant though it had been, yesterday's storm had cleared the air.

A telegram from the French Military Attaché in London was produced. It stated that the number of French troops embarked in twenty-four hours amounted to 5,000. Could I explain this?

I could not. The total numbers were of course much higher. Here I looked at Darlan, who made no sign. I hazarded a guess. "The French Military Attaché only knows of Frenchmen landed in England. Is it not at least possible that considerable numbers are being landed direct in France? I imagine," I went on, "that French ships sail direct for French harbours." I added that on the telephone the previous evening the Prime Minister had said the British authorities did not believe there were anything like as many French troops in the perimeter as the French supposed.

I was then told that the Military Attaché's telegram also stated that the ships carrying Dunkirk Frenchmen from England back to France were carrying a similar number of British troops from France to England. "What does this mean?" asked Weygand. I pointed out that his headquarters had been fully informed concerning the lines of communication and other troops we were bringing home.

"But why are you taking troops back to England if you mean to return them to France?" asked Reynaud.

Once again I explained why all these odd elements, these details, must be sorted out and re-allocated to new formations. "It is the only possible thing to do." I pointed out that the French themselves would, in the first instance, send their men from Dunkirk and elsewhere to depots where they would be regrouped. Our depots were in England. We could not improvise new ones in France overnight. Far from losing time, we were gaining it. At this stage improvisation meant chaos.

But Weygand persisted. "You tell us you will be sending new divisions soon. Send the odd formations you have in France to the harbours where these divisions are to land. They can be integrated there with the new divisions."

As patiently as I could I went over the old ground again. "Surely no one knows better than the Commander-in-Chief that you cannot throw packets of men at divisions as you slap plaster on a wall? A military formation is something more than a flock or herd made up so many bodies."

"The embarkation of British troops is bad for French morale," said Weygand with an expression that looked uncommonly like a snarl. I could quite see that, I said, but there were more important things than bolstering up morale in this locality or that. The truth could be explained. In any case, the best way of keeping up morale was success. This we were unlikely to achieve with odd elements brought together by accident only and neither properly officered nor staffed. As the General persisted I finally said: "We have a plan: that plan aims at getting fighting units back to France as soon as possible. To interfere with it would not gain but lose time. And," I added, "I am sure there is no chance whatever of the War Office agreeing to any measure likely to jeopardise its arrangements."

Nevertheless I was asked to ascertain how many troops, other than those at Dunkirk, we proposed bringing home to England, and I said I would pass on the request.

General Weygand then said that, according to the papers he had found on taking over, three new British divisions should have been on the point of arriving in France about now.

He begged me to request the Prime Minister to send over these formations without a moment's delay—"*de toute urgence*". There were, he said, very ominous concentrations north of Reims. I told him the Prime Minister had assured me over the telephone the night before that he (Weygand) would receive a programme very soon. But Weygand nevertheless repeated again and again how urgent was the need.

In this, at least, I was in complete agreement with him, and promised I would convey to Churchill how vitally important he considered the matter.

Weygand then referred to the importance of seizing the opportunity of hammering the German armoured divisions by air attack now that they were refitting.

I was able to assure him the matter was well in hand. The plans showing the points of concentration of these divisions had been transmitted to London as soon as received. I had been called up during the night on the subject.

Weygand went on to stress the enormous importance he attached to having adequate support from British fighters during the battle about to open on the Somme.

"We shall hold the enemy or we shall lose the battle according to whether we have or do not have enough *aviation de chasse*," he said. "As British fighters cannot intervene effectively in the fighting as far east as Reims if based in England, we are ready to place French aerodromes at their disposal." He gave me a list of the aerodromes which could be handed over, or which we might use.

I said I would transmit this message forthwith, but must inform the Council that, when transmitting a similar request, I had been given to understand that the risk of our machines being destroyed on the ground when refuelling in France was very great and might make the suggestion impracticable. And I emphasised a truth as great as the French need: we had not a machine to spare. Though I did not say so, I remembered that the Prime Minister had told me that at Dunkirk our fighters were bringing down German machines in the proportion of six to one, and that we simply could not accept conditions which would bring the proportion below three or three and a half to one. If we were to survive, our airmen must shoot down at least three enemy machines to one of their own.

Darlan then intervened to ask me to draw attention to the fact that, France having lost so large a part of her industrial area, the Germans would of course be fully aware of her need for greatly increased imports. They would in consequence intensify their attacks on French harbours. He therefore asked, as a matter of great urgency, that we should reinforce our anti-aircraft defences, at least in the harbours we were using, St. Malo and St. Nazaire, and afford what help we could in strengthening the defences of other French harbours.

Weygand then said that Nice and Bron (*sic*) had been bombarded that morning, he thought by German planes.

A telegram from Reynaud to the Prime Minister was then drawn up. It ran:

"The battle about to be waged on our front is of so capital a character for the common cause that I wish to draw your attention anew to the double necessity of the co-operation of the British Army and Air Force. Concerning the Army, General Weygand draws attention to the fact that the B.E.F. was to have been expanded during the current period to 14 divisions. It may be deduced from this that three divisions should be available and ready to be embarked. I might add that the 194,000 men you have just recovered from the northern front should enable you to follow the dispatch of the three available divisions by reconstituted units of proved fighting value.

"As regards the aviation, we need the support of both the bomber and fighter forces.

"We request that the British bomber force should provide before and during the battle about to be engaged action at least as powerful as that which it has provided in the battle in the north. It would appear that that support can be provided without your bomber force being based in France.

"As for the fighter force, whose role is decisive, since to concede air supremacy to the enemy would be to compromise the issue of the battle, I request you to co-operate with us to an even greater degree than was the case in the north. There is little doubt but that this force cannot act if based on England. There seems therefore no choice but that you should be good enough to decide that for the duration of the battle it should be based on aerodromes in

France. Orders have already been given by us to place some of our own aerodromes at the disposal of the British fighter force (these were in Beauce). We are preparing new landing grounds for our own aircraft. A note on this subject and a map have been given to General Spears so that he should transmit these to you immediately. The effectiveness of British co-operation, both on land and in the air, will depend in a great measure on the speed with which it is provided. We have indications of an early attack on various points of the front."

As I left, Reynaud told me he was going to visit the Somme front. He seemed relieved and pleased to be leaving Paris for a few hours. I shared that feeling so strongly that I was sorely tempted to ask to accompany him. The pretext I gave myself was that it would be valuable to see what preparations were being made to hold the German attack, and I longed to see French fighting troops. It seemed to me that, if in contact with them, I could, as in the past, quickly assess their morale. But reason told me this was not my job. There was no one to answer for me. I must remain in Paris.

That afternoon I walked from the Ministry of War to the Ritz and later from there to the Embassy. The Place de la Concorde was strangely empty, as it sometimes was at the height of the holiday season in August. But the trippers, the foreigners then to be seen in fly-like clusters were absent also. That beautiful expanse has always had a peculiar appeal for me. It offers to the eye the beauty, the symmetry and the space that is France.

I had every reason to know its moods: on my way to the Riviera as a child, standing by my tutor on the steps of the Madeleine, I had seen guns drawn across the bridge and the cuirassiers clearing the rue Royale and the boulevards during the Dreyfus riots. I had seen mounted troops charging across it in 1919, and again in 1934 when the *Croix de Feu* tried to rush the Chamber of Deputies. I had driven across it with Clemenceau, Joffre and Lloyd George, walked there with Lord French and Lord Bertie, and how many others? Happy or sad, I never once failed to sense its beauty or to feel the touch of its past. Today, in its sunny vastness, it gave me the impression of waiting for yet one more of France's dramas to be played there. What would the next act be? I had seen the victorious Allied armies marching here in 1919, and I had known old men who remembered the bearded Prussian columns of 1871 debouching from the Champs Élysées to the shrill notes of fife and flat drum. In spite of the heat of the day I felt cold, and shuddered. The Place Vendôme and the rue du Faubourg St. Honoré were as empty as the numerous expensive hotels. The people still about were those who could not afford to go. They were part of the fixtures, and seemingly as placid and expressionless. Their faces revealed nothing.

One of my most reliable and best informed French friends, a man in the closest touch with opinion in the highest spheres, was waiting to see me. I asked him whether the French Command had lost all faith in their Air Force. My own conviction (which I kept to myself) was that this must be the case since the tenor of all the messages given me implied it. Weygand was evidently trying to get the R.A.F. to substitute itself for the French Air Force.

My friend said he feared this was so and asked me if I knew General Vuillemin, the French Air Force Commander. I said I had met him, and we considered together the picture he had left in my mind.

Vuillemin certainly made a poor impression. He looked what he in fact was, a pilot of the last war who had gone to seed. N.C.O. was written all over him. Rather fat, rather pasty, bursting out of a uniform several sizes too small, which is a common failing of both French airmen and sailors, his bovine blue eyes had the same expression of rather hostile bewilderment to be observed in oxen as they watch the trains go by.

He had a fine war record. This one accepted without question, regretting only that the brave are not necessarily intelligent. When I had seen him with Reynaud, he had not uttered a word.

"He is very inadequate," said my friend, "and no one knows it better than Weygand"—words I was soon to recall.

Then Rollin, Minister of the Colonies, asked to see me. The Chief of Staff of the Colonial Army was with him.

I told him of the expected visit of Lord Lloyd, our Colonial Secretary. The Minister said he had wished to see me in view of the possibility of an Italian attack on British African territories. His department held that the best way of neutralising Italian action was to foment and encourage revolt in Abyssinia, and he gave me a list of places where the Italians were already having trouble.*

For the revolt to spread, it was essential that the Allies should not

* These were: Abane, Lidy Joannes, Abebe, Areghai, Cherasi, Arussi, Sciacca, Baccale.

suffer a set-back, but their position was difficult, since they had to defend two widely separated points, Berbera and Djibuti. The French thought the Italians were more likely to attack the former as Djibuti was strongly defended, and their Colonial Staff believed the Italians would endeavour to reach Khartoum and the Port Sudan railway.

The Minister and his military adviser begged that every effort be made to reinforce the defences at Berbera with troops from Kenya and South Africa, insisting again and again on the importance of denying the Italians, who they believed had 220,000 men and 380 planes in Libya, a success in this region.*

In the evening I saw Pétain. The old man was tired, having accompanied Reynaud beyond Compiègne, which had been his headquarters at one time during the last war.

He was not only tired, he was cross, which led me to think he had not been pleased with what he had seen. His querulous references to Weygand confirmed this view, for he spoke of him as if some of his old rancour, only submerged in the very recent past, had come to the surface again. He made one or two sharp comments concerning the defensive measures the Commander-in-Chief was taking. Then, following the not very definite path of his thoughts, in which there were gaps that evening, he said rather peevishly that the British were providing the Commander-in-Chief with a smoke screen behind which to conceal his deficiencies.

"But how, *Monsieur le Maréchal?*" I asked in astonishment. It then came out that Weygand had at that morning's Council Meeting made a bitter attack on Churchill. He had described him as a

---

* The Italian forces were reported to be in two groups referred to by the French as Packets A and B.

Packet B, by far the stronger, was at Harrar. It comprised:
- 4 Battalions of Blackshirts.
- 3 Colonial Brigade Staffs.
- 10 Battalions of Colonial infantry.
- 66 Light Batteries.
- 4 Heavy Batteries.
- 15 Tanks.
- 2 Groups of Banda (3,400 men).
- 100 Planes, many in bad condition.

Packet A at Sardo. Probable intention to advance in the direction of Dikkil to turn the French defences on the position Dikkil, Ali, Sabich. Strength:
- 2 Meharist Batteries.
- 1 Battalion Colonial infantry.
- 4 Banda. One of which is Meharist.

producer of fine speeches, a maker of promises which he did not keep. "If you do not play your part to the full, you are providing General Weygand not only with an excuse for a possible failure, but are turning yourselves into a most convenient whipping-boy. It will all be your fault. Not that I do not think there is much to be said for Weygand's point of view. For one thing, he is certainly right in considering the position to be extremely grave. For another, we have not obtained a definite promise of any kind from Churchill or any-one else. Weygand is quite right there. It is difficult for Frenchmen to believe the British Government have taken in all the implications of the situation."

The Marshal was right, I said, in so far as General Weygand's evident intent appeared to be to lay all the blame he could on the British. Did the Marshal not read the telegrams and reports? I asked. We had concealed nothing of our situation or our plans. If at times we seemed non-committal, it was because there was so much we did not know. It would surely be very wrong to make promises we could not keep. "Our difficulties in the north are largely due to faulty French Command," I went on, "we all know that now, but I have heard nothing but praise of the French commanders from General Weygand. Not a word of recognition for the role played by the British. He has never mentioned the British defence of Boulogne and Calais, yet a child could see the defence of Calais has made the evacuation of Dunkirk possible. Not a single man of the British garrison has come back to tell the tale, there has been no surrender, and now Weygand is trying to make out we are running away from Dunkirk under cover of a heroic French rearguard!" I spoke sharply: my anger grew as I realised the full implication of the attack on the Prime Minister until I found it difficult to control myself. "No doubt the French are fighting bravely, but if I hear any more of Weygand's sneers about our people, I shall tell him what I think of him to his face and then return to England. I hope this will not happen, it is not what I was sent out here for, but he is poisoning Anglo-French relations by his constant sneers and innuendoes. This attack on the Prime Minister, the best friend the French ever had, is really too much. I just won't stand it."

"I ought not to have said anything about it," said the Marshal. "At the same time, you should know what Weygand feels and how things appear to us."

I then told him that of course we realised how infinitely more tragic the situation was for the French than for us, but that it would not enhance French morale to depict us as unreliable allies, whilst the effect of such propaganda on British opinion would be wholly unpredictable.

I had every reason to believe Weygand heard of this conversation from the Marshal or from someone in his entourage. It was probably conveyed to him as a hint that the British resented his attitude towards them, in the hope of moderating his attacks, but it only served to add venom to his spite.

I began to understand then that Weygand was living in a kind of demented dream conjured up by his vanity to rescue his self-esteem. He could find no remedy to the disaster, no solution occurred to him. The splendour of fighting to the end à la Vercingetorix was a vision not vouchsafed to him. As neither he nor the General Staff could be at fault, as the French Army could only be the best in the world, then the explanation must be that France was betrayed—betrayed by the freemasons and anti-clericals, betrayed by the *Front Populaire*, stabbed in the back by the Communists, tripped up by her allies, let down by her own odious politicians. And so he spared himself the labour of seeking the solutions of which his mind was denuded. Like an empty wrinkled toothpaste tube, there was nothing to be squeezed out of it, so he turned savagely on others to avoid looking inwards and reckoning up his past responsibilities.

In an effort to leave the Marshal on a pleasanter note, I said it would not come amiss if some people could be reminded that once upon a time French and British troops had won a joint victory at Dunkirk—was it not called the Battle of the Dunes? "Yes," said the Marshal. The name had struck a note, and to my astonishment he added: "June 14th, 1658. There Turenne beat Condé and Don Juan of Austria, a very important battle; it led to the end of the war with Spain. It is curious that Cromwell should have sent a contingent to help Louis XIV. French history pays homage to the bravery of the Puritans." I stood in open-mouthed amazement at the old man's feat of memory. He himself was evidently pleased and smiled, which I had not seen him do in a very long time. I wondered whether the fact that he had himself been born in the land of Picardy, bordering on Flanders, was the reason why that engagement was so clear in his memory. My own most vivid impression of the battle, I told him, was derived from a picture I had once seen in a French child's book representing Cromwell's soldiers climbing a sand dune so steep that every man was sitting on the head of the man below. "Sand dunes are horrible things to fight in," said Pétain, "but they afford wonderful protection against shell splinters" (a truth borne out by the survivors of Dunkirk), and he went on: "It is strange that your Cromwell should have sent his men to help the King who was to revoke the Edict of Nantes. The morality of it is hard to discern, but you English, *vous autres Anglais, vous êtes de grands politiques.*" There was a *soupçon* of sarcasm in his voice. It was easy to discern his meaning: then as now, as always, the British followed the policy of their own interest. They could be relied on to produce high moral motives for whatever they did. The Marshal had not invented this. It has been the verdict the French have pronounced on the British since the two have emerged as nations on either side of the Channel.

As I drove away it occurred to me that the Marshal had perhaps been very clever behind the mask of his age and deafness which he assumed so conveniently when he wished. It was possible he had been glad to have a slight tilt at Weygand, thus disengaging his own responsibility, whilst preparing us for bad news on the Somme front. And it was not impossible that he had quoted the Commander-in-Chief as a means of expressing his own views. I asked myself whether, had this possibility occurred to me at the time, I should have spoken differently. No, well then, what matter? But the old man must have enjoyed seeing how I rose to the bait, how successful he had been in enraging me.

Late that evening a call from London informed me that Weygand had telegraphed to the French Military Attaché in London asking him to insist that the French rearguard at Dunkirk should not be sacrificed. Nothing would make him believe the French were not being offered up, a holocaust on the altar of British selfishness.

Later still, I received from Reynaud's office a copy of a telegram which was probably the one London had summarised to me previously. It was from Weygand to the French Military Attaché in London, and ran:

"Admiral North (Abrial) has telegraphed that, excluding the 25,000 Frenchmen who are defending the Dunkirk bridgehead, there remain about 22,000 French. All the British will leave this evening. As we may hope to evacuate these 22,000 Frenchmen tonight, there will remain tomorrow morning the 25,000 defenders.

"Consequently, Admiral North has declared he will remain at Dunkirk and has postponed the blocking of the harbour. He asks that every available support, naval and air, be given him tomorrow night (Monday) so as to evacuate the 25,000 fighting troops which, by remaining behind, have permitted the last British contingents to sail.

"Insist in the most urgent manner, in the name of the Commander-in-Chief, that satisfaction be given to the request of Admiral North. Emphasise that the solidarity of the two armies demands that the French rearguard be not sacrificed."

Meanwhile Darlan was as anxious to close down Dunkirk as was our Admiralty. He telegraphed to Abrial: "Make every effort to terminate the embarkation tonight. Five out of nine large torpedo boats sunk."

That night the Ambassador told me that Italy's entry into the war against us was a matter of days, perhaps of hours. He also said that Eden had broadcast saying four-fifths of the B.E.F. was safe. Thank God, thank God for that!

M. Paul Reynaud with General Weygand, Baudouin and
Marshal Pétain

Air-Raid Damage in Paris

CHAPTER III

Monday, June 3rd

Ismay and Churchill complain of French delays in embarking at Dunkirk—Churchill promises a last effort to bring the French troops away—A scene at the War Committee— Redman and I perfect our liaison arrangements—Count Horodyski—A German air-raid on Paris—Air Commodore Colyer on the behaviour of the French Air Force at Villacoublay—Reynaud's answer to Churchill on Dunkirk— He tells me of his visit to the front—Georges Mandel on the Belgian surrender—His plans to deal with the pro-German politicians—His opinion of Daladier—His contempt for political irresponsibles—Delbos fears for Léon Blum's safety.

In the early part of the morning Ismay called up several times, and the Prime Minister spoke to me at least twice.

From these talks I gathered that much ship space reserved for French troops the night before had not been used. Some ships had waited for a long time, then sailed away empty. Not unnaturally, feeling ran high in London about this, because of both the unnecessary risk to our men and ships, and the constantly implied suggestions that we were deliberately leaving the French behind. Nevertheless I went on pleading in favour of persisting in the endeavour to carry more Frenchmen. We could play little part in the battle which must very soon develop, so let us help where we could while it was still possible to do so. The Prime Minister needed no convincing. He had, I think, already made up his mind to make yet one more effort to embark as many as possible of the forces remaining in Dunkirk, and no annoyance, no wounding criticism could divert him from his endeavour to maintain Anglo-French co-operation.

I also learnt that, contrary to French reports, there were still some thousands of British troops defending the perimeter (it turned out later to be 4,000) and that on June 1st we had lost over thirty ships at Dunkirk.

Then at 1.20 p.m. I received a most immediate telegram from the Prime Minister for Reynaud and Weygand.

It said in effect: "We are coming back for your men tonight. Please ensure that all facilities are used promptly. For three hours last night many ships waited idly at great risk and danger."

Darlan was also informed.

That morning, while busy dealing with an infinity of details that were more and more coming my way, a scene was taking place at the War Committee of which I was totally unaware until I read of it in Baudouin's book.

In the main this book, which is written in the form of a diary, agrees with my own notes concerning this period, so I have no reason to doubt the accuracy of this account.

Baudouin writes under date June 3rd:*

"General Weygand indicates that at Dunkirk 282,000 men had been embarked, 65,000 of whom were French. Contrary to what had been settled at the Supreme Council, the rearguard is French. General Weygand is not in the least surprised at this. He adds that it is now certain that if the British, some 10 days ago, ceased to march in the direction of Arras, it is because they received orders from London in that sense. Since May 16th, Churchill has been playing a double game. He has abandoned France to her own resources. General Weygand affirms that the manœuvre aiming at a junction between the Armies of the North and the French forces on the Somme would have succeeded if the British had not continually looked back towards the sea. 'They do not know how to resist the call of the harbours,' the General declared. 'Already in March 1918 they wanted to embark.'

"Reynaud at this said he would inform General Spears of these reflections, whereupon General Weygand protested and went on to say he was on the coldest terms with General Spears at the end of the other war. General Spears was not in his view '*un esprit droit*', and he could not forget he had been a doubtful agent working for Lloyd George."

. . . . . .

* *Neuf Mois au Gouvernement*, p. 118. Baudouin's account of later events contains serious inaccuracies.

In view of the conclusions I had formed at the time as to Weygand's attitude, this outburst did not surprise me when I read it; even the accusation that Churchill was guilty of double-dealing was in keeping with the scenes of which I had been a witness.

I was, however, taken aback to learn that Weygand considered me to have been 'an agent of Lloyd George' in the First World War. When Sir William Robertson, the C.I.G.S., had appointed me Head of the British Military Mission in Paris in 1917, it was in the teeth of Lloyd George's opposition, because Wully Robertson could do no right in his eyes.

It may seem strange that it was only on this day that Redman and I solved the problem of keeping each other fully posted on the reports each was sending home. It was important, yet not easy, to avoid duplication. It was difficult even to keep in touch without messengers or dispatch-riders, and we only had our personal transport to depend upon. But most difficult of all had been to find means of not infringing the very proper security systems of both the Foreign Office and the War Office. It was at last agreed that I should be allowed to give Redman daily copies of my own messages.

The difficulties and dangers that can ensue from bad liaison arrangements even in such comparatively simple matters as communications within a single city can be very great. There are two aspects of security. The one concerns the plans and intentions of Governments and Commands. These are long-term projects and in their case security predominates overwhelmingly over speed in transmission. The opposite is the case concerning information about your own troops or the enemy's action. Then speed is, or should be, the governing factor. Many disasters have resulted from over-rigid security measures delaying news.

I was very late for my lunch with Count Horodyski in his flat at the top of a high building not far from the Champs Élysées. A strange, sad, interesting man, this Pole, who had once been reputed to stand high in the esteem of our Intelligence services. I always believed it was he who had followed up and reported on the German plan to send Lenin in a sealed wagon to Russia, there to instil his deadly doctrine.

Horodyski was fat, sleek and extraordinarily good company. Moreover, he had an excellent chef. The nephew of a General of the Jesuits, he was very discreet, and one might have thought he was merely a gifted observer had he not at times revealed an amazing insight into this or that international intrigue.

There were a number of interesting people at lunch, drawn from those who had been unable to leave the capital, and, as is generally the way in Paris when an exquisite meal is being served, the only serious concern of those present appeared to be, apart from enjoying it, to season each dish with biting or libellous commentary concerning every single acquaintance or person in a responsible position not present at table.

We were enjoying a superb *entremets* when the heaviest German air-raid yet began. In a moment Horodyski and I found ourselves alone, facing each other. We laughed and he, always a perfect host, giving me a glass of remarkable cognac, suggested we should adjourn to the balcony. My own thoughts flew back to a dinner I had given at my penthouse flat on top of one of the highest buildings in Paris, near the Trocadero, in 1917, soon after I had taken over my post. Fresh from Nivelle's murderous offensive of mud, blood and death, I could hardly believe in the reality of this charming world peopled with lovely butterfly women who carried on such a pleasant life of discreet luxury, so little affected apparently by the conditions of the only war I knew.

That dinner party I shall never forget. Then, as now, there had been an air-raid. Then, as now, the guests had vanished. The old Ambassador, Lord Bertie, had alone remained. I loved that delightful, stubborn, snow-haired old man, but never more so than when he stepped on to the roof garden that evening in the crash and noise, and there, with the building swaying under his feet, had beaten a tin tray with a soup spoon as hard as he could in loud defiance of the enemy.

This present raid was quite heavy, but no bombs came our way, and from our high point of vantage we could see there was no panic in the streets near-by. The great Citroën works were on fire, and there was much smoke from that quarter. We learnt later that Renault's works, though attacked, were not hit.

It also transpired that a bomb had dropped very near the Air Ministry, interrupting another lunch party there. It had not exploded and, as no one in Paris knew what to do in such a case, this was awkward. The area was roped off and guarded by police, very inconvenient for officials who had left their spectacles on their desks or for zealots anxious to refer to files.

It seemed that the strength of the attack was differently estimated by the British and French Air Forces. The French said that 300 enemy planes had taken part in the attack; we thought the figure was not higher than 200.

I saw Air Commodore Colyer, the Air Attaché, in the afternoon. He had been at Villacoublay awaiting Air Marshal Sholto Douglas when the raid occurred. He said the French defence was nil. Only three planes went up and these were content to patrol up and down over the aerodrome, never firing a shot. I reported: "This lethargy of the French Air Force is extremely disquieting." This was an official view. As an individual I was angry because disappointed and bewildered. I could only think of the French Air Force in terms of the last war, when it had been a rather casual entity perhaps, pre-ferring improvisation to planning, but gay, gallant and always spoiling for a fight.

Later that day I was assured on good authority that no machines had gone up to defend the Marseilles area when it was attacked the day before. The spirit, the morale, were extremely bad in the south, I was told. Well, it was always worse there than elsewhere.

In the afternoon Reynaud asked me to come round, and gave me his answer to Churchill's earlier telegram on the subject of that night's evacuation from Dunkirk.

It ran: "I thank you for having given orders to send ships to save the rearguard, which has played a decisive role in the evacuation. I am giving instructions to Weygand and Darlan to take advantage of these facilities with the minimum loss of time, and as far as the fighting will permit." He added: "Paris and the suburbs have just been bombarded by 300 German planes. Similar treatment in-flicted on the Berlin region would be greatly appreciated." The last words were in English, and the Premier was pleased at having introduced this touch. The quiet irony that became him so well, and was as characteristic of him as his neat black jacket, was as per-ceptible as would have been a flower in his buttonhole. He had some caustic and funny remarks to make concerning the interrupted lunch party at the Air Ministry, and then asked me if I had had occasion to note the behaviour of the population; I was able to tell him with perfect truth that the people I had seen, although not in an affected area, had been perfectly calm. I might have described them as disdainfully inquisitive and annoyed as by an unseemly display of bad manners in the street.

I then told him I must report to him what Colyer had seen at Villa-coublay. He looked worried. I had the impression that he had had other reports of the same kind which he, essentially a brave man, would not allow himself to believe.

Quickly changing the subject, I asked him about his trip of the previous day.

"Do you know General Besson?" he asked. Yes, I did, we had seen much of each other when we were both Captains in the last war. "He was a pleasant, round little man with a nice chuckle, a good officer," I said. "He now commands the Third Army Group," said Reynaud. "He made a good impression on me. General Frère was also there," he went on. "I know him, too. He received Churchill and me at Strasbourg last year and we had a long talk with him. He is a magnificent type of soldier. Very striking, but he was badly wounded in the last war. Can he stand up to the strain?" I asked. "He is doing so," said Reynaud.

I gathered that the troops had made a good impression, and this had cheered him, but his face darkened when he said that mechanical means for digging were entirely absent. There was a note of ex-asperation in his voice when he said the Generals complained of not having the necessary workers to prepare a second position, "and there are thousands available, thousands," he went on. There was a glint of anger in his eyes when he added that the Ministry of War was at times his greatest problem, his heaviest cross. "How can I put this right with a third of the Army out of action and an enormous attack impending?"

I knew by then he was extremely critical of General Colson. I was not in a position to judge but feared he must be right. As the General was a friend, I was grieved by what I heard. But it seemed un-pardonable that manpower was so badly employed.

I thought of the men widening the road in the Bois. I also knew that, as in 1914, there were no real defences of Paris and only 15,000 *Gardes Mobiles* to hold the northern approaches.

In the late afternoon Georges Mandel asked me to see him at his Ministry. He was very annoyed because the Ministry of War had stopped the telephone service during the air-raid, with the result that at 4 p.m. he had not yet heard what the casualties had been at Suresnes. But evidently that was not what he wanted to talk about. The British attitude towards the Belgian King rankled with him as it did with Reynaud. A number of Belgian aristocrats were loudly defending the King's action. Loyalty was no doubt a fine thing, but there were hundreds of thousands of Belgians in France. They must on no account be disaffected. Many were being enrolled in labour units. If the impression gained amongst them that the King's surrender was justified, they would no doubt feel there was a good deal to be said for following his example.

He intended interrogating a number of these Belgians whose importance was purely social and therefore of no account under present circumstances. If need be he would lock them up.

He said he wished me to know this, and added that he had caused a number of Frenchmen of the *monde*, that is, men about town, to be arrested. "What sort of people?" I asked. "People whose patriotism has faded of late in the blaze of Nazi success, people who see in Hitler a protector against Communism. Queer," he added, "after the Russo-German Agreement."

I asked him what he thought about those politicians who had in the past blazoned their pro-German tendencies.

Laval? Flandin? Bonnet? He named the three.

"Laval is by far the most dangerous. He is really dangerous, and clever too. No scruples of any kind.

"Flandin is next in importance on the dangerous list."

"He was my friend until he sent his telegram to Hitler on Munich," I said. "He and I were opposite numbers, each the Chairman of the Anglo-French Committees in our respective Parliaments. When, as a result of his telegram, the British Committee would have nothing more to do with him, he tried to work up an intrigue against me in my own party. Funnily enough, it was the Socialists who heard about it and exposed the whole thing. But he has courage and is a genuine leader," I added.

"I know," said Mandel. "But neither he nor Laval are dangerous so long as the Government is in Paris. If the Government leaves and they remain behind, one or the other or both might attempt to form a new Government. The answer is simple, they shall not remain behind."

"And Georges Bonnet?" I asked. "You named him in your list."

"Did I?" said Mandel. "Well, only because I thought you would have him in mind as he is one of the few French politicians whose name is known in England. But he is utterly and completely negligible. You surely know that from Munich. His long nose sniffs danger and responsibility from afar. He will hide under any flat stone to avoid it."

I asked why Daladier was still in the Government. He was in disagreement with the Premier over Italy, and his subterranean opposition, which tended to fuse the pro-Italian elements with the defeatists, certainly enfeebled the Government. Furthermore, the military leaders rightly or wrongly laid the incredible lack of preparations at his door. This was certainly Pétain's point of view.

Mandel said the over-advertised quarrel between Daladier and Reynaud had really compelled Reynaud to keep his enemy in the Cabinet. His resignation would have been described as the result of a personal vendetta by the Premier's numerous enemies as well as by those who plotted the Government's downfall in order to bring into power men prepared to sue for peace. This would weaken Reynaud, which would be most unfortunate. A suitable opportunity would no doubt occur to get rid of Daladier, the sooner the better.

Mandel said the Chambers were to adjourn on the 11th. He told me, as an illustration of the average politician's complete inability to comprehend the situation, that the Deputy who was also the mayor of a district that had been bombed, I think he said Suresnes, went about the lobbies, screaming: "I will interpellate the Government on this outrage as soon as the Chamber meets!" And Mandel indicated his contempt for the many modern politicians to whom democracy meant just that, a speech, an interpellation, a parliamentary row, the dreary, shoddy trappings of popular representation, the whole divorced from reality. "Paris is bombed by the German? Let's shake our fists at our own Government." The other way, that of silently going off to collect a gun and have a shot at the enemy, was a solution that occurred only to a few.

How Hitler must have laughed, I told myself. He had plumbed the folly of French politics to its depth, describing France as a rotten pear, ready to drop into his hand. He was well informed, better than those of us in England whose affection had blinded us.

Before dinner I went to the Meurice to have a word with Duff Cooper, who had come over to deal with propaganda questions.

I dined with Yvon Delbos, my opposite number as Chairman of the Anglo-French Committee of the Chamber, who for once was not in the Government. He was a charming man whom I greatly liked, but the evening was unreal, though the dinner at La Peyrouse was superb. Was the perfect food the reality and the Germans on the Somme a nightmare, or were Delbos and I dreaming a pleasant dream vouchsafed us as a relief from the horror we were living?

It was nothing so imaginative. We were merely exemplifying a rule I have repeatedly observed in war. People will go on doing what they have always done until prevented from doing so by physical force. The cook went on cooking because it was his *métier*. He could do nothing else so well. He would draw his salary as long as he could, and so would the waiter and the *sommelier* who poured out such good wines. And I suppose we dined there because it was good manners for a well-to-do Frenchman to give an expensive meal to a visitor from abroad, while I accepted because it was the custom, and in other circumstances would have given him in London as good an imitation as possible of the repast I was eating, with, I suppose, the same greedy reactions and unreasoning pleasure. But this was not always the case. Later, at Bordeaux, I remember quite distinctly that the exquisite food of the *Chapon Fin* on one special occasion tasted like sawdust.

Perhaps because I had to be so reserved for fear that even a friend might quote me and start a rumour, for naturally everyone knew I was living in the very heart of events, we spoke little of the war. Yvon Delbos, however, untrammelled by official secrets, told me freely his views concerning the French political scene. We both agreed as to who were the dangerous men, but he thought Mandel was not being nearly ruthless enough in dealing with them. He considered more arrests of dubious and defeatist leaders should be carried out.

He deplored the weakness of the French Air Force and told me he thought nothing of Vuillemin. "He is quite inadequate," he said. "*Pas à la hauteur.*" He then spoke of Léon Blum. They lived in the same old house on the Quais and he feared for Blum's life. "His life is really in danger," he said. "To many who yearn for a capitulation and hope to make friends with Hitler, he stands for that section of the population which will fight on at any cost. That is a dangerous position to be in today."

CHAPTER IV

Tuesday, June 4th

Churchill's wish to announce the numbers evacuated from Dunkirk—The French Naval Attaché reports the British achievement on the last night—The Ambassador delivers Churchill's telegram to Reynaud—Weygand transmits to Reynaud and endorses Vuillemin's demand for twenty British fighter squadrons—The Germans claim 1,200,000 Allied troops lost, and over 3,000 planes—French and British losses at Dunkirk—My report on the air-raid on Paris—General Koeltz's plea to Redman for British help—Kerillis on the Réduit Breton—The improved morale of the French infantry —Ybarnegary—The German Fifth Column—Jeanneney— Information from Reynaud's Secretariat about French resources and plans—French troops evacuated from Dunkirk not to be used for at least a month—Redman on Vuillemin's demands—Churchill's great speech in the Commons.

LATE the previous night I had received a telegram from the Prime Minister instructing me to ask Weygand whether he saw any objection to mentioning the figure of 300,000 men as having been successfully evacuated from Dunkirk, provided nationalities were not specified. He thought that to do this would be helpful.

I got hold of Redman and asked him to put Weygand the question.

Early in the morning he told me he had not been able to speak to the Commander-in-Chief the previous night as he was in bed, but had done so before 7 a.m. Weygand thought that it should now be possible to give a higher figure than 300,000. He saw no objection to a figure being mentioned, but added, quite rightly, that Reynaud should be consulted. Redman asked me to do this and inform London direct.

Before I left the hotel I received a copy of a telegram sent me by Campinchi, the Minister of Marine. The message was from the

32

French Naval Attaché in London and ran: "Approximate figure evacuations last night probably 25,000 (i.e., French). The operation was carried out with not a moment to spare. It began with the Germans in the suburb of Rosendæl and ended under the fire of enemy machine-guns. Nothing more can be attempted. Admirals Abrial, Platon and Leclerc are at Dover with General Fagalde. Admiral Abrial considers the work of the British was magnificent tonight."*

It was a nice thought, and I thanked Campinchi, asking him to make sure Weygand saw this message.

I drove to the Ministry of War and, to my surprise, saw the Ambassador's car there.

He was with Reynaud when I was shown in. He told me a telegram from the Prime Minister addressed to me for transmission to Reynaud had arrived at the Embassy, that an unsuccessful attempt had been made to reach me by telephone, and so he had delivered it himself. "But I have not moved from my room this morning," I said. It was slightly embarrassing, and I knew this crossing of wires held real dangers of confusion and misunderstanding. I said nothing, however, knowing Sir Ronald Campbell was only guided by the desire to act for the best. Later in the day he showed me a long telegram he had sent to the Foreign Office giving an account of this interview, emphasising the part I had played. It was very well meant. Before dealing with the Prime Minister's message, Reynaud told me, as he had no doubt told the Ambassador before I arrived, that he was immensely relieved by the result of the Dunkirk evacuation, and that he wished to acknowledge in the name of France that well over 100,000 French soldiers had been saved by British ships under the protection of the R.A.F. It was nice to hear him say this. His generosity in acknowledgement and his sense of fair play were in glaring contrast with what we experienced in other quarters.

The telegram from the Prime Minister brought by the Ambassador said in effect that Reynaud's message of the previous day requesting

---

* On this day 26,175 Frenchmen landed in England, over 21,000 of them in British ships. (Churchill, *The Second World War*, Vol. II, p. 101.)

Admiral Darlan caused the Vichy National Radio to state on January 8th, 1942: "Our light vessels sacrificed themselves (at Dunkirk) to ensure the embarkation of the British Army in spite of the fact its leaders had put themselves outside the pale." (Quoted by Reynaud, *La France a sauvé l'Europe*, Vol. II, p. 255.)

military and air assistance had been most carefully considered by the Government and the Service Chiefs. The British Expeditionary Force would of course be reconstructed as rapidly as possible in spite of difficulties due to lack of equipment. The problems facing the Air Force would be even greater than those of the Army owing to the occupation of the Channel ports by the enemy.

Churchill closed by saying he hoped the final decision of the Cabinet might be telegraphed that day; meanwhile he could assure Reynaud that no time was being lost.

It was only when I returned to the Embassy that I saw the telegram had a personal postscript for me telling me to prepare the French for a favourable response as regards the Army, but a disappointing one concerning the air.

Reynaud readily gave his agreement to the Prime Minister naming a figure for the Dunkirk evacuation and read out and handed to us a copy of a letter sent him the previous evening by Weygand. It ran:

Monsieur le Président,

I beg to send you immediately this very evening for your most urgent attention a most immediate letter I have received from General Vuillemin. This letter reinforces the most pressing appeal which you were good enough, at my request, to forward yesterday to Mr. Winston Churchill.

Its conclusions are in no way exaggerated. In order that our troops should not fight tomorrow's battle against too unequal odds, they must have the powerful support of fighter aircraft. No one who has taken part in the recent battles fails to assert this.

Our own Air Force is incapable of giving our troops this indispensable support. It can only do so if supported by the British Air Force.

In view of the gravity of the circumstances, I have the honour to request you to insist anew with the British Prime Minister, calling his attention to General Vuillemin's arguments. His letter has already been communicated to the Air Marshal Commanding the British Air Forces in France, and to his Liaison Officer at the Air Ministry.

Please accept, *Monsieur le Président,* the assurance of my high consideration and of my respectful and devoted sentiments.

WEYGAND.

We were then given a copy of Vuillemin's letter referred to in Weygand's covering note.

It began by referring to a letter Vuillemin had sent to Weygand on May 31st on the same theme. (Neither the Ambassador nor I had seen this letter, which had been sent to London direct, where, as we discovered next day, it caused much trouble.)

It appeared that he had requested therein a "massive" intervention of British fighter strength in France.

The letter went on: "The evolution of events, which include the intervention of important German bombing forces in the South-East and the eventuality of Italy's participation in the war at a very early date, emphasises still further the critical character of the situation I exposed to you.

"I have the honour to give you now my ideas on the subject in greater detail: If, as is probable, the enemy launches shortly a new and massive attack of tanks and aeroplanes against the defensive front now in process of organisation, there is no reason why he should not again break through our front and proceed to rapid and deep exploitation of his success, which it will be impossible to prevent if we have not the means of neutralising the German bomber forces by a massive intervention of British fighters at the very moment the enemy launches his attack.

"This massive intervention requires, as a minimum, half the fighter force now based on England. This is all the more necessary in that the German action in the South-East and the eventuality of Italy's entry into the war, compared with the *extreme weakness* of our Air Forces based on the South-East, which are ridiculously inadequate when compared with the threat we are considering, means that these must be reinforced the moment Italy enters the war, if all our South-Eastern territories are not to be abandoned defenceless to Italian action.

"This action may consist in the same combined air and tank attacks which will achieve the same success as the German operations did in the North-East.

"It is not necessary to dwell upon the gravity of the situation exposed above.

"Not to obtain from the High British Authorities the complete and immediate support requested would mean the probability of a defeat of the French forces and the loss of the war by Great Britain and France. The enemy having the choice of the hour, the support asked for can only be immediate if the British Air Forces take up their stations in France before the attack takes place.

"I have the honour, therefore, to ask you to be good enough to insist with the High British Authorities that their support be governed by the following conditions:

"1. The immediate dispatch of ten British fighter squadrons which would be stationed in the region of Evreux–Dreux, which would assume responsibility for the protection of the French land forces between the line Pontoise–Péronne and the sea.

"This measure would enable us to dispose of greater strength on the remainder of the front, taking into account the forces I should have to withdraw to strengthen the South-Eastern front.

"2. The preparation of the very rapid dispatch to France of a second series of ten squadrons which during the first days of the fighting would be based on the aerodromes already occupied by the British.

"3. As these squadrons would be established on bases already occupied by the British in France, it would not be necessary to move their ground establishments.

"If by chance the enemy committed the strategic error of attacking Great Britain before undertaking new offensive operations against France, these squadrons could, within the day, return to their bases in England; furthermore, they would thus probably have escaped the systematic bombing of fighter aerodromes by which the enemy will open his operations against England.

"I beg to affirm that the *immediate* satisfaction of these demands is a question of life and death for Great Britain as it is for France."

As I reported by teleprinter immediately after the meeting, we had not seen the appeal of the day before (3rd) referred to in Weygand's letter, though we did later, but both the Ambassador and I poured cold water on the request made by Vuillemin in the letter just given to us.

We begged Reynaud to remember that the entire Air Force we had maintained in France and which had been constantly reinforced was now to all intents and purposes destroyed, and that the losses at Dunkirk which we could not estimate must have been very heavy.

He must, we said, bear these facts in mind, for they were bound to affect the answer he would get, as they would of course have to be taken into account by our Government.

As we left, I asked the Premier how the defences between the Somme and Paris were shaping; he made a quick movement of exasperation and I gathered he could not get the General Staff and General Colson even to ask him for the civil workers he could have provided. Later I found the same feeling echoed in his office.*

Walking down the broad steps of the Ministry into the sunlit court-yard, I realised with sudden relief that Dunkirk was over. Our men were safely home. That there were immense dangers ahead was evident enough, but a gaping wound had closed and I believed that somehow the returned soldiers would provide the necessary leaven to knead the nation into a resistant mass Hitler could bite into but never digest.

Dunkirk was indeed the beginning for us. This I felt vividly with a renewed sense of confidence.

But what of France? I hoped, or tried to, that the fighting men would collect somewhere, somehow—in Brittany, in the Plateau Central protecting the Mediterranean harbours, in North Africa—and, combining with us, would reconquer their country. And meanwhile? The invasion would sweep the land clean of the scum that had ruined it. The people would at last awaken and there would be an end to this fatalism, this resignation, this apathy that had for so long condoned immeasurable shortcomings in every department of the State and had drugged that beautiful and gallant embodiment of all civilisation called France.

The Germans next day also claimed that the first chapter of the campaign was ended. They declared the Allied losses amounted to 1,200,000 men, that the material captured could arm from 75 to 80 divisions, that 1,800 planes had been destroyed in the air, and from 1,600 to 1,700 on the ground.

They admitted to 10,252 killed, 8,463 missing, and 42,523 wounded, but to the loss of only 432 aircraft.

These figures of our losses were of course greatly exaggerated.

A French General Staff note of June 6th, 1940, gave the French losses in Belgium and at Dunkirk as 370,000. It was claimed that 150,000 escaped, of whom two-thirds were evacuated from Dunkirk and the remaining third fell back behind the Somme.†

* "To General Colson, Chief of Staff of the Army (Interior), I said, without success, however: 'Ask me for 50,000 men to dig anti-tank ditches, to mine the houses in the villages which should collapse on the panzers.'" Reynaud, *La France a sauvé l'Europe*, Vol. II., p. 265.

† On all fronts the French lost a quarter of their '75' guns, a quarter of their heavy and light tanks, three-quarters of their medium tanks, as well as the greater part of their motor transport.

The British losses in the whole campaign were 63,386.

The Admiralty announced that 222 naval and 665 other British ships had been engaged in the Dunkirk operation, and that six destroyers and 24 lesser war vessels had been lost. A total of 226 other British craft, large and small, were sunk as well as 17 Allied craft.

The Germans boasted in their communiqué, and with reason, of the boldness of their scythe-like operation. What they did not foresee, and what we did not guess, was that they were to be finally destroyed by the same deadly strategic stroke. Speed, boldness of manœuvre, overwhelming armour and air preponderance brought victory to the Germans at the beginning of the war and to the Allies at its end.

It is strange how often the great reaper elects to use against him who fashioned it the tool with which he compassed the downfall of his neighbour.

Back in my office, I collected and sent on to London more information concerning the previous day's bombing of Paris. The Germans had evidently tried to hit the Renault works but had missed them; the Citroën works on the other hand had been fairly seriously damaged, and it had taken some time to gain control of the big fire which had been started. Trenches had not proved satisfactory against a near-by explosion. At Villacoublay one had closed in, killing the eight soldiers who occupied it. In another a good many children had taken refuge. It also closed in, flattening out all the small occupants beyond recognition. Nevertheless, one thing was certain: the population had not been upset, there had been no panic, not even excitement. The people of Paris could take it.

Redman sent me a report of a conversation he had had with General Koeltz the day before. This officer, whom I have already referred to,* had had a meteoric rise. Now assistant to Weygand, as he had been to Gamelin, it seemed to me but a few years since, as a very modest Captain in the Historical Section, he had been summoned by Marshal Franchet d'Esperey to accompany him on a visit to the Marne battlefields to which he had invited me. I could never see Koeltz otherwise than as a deferential figure bowing awkwardly to the impetuous Marshal. He had explained modestly one morning that he was the son of a gendarme, which made his achievement in rising to his present high position all the more noteworthy. But he

* See Vol. I, pp. 243, 269–70.

General Weygand

Marshal Pétain in 1917

knew the Marne battlefield in an uncanny way. I hoped his detailed historical knowledge would help him today. Koeltz had told Redman the French Intelligence reported that the Germans intended to block in turn all the harbours on the Channel and Atlantic coasts of France, with the object of cutting England off from France and preventing American supplies coming in.

He had repeated the request made to me by Darlan on the 2nd, that the British should assume responsibility for the anti-aircraft defence of the harbours they used.

Koeltz had also tackled Redman on the subject of British air support, using much the same arguments the Ambassador and I had heard that morning. He said the German attack was to be expected on the Reims–Châlons–South Marne front.

Redman reminded Koeltz that at the last Supreme War Council the British had promised to examine with the greatest care what they could possibly spare both in land and air forces for the fighting in France, and to send an answer as soon as possible. He explained once more the difficult situation in which the British were placed. They wished to assist France to the utmost, but felt they must keep in Britain the mimimum force essential to its defence. He pointed out to Koeltz that ten additional fighter squadrons had been withdrawn from the exiguous resources of the air defence of Great Britain and thrown into the battles in the north. These ten squadrons had been practically annihilated. This, said Redman, left a very reduced force for the defence of Great Britain, and speaking personally he thought the British Government would probably find it very difficult to provide much in the way of fighter support, especially for a battle that would be fought far beyond the range of fighters based on England.

General Koeltz brought up all the arguments we were now so familiar with in favour of stationing British fighters in France, but Redman exposed the fallacy of the contention that our fighters were as well placed to defend England from French bases as from their own. If the French argued they were too far away in England to participate in the battle of France, then surely they must be too far away if in France to take part in the battle of Britain. Further, it showed little knowledge of air warfare not to realise the essential importance of meeting a raiding force on its way in to attack, and that if it were not thus intercepted and attacked, our aerodromes would be destroyed and with them all hope of defending our country.

In the course of the morning Kerillis called up, saying he wished to see me and would I lunch? I was glad to accept, for it was a tonic to be in his company. Defeat did not damp his courage nor the poltroonery of so many dim his faith. He was convinced the Government should evacuate to Brittany and that a *réduit* ought to be formed there without delay. He had strongly urged Reynaud to do so, but felt the Premier believed it was already too late for this. He thought that in any event the Government should leave Paris now, when it could still do so in good order. Anything would be better than a higgledy-piggledy flight at the last moment under bombs and possibly even machine-gun fire, the whole combined with parachute landings.

It was not at all unlikely, he said, that there was a strong Fifth Column in Paris. If that was the case the western and southern exits of the city might well be closed, trapping the Government. But, in his view, the great advantage of leaving forthwith was that all politicians would have to go, none could remain behind unnoticed. He believed, as did Mandel, that if the Government fled under duress some would remain behind. Should this happen it seemed to him that there was every chance that Laval or other defeatists would set up a provisional Government and treat with the enemy.

I asked his opinion about Baudouin. He was a sinister influence, he said, George Bonnet's man.

Why did Reynaud, who was quite sincere in his desire to co-operate with the British, handicap himself so? I asked. Kerillis shrugged his shoulders and returned to the subject of Brittany and the *réduit*. In the opinion of soldiers he trusted, who confirmed his own view, Brittany presented, he repeated, very marked advantages as a *réduit*. It had numerous points of access to the sea and, in part at least, was very difficult tank country.

I asked him how long French troops would go on fighting in Brittany, with their wives and children in territory occupied by the enemy. The question troubled him. He was as honest with himself as with others. "It is a moot question," he answered, after a rather painful pause.

As the matter was one of considerable importance and might well influence the decision whether a stand should be made in Brittany or indeed anywhere in France if the present line was broken, I put the same question later that day to a man in touch with Reynaud who was one of the strongest advocates of the plan and a genuine die-hard. He was as disturbed by the question as Kerillis had been. "We should endeavour to evacuate all women and children to North Africa or to the New World," he said.

If that is the answer, I thought, if all the women and children of France must be placed in safety to ensure that the Army will fight, then there cannot be much hope of resistance, for it would take the entire shipping of the Allies many months to carry out such an operation, even if there were anywhere for these millions to go where they would find shelter and food. But I would not accept this point of view, for I knew that, however cruel the strain had been, the Army of the last war had fought on, unaffected, although a whole chunk of France had been occupied by the enemy for years.

As a result of these conversations I reported to London in the afternoon that it might be well to suggest to the French Government that if they intended to leave Paris they should do so at once, and that if it was intended to hold Brittany in case of a retreat from the present line, measures to that end should be taken forthwith.*

We were, I thought, fully entitled to make these suggestions as they profoundly affected our own plans, as regards both the location and organisation of air bases, and the harbours we should use for bringing in reinforcements.

Nothing revealed the lack of grip of the French Government better than its inability to take a decision on these vital issues.

To move the seat of a Government was no easy task. The housing of departments, and above all their communications, presented enormous difficulties, and time was evidently very short. Then the defence of the Brittany isthmus must of necessity involve grave problems, none of which had been seriously considered. The line which was to be held if this project was adopted had not even been selected. I reported further that I could find no evidence of a real effort to prepare a second line of defence or points of resistance anywhere further away than within a short, that is to say tactical supporting, distance from the present exposed front. The Premier had utterly failed to shake the military machine out of its bureaucratic strait-jacket. Routine held the Ministry of War by the throat,

* General Weygand (*Rappelé au Service* p. 152), writes that M. Reynaud had sent him a note on May 31st asking him to study the creation of a *réduit* to include the Brittany peninsula, in the event of a further German breakthrough on the line Abbeville–Switzerland. General Weygand makes it clear that, although he gave instructions to have the matter studied as M. Reynaud requested, he did not believe in the idea.

and it seemed to me increasingly evident that Weygand had no plan to fight on a new front. If he had, the considerable resources in manpower still available would surely be employed in its preparation.

On the other hand it was with relief and joy that I was able to report that all my information, and a good deal was coming in now, tended to show that the morale of the infantry was recovering fast, and that it might yet give a good account of itself under good leadership. But I gave warning that it was essential for the men to be provided with some weapon upon which they could rely for use against tanks.

It is a dreadful thought that, unknown to us, anti-tank weapons were in fact available but were never used by the French, though the Germans later found them handy against the Russians.*

There were a number of items of news that afternoon, some worth reporting and others not. I was, for instance, interested to hear that Ybarnegaray, a junior member of the Government, a well-known right-wing Deputy and at that time considered a die-hard, had joined hands with Mandel in tracking down and arresting both real and alleged Fifth Columnists. He was the more useful and his action was the more meritorious in that the most dangerous of these belonged to his own right wing rather than to the left.

Some of the victims were well known in society, and I found I knew several quite well. But more important personages were outside Ybarnegaray's field. Only Mandel and Reynaud could have dealt with Laval, and although both felt he should be placed out of temptation's way, that is, taken into custody, they threw back at each other the responsibility for so drastic a step which neither had the courage to take.

I had at last time to amplify the information I had collected concerning German Fifth Column activities, some of which I had already briefly reported on.

---

* Daladier stated at the Riom Trial that: "The Germans found 750 unused 25-mm. anti-tank guns in the depots, and over 2,000 tractors (*chenillettes*) unused." It also came out in evidence that there seemed to have been serious differences of opinion between French Commanders on the subject of anti-tank gun traction. General Besson regretted that these were drawn by horses, General Mittelhauser, on the other hand, regretted they were not all horse-drawn.

General Ricard stated: "On the Somme the Army Corps received 4–5,000 mines but used them badly owing to lack of instruction." *Général de Brigade* Conquet stated: "We received on the Ailette 1,800 mines for a front of 15 kilometres. This number was required per kilometre."

It was clear from the information received from many sources that the Germans had evolved a brilliantly organised system of deception, whose instruments were believed to be specially-trained and highly-paid Swiss and Belgians who could pass as Frenchmen. The French Intelligence said there were two schools for these agents. One was near Berlin. They were directed by men familiar with the intentions of the German Command and who certainly knew how to further them. Perhaps the most effective action consisted in intelligent use of the telephone for sabotage purposes. For example, a Prefect or other high official in the provincial administration would be called by an individual who said he was speaking for some senior military authority (there was seldom, in the general confusion, any means of checking the authenticity of the speaker) and ordered him to destroy all the petrol in his region, only to find that as a result the Allies were deprived of supplies they had been relying upon; or the contrary might be the case and the official was ordered to accumulate supplies at a point where the Germans found it convenient to collect them.

The most common as well as the easiest way to cause confusion and embarrass the Allied armies was to send telephone messages ordering the civil authorities to evacuate the civil population. As this corresponded with its instinct to fly, such orders were obeyed with alacrity, and the roads were soon covered by helpless masses of people choking communications, devouring supplies and paralysing military transport. It was but an additional artist's touch from Hell's academy, a splash of colour mixed on the Nazis' fiendish palette, to machine-gun these columns of helpless, terrified human beings.

It must be remembered that the refugees of today were but yesterday ordinary people pursuing their daily avocations, sleeping each night in their own houses, held by deep roots each one to his own place. Now they were no more than units amongst thousands going they knew not where, driven forward by fear. Imagine the effect on these demoralised columns of incidents such as this: A large pantechnicon catches up with the column and slowly, as opportunity offers, gains ground until it is wedged in the thickest traffic. The sides then fall open revealing machine-guns, which rake the wedged-in mass of humanity.

A quite usual proceeding of the sabotage organisation was to send imperative orders to destroy the post-office installations as the

Germans were about to enter the place, thus depriving the French military and civil authorities in a whole region of every means of communication. As the French Army was singularly lacking in wireless, this proved disastrous on many occasions. The German organisation was so thorough, the experts engaged so superlatively good, the plans on which they worked so meticulously thought out, that the confusion they engendered led to stupefied bewilderment over wide areas. From prefects to village mayors no one knew whether to believe or disbelieve, obey or disregard an order.

The following incidents were reported to me by reliable French officers. The Germans commonly used agents in the uniform of French dispatch-riders or Staff Officers who dashed up to a commander, called out a message or order and were gone. One French Colonel of undoubted capacity and courage received three such false instructions in one day. On the first occasion he was ordered to evacuate the position he held, on the second to lead his regiment into a defile choked with refugees where it well-nigh lost its cohesion, and on the third to occupy a support position found to be held by the enemy. It was later verified that no such orders had been issued by the Command to which the regiment belonged.

I was told, and could well believe it, that complete confusion reigned in the division concerned, and subsequently it was only possible to ensure that orders were obeyed if they were carried by officers known to the recipients.

Worst of all, a group of the best heavy guns in the French Army, the 155-millimetre Rimaillots, was halted near Laon when a pale-faced Staff Officer appeared declaring he had come post-haste from Corps H.Q. to say that a German panzer division was converging on them and would be there in a matter of minutes, and the Corps Commander adjured them as good Frenchmen not to allow their guns to fall into enemy hands. Within a few minutes 35 of these priceless guns had been damaged beyond repair. No such order had been sent from Corps H.Q. This incident was told me by St.-Exupéry, who said he could vouch for its truth. As can be readily imagined, cohesion could hardly be maintained when the authenticity of messages and orders could not be trusted. Orders cannot always be transmitted by means of people known to each other, and the tendency therefore was to disregard instructions until they had been verified, which led to hopeless delays on an already disorganised front. There were many cases, I was assured, of motor-cyclists carrying orders who, on being told to stay until their identity had been verified, bolted at top speed. The general sense of insecurity and nervousness that these methods added to the moral blow of a terrible defeat need not be stressed.

There were, however, occasions when the Germans became careless. One was reported to me by the people to whom it occurred. In a great crowd of refugees amongst whom there were a few soldiers, a boy noticed that a soldier in French uniform did not have the regulation buttons on his tunic. He turned out to be a German. This was carelessness indeed, for by that time the enemy had enough French uniforms at his disposal to clothe whole army corps.

In the late afternoon I called on Jeanneney, the President of the Senate. It was always refreshing to talk to this high-minded, high-principled collaborator of Clemenceau whom I had known for over twenty years. Aged, slight, bearded, perfectly courteous, he looked at me sadly through his pince-nez.

One of the best things about France, one that tends to give confidence in her essential moral soundness, is that, in spite of the buffoons and charlatans so apt to steal the political limelight, the solid middle and intellectual classes assert themselves by placing power in hands such as those of Jeanneney. And in doing so they have the approval of the whole country, for the French have a fundamental, ineradicable respect for wisdom, science, age and that moral rectitude which people like to know exists although they may seldom feel inclined to practise it themselves. He was typical of the *haute bourgeoisie*, a meaningless term in England where its counterpart does not exist. I cannot imagine an older member of that class relaxed, or having a good time, or clad otherwise than in sombre town clothes with very stiff collars, simply because I have never seen one who did not answer this description, or who did not move about amidst heavy, sombre furniture.

I shared to the full the universal respect for Jeanneney and on this day, as on more tragic ones, found solace in his company. He was so sound and straight that, when with him, it was impossible to believe the defeatists would prevail. I found too that if he approved of views and ideas I submitted to him, he would pass them on to those quarters where they would be of the greatest use. On this occasion, after telling him what I knew of the general situation, much of which he was not aware of, I drew his attention to the incredible defencelessness of Paris and the lack of steps being taken to remedy it. I compared this with the way the British people were making ready to resist invasion. Barriers were being erected everywhere, signposts torn down, names of stations obliterated so that low-flying machines could not verify their position. No step that implacable determination could dictate was being neglected. Could not the same spirit be infused into the French people?

Jeanneney looked sad and bent as I left him.

At the Premier's Military Cabinet, where I called next, I was given some interesting and, on the whole, encouraging information.

The present French forces, either in or coming into line, amounted to seventy-two divisions including three from North Africa. This was much better than they had hoped to achieve the previous week.

This figure did not include the divisions to be formed from the Dunkirk troops, which might amount to three or four, or the oddments being collected throughout the country from which it was thought two or three further divisions might yet be created.

Then I was assured, but this alas turned out to be but wishful thinking, that the French were getting on well with the formation of anti-tank units. These were each to comprise eight anti-tank guns, later to be raised to twelve, to provide defence in depth. The escort was to be of the strength of a squadron. Each unit was to include machine-guns for immediate protection, motor-cyclists and machine-guns on side-cars, as well as A.A. defence. They, in contrast with the rest of the French Army, were to have efficient wireless equipment.

Corps Francs units of thirty men, transported in lorries carrying anti-tank devices and explosives, were being formed, I was told.

The Intelligence reports collected by the armies tended to show that all the vital ancillary vehicles of the German armoured divisions were either worn out or destroyed. This led the French General Staff to conclude that should the Germans break through in the forthcoming attack they would be unable to penetrate very deep. From which the further conclusion was drawn that the German onslaught would take the form of an infantry attack preceded by barrages, much after the fashion of the last war. It is incredible what a short time it takes fools to create a paradise.

One piece of information caused me intense annoyance: the French Staff had not the least intention of employing the troops recovered from Dunkirk for at least a month. This was considered the minimum period required to reorganise and form them into the new type of light division.

Nothing could have been truer and the time suggested was an underestimate. I said nothing, for my informant did not know the pressure that had been put on us to send our Dunkirk troops straight back to France from Dover to hold positions behind the Somme front.

When reporting this to Ismay, I suggested the Prime Minister should not be told; it could but hurt him to find the French General Staff had two rules, one for themselves and another for the British. It might also undermine his confidence in the validity of French requests, for he was painfully aware of the clamant pressure put on him by Weygand to send our men back to France, armed or not.

It has occurred to me since that the proposal was a further and quite authentic manifestation of the strange self-deception that led Weygand, and the French professional officers generally, to believe that their Army alone excelled in war, that fundamentally our men were not soldiers, whereas the French were. It is an automatic manifestation of a sense of inferiority to belittle him who has often had the better of you, and fondly to believe the world at large is not aware of the fact.

I received another shock of the same order in the form of a pencilled letter from Redman that evening.

He wrote that it was most important that General Vuillemin's letter be seen in its entirety by the three Chiefs of Staff. "The trouble is," he said, "that the French do not play fair with us over the available strength of their aircraft," and he went on to explain that Air Marshal Barratt, on an urgent request a day or two ago for all possible fighter support, produced from his 27 remaining fighter aircraft the amazing total of 127 sorties in one day. The French had over 300 fighter aircraft available that same day, but only achieved 80 sorties in all.

He went on to say that Vuillemin's request for ten fighter squadrons followed by another ten did not seem to him in any way reasonable. Nevertheless he thought there would be utter alarm and despondency and much recrimination if none or even only a few were made available. He thought most people felt that a real gesture was needed to encourage the French and would have great political significance.

During the evening we heard of the Prime Minister's speech in the

Commons that afternoon. "WE SHALL FIGHT ON THE BEACHES, WE SHALL FIGHT IN THE FIELDS, WE SHALL NEVER SURRENDER"; the words billowed and roared from the island over the sea in a challenge such as the world had never heard; no wild climax of sound conceived by a great musician and executed by an immense orchestra ever caused more emotion and more awe amongst those who heard, and the peoples of the earth were listening.

To us, who had the honour of being members of the threatened nation, whose eyes were riveted on Winston Churchill, now recognised as the supreme leader who would give each and all of us the impulse we expected and awaited, the words conveyed a hidden meaning. Like a password, the significance of which only we could grasp, it bound us in a great secret understanding. No further need for words between us now, no room for private sorrow or partial interest, no regrets, no fears. We were held together in the knowledge that there was to be no looking back, that each one of us was to give ungrudgingly all that he had to give, looking forward to only one thing, the survival of the nation. Our generation has suffered much and endured a great deal, but we are to be envied by the world, for we once passed through an intense fire and light that burnt out everything mean and selfish in us, leaving only a common purpose and a common unity, fusing us into the single soul of the British people.

That night, very late, I dined in an old house with some French friends in whose company I had hitherto felt in complete communion with France. The beautiful objects, the familiar setting, were the same; a long and intimate friendship, common experiences, similar tastes, had long bound us together. We knew the same people, liked the same things, spoke the same language. Similar incidents moved us to laughter or to criticism. It was rare and easy, and it had hitherto been inconceivable that anything should divide us or that any of us should violate the impalpable code of taste governing our relationship.

But that night there was a rift between us, a slight crack in the crystal cup sufficient to change its sound when touched. I had my password and they did not have theirs. We no longer belonged to one society bounded by the same horizon. A lifetime steeped in French feeling, sentiment and affection was falling from me. England alone counted now.

CHAPTER V

Wednesday, June 5th

The German attack begun—The alignment of the French Armies—Weygand's complaint against the British—Churchill's telegram in answer to Reynaud's plea for reinforcements—Weygand and Reynaud disappointed—I read them Churchill's speech to the Commons—Reynaud's reply to Churchill's telegram—Weygand on German intentions—The French War Committee's anxiety about the defence of Le Havre—Reynaud on the consequences if Paris falls—His strictures on Weygand—Churchill's statement on King Leopold—British resentment of Vuillemin's letter—London's reply to Reynaud's telegram of June 2nd—French defensive tactics — General Héring — The French infantry's fine performance—Churchill's irritation at vagueness of French demands—Reynaud reshapes his Ministry—The British reply about Le Havre defences—Refusal of a single Anglo-French Air Command—A sharp message from Churchill to Reynaud—The new French Ministers—De Gaulle appointed Under-Secretary of War—A telephone conversation with my wife—Churchill agrees to my returning to London to report.

BEFORE 8 a.m. I learnt that the General Staff was convinced the great German onslaught had begun. The enemy was driving out from his bridgehead at Péronne on the Somme with tanks. He was evidently taking advantage of a factor extremely favourable for him: that the Somme formed a right-angle at this point, with the town and his bridgehead in a re-entrant, which meant the river afforded protection to both his flanks.

After the first news there came a long pause, as is always the case, filled only with echoes and rumours, but one thing seemed established: the Germans had not driven straight through. That fact alone was sufficient to afford relief, almost satisfaction.

The French Army facing the Germans was divided into three Army Groups. The Third was stationed below the Somme and the Aisne, as far as Neuchâtel, the Fourth lined the Aisne, the Second defended the Rhine and the Maginot Line. The Third Army Group was commanded by General Besson, to whom I have already referred. It included the Tenth Army, which extended from the sea to a point south-east of Péronne. The British forces in France formed part of this Army, which was commanded by General Altmayer. It was much stretched; the 51st British Division alone holding a front of 16 miles.

In my book *Prelude to Victory* I described Altmayer as "a stern, tall, thin individual with blue eyes and a cadaverous face, a Don Quixote in blue. Nothing could deflect him from carrying out his orders, he was the embodiment of will at the service of unquestioned military authority."

Next in line was the Seventh Army, under General Frère. It extended to Coucy, and beyond it came General Touchon's Sixth Army holding the line to Neuchâtel.

The Fourth Army Group, next to the Third, commanded by General Huntziger, comprised two Armies. The Fourth, under General Réquin, extended from Neuchâtel to Attigny, and the Second, under General Freydenberg, from Attigny to Longuyon. Thence to Switzerland extended General Prételat's Second Army Group.*

As I looked at the map I thought that if this attack was the major operation anticipated, then it was evident the Germans were making for Paris and attempting to reach the traditional channel of invasion, the Oise valley. The French Staff would in that case be proved right, for they had been watching this part of the front with particular anxiety, as they always did any sector from which Paris could be threatened. The Oise valley was the corridor that led straight to the capital.

By 7 a.m. the first part of a telegram sent me by the Prime Minister had been deciphered, but the second part was only decoded soon after 8 a.m. When I asked to see Reynaud to deliver it, I was told

* All this immense line, in which there stood at this moment nearly one and a half million men, or perhaps 65 divisions, was now to be assaulted by one hundred and twenty-four German divisions, also formed in three Army Groups, viz: Coastal Sector, Bock; Central Sector, Rundstedt; Eastern Sector, Leeb.

this was impossible, but would I attend the War Committee meeting, as on other occasions, at 10.45. As I walked in by one door, Weygand came in by another and handed the Premier a note, which he read and handed to me. It ran:

"The Commander-in-Chief is compelled to observe that the appeals to the British Government have been without avail. The German attack against us is being launched without our having received any further help from the British; neither fighters nor fresh divisions."

To say that I looked at Weygand with dislike after reading this note would perhaps be an understatement. Addressing Reynaud I said: "*Monsieur le Président*, I do not think the Commander-in-Chief is helping the cause of the alliance, or even that of France, by his habit of making unjustified complaints against us."

Weygand then said in a voice that was, I suppose, meant to convey a sense of aggrieved innocence, but which grated on my ears like a nail scratching on a blackboard, that he was not criticising the British Government. "There is no difference between the Government and the Army," I answered. "The Prime Minister would be the last to countenance such a suggestion. Mr. Churchill speaks another language," I went on, and referring to his speech of the day before in the House, parts of which I had translated into French to show Reynaud, I read: "We shall not be content with a defensive war. We have our duty to our ally." There was a silence, then I said: "*Monsieur le Président*, I have an important telegram for you from the Prime Minister, may I read it?"

It was to the effect that, in answer to his request transmitted by me on the 2nd, he (Reynaud) had been assured, without however any definite promise being made, that the British Government would immediately consider what reinforcements could be sent at once to France, and what air support could be given in the forthcoming battle. The Prime Minister felt it necessary to underline certain general points. In the first place it must be realised that the troops recovered from Northern France would have to be entirely re-equipped before being re-engaged. In the second, the three British divisions alluded to in Reynaud's message were not yet fully equipped. The original plan we had been working to aimed at sending the first of these to France towards the end of June.

Reynaud was also asked to consider that almost the entire R.A.F. fighter force had been engaged in the recent battle, that the struggle had proved of quite unexpected severity and that losses in machines, and particularly in pilots, had exceeded all previsions. He was invited to give earnest attention to these matters since they materially affected the assistance Great Britain was in a position to give.

The steps the British Government intended to take were, as regards the Army, to re-establish a B.E.F. Headquarters in France and rebuild that force as rapidly as possible.

One division would begin to embark within seven days. A second division of regular troops, recovered from Dunkirk, was being re-equipped with the utmost urgency to follow the first with the least possible delay. Corps troops were also to be dispatched.

No date could be given for the dispatch of a third division but not a moment would be lost. The Prime Minister added that the date of the dispatch of this division would probably depend on when its artillery could be provided. Could the French help in this respect? He also said that the appropriate army co-operation aircraft would accompany the division.

The Prime Minister then dealt with the question of the Air Force. The three squadrons of fighters in France were to be brought up to strength immediately, but in view of the extremely serious losses of the last three weeks some little time must be allowed for overhauling the squadrons and replacing losses. A short time must also be allowed to determine the nature of the help that could be provided and its extent.

The extreme urgency of the case was fully appreciated, said the Prime Minister, and he pledged himself to communicate further with Reynaud at the earliest possible moment.

Dealing with the bomber squadrons, Churchill said that the six squadrons already in France would be brought up to operational strength as early as possible. The remainder of the bomber force would remain based in Great Britain, but would continue to give the same support as in the past. Priority would be given to battle-field objectives and to those selected by the French High Command.

Weygand, having listened with every sign of impatience, exclaimed that this support was absurdly inadequate (*dérisoire*—a more exact translation of the term would perhaps be "laughable") except as regards the bomber force, which would, he assumed, operate according to his directives. It was clear, he declared dramatically, that France could not rely on effective support from England in the battle which had opened that morning. Reynaud broke in to say he also was most disappointed by this message. If it had been necessary to prolong the air battle over Dunkirk to save British troops, the R.A.F. would have continued fighting in spite of its losses! I interrupted to point out that the R.A.F. had indeed gone on fighting to the end at Dunkirk—for what purpose? To save the last French troops. This point was not taken up, and Reynaud said that it looked as if the British were committing the fatal error of considering the defence of England as the capital issue, whereas the Germans were marching not on London, but on Paris. This, he declared, was his reading of Mr. Churchill's speech of the previous day in the House of Commons.

Such would not have been his conclusion had he seen the full text, I said. Of course Mr. Churchill had referred to a possible invasion, how could he have shirked that issue when speaking to the British Parliament? But he had not emphasised that contingency. He had in fact dismissed it rather lightly. Far from showing apprehension, he had growled defiance. Had it not been noted that he had quoted to the House someone's phrase to Napoleon when his Grand Army lay at Boulogne, "There are bitter weeds in England"? Had the fact that Mr. Churchill had pointed out the immense strength of our untouched sea defences passed unobserved?

If, I went on, Reynaud had been led to believe that the speech indicated the least trace of a defensive policy he had been misinformed. Nothing could be further from the fact. On the contrary, Mr. Churchill had outlined a further maximum effort in France. It was surely wise to make Parliament feel there was no immediate threat of invasion, otherwise the wisdom of sending every man we could spare to France might have been questioned. He had completely identified the cause of France with that of Britain, and I read a marked passage in my text: "The British Empire and the French Republic, linked together in their cause and in their need, will defend to the death their native soil, aiding each other like good comrades to the utmost of their strength." What stronger pledge could be given or what more convincing proof, I asked, than this assertion of our identical interests?

I looked round. No one said anything, so I went on, as I had hoped I should have a chance of doing, to read the Prime Minister's concluding phrases: "We shall go on to the end, we shall fight in France, we shall fight on the seas and oceans . . . we shall fight on the beaches, we shall fight on the landing grounds, we shall fight in the fields and in the streets, we shall fight in the hills; we shall never surrender." "We all feel like that," I added; "Parliament made it clear by its enthusiastic reception of the speech that Churchill was expressing the feelings of the entire nation."

Momentarily the atmosphere of the meeting had completely changed.

"Your Prime Minister was speaking for France as well as for England," said Reynaud, who was visibly and deeply moved by the magnificent sentences even though I feared they had lost much in my hasty translation into French.

These splendid words had swept the room clean of meanness. Base and contemptible thoughts had scuttled back and hidden in the hearts where they had been hatched. What was good and clean like the innate loyalty and pluck of the Premier stood out, burnished by the scalding sentences. But the effect was only fleeting.

There was silence and I realised the Premier was looking hard at Pétain through his slit eyes, but the old Marshal was staring down with a wooden expression. Perhaps he has again not heard, I thought, but I was sitting next to him, and had certainly not been whispering. Reynaud was speaking again. I perceived that the effect of Churchill's words was already evaporating. His voice was hard. He had returned to his theme and to his sense of grievance. "Mr. Churchill's message requires an immediate answer. There is simply not a moment to be lost. He must be made to realise the gravity of our position."

So, seizing one of the immense sheets of foolscap headed *Présidence du Conseil* on his desk, he began writing, consulting by a glance Weygand and Darlan as he spoke each sentence before putting it on paper. At first he looked at Pétain also, but the old man sat on, with bent head, expressionless, as if he had not heard. He had heard, however, for later, to everyone's surprise, or at least to mine, he chimed in. The Admiral made but few comments. Weygand on the other hand discussed every phrase, made proposals, suggested words, sentences and even whole paragraphs.

I also intervened, making suggestions with the object of toning down some of the expressions which were too sharp in tone and would have given offence. The two last sentences were inserted on my suggestion.

The text of the message as it finally emerged was as follows:

1. *British Divisions.*

General Weygand's opinion is that, if he has not got the means of feeding the battle, there will be the greatest risk of its being lost.

It is therefore necessary to hasten the dispatch of the British divisions.

You inform me that the first division will only embark seven days hence.

But eight days will be required between its landing and its employment at the front. Even this first division risks arriving too late.

My conclusion is that, in view of the new factor created by this morning's offensive, the dispatch of the British divisions must be hastened to the maximum.

2. *Fighters.*

You state that, in view of the heavy losses suffered by the British fighters, you can at present only re-complete the three squadrons at present in France. You therefore reject the request put forward by General Vuillemin on June 3rd and transmitted by me yesterday, June 4th, to Sir Ronald Campbell, to send to France:

1. *Immediately* ten fighter squadrons.
2. As soon as possible ten further squadrons.
   (These twenty squadrons representing half the fighter force based on England.)

I cannot believe that your decision will be persisted in in view of the new factor of the German offensive.

I recall that in his letter of June 3rd to General Weygand, a copy of which was sent to the British Government, General Vuillemin said:

"If, as is probable, the enemy launches shortly a new and massive tank and air attack against the defensive front now in process of organisation, there is no reason why he should not again break through our front and proceed to a rapid and deep exploitation of his success, which it will be impossible to prevent if we have not the means of neutralising the German bombers by a massive intervention of British fighters at the moment when the attack is launched."*

General Weygand concurs with this statement: it is useless to stress the extreme gravity of the situation. If the British air fighter force does not render our Army the support asked for by General Vuillemin, it is to be feared that the battle will be lost and Paris will be occupied by the enemy.

* See Chapter IV, p. 35.

It was at this point that Pétain suddenly looked up and spoke: "You must make them realise what that means," he said, and then looking down again resumed his absorbed study of the carpet pattern.

"The consequences of the loss of this battle and the occupation of the capital are known to the British Government," said Reynaud slowly, embodying the Marshal's thought, scanning every word as he wrote.*

3. *Bomber Force.*

I thank you for your declaration, which gives us entire satisfaction.

The French Government has complete confidence in the spirit of total solidarity of the British Government and its Chief.

The stating of the case had again changed the atmosphere. The reality of the danger stood out the more starkly divested of histrionics. Moreover it began to appear, as British help was so badly needed, that it was worth while attempting persuasion even if it meant sacrificing the more congenial method of hectoring.

The sensation of the storm about to break on the front of the armies was as perceptible in that room as is the hush before a great onrush of wind and driving rain. It eliminated all other feelings, and Weygand and I found ourselves talking as if there had never been a shadow of difference between us. He explained that he believed the Germans were probably trying to draw the French reserves to the Oise, to oppose a thrust on Paris, but that their main attack would probably take the form of two break-throughs, the one directed on Rouen and Le Havre, the other from Rethel, aimed at the Marne. He thought the Germans might be planning to

---

* Cordell Hull writes in his *Memoirs*, quoted by Churchill, Vol. II, p. 126, that "Bullitt (the U.S. Ambassador in Paris), outraged by this decision (that of the Prime Minister not to send planes to France), communicated to the President and me on June 5 his fear that the British might be conserving their Air Force and Fleet so as to use them as bargaining points in negotiations with Hitler. The President and I, however, thought differently. France was finished, but we were convinced that Britain, under Churchill's indomitable leadership, intended to fight on. There would be no negotiations between London and Berlin. Only the day before Bullitt's telegram Churchill had made his magnificent speech in the House of Commons."

I am convinced, and all internal evidence confirms this, that Mr. Bullitt got no such idea from Reynaud. I do not believe it crossed his mind.

encircle Paris rather than attack it frontally, in which case the two advancing columns would rendezvous about Orléans.

He told me the need was so great that he was bringing up behind the point of attack some divisions without any anti-tank guns, others with only one or two. He said: "I beg of you to tell the Prime Minister that my formula is this: 'The battle is lost if it is not prolonged, and it is unlikely we can prolong it without fighter aircraft!' " This I did.

Hardly had I got back to the Embassy when I received a message asking me to return immediately to the War Council. There I was told that a message timed 9.20 that morning had been received from Le Havre to the effect that the British were shipping back to England the searchlights they had installed there. Darlan said: "Pray ask your people to realise that if Le Havre is not defended Paris will be asphyxiated."

I was requested to ask that the anti-aircraft defences and balloon barrages should not be weakened.

Darlan added that once before he had had to use his influence with the Officer in Command at Le Havre to prevent the British from embarking. I said I knew nothing about this, but did not believe such action would have been in accordance with the British Government's intentions. The only thing I was aware of was that a few days earlier I had forwarded his request that we should strengthen our anti-aircraft defences in the harbours we used as bases.*

Reynaud's reply to Churchill was sent off by teleprinter at 1.30 p.m. I also sent as a special communication Weygand's note concerning the "unavailing" appeals to the British. I had no choice but to do this since it had been handed to me, but as when I left the conference he told me this paper was not meant to be a complaint against the British but was a statement of facts to his political chief, I underlined this, for it was important as showing that he did not wish to advertise hostility to the British. I did not refer to the passage I had had with him on the subject, but I did say the reference to the consequences of the fall of Paris had been inserted on Pétain's intervention.

It is much to Reynaud's credit that in later years he wrote that Churchill would have committed the gravest ·of errors had he sacrificed the totality of Britain's air force in the battle of France. He says he did not perhaps realise either the danger involved in

* See Chapter II, p. 15.

risking England's defeat or that Churchill had gone as far as the joint interests of France and Britain allowed. He describes his responsibilities and anxieties and offers them as an explanation for having sponsored Weygand's requests and as an excuse for his constant pressure on Churchill for more help.

His was the chief responsibility for the safety of France, and one can both understand and honour his motives and his actions. I, who was the witness of his dreadful anxieties, have only admiration for the way he defended the interests of his country as he saw them. I respected and appreciated the line he took, though I had to oppose him at times.

This was not to be an easy day, even by the trying standards of the period, and greater trouble lay ahead than had been encountered during the morning, but this was dealt with without ill-feeling, although I had to deliver some pretty sharp messages to the unfortunate Premier in the course of a number of meetings. One of my chief anxieties was lest Churchill should at last lose patience with the French. Late in the evening he spoke to me twice on the telephone. At the moment they were trying him almost beyond endurance, but the mood did not last. His sublime understanding of their difficulties, his imaginative pity for their distress, soon obliterated such annoyance as he had felt that day.

On the occasion of my first call after lunch, Reynaud, referring to his message of the morning, asked me to tell the Prime Minister that the sentences dealing with the possible fall of Paris and its consequences had been inserted at Pétain's suggestion. I told him this had already been done.

He went on to say that many reasonable men, both politicians and soldiers, had told him that resistance would be hopeless and should not be pursued if Paris fell. Pétain was most emphatically of this opinion. "And you?" I asked. "I shall fight on, but I may be replaced by others differently minded," he answered.

He told me Weygand was opposed to falling back on Brittany. He did not consider it a military proposition.

"He has no ideas," said Reynaud, "beyond fighting it out where the Army now stands and, if the front is broken through, allowing the different sections to stand their ground as long as they can. It is a simple strategic conception such as you might expect from a simple business man, a Director of Suez," commented Reynaud sarcastically, referring to the fact that the General was a director of the Suez Canal Company.

He added that nevertheless he himself had given General Colson positive orders to carry on with plans for the defence of Brittany, and, in particular, to see to it that both telephone and wireless communications were installed.

"Why," I asked, "does not Weygand, who says he is so short of troops, drain the Maginot Line and North Africa to feed his defensive front? The actual fortress troops are not mobile, but he is fighting a defensive battle. It is extraordinary that he should ask us to send unequipped troops fished out of the sea at Dunkirk to his front whilst the fortress line is packed with men, with God knows how many active troops as well." "I am not the Commander-in-Chief," answered the Premier, "nor have I the constitutional right to interfere with him, and he is fully alive to that fact. But I must confess I do not understand his policy of reinforcing his line in driblets".*

* Theodore Draper points out in his *Six Weeks War* (p. 38) that at the time of the German break-through "62 divisions, or 60 per cent of the total forces available on the north-east front, were immobilised in fortified sectors where there was no fighting, while the fate of the Allied Armies was settled in Belgium on the basis of only 40 per cent of the total forces—in fact, there were 41 divisions in Alsace and Lorraine against only 40 in Belgium"; and further (p. 123): "It should be pointed out that the Armies in the Maginot Line were left intact all through the break-through. Even now, however, after the damage was done, the French Command could not bring itself to make any very drastic withdrawals from the Maginot Line. Only three divisions were taken from the III Army, which had ten (on an 18-mile front), only three from the V Army, which had nine (in the heavily-protected Bitche–Sélestat sector), and only one from VIII Army, which had another nine. Only the III Army, at the northern end of the Maginot Line, was relatively close to the danger zone."

Weygand writes:

"On June 4th the II Army Group, holding the front from the Moselle to the Jura inclusive and whose function was to support the fortified positions and to meet a possible attack through Switzerland and across the Upper Rhine, comprised 17 divisions (one Active, one Series A, ten Series B, three Fortress Divisions and two Polish Divisions)." (*Rappelé au Service*, p. 577.)

Weygand makes it clear that the Generals concerned, as early as June 2nd, favoured the evacuation of the Maginot Line. This is what he writes:

"On June 2nd I had an important conference at Châlons with General Georges, the Commander of the II Group of Armies, and the Commander of the II Army. General Prételat told me of the situation of his forces, reduced to a minimum by the calls I had made on them and without reserves, which it was not possible to build up out of fortress units. The possibility of an attack at the junction of the II and III Army Groups would create a very dangerous situation. General Prételat, as also General Huntziger, wondered whether it

Continued on p. 60

I drew Reynaud's attention to the passages in Churchill's speech concerning the King of the Belgians. He had now been given full satisfaction, I insisted: the Prime Minister, talking of the King's surrender, had spoken of it as a pitiful episode. The Press had greeted these as "withering words", and so they were.

As I left, the Premier told me he was reshaping his Government. I put him no questions, but knew well enough that this must mean the elimination of Daladier, and (I hoped) of the pro-Italian Ministers.

Later I heard he had had the extraordinary idea of offering the Foreign Office to Pétain, which, fortunately, the old man had refused.

That afternoon I had the explanation of a fact that had puzzled the Ambassador and me for some days. We had seen references to a letter of Vuillemin's to Weygand which had got to London without our seeing it (it must have been sent direct to the French Military or Air Attaché). Now Ismay sent me the text and I could see why it had been so resented. The Ambassador was as angry about it as I was.

The demands made on the R.A.F. we were familiar with, since they were repeated in the recent documents I had handled, but this one contained a request we had not hitherto heard of, which was that the totality of the British fighting force should be detailed to take part in the forthcoming battle (leaving nothing for the protection of Britain) and that half of it should be based in France.

That was a pretty tall order, but added to it was a sentence of insufferable impertinence in its complacent fatuity.

As has been seen, we had thrown into the Battle of the Bulge, as the break-through on the French front was called, a greater proportion of our fighter strength than prudence allowed, and that force, engaged immediately, completely, and regardless of consequences, had been to all intents and purposes destroyed, yet this is how General Vuillemin described the support we had given: "*Such reinforcements, although produced tardily and in insufficient numbers at the time of the battle which started on May* 10*th, proved however to be of value.*"

---

was wise to cling to the Fortified Region, or whether it would be better to carry out a strategic retirement before being forced to do so under enemy pressure. I answered that I had considered this hypothesis with the other but had renounced it.

"My decision was taken. The risks were known and had been accepted by the Government, who were fully aware of my plan of action." (*Rappelé au Service*, p. 156.)

Ismay's covering letter contained the following instruction: "The Prime Minister would be grateful if you would find a convenient opportunity to invite Reynaud's attention to the terms of this letter, and to tell him that it has created a very unfortunate impression on the minds of those Ministers and officials in this country who are doing their utmost to give the French the greatest possible help."

The suggested opportunity I took later that same day, and I was glad to see the Premier was shocked. He said he quite agreed that the tone and the terms used by Vuillemin were quite inadmissible.

Had we known that the pilots of Corap's Army, whom our fighter pilots had sacrificed themselves to save, were at that moment sitting idle near Tours, 30 kilometres from a number of Potez 63 aircraft which had been collected but were never handed over to them (these machines were eventually evacuated by lorry to the south), I can imagine what the reaction would have been.*

* At the Riom Trial (it is to be noted that in no public library in France are the accounts of this trial available; the contemporary French papers are useless as all the more important parts were censored) Monsieur Guy Le Chambre, ex-Air Minister, interrogated on June 9th, 1941, quotes General d'Harcourt as saying: "Judging by the machines stocked in my command, there were enough to satisfy, to a great extent at least, the needs of the Armies."

General Massenet de Marancourt, giving evidence, stated: "At Tours there were 200 war planes including monoplane fighters at the disposal of Air Force G.H.Q." In January 1940 he asked to have the use of 20 of these for training and town protection. He said that this would enable him to provide fairly quickly trained teams. This request was refused by General Picard, who said Air Force G.H.Q. refused a single plane. On May 10th, 150 Bloch 151s were still at Tours, fit for flying. He took upon himself at once to constitute fighter patrols. There were neither guns nor machine-guns. He sent cars to Châtellerault, where he found all he wanted, which proved nothing was missing.

In June 1940 his patrols fought over Tours and won two victories without loss, "which shows," he declared, "that the unused material was usable." He went on: "About May 15th there arrived in the region of Châtellerault, near Tours, all the squadrons of Corap's Army, over 400 kilometres as the crow flies from where that Army had been engaged. These units had lost their Potez 63s, destroyed during the bombardments owing to their having remained grounded under conditions upon which I will not insist. But these units had their pilots and all their transport. At the same date I received from the Air Minister the order to collect all the Potez 63s from the schools, to equip them and hold them at the disposal of Air G.H.Q. Forty-eight hours later some 30 of these machines were collected south of the Cher and a few kilometres from the air units of Corap's Army.

"A month went by, no order was received. The squadrons remained without aircraft and the Potez 63s without pilots. At the moment of the 'débacle' I had to have the Potez 63s evacuated by lorry on the roads."

(This evidence was censored by Pétain's order.)

Monsieur Guy Le Chambre also quoted General Mouchard: "There were

Continued on p. 62

I was unaware, as was the French Government, which was a pity, that fighter squadrons which had refuelled in France on May 17th, 18th and 19th, but had not done so since, took the risk, in view of the emergency, of refuelling in France once more this day [June 5th], when two Fighter Command squadrons were sent to the aerodrome of Rouen-Boos to operate a refuelling base.

I also received during the afternoon London's comments on Reynaud's telegram of June 2nd (p. 15).

These pointed out that the first reinforcements for the original B.E.F. were still in France. It had been intended to re-embark them so as to amalgamate them with the troops recovered from Dunkirk. General Weygand having personally asked the C.I.G.S. to leave them in France, his request had been complied with, although this involved a serious handicap.

No promise whatsoever, I was told, had been given that there would be three more British divisions in France by now. Under the original programme the first of these was to have been dispatched toward the end of this month (June), and I was reminded that the matter was being pressed forward as fast as possible.

The question of possible fighter support was receiving consideration. The map and information concerning aerodromes I had sent was in the hands of the Air Ministry, who were dealing with it.

As the information concerning the German attack launched that morning was not actually bad, since the panzer divisions had not broken through, the sense of relief grew. Not to be beaten was almost good news, so true is it that everything is a matter of contrast. Nevertheless, with an anxiety all found hard to conceal, every scrap of information from the front was sought for and eagerly scanned, each one comparing notes and impressions with his neighbour.

I knew that General Georges had been working hard at a new theory of defence which he had been trying to impose on all

---

in the interior modern planes whose place should have been with the armies. After May 10th these planes appeared suddenly and were thrown into the battle piecemeal and under improvised conditions which were both regrettable and fruitless."

Such were the conditions under which the utmost pressure was being placed on Churchill to send to France the few aircraft available for the defence of our country. But, not knowing these things, we all believed the French had used up their last reserves and that it was incumbent on us to run the gravest risks on their behalf.

formations. Weygand had accepted the very simple principles involved and had used his authority in support of them, but, obvious though they were, it was hardly possible that an army battered as was the French should, in spite of its amazing adaptability, put these new ideas into practice in a matter of days, even though they afforded the only possibility of a successful defence.

The problem was to get into the heads of all concerned that linear defence was a thing of the past, and that its place must be taken by defence in depth.

The French Army had been trained on the "continuous line" conception of the last war. If the front was broken, then it must be re-established further back, always as a continuous line. As it was now certain that German armour could, if sufficiently concentrated, break through a line at any point, and if the only answer to this was to fall back and reform a line beyond the furthest point the armour had reached, the French Army would soon be defending the Pyrenees. In fact, no new line would ever be formed, for the armour would certainly attack again before one was re-established. This was obvious, but so ingrained was the conception of linear fighting both amongst the public and the Army, that each talked of the battle now engaged as the battle of the Weygand line.

It was understandable, for as the front was continuously held, it was in that sense linear, but there was a fundamental change in conception, for it was no longer an immense line that was to be held at all costs, but a series of strong-points along a line supported by other strong-points in the rear. In other words, a defence in depth.

Cadrillage the French called it, chequer-board. These strong-points were mainly fortified villages selected so as to prevent the German armour from using the roads. But Georges' conception was not a defensive one. Every attack was to be met by a counter-attack. The enemy was to be driven out of any point he might occupy, and it was laid down that, above all things, should a unit find itself cut off from its neighbours it was not to withdraw but to fight on, holding up the enemy and endangering his advance. The utmost effort was to be made to deepen the zone of the defence.

Of course this was not new. It embodied the principles of Pétain's defensive battle of Champagne in 1918. But the conception underlying that great and successful battle had been lost sight of for too long.

Georges now rightly laid it down that every strong-points hould include anti-tank and 75 mm. guns. The French troops, who always hated digging, were adjured to do so, it being pointed out that the slit-trench provided the answer to the dive-bomber.

In quest of news I went to see General Héring, the Governor of Paris, in the late afternoon. I had known him during the last war when, as a major, he had been liaison officer to General Rawlinson's Army. What I remembered best about him was his dislike of politicians, a dislike which he shared with all professional officers save those who relied on political favour for their advancement.

His personal views on this subject were made clear when in 1917 a German delayed-action bomb blew up a couple of French Deputies together with a number of our men in Bapaume Town Hall. He would enquire every day with mock solicitude if they had been found, but his overriding fear was evidently that they would be disinterred, and his cheerfulness grew as the likelihood of this happening receded.

He was moderately confident. He had, he said, telephoned to General Frère in the late afternoon, who was fairly happy, though the *massif* of St. Gobain had been lost.

In·the last war this would have been considered a major disaster, but values had changed. If the enemy had broken his teeth on a great obstacle and then been stopped, a positive advantage had perhaps been gained. I did not, however, feel very reassured, because we were only talking in terms of the attack by armour, and supposing this was held at the cost of immense sacrifice, what would happen when the terrific blow of the German infantry following close behind was delivered? How could the depleted French Army, shaken by the assault of the German tank divisions, and for which no reserves appeared to be available, cope with a more numerous and practically fresh army? And what of the Stukas? No defence in depth affected them, and we were not far from the moment when we should have nothing with which to oppose them. Still, at times such as these the only thing to do is to concentrate on the dangers of the present, acting on the principle that there is only one kind of success that matters, and that is the success of the moment. Hanging on today might mean victory tomorrow.

Most encouraging of all, French liaison officers came in with moving and stirring tales of how the French infantry was resisting desperately, fighting back magnificently, making great ravages amongst the German armour, holding up the following infantry.

No news could have given me greater joy and pride. The French defeat had been to me very like a personal humiliation. I had been bewildered, for the French soldier of the First World War had been my pal and I had retained in the intervening years a respectful and deep admiration for his simple, stoical qualities. I could neither accept nor believe that the sons of my old friends were unworthy of their fathers. Now that it was being proved that this was not the case, I was deeply stirred, and as I rushed from one task to the other, telephoning to London, computing reports, writing telegrams, I felt a greater ease than I had since I arrived in Paris. All the horrible defeatism in high places, the arrogance of the French General Staff, the ineptitude of Weygand, were being redeemed, as often before, by the simple heroism of the common soldier and the regimental officer. After all, I recalled, very much the same scenes had been enacted in Paris time and again between 1914 and 1919.

That evening I remembered a poem written long ago by a French officer I knew which expressed all the simplicity of a *poilu*. The old fellow had been killed, as most of them were, and was terrified when he found himself standing before the saints. When he beheld Joan of Arc in her armour he was convinced he was facing a court-martial and that he was being accused of all the crimes he knew he had committed, such as stealing a chicken now and then, mislaying his gas-mask. . . .

My fleeting exhilaration was not shared by the authorities in London, who were evidently perturbed at the paucity of news of the fighting; I was called up several times, and so was Redman. But my information amounted to little more than hearsay. Here again liaison failed. In the first war we would have had reliable liaison officers on the spot whose job it would have been to know and to report. The Prime Minister himself, realising the fate of the war was probably at stake, spoke to me at least twice on the telephone during the evening and again during the night. He was irritated less by the lack of news than by imperative but vague demands for help with which our military and air authorities were apparently being assailed on all sides. His attention was focused on a German attack which had developed in the region of Abbeville concerning which I had no news: nor could I obtain any in spite of the urgency of his enquiries. On the other hand he had heard nothing whatever concerning the fighting about St. Quentin.

Just before 8 p.m. I received a most immediate telegram for

Reynaud and Weygand which expressed the Prime Minister's anxieties and perturbation. Its gist was that we had that morning received, in general terms only, a request for air assistance over the area of the Abbeville second-line front. There had been nothing to indicate the form of assistance required or where precisely it was needed.

We were holding four squadrons of bombers and two squadrons of fighters at full strength, said the Prime Minister, ready to intervene from England as soon as we were told where they were expected to operate. He pointed out that to collect this force, which had up to the moment of his telegraphing not been called upon, it had been necessary to break up many squadrons and suspend the whole process of reorganisation after Dunkirk.

Meanwhile we were dispatching reconnaissance aircraft over the supply area of the enemy. If good targets were revealed they would be attacked by bombers escorted by fighters. If no suitable targets were found, the fighters would be sent in any eventuality to intervene in the battle area. All these operations were in addition to those undertaken by the R.A.F. stationed in France and were quite apart from the attack to be carried out that night by strong bomber forces on objectives chosen by the French.

I gave this message to Reynaud. Although he was in the very midst of the unenviable task of recasting his Government and had just seen or was about to see Daladier, he listened carefully and, as always, intelligently to what I had to say. He detected the note of growing exasperation in this and others of Churchill's messages but showed no irritation in return. Better news from the front was naturally a powerful help to him. The prospect of getting rid of double-dealing colleagues no doubt gave him an assurance, a self-confidence he had inevitably lacked when he felt the dagger passing from hand to hand under the Cabinet table, sure only that someone was ready to plunge it into his back at the first opportunity.

"The General Staff is certainly not working as it should," he said. "It is as remarkable as it is unfortunate that liaison between the British and French Commands is so poor. It is a pity," he added with a wry smile, "that neither of us was doing his present job earlier in the proceedings."

The way in which this telegram was received by Reynaud's military staff showed they did not even grasp what was meant by such terms as "breaking up" squadrons, and "reorganisation after Dunkirk". A well-organised Air Force was something they had no conception of. No pains had been taken to study ours, owing to the fatal blindness engendered by the belief that in all matters appertaining to war the French must know best.

There was at the Embassy what we took to be good news from Rome. Our Embassy there had heard the Germans were very short of petrol, so much so that they were planning to invade Rumania. If only this could mean their attack would be slowed down for lack of fuel! Could we but be certain they were not collecting considerable supplies in France!

I was to see Reynaud yet once more, about 10.30 p.m. at his flat.

I had several messages for him. The first was an answer to the French query concerning the defences of Le Havre.

It was to the effect that the Chiefs of the Imperial General Staff had issued strict orders that the anti-aircraft defences of Le Havre were not to be weakened in any way. I was also to inform both Darlan and Weygand that the provision of anti-aircraft defences for other harbours was being urgently considered. This information gave real satisfaction. It did something to counteract the fixed impression of the French that we were only interested in our own defence. I kept to myself yet another message, that it was presumed the French realised that we also depended on imports from overseas and on having secure harbours.

I also gave Reynaud the answer to a question he had put earlier that day concerning the possibility of establishing a single Anglo-French Air Command. Curiously enough there had been a hint in the French suggestion (for which Reynaud was not responsible) that such a Command should be French on the ground that Weygand controlled all the land forces.

The answer was short, and conformed with the discussions I had had with London.

1. Unity of command of the bomber forces was possible—under a British Air Force officer.

2. Unity of command was not practicable in regard to the fighter forces.

Reynaud took this answer philosophically. I do not think he expected anything else, nor do I think he would have been averse to a single command under a British officer. I also handed him a private and personal message from the Prime Minister, in English. It was unusually sharp in tone.

Private and Personal.
1. Your comments will be examined by the General Staff, who have orders to send the two divisions as soon as possible. Permit me to observe that your divisions picked out of Dunkirk are not to enter the line for a month. We are trying to send one of our seasoned divisions in a fortnight.
2. Fighter aircraft. General Vuillemin's demand was altogether unreasonable and his letter made the worst impression on everyone here and greatly increased my difficulties. Kindly look at paragraph in which he refers to the assistance we gave in recent battle. You do not seem to understand at all that British fighter aviation has been worn to a shred and frightfully mixed up by need of maintaining standing patrols of 45 fighters over Dunkirk without which the evacuation would have been impossible. The mere sorting out of aeroplanes from the different squadrons practically paralyses the force for four or five days. However, I have sent you this morning a telegram saying that we would hold four squadrons of day-bombers and two of Hurricane fighters available for the operations this afternoon in addition to the nine squadrons you have already, and I shall try to maintain the same tomorrow, when I will telegraph again.

Reynaud frowned as he read it, then said: "Leave it with me, we will discuss it tomorrow morning. There is a meeting of the full Cabinet presently at the Élysée (this meant that the President of the Republic would preside). I simply have not time to deal with it now. I am in the midst of reconstructing the Government." But as I left he repeated what he had said earlier concerning his disapproval of Vuillemin's attitude.

I saw Baudouin at Reynaud's flat and learnt with some astonishment, which I tried to conceal, that he was to be Under-Secretary of State for Foreign Affairs. He had no qualifications that I knew of for the post, though many for that of Minister of Finance. I enquired who was replacing him as Secretary to the War Committee. To my further surprise he said he was to combine the two functions. On reflection I concluded that Charles-Roux, the able permanent head of that department, would be virtually in charge and that Reynaud intended Baudouin to be the link between himself and the Quai d'Orsay.

Monsieur Prouvost, another of Madame de Portes' protégés, was also there, and I learnt he was to be Minister of Propaganda. He was popular amongst, or at least considered useful by, a whole band of young women of the highest society who liked meeting each other and enjoying the excellent food at his superb flat at the Trocadero. He was very rich, and generous when flattered by feminine charm or high-sounding names. His fortune came from textiles in the dreary north-east, a part of France no self-respecting man or woman of the world he now entertained in Paris had ever been to, where smoke and dust merged with similar unpleasant products generated by the rather *drôle* Belgians in their own flat country just over the way.

But Prouvost also owned a paper, *Paris-Soir*, which gave him authority. People are always impressed by a newspaper proprietor; they have a vague idea that he can make or mar a man, or indeed a woman on occasion.

Though I did not particularly like him, I had none of the reasons for holding him in contempt which arose later. On the contrary, I was on friendly terms with him and had met some very charming people at his house. Strange to think what became of them all. Most, I think, weathered the war by drifting as the prevailing wind ordained, but on the other hand the patriotism and courage of some of these delicate, beautifully-dressed creatures, the lovely idols of pre-war good fortune, was beyond all praise. One, a Duchess, young in spite of a grown-up son, lost him in the war as well as her husband tortured to death by the Germans, whilst she herself spent long months in a French gaol, emerging at last disfigured by lice.

Prouvost and I said we would keep in touch, and voiced the nice things we both thought of his opposite number, Duff Cooper, but we never met again. I would not have had any dealing with him at Bordeaux for all the gold in South Africa.

I also heard that Colonel de Gaulle, of whom Reynaud had often spoken in the highest terms, was to become Under-Secretary of War. This was good news. He was one of the very few European technicians on tank warfare. His book on the subject was remarkable. That the General Staff distrusted him was no matter, since he would be in control. Other advantages were that he favoured defending Brittany and was not in Madame de Portes' orbit. Best of all, he had proved his worth as a fighting soldier. Everyone agreed he had led the 4th Armoured Division with great distinction in the recent fighting at Abbeville.

How would he get on with Pétain? Long ago he had been on his staff, but the old Marshal was said to have disapproved of his ideas on mechanised warfare.

Late that night I spoke to my wife. She was no longer living in her dream. It had come to an end with the departure of the omnipotent and kindly patron of her unit, General Réquin. She was, I realised, rather bewildered, rather frightened at the decisions she must take. The responsibility for all those girls weighed heavily upon her. No talk of painting now. Nor was I as sure as I had been that she should stay where she was. I was no longer certain she could reach the Mediterranean if the Germans broke through, and I did not want her and her hospital to be forced into Switzerland and cut off there.

Even in the midst of the anxieties of the moment, it gave me a pang to hear her say in a small voice that she wanted to come and consult me. Nothing could have revealed more clearly that her confidence was shaken, and that she could not tell under the dark clouds she at last perceived where her erstwhile sunny little world was drifting. One thing I was certain of: her courage would never fail her. It was, in fact, of too positive a kind ever to be reassuring.

Concerning her trip to Paris I tried to convey, without either frightening her or giving any information away, that she should follow a southern route. Also she must hurry. At any moment, any day, I might have to return to London to report.

It was just as well that I said this, for in the early hours the Prime Minister called me up. The French picture, both political and military, presented such a tangled skein he wanted to get it in focus. His confidence in the French Command was evidently much shaken. Was there a real plan? he asked. What would the French do if their line was broken? Was there anything in the Brittany project? Was there an alternative?

He was obviously disappointed, distressed, puzzled and rather angry. It was, I said, very difficult to report adequately or effectively over the telephone or by telegram, and suggested I should return to London for a short time. He said he fully agreed, he had himself thought of this. After all, that was what I was supposed to do. When could I come? Tomorrow? I pointed out that Reynaud ought to be consulted. He would in any case probably expect me to attend the War Committee meeting in the morning, and had told me he wished to discuss his (Churchill's) private and personal note of the previous evening. Other appointments had also been made for Thursday. Would Friday be all right? "Friday, then. I shall want you to see the War Room people, and there are others who will wish to talk to you as well."

CHAPTER VI

Thursday, June 6th

(1)

The composition of the new French Ministry—A request from Darlan—Meeting of the War Committee—Weygand's attack on General Fortune—His outburst against the British—I arrange for him to meet Air Marshal Barratt—His defence of Vuillemin—The Committee renews its appeal for British help—Weygand calms down—My letter to Reynaud—The Ambassador's support—Reynaud's optimism concerning the battle—His decision about the defence of Paris—I call on Pétain—His pessimism—His poor opinion of de Gaulle—He reads me an old speech about Joan of Arc— and shows me a statuette—Afterthoughts on a strange interview.

As Reynaud had said he wished to discuss Churchill's private and personal message of the previous evening in the morning, I asked when he would receive me for that purpose, but was told he could not do so before meeting the War Committee, which he would expect me to attend. This was a pity, for I should have liked an opportunity of smoothing over in a *tête-à-tête* talk the growing asperity of the communications between London and Paris.

I had foreseen that if Churchill heard that the French, whilst pressing us to ship our Dunkirk troops straight back into the battle, did not intend engaging theirs for a month, he would be furious. I had suggested that he should not be told, but he had been, and was now as angry as I had imagined he would be. I shared his exasperation but I thought it should not be allowed to rankle.

The composition of the new French Cabinet was an interesting study. Defeatists and non-defeatists seemed about equally balanced.

72

Mandel of course remained in office, and so did Campinchi, Marin, Monnet and Rio. Daladier, against whom the whole manœuvre was mounted, was eliminated. No paper mourned him. Chautemps continued as Vice-President of the Council, a choice which soon proved to be a fatal mistake. De Monzie was fortunately dropped. The appointments of Colonel de Gaulle as Under-Secretary for War and of Baudouin and Prouvost were confirmed.

There was a newcomer, Ybarnegaray, a Deputy of the Right, believed to be stout-hearted, but who turned out to be the opposite.

A great surprise to me was the dismissal of Lamoureux from the Ministry of Finance. He was a cheerful little man, and I knew him to be able. Later that day I was told his services had been dispensed with because he had been in favour of making peace overtures. This was news to me.

My friend Delbos was once more set the task of educating young France, in place of the apoplectic Sarraut, whom Pétain had, I heard, been working against for some days, as he had been against Daladier. Well, Reynaud could afford under the circumstances to offend the powerful *Dépêche de Toulouse*, edited by Maurice Sarraut, the ex-Minister's brother. Nobody was worrying at the moment about the Radical Socialist party and their powerful organ.

I did not know the new Minister of Finance, Bouthillier, who had been the senior official of that department. Reynaud, of course, knew him well, having been political head of the Ministry. His confidence turned out to be misplaced, for the new Minister was soon to prove his bitterest enemy, which was all the more discreditable in that Reynaud had rescued him from the obscurity to which an earlier Minister of Finance had relegated him.

Before going to the War Committee meeting I wrote to Ismay telling him I should probably be in London the next day, and also asking him to send all telegrams to me via Redman. This would save much time on two counts: the first was that if they dealt with any questions affecting the Commander-in-Chief, Weygand would be informed, and the other was that the Embassy cipher staff, which was apt to include practically everyone in the Embassy, was so overworked that there were inevitable but serious delays. Furthermore, I desired to avoid any possible awkwardness resulting from my telegrams being dealt with by anyone but myself.

I then received a message from Darlan that he wished to have a word with me before the Committee met. It was to say that some of the British anti-aircraft guns at Le Havre had already been taken away. With a calmness for which I was thankful, he said he would be most grateful if they could be returned. Would I do something about it? I promised to deal with this immediately.

A month earlier Paul Baudouin had described Darlan as full of contempt for his British colleagues, "*plein de mépris pour ses collègues britanniques.*" That attitude was now noticeably changed. He probably did not like them any better but his contempt had evaporated.

The War Committee meeting was attended as usual by Pétain, Weygand, Darlan and Baudouin. General Vuillemin was not present on this occasion. Sometimes he was, at others not. It made no difference, for he never contributed or said anything, but just looked on with the bewildered washed-out eyes of an ancient celluloid doll floating on the opaque waters of the bath it seemed bewildered to find itself in.

"*Vuillemin, nul comme d'habitude,*" a cypher as usual, says Baudouin somewhere, not inaccurately.

Reynaud opened the proceedings by saying he had had a talk with Present Roosevelt late the night before, and that it had given him keen satisfaction; his manner and expression showed this to be completely true. A new confidence radiated from him; this talk, combined with having got rid of his most dangerous colleagues, had renewed his self-reliance. President Roosevelt, he informed us, had told him he was going as far as the law would permit to help the Allies, and even a little further.

The pleasant impression this gave me did not last long. It soon became evident that Weygand had seen the Prime Minister's message of the previous evening to Reynaud and deeply resented it. His face of taut parchment was working as if it would crack. Watching him carefully, I thought I read real malevolence in his expression, and prepared for the worst. I was not mistaken, but was surprised by the new line of approach his unflagging hostility to the British led him to take that morning.

This time, General Fortune, commanding the 51st Division, was his target. He had, it seemed, fallen back without orders. It was quite intolerable. How could he, Weygand, conduct operations when such elements were included in his own reliable and disciplined forces? What had I to say?

"Nothing," I answered, determined both to ignore the insult and to keep my temper, an extremely difficult task, for one of my most notable failures in life has been to earn the reputation of being long-suffering. "I do not know anything about General Fortune's orders, or his movements. These lie entirely outside my duties, which are to represent the Prime Minister, in his capacity as Minister of Defence, with M. Reynaud. It is a matter to be settled between yourself and the British General Staff. If M. Reynaud, when fully informed of the facts, chooses to draw Mr. Churchill's attention to them, then I will take action, not otherwise."

But Weygand wanted a row, and presently he got it, but not yet. General Fortune was behaving exactly as Lord Gort had done, as the British always did, he was now saying. "I wish you to know that in my mind there is no doubt that General Blanchard was never able to obtain that the British Army should attack southwards. I am certain," he went on, "that the British Government ordered its Army to re-embark without informing the French Commander-in-Chief. Your General should be called 'Misfortune'," he added amiably.*

I sat there wondering what sin I could have committed in a previous incarnation which must now be expiated by having to listen to this venom being regurgitated on our Army. But still I held on, maintaining what was intended to be an impassive mien, and I must have been successful, for I have read a French description of the scene in which it is said "*Le Général anglais demeure impassible.*"† All I did was to turn to the Premier and say, in a voice which I hoped sounded natural, that I thought there was little point, situated as we were, in going over old ground. Our information concerning events in the north was totally at variance with that of the Commander-in-Chief. We did not accept his as correct, and the British Government would deplore his conclusions. We, however, hoped not to be compelled to produce our version of the facts. And I could not

* The following passages occur in *Strange Defeat*, by the French officer, Marc Bloch (p. 110): " 'Do anything you like, sir, but for Heaven's sake do something.' In those words, according to one of my colleagues who was present, a Corps Commander on one occasion addressed General Blanchard at Lens"; and further he writes that on the night of May 25th–26th "I distinctly heard General Blanchard say, more calmly than I should have thought possible: 'I have not much doubt what is going to happen—double capitulation.' At that time it was only May 26th, and we had the means, if not of saving ourselves, at least of putting up a long, heroic, and desperate resistance, às whole islands of men had done in 1918 when they were surrounded on the Champagne front . . ."

† *Aurore* 27.11.49: "The Secret Communications of the French General Staff".

resist adding that if he were not informed of these this could only be due to poor staff work, excusable under the circumstances.

"But," I asked Reynaud, who evidently did not approve of the line Weygand was taking, "is there nothing to discuss this morning beyond past events?"

The Premier was glad to change the subject to the question of air support. That was the major problem at the moment, he said.

He can have little realised that these were the magic words that would open the flood-gates of Weygand's hatred, which now poured from him like lava, with the doubly surprising effect due to such a phenomenon occurring in an extinct volcano. He was determined to link our alleged failure to support the French in the air to the pre-Dunkirk period. He was now literally yelling, in a high-pitched broken voice. "What is happening in the air now is but a repetition of what happened in the north when the British refused to attack on Arras," he screamed. "I support and endorse every word that General Vuillemin has written" (so much for the Prime Minister's comments). "Mr. Churchill may think General Vuillemin's demands unreasonable. Perhaps if he saw the condition of our Army he would think we were unreasonable to go on fighting." (Then what of the undisciplined Fortune marooned amongst the reliable and disciplined French?) But there was something real and ominous under this spate of vitriol, and that was the clear indication that, before the fate of the present battle was cast, it was considered lost by the Commander-in-Chief and his excuse for this was British duplicity and delinquencies.

"I will not accept," Weygand was screaming, "that *La Royale Air Force* should send out reconnaissances of its own and bomb objectives of its own choosing. I, the Commander-in-Chief, I alone am the person to select targets."

This was something actual that had to be dealt with, so I weighed in. "*Mon Général*, we have not got pet objectives of our own, we are trying to strike where it hurts most. Again this is not my business, but have you indicated to Air Marshal Barratt the targets you have in mind, or the reconnaissances you require?"

Weygand stopped screaming. He was now not even gesticulating. He looked blank.

"When did you see the Air Marshal last?" I asked. No answer. "Do you mean to say you have not seen him at all, have never seen him?" It was my turn to be struck with open-mouthed amazement. Here was the Air Marshal in command of our Air Forces in France, endeavouring as best he could to support the French, in touch no doubt with General Georges, but whom the Commander-in-Chief, endlessly complaining about the R.A.F., had not even seen! I perceived I had scored a point. Turning to Reynaud I asked if I might suggest that General Weygand should meet Air Marshal Barratt as soon as possible. I should be delighted to arrange this.

As there seemed an opportunity of getting the situation in focus, I went on to say that if General Weygand had made requests to the Air Marshal, and he had refused to comply, there would be justification for the complaints to which he had given the form of accusations. But as he had not even seen our Air Commander I did not admit that he had the least ground for the severe strictures he had made. Turning to Weygand I added that I thought I could arrange for Barratt to see him that day. Did he agree? He nodded. This I was able to do, and they met that afternoon.

Weygand's rage was now overflowing again, but in a new direction. "Monsieur Churchill's criticism of General Vuillemin is intolerable," he said. "General Vuillemin is my subordinate. I take responsibility for all his actions." I protested. "Mr. Churchill has complained of a dispatch of General Vuillemin's which is a gross insult to our Air Force and moreover is untrue. If that represents General Vuillemin's real view, all it can mean is that he has no idea of what is going on." I was started now. "If General Vuillemin got into a plane and visited the front, he would no doubt be enlightened," I said, probably grinding out the words with a cold acidity for which I have often been criticised. "Mr. Churchill only complained because General Vuillemin's taunt is likely to detract from the effort he is making to give the French maximum air support."

The fat was now fairly in the fire. "If the British are sincere," Weygand shouted, "they will place their Air Force under General Vuillemin. I demand that the British send over their fighter force to France, where it will operate under General Vuillemin under my direction."

Recalling Colyer's description of the French aviators at Villacoublay going on with their lunch, refusing even to lend our pilots their machines to go up and attack the Germans overhead, the idea struck me as so absurd that I regained my temper.

"That is impossible," I said. "Our Air Force is not part of the Army, it acts independently in furtherance of a general plan." But Weygand would not have it. "It would be of more practical use if it were part of the Army," he went on. "It is of no use now. It's fine feats are told by you. They have not been reported to me." "Perhaps because there were no French airmen there to witness them," I retorted, angry once more. "It is strange that you have not seen the French reports on the Dunkirk evacuation. Your suggestion is not only impracticable, it is absurd. Furthermore, I should not be surprised to hear that the R.A.F. have not unlimited confidence in the French Air Command."

Weygand was now grey with rage. His voice sounded to me like a number of cats engaged in a feline Waterloo. "This is a personal attack on General Vuillemin," he fulminated. "I named no one," I said. "Yes you did, yes you did. Here are the English dictating to us who our Commanders are to be. The French are masters in their own house" (I wonder if a few months later he remembered saying that) and so on and so on.

My detailed notes made within half an hour say just that, "and so on and so on."

By now there was no trace of anger in my mind. On the contrary I felt cold as ice as the sense of responsibility grew. The stakes were too high for quarrelling. In the awful predicament in which we found ourselves this was just the sort of thing that should be avoided. If it was a question of high tempers I had a pretty heavy responsibility myself. Above all things, I must not let the Prime Minister down. It would perhaps have been wiser to have said nothing.

I turned to Reynaud and said that there were evidently serious divergences of view on the employment and control of the air forces. This was perhaps not the right place to discuss them as no conclusion could be reached. I would endeavour during the day to put our ideas in writing and send them to him.

But Weygand had one more shot in his locker. He could not, he said, either tolerate or accept the British attitude, the evident object of which was to place on the French Command the responsibility for a complete lack of good will for which the British leaders were entirely to blame. I did not answer, so, after all, Weygand had the last word.

Reynaud, who for some time had been trying to stop Weygand, was evidently relieved at the sudden end to the dispute. Making

Some Members of Reynaud's Government

(*left to right*) Paul Reynaud, Frossard, Yvon Delbos, de Gaulle

General Fortune, Commanding British 51st Division, with
General Fagalde

use of my last remark concerning the employment of the air forces to return to the subject which he considered of prime importance, he said: "Certainly. But what are you really going to do for us?"

Wearily I turned to Churchill's last messages and read them over again. My French audience was as familiar with them as I was. "That is all I can tell you," I said. "Can nothing more be done?" asked Reynaud. "It is very little in view of so desperate a situation. Are its full implications really grasped in London?" he asked. "They certainly are," I answered, "and by none better than by Mr. Churchill, with whom I spoke twice last night."

"What will a large fighter force avail you in England if France is beaten to her knees? Please ask Churchill to reconsider the situation." I told him that from my talks with the Prime Minister the previous day I was certain there was not a consecutive half-hour during which the position in France was not being considered by him, always with a view to giving the maximum help. All I could be certain of was that more and not less than had been promised would be given. I also imagined that, as two squadrons of fighters had refuelled in France the previous day, they might do so again today. I had no authority whatever for saying this. It was pure surmise. If they could do so it would be a powerful help, since on the Abbeville front fighters based in England could only remain 20 minutes over the target. This was a matter I promised to take up again with the Prime Minister.

"There can be no limit to human effort," said Reynaud, "if it is a question of living or dying, and that is the truth staring us in the face since the decisive battle was started yesterday."

Then Weygand spoke again. His attitude, voice and appearance had changed. He was now practically normal. There was nothing unusual in the slight whine in his tone. "Please tell your Prime Minister," he was saying, "that if he could see the condition of the men and the divisions we are throwing into the battle, he would then perhaps not hesitate to engage fighter squadrons however imperfectly organised. We are forming the Dunkirk troops into divisions as best we can, but these will have only six battalions instead of nine. They are miserably equipped and are very poor in artillery. There is, however, no choice, we are in mortal peril."

I assured him I would give the Prime Minister his message word for word, which I did.

Reynaud walked with me to the door. "You know I have complete confidence in Churchill," he said as I crossed the threshold. "Yes, I know," I answered. "You can rest assured that he is straining every nerve on your behalf." "*Il fait l'impossible.*"

And indeed he did, for two fighter squadrons did operate from Seine bases on the 6th and 7th. It was then decided that four squadrons should operate from them. Three did so on the 8th, but that evening the threat to the airfields they were using was such that it was decided to refuel no more home-based fighters in France.

I returned immediately to the Embassy and drew up an almost verbatim report of what had occurred at the War Committee meeting, and then dictated the following letter to Reynaud:

PRIVATE AND CONFIDENTIAL

June 6th, 1940.
My DEAR PRESIDENT,

With reference to what General Weygand said this morning, there are some points I should like to develop. I did not do so at the time in order not to emphasise differences of opinion.

There is a real difference of outlook between the French and the British Air Forces, which is in no way dishonourable to either, but which does make for lack of confidence based on different doctrines. The French Air Force is naturally considered an adjunct to the Army. It is just another weapon in the hands of the Commander-in-Chief. With us this conception only applies to a section of the Air Force—that attached to the Army. The remainder—that is, by far the greater part of our Air Force—has a strategy, a policy and a point of view of its own.

It is inevitable that an Air Force with this point of view must fear being bound to a Command whose outlook is so different from its own.

I am bound to say that if General Weygand presses his point, that the role of our Government and of our Air Force should consist solely in making available and handing over to him the maximum number of our air forces, to be employed by him without query or question according to his conception of the use of air power, I fear that we shall be faced with the worst kind of trouble. Our Air Force is not a machine like a new and efficient tank that can be handed over by the manufacturer to the Army to be used as the Generals may deem fit.

I was extremely glad to see you put your finger on the most obvious defect of the whole present organisation—that is, lack of liaison. I could hardly believe my ears when I heard that General Weygand had not seen Air Marshal Barratt yet. If for any reason Barratt cannot be in close daily touch with General Weygand, then a really good liaison officer should be appointed. What is evidently required is that General Weygand's very real needs and requirements in the air should be translated into British air terms and mentality by somebody standing beside him. And it is also evident, as I said this morning, that the situation expounded by one of our own Air officers would be more readily understood and appreciated by our own Command than were requests for support put forward—as was obviously the case yesterday—in a way that was ill-understood and led to misapprehension in England.

Yours very sincerely,

E. L. SPEARS.*

Monsieur Paul Reynaud,
Président du Conseil.

As soon as this was typed I saw the Ambassador and read it to him as well as my notes on the Council Meeting, adding my comments much as I have written them here. He was incensed by Weygand's attitude and thoroughly approved my letter. When I told him I meant to hand it personally to Reynaud as soon as might be after lunch, he offered to accompany me, thus showing in the most positive way his approval of my action. I gratefully accepted. Nothing was ever more effective than such demonstrations of solidarity on the British part. It proved we were one solid homogeneous whole. I had meanwhile arranged for a meeting between Barratt and Weygand, so when we called on the Premier the talk was mainly on this subject. I gave it as my opinion that once liaison had been established between Weygand and Barratt a good many difficulties would disappear, and regretted this had not been done long ago. Reynaud agreed, saying he had been as surprised as I was that contact had not been established long since. My memory is that Weygand's attitude was not referred to, but I knew the Ambassador's presence was not lost on Reynaud. He was aware that Sir Ronald knew what had transpired and that his gesture in accompanying me

* Translation of French text.

provided more eloquent support than any words could have given. Reynaud seemed rather optimistic as to the way the battle was going. We fervently hoped he was right. I had heard that the Germans were gaining ground rather fast towards Roye on General Frère's front and towards Rouen. Still, it was all very vague, and in operations of such magnitude what occurred at one point was no guide to the whole situation.

Reynaud told us he had taken a big decision regarding the defence of Paris. The military authorities had been offered a very large number of civilian workers, 100,000 I think it was, who presumably would in the main have been Belgians, but had answered they could only utilise four companies of 200 men apiece as they could not house, feed or transport more than that number. The Premier had taken the amazingly courageous step of placing all the military engineers of the Military Government of Paris under the head of the Public Works Department of the city.

It was really very plucky and imaginative thus to fly in the face of tradition and military hierarchy. I learnt later that within a couple of days 10,000 men were at work. He also referred to his plan, which he had mentioned to me before, of mobilising at once the next two classes of recruits to be called up and sending them to North Africa. They would be safe there and could be trained under peacetime conditions.

But General Noguès, commanding in North Africa, was raising all sorts of objections. There were not sufficient barracks, the African summer would not be good for the health of these young Frenchmen (as if masses of them did not serve in Africa anyway).

I was amazed. So this was General Noguès of whom we had heard so much and whom Lord Dillon, our liaison officer with him, held in such high esteem, describing him as a "tiger straining at the leash".

Noguès only put forward one valid objection and that was not within his purview. It would take months to transport the numbers involved, he said. This I thought a very strong reason for beginning the movement at once; all the more so that probable intervention by the Italians later might further complicate the operation.

Reynaud told us that he was determined to send over at least half a class at once, say 120,000 men. The French General Staff said they could only transport 20,000 men a month, so he was sending General de Gaulle to London to ask if the British Navy could help.

This visit would also provide the new Under-Secretary for War with an excellent opportunity of meeting the British leaders.

I had made an appointment to see Pétain, and went to see him after I had taken my letter to Reynaud. I did so because I felt these morning conferences were becoming impossible. I could rely on the Premier for fair play as far as he was able to give it, but it was increasingly evident that he was daily more isolated in his desire to fight on with us. It took no prophet to see that Weygand would turn on him if things did not improve, and it was all too clear that Pétain did not believe success to be possible. Reynaud was, therefore, in too weak a position to do much to restrain the Commander-in-Chief, especially as he had no control over him in the military sphere.* What I hoped to achieve by my talk with the old Marshal was that, as much on the grounds of our old friendship as on any other, he would endeavour to restrain Weygand and point out that nothing was to be achieved by blackguarding England and everything British on all occasions. If the old man persisted in believing all was lost, I hoped to win him over to the thesis that we should at least die well, *mourir en beauté*.

So I left the Ambassador and went to the Marshal's office in the Boulevard des Invalides. I knew the low two-storeyed building well; he had occupied it since 1931. Its entrance was next to 4 bis Boulevard des Invalides, where the *Conseil Supérieur de l'Armée* was housed, and where I had had my own offices at the end of the last war.

The door gave on to a long, rather narrow courtyard, and you walked into what had probably once been the dwelling of some official in imperial days. At the head of the stairs sat a soldier, a *planton*, the only young creature in the place. A pleasant man, the A.D.C., who might with equal justification have been selected to serve the ancient Pétain because of his mature years or for his good manners, at once appeared and led me into the Marshal's study; a long, low room, shaped like a reversed L, the desk in the short arm, the several windows of the long arm giving on to the sunny courtyard.

The Marshal's greeting was friendly, almost paternal, as it invariably was. I always thought that when he was alone with me a connection was established in his mind with the times he preferred to remember, the days when he commanded a corps facing the Vimy Ridge.

* See Chapter V, p. 59.

His deafness, so apparent at the morning sessions of the War Committee, had disappeared, so had his surly, expressionless mask; he almost smiled, his face was almost animated.

"Now come here," he said, and without further ado sat down at his desk, beckoning me to a chair beside him. "Look at this map. This is like old times, but we have never looked at anything like this." He adjusted his pince-nez, and his strong forefinger with its straight cut nail began to follow the line along which the battle was raging.

"Abbeville to Rethel. That is well over 200 kilometres, and the Germans are attacking or may attack at any moment anywhere along that line. Nor is there anything to prevent their attacking elsewhere if they choose.

"They have certainly not got less than 10 panzer and 120 infantry divisions. Against what?

"Sixty of ours, one of yours. And in what condition, I ask you?

"You cannot even help us in the air."

I felt smitten at this. It was terribly true that we were both suffering for the faults we had each committed, but it was the inescapable fact that the French were footing the joint bill at the moment.

The Marshal went on speaking as, head bent, his finger moved from point to point on the map.

"In all our battles in the last war there was time; if caught unawares, by making a great effort, and maybe by sacrificing ground, in a short time we collected troops to close the breach and, presently, to counter-attack. This time there are no reserves, *vous m'entendez*, no reserves at all. It is hopeless—*c'est sans espoir*." His voice was cold. He seemed detached as a judge pronouncing a sentence. Then he went on: "No doubt the men are fighting well, they have got over their first surprise as they did in 1914, but they are fighting one against two and many of their weapons have been lost."

He went on to say that, as if this were not enough, the *Président du Conseil* (Reynaud) had undermined morale by a speech he had made a week or two before, implying that the defeat was all the fault of the Generals. If our men did not always fight as they should, it was not the fault of the Generals, but of the schoolmasters, above all of the politicians. "The country has been rotted by politics. The people can no longer discern the face of France through the veil politicians have thrown over it. As you know, a matricide is led to the guillotine with a veil over his face. It is that sort of veil, but it is over the face of the mother. The murderer has thrown his veil over his mother's face."

I was taken aback by the glacial fury in the Marshal's voice. My memory, delving into the past, searched for the record of a similar note. I seldom forget a sound, a faculty also enjoyed by parrots, and there was indexed in my mind the fact that I had heard this one before. Then, startlingly, I had it. I heard Pétain's voice of twenty years ago. The words were lost, but the tone was the same, and he was speaking of Weygand.

There was a pause. I could see that the Marshal's anger was not abating. He was looking down at the map, but not studying it. "Then this appointment of de Gaulle is not going to help matters. Do you know him?" he asked.

"No, but I thought he was highly spoken of; has he not done very well in command of the Armoured Division at Abbeville?"

"He thinks he knows all about the mechanics of warfare. His vanity leads him to think the art of war has no secrets for him. He might have invented it. I know all about him. He was once on my staff and wrote a book, or at least I told him how to do so. I gave him the outline and corrected it, in fact annotated it in my own hand. When he published it he did not even acknowledge my contribution. Not only is he vain, he is ungrateful," and he concluded, "He has few friends in the Army. No wonder, for he gives the impression of looking down on everybody. They called him 'Le Connétable' at St. Cyr." The word conjured up the picture of a Connétable de France I had once seen, long face resting on a ruff, long nose, receding chin barely concealed by a pointed beard, heavy drooping hooded eyelids under which a piercing glance seemed to escape diffused, like water held by a finger under a tap.

All this was interesting but had little connection with the purpose of my visit. I felt I must make it clear that the British would not accept his conclusions concerning the prospects of the battle. It was not easy to argue with the implacable old man, so obviously anchored in defeat. There was sand in my throat as I urged that failure only came to those who accepted failure, and I quoted well-known French authorities who had asserted this.

"You were saying, Monsieur le Maréchal, that we had time in the last war which we do not have now. But time can be gained. If all France resisted invasion desperately everywhere, as the British will surely resist when their turn comes, then there would be delay. Why are not the great forests of France cut down and their trees laid across every road? Why is not every bridge and culvert blown up? Why are the villages not destroyed to block the roads the panzers must follow? The will to resist if it existed would inspire these measures as it inspired the victories of the ill-armed armies of the Revolution. The panzers only move quickly under ideal conditions. Eliminate these, and there is only infantry and artillery left. We dealt with them in the last war." "And aeroplanes," interjected the Marshal. "The U.S.A. can provide those," I answered, "if we gain time and, above all, fight back."

As I recall the scene I think I was almost crying, not visible tears perhaps, but the desperate inner tears of one pleading on behalf of a love that is dead. I knew it was hopeless, but I persisted as a man will, although he knows the gates of hope have been closed against him. I saw France as a person, and she was not dead; it was far worse, she was alive but did not remember her own past, that noble, ample past, so great and generous that every civilised man had a claim on her because of his own civilisation.

The situation recalled to my memory verses that seemed to describe the situation better than could my own thoughts:

"Dans le vieux parc solitaire et glacé
Deux ombres ont évoqué le passé"

and Verlaine's infinitely sad and hopeless poem dropped silently into my ears the agony of its ice-cold despair.

The Marshal was speaking now. What he was saying I do not remember. Perhaps I was not listening very carefully. I only know he seemed to have fallen back into the old age from which he had for a moment emerged. He was certainly not answering the points I had made. I should have remembered that, cherished every word that suggested resistance.

I had hoped, or tried to hope, that he would do something, seize Rude's trumpet from the Angel of Victory at the Arc de Triomphe and awaken France to life, to desperate resistance. He could have done it, for his power over the people was very great, but I saw he would not, could not, he was too old; and, recalling what I had tried to forget, I saw that clear, enthusiastic courage had never been a characteristic of his. His power over the Army was due to other causes; the men had trusted him as a leader who, unlike most of the Generals of his period, was sparing of men's lives and watchful of their welfare.

He was now talking of the German attack in the Abbeville sector. If they got through they would soon be on the Seine, at Rouen.

The name of that city, dropped into the channel of my thoughts, deflected them into an associated vein.

Very sadly I said: "What France needs today, *Monsieur le Maréchal*, is another Joan of Arc." His reaction was startling. Once more he was all animation, his face lit up. "Joan of Arc! Joan of Arc!" he exclaimed, "Have you read my speech on Joan of Arc?" "No, *Monsieur le Maréchal*." "Now that is too bad, it should have been sent to you. I made it at Rouen; now when was it, in 1937, '38? It was an extremely fine speech, I may say. I shall read it to you."

To my amazement, not to say consternation, he went to some bookshelves between two windows, pulled out one or two bound volumes of typescript, did not find what he wanted, then bent right down to look at the lowest shelves. The effort was considerable, he straightened stiffly, and said: "I shall have it found, it is certainly here," and, moving back to his desk, rang a bell. In a moment his Chief of Staff, General Bineau, appeared. He was almost as old as his chief (age was a major quality in the Marshal's eyes) and, I think, very lame.

The problem was explained, and with courteous apologetic haste the General began to hunt for the speech.

It was presently found. "*Je vous remercie*," said the Marshal, as, adjusting his pince-nez once more, he settled himself in a stiff arm-chair with his back to the window.

All I remember about that speech was that it was very, very long and that he read it in a monotone. I cannot recall a single sentence, or even its gist. What I do remember was the terrible sadness I felt as I watched him, a sadness now based on pity for a very old man for whom I had, till so recently, felt the deepest affection and regard. He was infinitely pathetic in his childish satisfaction as he read. I do not think he was really proud of that speech as of a great achievement, for he did not caress it by inflections of voice as a sculptor might stroke a statue he believed to be a great work of art. He was recalling rather the pomp and circumstance of its delivery, the applause, and he wanted to include me in that admiring audience of years ago.

As the interminable recitation went on, I felt that I could not bear
it. I thought of France and of the people of France. There could not
be a man or a woman in the country who, several times each day,
did not say to themselves or to each other: "Things certainly look
bad, but they are bound to turn out all right in the end, for Pétain is
in the Government, he is at the head of affairs, he will save us as he
did at Verdun."

If they could have seen their hero, at this perhaps their darkest
hour, reading an old speech to a foreign officer, then they would have
thought themselves the victims of a cruel hallucination, or that the
fates themselves had gone mad. It was impossible, they would say,
that France should end thus, fading out on an old man's tremulous
evocation of a heroic past.

I noted in the plane next day that I had felt as if tears were falling
on to my heart, slowly, one by one, audibly. Some may have welled
into my eyes: but the Marshal was reading on.

Then at last he had finished and I thought my ordeal was over.
But it was not so. "Joan of Arc was a peasant of France," he was
saying. "Our peasants are part of the soil of France. Have you
peasants in England? I doubt it—sailors, yes, but it is not the same
thing. It is a great misfortune not to have peasants. I made a very
fine speech on the peasants of France—now let me see, it was some
time back; you must see it, I shall read it to you." Again the bell
rang. "*Trouvez moi mon discours . . .*"

Genuine alarm brought me back to realities. Time was passing, I
had endless work to do. The London telephone was certainly
calling. How could I get away? My resource failed me. I could
only think of saying I would spare the Marshal fatigue by reading the
speech myself. So I looked at each page, which was a blank to me,
for the minimum time permissible, stealing a glance at Pétain now
and then in fear that he might think I was turning the pages too fast.
Each time I looked, his gaze was fixed on me with bland interest.

On the last page I saw a reference to another speech. Had I
wanted above all else to read this one also I could not have spared
the time to do so, and in fear the Marshal would note the reference I
closed the bound typescript and told him I must return to the
Embassy.

So far I had not succeeded in raising the question about which I
had called, Weygand's attitude. As I rose I attempted to broach it.
"Do you not consider it regrettable, *Monsieur le Maréchal*, that at

our morning meetings General Weygand so persistently attributes the worst motives to the British, and is so rude about them?" The Marshal was walking towards the door, intent on fulfilling his role of polite host punctiliously, so much so that he seemingly did not hear what I had said. His face was blank, and he did not answer. It was no good.

As I stood with him in the hall, after having failed so signally to elicit any reaction on the subject of Weygand, I spoke of Britain's attitude to the war, and he listened patiently as I asked him to realise that the British were in deadly earnest when they said they intended to fight the war to its bitter end. I told him I feared I had sounded rude when I told him after the Supreme War Council that we would bombard French harbours if they sheltered Germans, but it was a fact, and had to be faced. If France stood between us and our enemy, then we should regretfully, but of necessity, strike France down so as the better to drive home our blows. "If France should ever side with the Germans, which I cannot conceive, not only would she lose her honour, but she will never recover physically. She would be bound to a Germany on whose windpipe our thumbs will soon be closing. The French forget from generation to generation what implacable foes we make."

I then developed the theme that so long as we held together, did not break the link uniting us, our joint victory would one day compensate us for all we were losing today or might lose tomorrow.

"It is possible that one day, and for a while, France may be driven to fight back from Africa, as we may be to fight back from Canada and the remainder of the Empire." And I told him I hoped and prayed that if this should happen he would be with us, giving inspiration and confidence to all those who, perforce, would be left behind.

The Marshal did not answer. His expression conveyed that he had tried to hear but failed, but that, as I had listened to him for so long, politeness required that he should allow me to have my say. Instead of answering, and as if what he proposed had nothing to do with our conversation, he led me to a small room, saying there was something he wished to show me. On a pedestal, shoulder-high, stood a beautiful bronze or bronzed terra-cotta group. It represented the Marshal himself on horseback bending forward towards two very typical *poilus* of the last war who beamed up at him in fond and trusting respect. It was extraordinarily striking. Affection and solicitude on the one hand, complete confidence on the other. I have never seen in any form of art, written, painted or sculptured, so perfect an interpretation of the idealised relationship between officer and man.

"That is the epitome of the 1917 mutinies," I cried. "It is the whole story of the way you handled them." This time the Marshal had heard. "You understood the meaning of the group at once," he said. "Not many people do. I was right to ask you to write the story of that period." I had wondered if he remembered doing so, and rather expected him to ask for the return of his papers. "I wish that group to commemorate me to the French people one day," he said.

When I had left him and was on my way to the Embassy, I realised that perhaps the Marshal had wished his statuette to convey another meaning to me. The part he had played in quelling the mutinies was far more important to him than his defence of Verdun. That was clear. But there was more to it than that. Those little figures expressed the indissoluble bond between Marshal Pétain and the Army of his time, the heads of families of the France of today. They trusted him, he was often spoken of as the Father or Grandfather of the country. A grandfather does not abandon his grandchildren whatever the motive may be. No urge of higher policy or of ultimate good can justify the breaking of the elemental necessity which imposes on the old the duty of protecting the young.

I was convinced that this was what I was meant to understand when I was taken to see the little group, and next day told Churchill I was certain Pétain would never leave France.

It is, of course, possible that I was mistaken, that the impression conveyed was accidental and simply served to crystallise into conviction a conclusion I had already half formulated.

Pétain's natural pessimism had already led him to accept defeat. This much was certain. He neither believed in miracles nor sought to create situations in which miracles become possible. Such was not his character. But had it not been for the bond of affection, respect and trust between him and the French people which was soon to prove itself such a reality, it is conceivable though unlikely that he would have consented to leave France with the intention of exacting better terms from North Africa. But as he would not leave France his endeavour was, perhaps inevitably, to make it impossible for others to do so.

During the later years of the war when Pétain was an opponent and I was advocating a stronger line against Vichy than sometimes commended itself to the Government, convinced as I always have been that there is no such thing as a half, still less a quarter, friend, I often described this interview with the Marshal to both French and Englishmen. Several said he had been fooling me, since he had told me nothing that was not common knowledge, including his own point of view on the situation. I do not believe this. Why waste his own time, not to mention mine, when he could quite simply either not have received me, or brought the interview to an end after a quarter of an hour's generalities?

It is, however, possible that, while indulging his old man's foibles, he had intended to convey a meaning, and was satisfied that I had grasped it. But this thought only occurred to me much later.

That evening, although too busy for consecutive thought, when my mind went back to this interview which had moved me so deeply, I felt humiliated at having failed to carry out my intention: my discourse on Britain had not been allowed to penetrate; my attempt to persuade the Marshal to curb Weygand's furious Anglophobia had met with no response. Had I been more astute, I thought, I should have been able to do this, as fundamentally Pétain the Picard hated Weygand the Belgian. Although they were both working, all too obviously, towards the same dreadful objective, I had hoped to isolate Weygand in his hatred of England. In this I had failed. Whether by accident or design the Marshal had steered clear of the subject and, when I had got within hailing distance of it, had been overcome by deafness, or overwhelmed me with old speeches.

CHAPTER VII

Thursday, June 6th

(2)

Churchill's telegram on British reinforcements—Reynaud's appreciation—Weygand's comments—His orders to his troops—My wife arrives from Lorraine—A note on General Picard—Italy pleased at Baudouin's appointment to the French Foreign Office—Mandel gives me a message for Churchill—A friend asks for news of her sons—Reynaud's broadcast—An unfortunate car smash—General Colson provides transport for my wife.

At the Embassy I found a telegram from the Prime Minister.

It said that the embarkation of the 52nd Division had been accelerated to the utmost. It was starting next day (the 7th) and, to gain time, two harbours were being used. The whole division should be in France by the 13th. To provide support more rapidly than could be done by sending a Dunkirk re-formed division, the Canadians were being sent over on the 11th. A third division would follow as soon as possible if the French could provide artillery. I was to find out about this and inform London.

The telegram also stated that our air forces from England were participating to the full in the Somme battle that day. Fighters were refuelling in France so as to remain longer in the battle zone. In addition, considerable heavy bomber forces were to carry on with their attacks on objectives specified by the French High Command.

This was indeed satisfactory, we were more than fulfilling our promises. The shadows of resentment were being dispelled by the fierce glare of a conflict that promised to take its place as one of the decisive battles in history.

I asked Redman to deal with the question of artillery for the third division, as I was leaving next day.

There was not much news of the fighting, which, in a defensive action of this kind, was good news. The Germans had gained some further ground towards Roye, but the strong-points appeared in the main to be holding out. Defence in depth seemed to be proving its worth. Best of all, the French infantry, now it was having half a chance, was fighting back very hard indeed.

That, to me, was the best news of all. Again I reflected that, not for the first time in the chapters of French history I had myself lived through, the example of the troops was imposing itself on the leaders of the nation. If the Army held we might yet see our Paris defeatists yelling "*À Berlin*," urging the Army on by their *résolution farouche*.

Reynaud was naturally very pleased by Churchill's messages. He beamed his appreciation. "*Ce brave Churchill, vraiment c'est un brave type.*" "He is always better than his word," I said. "*C'est vrai, non vraiment, c'est très bien*," from Reynaud. "You see," I went on, "he is throwing everything he possibly can into the battle. From what I can make out, there will be no troops left in England when the Canadians leave save the Dunkirk men who have not yet been sorted out or re-armed. We could hardly do more for Kent, were it invaded, than we are doing for you." Reynaud then read me a note he had received from Weygand. It ran:

(1) British land forces:
General Weygand received today General Pownall, General Gort's Chief of Staff, who informed him of the arrival of the 52nd Division, which will begin to disembark in France tomorrow, the 7th June, and will have completed the operation on the 13th June. At the same time a Corps Commander will arrive in France who will take over the command of all the large units which have landed.
As soon as possible after the landing of the first division there will arrive a second, followed by a third. As soon as there are four British divisions in France, Lord Gort will reassume command of the B.E.F.
This is an excellent programme, and it will be even better if it is pressed forward in view of the grave circumstances created by the new German attacks which are extending every day.
(2) General Weygand has today seen Air Marshal Barratt. He has satisfied himself, and has ascertained from Generals Georges, Besson and Têtu (representing General Vuillemin at General Georges' Headquarters), that perfect liaison exists between Britain

and France, by making most effective use of the British aviation placed at the disposal of our front, in accordance with French plans.

From now on the *total British bomber strength* based in France and in Great Britain is acting in support of our battle.

As for *the fighter force*, nothing is as yet finally settled as the British Government has not yet taken a decision (information at 5 p.m.). Air Marshal Barratt explained the difficulties to be surmounted. General Weygand asked him to consider the dramatic circumstances under which we are fighting this battle and to plead our cause in London.

To sum up, the British Government is giving us aviation and it will be well employed.

WEYGAND.

Weygand had added a P.S.:

This note was already written when I saw the telegram which the Prime Minister (Churchill) addressed today at 5.30 p.m. to the President of the Council (Reynaud). As the landing of the 52nd Division will finish on the 13th, and as the embarkation of the Canadian Division will begin on the 11th, we are beginning to be given satisfaction. I am having the question examined as to whether it will be possible for us to give artillery to the Dunkirk division. The solution of this question is bound up with the arrival of five hundred 75 mm. guns from the U.S.A.

The atmosphere was now relatively cheerful.

Weygand had issued orders with which no fault could be found. The sense of these was:

(1) The system of chequer-board defence adopted against tank attacks appears to be yielding good results.

Therefore hold on.

(2) Not only hold on but perfect the defensive system. Take advantage of every respite to strengthen existing strong-points and create new ones.

All artillery not already included in a strong-point should be used to form new ones.

(3) Be as aggressive as possible. This means use ambushes against tanks which have penetrated between strong-points, attack

them with gunfire, from the air, etc. Tanks that have thus advanced
are in a difficult position.

(4) The garrisons of strong-points must continue to receive the
necessities of life. In consequence both material and personal contact
must be re-established with isolated strong-points as soon as possible.

(5) See that all are informed of plans and objectives. Each strong-
point must be kept informed of the movements of French neighbouring units.

(6) Every step must be taken to ensure that each strong-point is
kept supplied with food and ammunition.

I was with the Ambassador in the late afternoon, discussing how
best to ensure his being kept informed during my absence on those
military questions I had been dealing with, and telling him of my
strange conversation with Pétain, when my secretary put her head
round the door to say my wife was in my office.

I can see her now as I walked into the low-ceilinged room. I can
see the windows level with the floor, the gravel courtyard, the low
stone building across it, once servants' quarters, now packed with
secretaries, and my wife sitting on the edge of a low sofa. She wore
the long grey cape lined with blue of her unit, and a nurse's *coiffe*.
It was very much like the kit she had worn when I met her in the First
War, but her cape had then been lined with red and was much
heavier, for it had been winter. She looked like a small girl who
knows she deserves a scolding and intends brazening it out. Her
expression was obstinate; she evidently had a plan and meant to stick
to it. I guessed what it was. She feared I would try to make her
withdraw her ambulance to safety.

Well, I had no such intention. She was in the war too, and must
do her duty as she saw it. Hospitals would have much work to do,
and she knew her job.

She had confidence in General Réquin, and he would certainly
look after her and her girls as best he could.

She was looking at me when her expression changed. Her round,
small-girl face assumed a look of astonishment, her mouth opened,
then her immense yellow-green eyes looked frightened.

It was only after the war, when I read her book (*Journey Down a
Blind Alley*), that I understood what had happened. My look of
exhaustion, the new lines in my face and eyes lacking sleep made her
suddenly realise the violence and strength of the merciless forces we

were attempting to hold in check. She was, she said, really frightened for the first time, and perceived that she had been living all this time in a dream. The questions she put were nevertheless ordinary enough. What was the situation? she asked. The curtain of security at once fell, creating a barrier of *gêne* between us. Although I did not realise the impression I had made on her, I knew she had read deeply into my mind. I tried to be reassuring without departing from the truth. The news was pretty good, I said. "In fact, Reynaud told me just now that he felt justified in making a rather optimistic broadcast this evening." "How is he doing?" "Never mind," I said. "And Weygand?" she persisted. But I would not be drawn and said very little. I gather from what she has written, however, that what I did say did not lead her to conclude that I had a high opinion of him.

"And you?" I asked.

She began telling me. Réquin had asked for her unit to follow him on the Marne; they were under orders to move at any moment, probably to the vicinity of Vitry-le-François. I felt a pang. There would certainly be heavy fighting there. For a moment I saw the place which had been Joffre's first Headquarters and where I had been projected into the 1914 War.

The Hadfield-Spears unit was about to be launched like a cockleshell into the torrent of the battle.

Only one thing was certain: my wife would not lose her head, or fail to fulfil the task assigned to her.

She was now telling me of her journey to Paris. She had been given an armed soldier escort and told to follow a route far from the front. What nonsense, she said, but she was watching me to see if perhaps it was not such nonsense after all. There was the shadow of a doubt that the kind of static war she knew was not the same as this.

Then I saw she was really tired by her long drive from Lorraine. I told her to go to the Ritz, order supper and wait for me. With any luck I should be with her by nine. When I told her she could have a hot bath, she cheered up like a tired child who is promised a treat.

Before going, characteristically, she remembered a grievance she had forgotten all about. "Do you know, I went to the Ritz first and they would not let me telephone to you," she pouted. "No one can telephone in Paris now, save on official lines," I said. "But you have a telephone in your room?" "You could not use that; the operator would have thought some unauthorised person was on my line and cut you off. The police would probably have come rushing in."

Silenced but not convinced, though smiling and relaxed, she stepped into the car and I closed the door.

Once more I fell to reading telegrams and reports, sending my own, forwarding dispatches from Government departments making requests of every conceivable kind and asking questions necessitating asking yet more questions.

More information concerning the lamentable state of the French Air Force came in. It was all too clear that the leadership throughout, with some brilliant exceptions, left much to be desired.

I had been asked for a report on General Picard. This is what I sent in:

"The *Chef de l'État Major de l'Armée de l'Air à l'Intérieur* General Picard held the position of *Chef de l'État Major de l'Armée de l'Air* at the French Air Ministry up to the advent to power of M. Pierre Cot. He was then retired since he had reached the age limit and remained out of the service until a month or two ago, when M. Laurent Eynac took office. General Picard is just over 60 years of age.

"Since his return to the Air Ministry he has shown signs of very definite Anglophobia which has got notably worse since the outbreak of the present battle.

"He has adopted a bullying attitude and has even suggested on occasion that we were trying to withdraw the A.A.S.F.* from the support of the French and several times has been quite indefensibly rude to senior British officers who were trying to negotiate with him.

"General Picard seems to be a man who has been thrown off his balance by the rapidity of events with which he is quite unable to cope."

Somebody came in to say that the Italian Ambassador, Guariglia, had called on Reynaud to tell him how pleased his Government were at Baudouin's nomination as Under-Secretary at the Foreign Office. The information was quite reliable, and left me wondering. The impertinence was insufferable in view of Italy's undoubted attitude. Here she was, about to declare war, yet making a point of emphasising that she had a friend in the French Cabinet, just when her other friend, de Monzie, had been kicked out.

The Embassy views about Baudouin were evidently sounder than mine had been.

Then Mandel called up. Would I dine with him? I feared that was

* Advanced Air Striking Force.

impossible, my wife had just come from Lorraine. Well, would I
come and have a word with him now?

I found him the same as always. He was the only Frenchman I
met who proved quite impervious to circumstances, who remained
detached, objective and even-tempered whatever befell. I have met
many men who did not shrink from calamity, others who bore
misfortune stoically, and yet more in whom danger kindled courage,
but very few of the kind you could not "rattle", whose pulse and
mind remained unaffected by events however unforeseen, sudden
or shattering. It is a reptilian quality, not endearing but wholly
enviable.

Mandel wanted to know what the British really felt about the
Réduit Breton.

He did not conceal his own feeling that it was impracticable. No
pretence could be made of governing France from Nantes, Lorient
or St. Nazaire. Besides which, no real effort, that he could see, had
been made by the military authorities to prepare a defensive line
across the peninsula. You could hardly blame them. Their every
effort was needed to strengthen their present line.

Had Weygand communicated with the British on the subject?
Not that I knew of, but then I was not responsible for military
liaison. He might have done so. All I knew was that Reynaud was in
favour of the idea and so was Churchill.

What, it seemed to me, weighed with both of them was that plans
should exist for continuing resistance somewhere should the present
line be broken. They wanted proof that Weygand intended fighting
on.

I felt sure that if a convincing plan was put forward for holding
out in the formidable Plateau Central and defending the Mediterranean harbours, Churchill would gladly adhere to it.

If the Alps and the Plateau Central were held, the Germans could
never get down the Rhône valley, I said. "North Africa would
become your base. After all, all that matters to us is that France
should remain in the war. We are absolutely convinced that one day
we shall win, even if we have to fight alone. Together the job can be
done in less time, that's our point of view."

"You will have to think of some very effective form of pressure to
keep Weygand in the war if the Germans break through the present
line," said Mandel. "He will have none of the *Réduit Breton*, which
he considers indefensible. He apparently thinks there would not be

enough troops to hold the Plateau Central." "That is surely non-sense," I said. "It is terrifically strong defensive country." "Well," went on Mandel, "he is on surer ground perhaps in saying it will be hard to fight if the Paris region, which produces seventy per cent of our war production, is lost, not to mention the north."

"You will have to depend on the U.S.A. In the case you are now considering your needs would also be less than they are today," I answered.

But Mandel was following the idea which was evidently the object of the interview.

"Weygand is opposed to fighting on in Africa, and either Noguès has been convinced by him or he has come to the same conclusion on his own. After all, the pair of them come from the same stable. Pétain has accepted defeat and for the first time in his life is sincerely supporting Weygand, whose every pessimistic utterance he applauds with both hands."

I then told him of my visit to Pétain that afternoon. *"C'est un 'Conquistador'*," said Mandel. But he pronounced the word as if it were four vocables, noun, relative pronoun, pronoun and verb (omitting the *t*), which was so funny that I laughed, though if anybody had bet me I would laugh that day I would have laid a hundred to one against.

As I left, Mandel repeated it was necessary to find some means of bringing pressure on Weygand. "Can you think of any?" I asked. "No, but Churchill is very resourceful." "I shall be in London tomorrow and will tell him," I said. "At least do not give Weygand any legitimate grounds for saying you are not giving him full support." "How?" I asked. "He has complained much about the British Air Force," he said. I told him Weygand had become practically lyrical on the subject, so great was his satisfaction, and gave him an outline of what had occurred that afternoon.

"You are flying?" said Mandel as he opened the door. "Be careful, and do not be away long. I mean that. Events are moving very fast."

Mandel had not asked me to see him without a purpose, and although he had been satisfied when I said I would tell Churchill next day, I felt that the sooner I reported our conversation the better, so back at the Embassy I drew up a telegram to the Prime Minister.

While I was at my office, a great friend of ours telephoned. How she managed to get on the official line I do not know. These things can always be arranged in France. She wanted news of her sons. One was on the Somme, the other had been at Dunkirk. "I must, I simply must find out," said the voice I liked so well. But it was distraught, angry. The eldest must be in England, had I not telegraphed, telephoned, done something? No, I had not because it was impossible. No one had the right to take up time on the overloaded lines or impose an extra burden on anyone just now. News would come in time. It was hard to wait, I knew, but there it was.

The voice now sparkled into hate, the hate that had been politely concealed but was so evident just before the war, the hate of the highborn and the rich against England who, they were convinced, had willed the war.

"I hate war," the voice was saying. "It is the fault of your country. You bear a heavy responsibility, *you* were a *belliciste*, like your Churchill. Won't you even try to find my sons?" The voice broke into a sob, the line was cleared for another call. As I listened to the next voice, I recalled a very pretty woman, exquisitely dressed always, whom I had known when we were both young. I had known the boys as little fellows, adjuncts to their mother they had seemed, just extra ornaments showing off her beauty. She had talked lightly of them when they were taken away by grave servants, as was the tea-tray in her perfectly-appointed house. But the boys must have mattered more than I had thought.

I had many such calls, but only remember the details of this one, which has left a scar. I never heard that voice again, and of what I had believed was an infrangible friendship only the bitter sound of a wail cut off as with a pair of scissors remains.

The sketchy news of the fighting that came in driblets in the late evening did not sound very good. The enemy had reached the Bresle River south of Tréport, and appeared to have gained a footing on the heights overlooking the Aisne. Again the Chemin des Dames of horrible memory was mentioned.

I had written a book about the fighting there. My wife's first hospital had gone through untold horrors in that area. Now she was going back to the same region, or rather beyond it, where, the reports said, great German forces were massing about Rethel, opposite Vitry-le-François. It is extraordinary how bad for morale the situation in which I found myself was. Anticipated anxiety certainly clogs the works.

Still there was no news of anything like a break-through, and the French reports inferred that the German forces which had gained ground were in no great strength; and counter-attacks were announced. In the main the German plan now seemed clear enough; it was taking the shape anticipated by Weygand, an immense pincer movement aiming to close south of Paris combined with a direct thrust on the capital; but it did not seem to be developing according to plan.

The defence in depth was yielding results.

That evening, listening to Reynaud's speech on the wireless, I was impressed, as were all who heard it, by his eloquence and virility. It was well calculated to encourage the people. His voice sounded confident, there was the echo of a clarion call in some of his sentences.

Considering the pressure he was being submitted to, the morass of defeatism in which he was struggling, the colossal ineptitude of the French Command with which he had been confronted, there was a touch of heroism in the way he was trying to make France believe in ultimate victory. He had little to build on, however, and I wondered if it was wise to praise as he did the leadership of the military chiefs in the north, which, he said, had been "magnificently demonstrated". "I received this morning Admiral Abrial, the defender of Dunkirk. Before such men France feels herself live again in them. She feels rekindled the eternal genius of the Generals of the Revolution and of the sailors of the Kings of France."*

He was on safer ground in quoting Weygand:

"I shall tell you nothing but what General Weygand has told me," he said. "General Weygand's words to me were: 'I am satisfied with the manner in which the battle has begun, and with the way in which my orders for resistance at any price are being executed'."

Reynaud was always a fine orator. The picture he drew of defeat for the benefit of those who affected to believe in Hitler's promises was striking. "It would be the Middle Ages again, but not illuminated by the mercy of Christ."

* "There was no fight in the senior French officers of both services who were in Cherbourg in June, 1940. It is charitable to suppose that they already knew of Pétain's request for an armistice. Otherwise there would be no excuse for the fact that they surrendered the fortress and 30,000 men to a single armoured division, barely 12 hours after it had come within range of the formidable fortress guns. . . . In the harbour was the undamaged transport of a British mechanised division . . . Amongst those captured were: Admiral Abrial and four other admirals. . . ." (*Rommel*, by Desmond Young.)

He spoke of his Government. "All members of the Government are animated by a common will—to conquer." Well, it was at any rate truer than it would have been yesterday.

He was on the target when he castigated Democracy.

"Democracy has for a long time been lacking in foresight and audacity. The idea of the Fatherland and of military valour has been too long neglected . . ." and then a true note of warning: "Only the propaganda of Herr Goebbels is interested in fomenting discord. . . . France is calm and proud like her ally . . . it is for the independence of all other countries that our soldiers are fighting on the Somme and the Aisne."

An olive branch was extended to Italy.

"There is no nation with whom France cannot settle by peaceful means the divergent interests which appear to oppose each other. France desires a settlement of these problems and the reconstruction of a Europe in which the prosperity and independence of each nation is assured."

The great merit of the broadcast was that he showed the people the extreme gravity of the situation whilst affording no excuse for despair. He had been, and had sounded, sincere, though I could hardly think he quite believed what he had said about the Generals in the north. On the other hand he probably did think Admiral Abrial had done quite well.

When I got back to the Ritz it was ten. How civilised it was, the well-appointed table in the sitting-room, the silence of the garden, and of the Ministry of Justice beyond.

My wife was rested, as good as gold about being kept waiting so long. It was refreshing to hear her chatter about the hospital and all its little problems. I made an effort to sort out the people she mentioned, to attach faces to all those names.

Where did I think the hospital would be sent? she was asking. She was full of plans, but very worried about her transport. "We won't be moving much after we are settled in," she said. Her terms of reference were those of 1917. 1914 had been before her time, she had never seen retreats, refugees, armies and populations rolling back together.

Then came a knock on the door. It was my wife's M.T.C. driver and the friend she was staying with. They had long faces, and no wonder. The girl announced that in the pitch darkness she had driven head-on into one of the road-blocks in the Champs Élysées, erected to prevent planes landing there. The car was beyond repair.

My wife was frantic at the thought of being cut off from her unit and the twenty-five British girls for whom she was responsible. They were awaiting orders to move. If this happened before she got back she might never catch up with them, and here she was stranded without transport. Would I help? I must help. She was almost in tears. Could she have my car? No, it belonged to the Military Government of Paris. Further, it was a town car quite unsuitable for a race of 250 kilometres across France.

Then I had an idea. I did not like doing it, but I would ask General Colson to help out. I felt sure he would. This reassured her. Would I call him up at once? But I was firm. Nothing would induce me to call him up before 7 a.m. next morning.

Then the telephone rang. The line was bad, but my wife's second-in-command was speaking very indistinctly from Lorraine. She was telling my wife to start back at once, that the ambulance had orders to leave at 8 a.m. for an unknown destination. This was too much for her. I saw that I must take this situation in hand. She could not leave before 8 a.m. and I would see that she did so then. I would find out where she could rendezvous with her ambulance. I got through to the *Médecin Chef* of the ambulance. He told me the previous call was unauthorised, and he had known nothing of it; furthermore the information was untrue, the ambulance was only to move at 1 p.m. next day. My conclusion was that the sudden intervention of so many ladies into my corner of the war had neither clarified nor eased the position.

I thought I could then get to bed, for it was after one, but the telephone rang again. There were messages coming through at the Embassy, so I went back there. I do not remember them all, but the military reports were disquieting. The Germans had gained ground in the north and it was not certain whether the refuelling base for our fighters on the Rouen front could be maintained. An attempt would be made to use it again on the 7th.

My wife was asleep when I got back. She woke me well before seven. "You promised to ring up General Colson," and I did. Cool, pleasant and efficient as usual, he said he would certainly have a car at the Ritz by eight. "*C'est la moindre des choses. Madame Spears a rendu et rend tant de services.*" "A car that will have her in Lorraine by one?" "It will be a racing car with two drivers." What befell her she has told. It seems I was telephoning to London when she left. I do not remember. She said I waved a distraught hand to her as she slipped out. I did not see her off or see the marvellous drivers who, it appears, averaged 60 miles an hour all the way on the long deserted *chaussées* of eastern France.

The roads of war are many, and wayfarers along them are soon lost to each other. In life you never know at which bend you have waved your last greeting. In war the path you follow has more sudden turnings than the one you saunter down or hurry along in peace-time, but in neither case do you know when you have exchanged your last farewell.

My wife and her ambulance were swallowed up in the war the moment she left the Ritz that morning. She was swept back pell-mell with the flying Army, with the uprooted populations, until, embarking in fishing-boats at Arcachon, she and her girls set out to find the British Navy, which duly appeared in the shape of H.M.S. *Galatea*. But I was without news of them, excepting for one telephone message when I was at Bordeaux, until they all landed safely in England on June 26th.

CHAPTER VIII

Friday, June 7th

*Reynaud seeks to counter anti-British rumours—Churchill's objections to publicity concerning British forces—His telegram to Reynaud on air reinforcements—The 51st Division—A French civilian does his bit—News of the battle—Moxton and the unexploded bombs—Dautry's achievement—Reynaud gives me a message for Churchill—Apposite quotations from Joffre and Foch—Good-bye to the British Embassy—Flight from Boucq in Churchill's Flamingo —Report to Churchill at Number 10—Sir Edward Bridges— The contrast between London and Paris—Churchill on bad liaison—*The Times *on General de Gaulle—Dinner with the Churchills—and Nelson—at the Admiralty.*

ON the previous day Reynaud had asked if the Prime Minister would have any objection to his giving the Army and Foreign Affairs Commissions of the Senate, which he was to meet in joint session on the 7th, the exact figures of Allied forces engaged on the 6th. His idea was to show the Senators how important a part the British were playing in the battle, especially in the air, and thus counteract the strong criticism the French were levelling at us.

In no country in the world would people not have been critical of an ally bearing so small a part of the common suffering and loss, but the French give way more readily than other nations to the temptation to criticise their friends. In times of stress they look for scapegoats among themselves, and are very apt to conclude that a section of their own population has betrayed them. In defeat the old cry "*Nous sommes trahis*" is not far from the lips of the commoner sort, who find therein an explanation covering their own deficiencies in the past and an excuse for such shortcomings as may be theirs in the future.

Rumours concerning the Dunkirk evacuation were rife. The most amazing stories were told and believed, in spite of the fact that all the

French troops available for embarkation had been taken off. Early messages from Dunkirk such as this one: "British officers, revolvers in hand, are threatening us, treating us as deserters", had received wide circulation. The truth was that these officers, unable to make themselves understood, had been trying to direct completely uncontrolled mobs of soldiers to the right beaches or points of embarkation.

And of course the Germans had done their best to describe the British to the French not only as ineffective allies, but as abandoning them in adversity.

The withdrawal from the Saar front of the 51st Division was proclaimed by German propaganda as just another example of the way in which the British discreetly withdraw from a tight corner. "*Ils filent à l'Anglaise*" (they are taking French leave) yelled the Traitor of Stuttgart, the worthy counterpart of our own Lord Haw-Haw.

Rumours and propaganda had their effect, weakening confidence, the most vulnerable link of all in the chain of Anglo-French unity, the one without which it must break, and to which therefore both Churchill and Reynaud attached major importance.

But no secret has ever been kept in Paris, and Churchill was alarmed at the risk, or rather the certainty, of the enemy soon becoming aware of any figure given by Reynaud to the Commissions. It would have been fatal to proclaim our weakness.

It was in consequence of this fear that I received a most immediate telegram from Ismay saying that the Prime Minister strongly objected to any information being given concerning the forces engaged that day and the day before. Nevertheless, so that Reynaud should be made aware of the scale of our efforts, I might tell him for his personal information that 144 British fighters had been engaged on the 6th and an even larger force would be operating today, the 7th. I was very glad to take Reynaud that message.

I raced back and forth several times that morning over the short distance between the Embassy and the rue St. Dominique. Most of it was taken up by the immense Place de la Concorde, and I tried to photograph in my mind a final picture of the scene I knew so well, with beyond it the lovely sweep up the Champs Élysées, framed by the horses of Marly. The sky overhead was as blue as that which spread over the Obelisk's sister monolith at Luxor, and it seemed to me the silence must have been comparable.

I was leaving for London in a few hours and felt very sad. In my heart I knew that only a miracle could save Paris, and I had learnt that miracles are only wrought in war by men determined to make them. In France, so far, I had met neither prophets nor miracle workers. I had a horrible vision of the great Nazi banners I had seen in Germany, reaching to the ground from the top windows of the Hotel Crillon and the Ministry of Marine. I wondered if Paris could survive such a desecration, and felt that if it happened she would never again be the same to me.

Later there was a further message from the Prime Minister for Reynaud:

"I can now tell you that during the last twenty-four hours we have increased our efforts in the air to help France. During the night our heavy bombers have attacked in strength, dropping 59 tons of bombs on objectives indicated by the French High Command.

"In addition medium bombers have, up to the present, made 60 sorties from England. Fighters operating from their bases in England and using the forward aerodromes south of the Somme have carried out, either as escorts to medium bombers or in independent fighter patrols, 192 sorties, without taking into account protective missions over troop transports between Southampton and Cherbourg, etc.

"Tomorrow (8th) we intend, by amalgamating three fighter squadrons, to send two additional fighter squadrons at full strength which will be based in France in the forward air fighting zone. These will be under the orders of the British Air Officer Commanding-in-Chief. Thus the strength of this fighting formation will be brought up to five fighter squadrons at full strength. In addition we hope to be able to engage every day four fighter squadrons based in England, but refuelling from advanced bases south of the Somme.

"Our recent experience shows that we cannot at present maintain a greater number of squadrons owing to the heavy losses suffered in the battle of Flanders.

"Thanks to an improvement in the communications which has taken place today between the Air Officer Commanding-in-Chief in France, and Great Britain, it is now possible to place the medium bomber squadrons in England at the disposal of the Air Officer Commanding British Forces in France with a view to co-operating with the British and French forces engaged in the battle. The

squadrons of heavy bombers will remain available for the attack on
night objectives selected by the French High Command.

"I understand that the French Air Attaché in London has transmitted a request for 74 barrage balloons, complete with equipment,
for the defence of Paris. We are sending forthwith 24 complete
balloon units and crews to carry out this mission.

"It should be noted that attacks have been made against objectives
in this country during the last two nights by about 100 planes each
night, not including important mine-laying operations carried out
from the air against our shipping.

"I am advising the War Office of your complaints concerning
General Fortune. He has had to hold an extended front and has
suffered very heavy losses."

Little did the men of the 51st Division realise that Weygand was
accusing them of fighting badly, or that they were, according to him,
the victims of "hide-bound exacerbated inefficiency". They moved
slowly, as is the British way, fought stubbornly, retreated reluctantly,
seldom got more than mildly annoyed with the Germans, only losing
their sense of humour if breakfasts were not forthcoming or tea not
available by the gallon. The French who saw them fight had no
criticism to make of them, nor had they of such Frenchmen as
participated in the same engagements. But that is generally the way
of fighting troops. Enduring the same hardships and perils, they
have not the opportunity to develop the critical faculties which come
easily to those judging operations from afar.

I was told of an incident that occurred at that time which is so
unusual that it is worth noting. The main body of a small rearguard belonging to a unit of the 51st Division was halted on the road
when it was overtaken by a French civilian on a bicycle. He was in
his Sunday best black suit and wore a bowler hat. A rifle was slung
over his shoulder. He dismounted and, without a word, sitting down
by the ditch, pulled an elongated loaf of bread out of one pocket and
a sausage out of the other. A large clasp-knife was then produced,
slices of sausage were spread on slices of bread and he began to eat
heartily if not delicately without so much as a glance at his Cale-
donian audience.

Then the fighting started. British patrols could be seen falling
back. The Frenchman went on eating whilst the British opened out
and lay down in the open fields.

Then the fire increased, a machine-gun could be heard joining in here and there, a few Germans could be seen running forward. The Frenchman wiped his mouth with the back of his hand, replaced the sausage and the bread in their respective pockets, loaded his rifle and sat down, tilting his bowler back and taking comfortable aim over a kilometre stone. His fire proved accurate and deadly, and he kept it up for some time. Then there was a lull and he stood up, slung his rifle, adjusted his hat, mounted his bicycle and rode off, saying no more when he left than when he had arrived. The *camaraderie*, if *camaraderie* there was, was entirely occult.

It was very sensible. Why, he may have thought, waste words on people whose language he did not understand and who did not even know how to make gestures which might serve to explain the incomprehensible sounds they made?

I have often thought with admiration of that civilian. Had there been more of his kind we should have had a different sort of war in France.

I was told Reynaud wanted to give me a message for the Prime Minister before I left. Meanwhile I went to the different departments to obtain such news as there was of the battle.

It was on the whole satisfactory. It was believed that between five and seven panzer divisions had attacked. In the main they had been held. The Germans had continued to gain ground towards Roye, but if they were really entangled in a maze of strong-points and could not pour through, the battle was anything but lost. What was so disquieting was the lack of reserves. As always, I asked about these. Generally there were but the vaguest answers, but today I was glad to hear that a division was on the move from the Alps. I wondered why it had not come up sooner. If it could be spared now that Mussolini was on the point of declaring war, then it could have come north earlier instead of running the risk of arriving too late.

During one of my calls at the Embassy I found waiting for me a man who interested me as much as anyone I have ever met. He had an introduction to me from London and wore a R.A.F. uniform that had seen better days.

His name, I think, was Moxton. He was youngish, his manner modest but quietly determined. It was his request that was extraordinary. I had reported that during the air-raid on Paris some bombs had dropped but had not exploded and that all that had happened was that the adjacent area had been cordoned off in the belief they might be time bombs.

Moxton asked if they had since exploded. No, I should certainly have heard if they had. They seemed to be causing considerable inconvenience.

Moxton's eyes glistened. Could I obtain permission for him to dig up those bombs? If he could only get one it would provide invaluable data. I might, I said doubtfully, with an all too vivid picture in my mind of what would happen if the bomb turned nasty on being disturbed.

"Had you not better leave these bombs alone? After all, it is a French responsibility. Even the Nazis did not so much as hope they would blow up an Englishman." But if ever a human being looked like a terrier begging for a bone, it was Moxton.

He was determined to have it, so, wondering and humbled by his simple unassuming courage, I sallied forth to see Dautry, who readily gave the permission asked for.

I took the opportunity of this visit to congratulate Dautry on the wonderful work he had done in sending up to the front defensive material without which resistance might have been well-nigh impossible; mines, explosives and material of all sorts must have reached the armies in great quantities. When it is remembered the short time he had at his disposal, the fact that much of industrial France was in German hands, and that the railways were congested by troop movements, the feat was astonishing.

Presently I went to bid Reynaud good-bye and collect his note for the Prime Minister. It went over the same ground as so many previous communications: the urgency of pressing forward the embarkation of the British divisions, the vital need of fighter support and of more fighter squadrons being based in France. I told him I thought it would help the Prime Minister if he were informed of the number of troops the French were bringing from North Africa and from Colonial garrisons generally. I told him we were bringing to England every battalion that we could lay hands on in the Empire.

The movement of the division from the Alps also prompted me to ask that we should be told of the extent to which it had been found possible to withdraw troops from the Maginot Line.

Reynaud said that Weygand was reasonably optimistic but nevertheless considered the situation very grave. Only about half the enemy's armour appeared to have been engaged. Even allowing for heavy losses and much wear and tear, further attacks must be expected. Weygand thought the enemy's principle effort would probably be made on the Aisne. He thought that if the enemy could be held for another week the attack could then be considered broken. "But he has no reserves—he never ceases saying he has no reserves—that is undoubtedly the most serious aspect of the situation." Once more I exclaimed: "Why, but why are there no reserves?" Reynaud shrugged his shoulders impatiently. "Because Weygand engages every battalion as it comes up. His has been the strategy of '*le pain à cacheter*'—a wafer policy—the device of a man who would try to stop water coming through a ceiling by sticking wafers on the cracks."

Then Reynaud gave me a personal message for the Prime Minister: he asked me to say that he would fight on. I was convinced of his sincerity and felt certain he would do so. Weygand's comparative optimism had evidently encouraged him and relieved the intense feeling of isolation resulting from finding that he and Mandel, with one or two other lesser figures, were alone in their hope of being able to continue the struggle.

I showed him as I left two extracts from the books of Marshals Joffre and Foch which I had been given the day before. I would quote them in London, I said. We were apt to forget that in the opening phases of the last war the situation had been as bad as, if not worse than, today, yet confidence and courage had snatched great victory from defeat.

Joffre had written: "From everywhere there arrived news of weaknesses which made me fear that the morale of the troops was broken; discouragement began to make itself felt in every grade of the Army, and even at my own General Headquarters. . . .

"Conditions are such that for the moment the British Army no longer exists. . . . It was necessary to inform the Government that probably in four or five days the German Cavalry would arrive before the gates of Paris. It was urgent to prepare public opinion for this eventuality, and to make everybody understand that our final victory was dependent on a determination to defend ourselves to the bitter end."

And Marshal Foch: "The enemy was advancing on Paris, the heart of the country, at furious speed. Our general offensive on the frontier had been thrown back and our armies in the centre and on the left wing were in full retreat, closely pursued and constantly threatened by envelopment from the west . . ."

When after the war I read President Lebrun's *Témoignage*, I found that he had quoted these extracts in his diary on June 9th. Perhaps the same person had drawn his attention to them.

The Ambassador was, I thought, sorry to see me go. I hoped it was because he felt that I had been of some help without in any way trespassing on his responsibilities. "So you are abandoning the sinking ship," he said with a wry smile. But I told him that was not the form. I had kept my rooms at the Ritz, for I did not expect to be away more than a day or so. Indeed, I had left a good many things behind, partly because I had not had time to pack, but also because I expected to return so soon. Those things I never saw again, and often, in the following years, thought with annoyance of a fine black-thorn stick, left in my room; I particularly disliked the idea of a German walking about with it.

The Ambassador sent me to the aerodrome in his Rolls, which was a friendly gesture. And so I heard the crunching gravel of our Embassy's courtyard for the last time. My final impression of Paris was the deadly quiet of the rue du Faubourg St. Honoré. Scattered groups of children were playing in the side streets and on the footpaths of that once thronged thoroughfare, outside the tiny antique shops long since closed *pour cause de mobilisation*. They were nearly all little girls playing what I have never thought could be a very amusing game, but which evidently holds hidden fascination for the French female child, hopping about on one leg from square to square chalked on the pavement, or bouncing a large soft rubber balloon against a wall.

At Boucq aerodrome I found the Prime Minister had sent his Flamingo for me. This was luxury indeed. No club boasted of more comfortable arm-chairs. During the innumerable journeys I was later to undertake, many in back-breaking discomfort, I often thought with regret of that machine. We made a wide detour, and the Channel was broad where we crossed it. The blue sky was innocent of Germans, so, landing without mishap, I walked into the garden of Number 10 Downing Street in the late afternoon.

The Prime Minister was sitting there with the keen concentrated look of one watching a target at which he has just fired. Marshal of the R.A.F. Newall, Chief of the Air Staff, whom I knew only slightly, was also there, together with my friend the Secretary of State for

Air, the argumentative but entirely lovable Archibald Sinclair, than whom I have never met a more charming personality, or, so it has always seemed to me, a better-looking man.

Sir Edward Bridges, Secretary to the Cabinet and Head of the War Cabinet Secretariat, was standing, evidently on the point of leaving. An admirable man who inevitably conveyed a very exact impression of his governing characteristic, unflinching rectitude. I always felt when with him that he carried the law of the Medes in one pocket and that of the Persians in the other. I had only had to do with him once previously, when, a couple of years before, I had had an argument with him concerning the reproduction of some documents in my book *Prelude to Victory*. He had wished me to omit them. I argued that they were printed in the French Official History of the War and could hardly therefore be deemed secret. He contended they were not printed in England, where but few people read the French history, and were therefore secret here. By the same argument the ten Commandments could be classified as a secret document because they were originally inscribed on tablets in Hebrew, and there are, unfortunately, individuals in England who have not read the Bible. Finally I was allowed to print my documents, and of my short meetings with Bridges only a pleasant if rather awed impression remained.

I was suddenly made conscious, by the expressions of the Prime Minister and Archie Sinclair, the two who knew me intimately, of something I had sensed in my wife's look when she first saw me the day before, and I felt annoyed with myself. Evidently I must be looking pretty ghastly, and I remembered the axiom that a Staff Officer must never, either in look or demeanour, convey anything but an impression of serene repose and confidence.

"You look as if you had not slept for a week," said Winston, with the extraordinarily round, warm, kindly intonation he sometimes uses, which is the equivalent of an arm thrown affectionately over one's shoulder.

He read Reynaud's message and I gave him the verbal one. He then put me some questions. These were in the main for the purpose of amplifying some of my reports: as regards the Army, I could speak only by hearsay; the French troops were certainly fighting much better now they had got over their initial surprise. The new defensive system was reported to be yielding good results. The new tactics were, I supposed, initiated by Georges, who had a freer hand than when under Gamelin. It remained to be seen whether there were enough troops and field-works for a real defence in depth.*

The lack of reserves was the gravest feature of the situation, and I repeated the conversation of a few hours before with Reynaud. On the other hand the effort made to strengthen the defensive lines and to provide material to defend strong-points was truly remarkable. No, I had not heard of any serious effort to defend Brittany, but then my means of information were very limited. Weygand had certainly no faith in the plan.

Then I told the Prime Minister of the men I had been in contact with in Paris.

What a contrast in atmosphere between this garden and the sunny Cabinet Room I had walked through, and the colourless, anonymous garden and shadowy rooms of the rue St. Dominique. The same sun drenched both places with light, indeed in the Concorde it had been blinding, but oh, so forlorn! Here everything was homely, easy. It was unbelievably relaxing. I might have been on any lawn in any house in England talking to friends about a riot I had watched from the window of my hotel somewhere abroad. There was confidence, ease, the sense of effortless trust born of the intimacy of lives that had flowed down similar channels.

Since I had landed in England I had met no one with whom I would not have left my life in trust, were lives things you could leave in boxes in other people's care whilst your soul went for a jaunt to the stars. No special care would be taken of it during your soul's absence, but it would be handed back safely on its return. That went

---

* "On the whole, the first day (of the attack in the Péronne sector) was not entirely satisfactory from the German point of view. Compared to their former behaviour the French were not doing badly . . . the difference between the fighting in Belgium and this action may be seen by the French losses. Of the French battalion at Liancourt, only 125 men succeeded in getting out. The 19th Division was wiped out. The 29th Division was reduced to a few companies. Many units simply fought to the last shell and bullet. . . . It is evident that the French troops were making every effort, not without success, to carry out Weygand's instructions. The German tanks were almost cut off and 'starved out' as Weygand intended. . . . Defence in depth was justifying itself, but the French forces did not have enough tanks, guns and planes to make it stick. Above all, they did not have enough depth. Weygand's depth was still very primitive. For 12½ miles as far as Roye and 6 miles as far as Chaulnes the defence zone was thickly knotted with strong-points. But once these sectors were taken, whatever the cost, the defence again collapsed. A power vacuum again developed in the rear . . . it is interesting to speculate whether the German tanks could have continued to by-pass strong-points for 25–50 miles instead of 5 or 10 . . ." (*The Six Weeks War*, T. Draper.)

for the pilots, the military chauffeur, the policemen, the servant who opened the door. Until these last few days I had always felt almost as much at home in France as in England, but this time I had left strangers behind me and was now at home. That is one of the most wonderful of all human sensations, the oneness with people and things, with the earth, with the sky, when the sound of the wind in the trees, the rumour of the town, are as much a part of the language as the words of your friends.

Presently I stood up to go. "You are in any case to have a long sleep before you return to Paris," said Winston; then he saw that my large revolver made my belt sag, and he launched forth against my slovenly appearance. He had never seen anything so untidy. XIth Hussars indeed! Had I had the good fortune to be brought up in the IVth Hussars I should never have presented so shocking a sight. But it was all Hore-Belisha's fault. It had been one of his more stupid ideas when at the War Office, to do away with the cross-belt.

I did not say it was Douglas Haig who had introduced the single belt for cavalry officers. But in his day, if you wore a revolver at all, it was a light one.

I was half-way to the door when the Prime Minister told me to sit down again. There were some points he wished to ask about. His expression was sometimes stern, at others extremely kindly, changing from one mood to the other quickly, according to the subject. Then he said such nice things about my work that fatigue fell from me, and I thought all the anguish had been well worth while. I knew from the way he spoke that his vivid comprehension had led him to understand completely what my difficulties had been. Becoming really angry, he inveighed against the bad liaison that had existed on all levels between Britain and France. He attributed much unnecessary anxiety and even danger to this source. Remembering how, ever since war had been declared, he had himself asked that I should be employed in a field I knew so well, he said bitter things about the system and the people who had turned a deaf ear to his suggestions, and had instead produced machinery that did not function, lines of communication that did not communicate, wires that crossed, men untrained and unsuited for the jobs. "In fact," he concluded, "liaison that did not liaise."

Once more I rose to go, but once more was called back, to be asked to dinner.

I went to my own office at Westminster. There were great piles of papers, some from my constituency. I must get some fellow-member to take up these questions for me. There were urgent matters concerning the businesses I was interested in. In one case there was trouble concerning some aliens we employed, key men, essential to the war production they were engaged in. Leave for them to reside in a prohibited area must be obtained. There were questions connected with a company whose chairman I was and which was of absorbing interest, for it made protective covers for aircraft tanks, ensuring they would not catch fire if pierced by bullets; but everything was really in hand, thanks to the wisdom and devotion of my secretary.

I looked at *The Times*. It contained an article concerning General de Gaulle, whom I had not yet met. I was curious concerning him, so kept the article. It ran:

"From the military point of view, the most interesting change made by M. Reynaud is the appointment of General de Gaulle as his assistant in the Ministry of National Defence. General de Gaulle was promoted to that rank only a few days ago, after distinguished service in command of an armoured unit.

"General de Gaulle came to the notice of the French military world a few years ago by his books, especially *Vers l'Armée de Métier*, which are mainly concerned with the influence of the machine upon the art of war. He is of a type which has not a strong appeal—perhaps not a strong appeal enough—to British military students, though one British military writer resembles him in certain ways. Rather aggressively 'right wing', intensely theoretical, an almost fanatical apostle of the mass employment of armoured vehicles, he is also clear-minded, lucid, and a man of action as well as a man of dreams and abstract ideas.

"Charles de Gaulle gave a series of lectures at the Sorbonne, and had to face a number of heated interruptions. His ideas—but probably much more his manner of expressing them—appeared inconsistent with democracy to people who associated tanks with Nazism and Fascism. One man, however, at once perceived their true value and tried to translate them into realities through the medium of Parliament. That man was M. Paul Reynaud, who has now called General de Gaulle to his side."

We dined upstairs at the Admiralty. It was a small party,

Churchill, Mrs. Churchill, Desmond Morton and a small black cat called Nelson, which constantly focused Winston's indulgent attention by its outrageously feline behaviour, as a very spoilt cat will. It was pleasant to see how the tiny animal provided the Prime Minister with some relaxation from worry, so much so that I, who had begun by thinking a good terrier would have been a welcome addition to the party, ended by feeling quite kindly towards Nelson.

Nothing important was said, but a word here and there threw light on the stupendous achievement of Dunkirk. It struck me then how very little this was known and appreciated in Paris.

There was talk about the German air-raids and the certainty they would be intensified. The Germans had a superiority of four to one against us in the air. In the face of this fact, the Prime Minister's unfaltering determination to help the French with all those extra fighters, thereby leaving us with little or no margin of safety, struck me as an act of immense courage. The courage of the man was, in fact, breath-taking. What enhanced the impression was that he was so completely unconscious of it himself. He was so sure, so certain, so single-minded in his decisions, so unconcerned with anything but the effect any given measure would have on the result of the war that the weight of his staggering responsibilities sat lightly on his shoulders.

His boyish exultation at feats of bravery in others emphasised the impression; it was clear he saw himself only as a member of an admiring audience debarred by circumstances from having the fun of doing something brave himself.

He told us several such anecdotes as this or that incident brought them to his mind.

He would then look either fierce and his eyes would flame, or, if it was a case of self-sacrifice, they would dim.

Soon he went off to his table laden with dispatch-boxes, and I groped my way home through the black-out of the sultry night.

CHAPTER IX

Saturday, June 8th, Sunday, June 9th and Monday, June 10th

Ronald Cartland, M.P., killed at Cassel—A day in the country—Grave news from France—Renewed appeals from Reynaud—Churchill's reply—De Gaulle in London—Lord Lloyd—Will the French defend Paris?—Attitude of the French Communists—French lack of communications—Ismay on the danger to the 51st Division—Weygand's proclamation to the Armies—Churchill's telegram on British air support— Eden suggests a meeting of the Supreme War Council— The War Room—Churchill on the military situation—He decides to go to France at once—The pretty housemaid and the uniform cross-belt—Difficulty in locating Reynaud— Our departure postponed—An evening with the Churchills at the Admiralty—General Dill on the defence of Brittany— Churchill in grim mood.

THE first thing I saw on Saturday morning was the announcement in *The Times* that my friend and parliamentary colleague Ronald Cartland was missing. It was thought he had been taken prisoner, but he had been killed when his battery most gallantly held up German tanks at Cassel.

I was saddened by this, and imagined him fighting the Nazis with the same gay smile with which he had fought for what he believed in in the House of Commons. Like me, he had detested Munich; we had both voted against our Party on the same issues. I set off for Whitehall with the picture of my tall, slender, dark, roman-nosed young friend in my mind, but it faded like everything else, even my anxiety concerning my wife, when I sat down to work with Pug Ismay. Then I saw Archie Sinclair and Anthony Eden, giving such information as I had and learning much myself.

118

That afternoon, on the Prime Minister's instructions, I went to our cottage in Berkshire and on Sunday slept and slept. My boy came over from Oxford with a friend.

Then, by a miraculous piece of luck, a lot of chicks hatched out of an incubator not long installed. To watch these tiny fluffy specks of life fight their way into a world in which they immediately took such a beady-eyed interest proved that life and therefore hope must somehow survive all hazards—the breaking through of a hard shell with a minute soft beak, or wading through the surf to a small boat off Dunkirk.

The June garden looked lovely. Care lovingly bestowed was yielding a rich reward, but its mistress was not there to enjoy it.

I was back in London by Sunday evening. The latest reports showed how grave the situation was. Such news as had come in by the evening of the 7th, the day I left Paris, had not been too bad, but in fact the Germans had forced the Somme front with two panzer divisions that afternoon, and one had continued its advance as far as Forges-les-Eaux, more than half-way to Rouen. A report dated the 8th stated that the other was apparently making for Pontoise, 32 kilometres from Paris. The information was of the vaguest; the only thing certain was that the enemy had certainly broken through towards Rouen. The news of this could only have reached Reynaud very late on the 7th or on the morning of the 8th, for on the evening of the 7th he had announced to the Army Committee of the Senate, as he had told me he hoped to do, that there was reason for confidence in the way the battle was shaping. On the Aisne on the right of the great battle front, the French seemed to be holding, though there was heavy fighting there too.

The three British fighter squadrons that had been refuelling near Rouen had had to pack up and return to England on the previous evening (8th) because of the threat to the air-fields they were using.

They must have been hard pressed, for Reynaud had begged that very day that they should not only be maintained but strengthened.

No one in London took offence at the French Premier's statement that in France they would yield their maximum result, as they would then benefit from the advice of French technicians.*

* Paul Reynaud to Winston Churchill, June 8th, 1940: "Rouen and Le Havre are directly threatened, and consequently the supplies of Paris and of

Continued on p. 120

Churchill answered at once: "We are giving you all the support we can in this great battle, short of ruining the capacity of this country to continue the war. We have suffered in today's air fighting very heavy and disproportionate losses, but we shall carry on tomorrow."

General de Gaulle, I was told, had been in London on the afternoon of Saturday the 8th to plead again for ever more fighters and for hastening the dispatch of fresh troops. He urged his case with conviction and force, but when the Prime Minister gave him the same answer I and others had been giving for days, because there was no other, de Gaulle told the Prime Minister he thought he was quite right, that it was the only decision Britain could take.

De Gaulle had made an excellent impression on all who met him: cool, collected, completely "unrattled". The British soldiers and Ministers were pleased and cheered that Reynaud should now have the support of this vigorous personality. But these eulogies were always accompanied with the remark that invariably qualified any wise measure, any innovation introduced in those days: "What a pity this was not done long ago."

De Gaulle, questioned concerning the *Réduit Breton*, had said he was in favour of it but expressed doubts concerning the possibility of holding it now. He had not had time to find out what had been done to prepare a position there. Very properly he had avoided becoming involved in any criticism of Weygand, but it had been clear enough that he did not think the Generalissimo believed in the plan or had taken any steps to make its realisation possible. It seemed strange that Weygand, who at first had looked upon Dunkirk as a bridgehead that could be defended, though this was an impossibility, made no real attempt to form one in Brittany which would have offered the chance of a prolonged defence had work been undertaken when the idea was first mooted.

I had a talk with Lord Lloyd, the Secretary of State for the

---

half the Army. I thank you for your efforts, but the situation demands still greater ones, in particular that the fighter squadrons should be based in France so that they should be able to furnish their maximum effort *as they would then benefit from the advice of our technicians.* (My italics.)

The nine fighter squadrons which you are good enough to promise us represent only a quarter of the 39 fighter squadrons which, according to your declarations at the last Supreme Council, you disposed of on May 31st.

It is my duty to ask you to throw your total strength, as we are doing, into the battle. PAUL REYNAUD."

Colonies. He was off to Paris next day. I imagine he had suggested to the Prime Minister he should go. Unimaginably dynamic himself, he just could not bear any slackening of effort in any direction. If anything failed anywhere, he had to dash off and see to it himself. Not so long before, when he was head of the British Council, I had sat beside him at a film put on by that body. Something went wrong with the performance, and I turned to find his seat empty. He had crept out on all fours to deal with the situation personally.

He told me, his tense voice vibrating like taut wire, that he had heard Reynaud was depressed; he was a friend of his, he would endeavour to cheer him up, tell him we were going to win the war. He would also see Weygand. I said I was sure his visit could but do good. Reynaud, I thought, also believed we would win the war in the end, but he was so alone, so isolated, that any manifestation of friendship and good will would be a tonic and an encouragement. As for Weygand, I should prefer to say nothing, but should be glad to hear his impression when he returned.

One question was constantly put to me: Would the French defend Paris? Would they, as Clemenceau had said in the 1914 War, "Fight outside Paris, inside Paris, behind Paris"?

I could not honestly say that if it came to the point I thought they would.

If they do not, how can they hold the line of the Seine? I was asked. To this there was no answer save to say that so long as they held the Aisne, Paris was covered to the right, and the Seine provided a powerful defensive line to the left. Whether they could hold the Oise north of the city, which connected the two rivers, I could not tell.

If they did hold this line, weak in its centre north of Paris, then the capital twenty miles back would be to all intents and purposes in the front line. If they lost the Aisne and retreated to the Marne, which falls into the Seine south of Paris, then indeed there would be fighting in the city itself, at first on the perimeter, but the obsolescent forts would not hold out long, so that the battle would rage from bank to bank of the river, from *quai*-side to *quai*-side, laying waste the finest agglomeration of monuments in the world outside Rome, rending and laying in ruins the magnificent bridges spanning the river. It was enough to evoke the picture to be certain the French would not fight in Paris. Certainly not the French of this generation. How could Reynaud do it? Even had he possessed the resolution and determination of Leonidas at Thermopylæ he was neither the expression of the country's will nor the leader of a great parliamentary majority which alone could have enabled him to impose or demand supreme sacrifice. He was no Clemenceau, nor did he hold France in an iron grip as had the "Tiger". In spite of his personal qualities he was but one of the passing shadows the Third Republic projected in rapid succession before an unconvinced and bored audience on the scarred screen of contemporary politics.

It would have been a stupendous undertaking even with the full and enthusiastic backing of Pétain and Weygand, the only two military leaders France recognised. In the face of their opposition he would, in the view of his compatriots, merely have proclaimed himself to be a lunatic, for to allow the destruction of Paris would be to tear a shrine out of the heart of every Frenchman, for whom the city stood as the sacred and beautiful emblem of France herself. France without Paris? you might ask a Frenchman and he would answer: "*Laissez moi rire*"—Don't be funny.

Then what happens if the French are driven back from their present positions? There is only the Loire, which is no real obstacle in summer, wide as it is. The river is just a well-defined topographical feature and infinitely longer and more difficult to hold than the others farther north.

There was but one answer. If the French lost their present position it became a question of holding Brittany, the Plateau Central, or withdrawing to Africa. Everything depended, I thought, on whether the new positions now being attacked were deep enough and sufficiently armed.

To believe anything else was to nurse an illusion.

I had to answer many questions concerning French morale, for people were sorely puzzled as well as surprised and disillusioned. I could add little to what I had reported.

About the action of the Communists I had formed a fairly clear idea. Those who held the view that the mass of the Communist workers would not make a maximum effort while Russia was supporting the Nazis were right. In many cases the workers did give of their best, but there were other authentic instances where men who worked harder than others because of the war had their tools hidden, or were otherwise made to suffer.

I lost no opportunity of drawing attention to the wonderful work of Dautry. There was real hope so long as one individual in the face of such unbelievable difficulties was able to do what he had done in so short a time. He had told me that not a single land-mine had been ordered before the war, although many thousands were now being delivered at the front. What he had done others might yet do.

One point I was sure of and lost no occasion to underline, for it was most important from the point of view of the equipment of our armies-to-be: whatever reasons there were for the French defeat, lack of communications of all sorts was one of them. This was sufficient to explain, in part at least, the breakdown of the French Command.

It was only in November 1939 that the French General Staff adopted short-wave wireless sets for tanks, with the result that there were hardly any available to the Army in May.

As I was leaving my house on Monday, June 10th, a message from Pug Ismay asking me to see him was handed me. When I walked into his office he pointed to a paragraph in the *Daily Telegraph*. It was headed "Paris never to yield—Destruction first". It went on:

> "Paris will never be Hitler's intact, according to a French Government spokesman today (Sunday, 9th). When I asked whether, if the worst came to the worst, the French would declare Paris an 'open' city in an effort to spare the world's most beautiful city, the spokesman answered:
> " 'Never. We are confident that Hitler's mechanised hordes will never get to Paris. But should they come so far, you may tell your countrymen we shall defend every stone, every clod of earth, every lamp-post, every building, for we would rather have our city razed to the ground than fall into the hands of the Germans.' "

"This hardly agrees with what you have been saying," said Pug. "I hope I am wrong," I said, "but I still believe I am not mistaken."*

The collapse of the French Command baffled Ismay and beggared his extensive vocabulary.

The case of the 51st Division was an example of the prevailing hysteria. Had it fallen back on Rouen as the War Office had wished, it would now be safe. The French Command had not allowed this,

---

* We now know that the decision to leave Paris was taken by the French Cabinet at the meeting held at 5 p.m. on the 9th, and that on the 10th Weygand took the decision to declare it an open city.

and the division was still at Dieppe on the 9th. Then, with the Germans already on the Seine at Rouen, General Fortune had been told by the French to fall back on Le Havre, which could not now be reached. Forces had been sent to cover its withdrawal, but Ismay doubted whether these would either arrive in time or be strong enough to achieve their task.

The news was extremely bad. The withdrawal of the French Army appeared to be taking on the proportions of a rout, which Weygand's proclamation of the day before was unlikely to stem. "For each man this is a fight without thought of retiring. . . . The German offensive is now launched along the entire front, from the sea to Montmédy. Tomorrow it will extend to Switzerland." (I wondered if he really thought that.) "We have reached the last quarter of an hour (*Nous sommes au dernier quart d'heure*). Hold on." "Well," I said, "if the *Réduit Breton* is going to be used, now is the time to make for it, if it is not already too late."

The Prime Minister had sent the following telegram to Reynaud:

"The British forces are giving the French Armies the maximum possible support in the great battle they are now fighting with indomitable courage. All available resources are being put into play to help you on land, sea and air. The R.A.F. is continuously engaged on the battlefields and during these last few days fresh British forces have landed in France to take their place by the side of those already engaged in the common struggle, while other important reinforcements are being rapidly organised and are on the point of starting."

Anthony Eden, whom I had seen the previous day, asked me to go to his office. We both thought it necessary there should be another War Council as soon as possible. It was too dangerous to leave Reynaud at the mercy of his defeatist colleagues at a moment when everything was collapsing in France. So we agreed I should put the suggestion to Winston. Just then a summons came for me to go to Downing Street, but it turned out to be from Desmond Morton, who said that, by order of the Prime Minister, I was to go to the War Room, where I was wanted.

This was my first visit to the curious and complicated subterranean abode which was later to become the focal point of the war.

The Service officers were, as is always the case, cool and collected.

I have on occasion (though not often) met stupid officers, less rarely individuals steeped in prejudice and hampered by routine, but only once or twice in two wars have I come across men who were not masters of their subject and completely calm.

The batch I met that morning under floors of concrete were mystified by the fact that there were no less than fifteen French divisions they could not account for. Needless to say, neither could I. Whether they had ever in fact existed or had been volatilised during the German onrush, I did not know. I had no idea whether the figures I had been given in Paris and had reported to London corresponded with those our Staff had obtained from the French General Staff. That there were discrepancies was not to be wondered at, since I had found that Reynaud's office at the rue St. Dominique had given me different totals from those provided by the Ministry of War in the Boulevard St. Germain at the other side of the same block. I had not attempted to solve the problem, as I had only asked for the figures for my own information, nor could I do so now.

I had asked to see the Prime Minister, and a message came whilst I was still in the War Room that I was to come at once.

He was in the Cabinet Room at No. 10. His looks reflected the gravity of the situation as he brooded over some reports. He did not say anything for quite a while. I have often sat with him thus. Having immense powers of concentration, he does not like his train of thought to be broken into until he has reached a conclusion. On the other hand he is not averse to the presence of someone he knows near him, someone who can answer a question if need be or be sent to seek information. Presently he questioned me about the Aisne front.

Yes, I knew it well, and not long ago had revisited it to refresh my memory in connection with *Prelude to Victory*, which I was then writing. "You remember," I said, "you wrote the preface."

"Yes, the Aisne was a serious obstacle, the French artillery should have excellent positions to defend its passage."

Who was there? he asked. The Fourth Army, General Réquin, did he remember him? He had been with Foch. He would put up a good fight, but his plans must depend on what the Sixth Army covering Reims could do. I could not think why Réquin's Army had not Reims in its sector. It should have been included in it. If the Sixth

Army fell back he would have to abandon the Aisne positions.*
"What reserves are there behind that part of the front?"
None, I thought. "Weygand kept repeating he had no reserves
anywhere."

I then told him, as had been agreed with Eden, that I thought there
should be a meeting of the Supreme Council that very afternoon. It
was neither right nor wise to leave Reynaud alone to face this
disastrous situation. We could be sure that every pressure would be
put on him to throw up the sponge now that Paris was directly
threatened.

Pétain had, as he knew, made up his mind the war was lost.
Weygand had neither ideas nor plans. He did not believe in the
Réduit Breton or in anything else. He just wanted to find a pretext
to stop fighting while he still had some sort of a personal position
and an army, be it only in name. According to Mandel there were
politicians ready to seize power and to treat with the Germans,
probably at our expense.

Winston reflected a moment, drummed the table with his fingers,
played with his multicircled ring, then said: "We will go to Paris
this afternoon."

"But you can't, Winston," I said. "The Germans have crossed
the Seine at Pont de l'Arche. They may be in Paris in two hours'
time. They might for aught we know get there as soon as you. The
meeting must take place south of Paris. There may actually be
fighting in Paris, though I do not think so."

The Prime Minister looked startled. It had not occurred to him
the position was as immediately desperate as that. "All right," he
said. "We must find out where Reynaud can meet us," and rang a
bell.

He gave orders to tell the Foreign Office to find out from the
Ambassador in Paris if Reynaud could meet us that afternoon and
where.

My personal problem now consisted in having my things packed
and brought to the Admiralty.

I got on to my house by telephone and explained the position to
our very pretty little house-parlourmaid, and was standing at the
entrance of the Admiralty when she arrived. She came running
across the courtyard clutching to her bosom every sort of article of

---

* The Reims sector was made over to the Fourth Army in the middle of the
battle. It was then too late.

male attire, her little apron fluttering. Not knowing what was really wanted, she had put several drawersful of my belongings into a taxi, but, that conveyance not being allowed past the Royal Marine sentries, she was rushing up the first consignment. The sentries presently relaxed and the taxi drove in, so we packed on its step. Alas, the cross-belt prescribed by the Prime Minister was missing, so the little maid was off again in the care of the enormously intrigued taxi-driver, intent and purposeful as if she were carrying a dispatch to a much exposed outpost. Soon she was back, waving an amazing assortment of leather straps, cartridge bags, belts, and even my old golden full-dress XIth Hussar cross-belt, which was much too high-class for this particular war. Happily the needed article was included in the assortment.

Funny how little things remain. That pretty, eager, intent face, the dainty apron, the quizzical expression of the taxi-driver, much keener and more interested than he would allow, are things I know now I shall never forget, since I remember them clearly across years over-full with events.

To say the Prime Minister wanted to meet Reynaud, and to carry out his wish, were very different things.

The direct telegraph and telephone lines were not functioning. Perhaps they were cut.

The impression grew that the French Government had already left Paris, though it transpired later that Reynaud went only that night.

The hours passed.

The day was dark and gloomy, in strong contrast with the brilliant sunshine we had had up to then. There was no fog, but a real darkness in the air; some thought it due to the clouds of petrol from the dumps on fire at Rouen.

I had an uneasy feeling that I should have remained in Paris. After all, my job was with Reynaud. 1 should in all probability have been able to do little there, especially now that communications had broken down, but I was of no use whatever in London.

It was not until 5.15 p.m. that it was decided it was impossible to fly to France that day.

The Prime Minister asked several times where the French Government was, but no one knew. The Foreign Office were without information. They could not even confirm whether it had left Paris. No reports concerning its whereabouts came in during the night, but there must have been some contact, for I noted that the impression was conveyed to the anxious observers in London that Reynaud was not very anxious to meet the Prime Minister next day.

I went over to Richmond Terrace and worked with Ismay for a while, then with some of his officers, always trying to sort out the French tangle and to plan what could be done in this or that eventuality.

The Prime Minister had asked me to dine. The party at Admiralty House included Anthony Eden and General Dill, the C.I.G.S. Mrs. Churchill and her daughter, Mary, were also there. I had always thought Mary Churchill when a child the most enchanting of little girls. Vigorous, gay, blue eyes for ever sparkling, she was always in movement, always laughing; she was of the type that gave the eyes that watched her joy, and the heart a respite from sadness. Now she was a child no longer, but a girl in her teens, promising great beauty. Mrs. Churchill was perfectly composed as usual, making as always the meal over which she presided a very civilised occasion. Anthony Eden and Dill looked tired, as well they might. It was no picnic to direct affairs at the War Office these days. Nevertheless the dinner was a real relaxation, and I can still remember it with pleasure. The Churchill family was so urbane, Winston so quick at detecting ridicule, such a master at clothing with apt words any idea that crossed his mind and so much enjoying doing so, that I thought of those Paris dressmakers who, with deft fingers and infinite taste, create out of their fancy, with a few wisps of material and a ribbon or two, an arresting or amusing figure out of the dullest female.

What was so astonishing and pleasing was Winston's power of seizing on a word or a fact most people would have passed unnoticed, lifting it up as a connoisseur would a glass of wine, revealing colours hitherto imperceptible, a bouquet unsuspected, smacking his lips at a taste so far unrevealed, until all were stimulated into thoroughly enjoying sensations which would but for him have remained dormant.

The C.I.G.S. had a thin, distinguished soldier's face. He had undoubted ability and persistency, but preferred, so long as he achieved his aim, the diplomatic to the direct approach. His mien was scholarly, and he was well versed in his profession. I knew he attached great importance to its forms, usages and codes, but these were not invoked that evening.

The sky had cleared as we sat in an upstairs drawing-room overlooking the Horse Guards Parade. The ladies left and conversation turned to the defence of Brittany. I felt and I fear showed ill-humour when, having discussed the lack of measures taken by the French to make the plan possible, it turned out that we had done nothing about it either. True, Brittany was in France and a part of Weygand's responsibility, but, I pointed out rather tartly, he had other things to do as well. The C.I.G.S. did, however, produce one argument against the French holding Brittany which was convincing. It would impose a terrible strain on the R.A.F., whose bases in England were too distant for fighters to cover the peninsula. But if this was true, why were we landing our precious divisions there as fast as we could? I thought, with some irritation, that the tendency of the War Office was to lay every fault and shortcoming at the door of the French, just as they blamed us for their own most glaring errors. It was natural, and the cataclysmal inefficiency and smugness of the French military authorities laid them open to every stricture, but there was danger in this, for it might blind us to our own serious mistakes.

It is strange how some lives always follow the same pattern. Mine is to defend unpopular causes, first on one side then on the other. I had spent the whole of the First War doing just that. Now, having fought bitterly with Weygand only three days ago, I found myself standing up for him. It had been the same thing with Gort, with whom I had had acrimonious discussions on officer manpower and liaison before the war.

Dill and Eden left to carry on their endless task of making bricks without straw at the War Office over the way. I stayed on. The news was bad, agonising in fact. The 51st Division was cut off on the coast at St. Valéry, west of Dieppe, together with the French IX Corps. Ships would, it was hoped, evacuate many of the men, but the equipment would be lost. The operation was to take place the following night, but it was feared there might be fog. Nature was threatening to play us this grim joke as if to underline the crass stupidity that had landed these fine troops in such unnecessary jeopardy. The elements were joining in to make us pay for our blindness. The gods of Hitler's Germany had taken charge of Heaven. Perhaps the old Norsemen were right in their belief that one day evil would prevail in the world.

I watched the Prime Minister at work throughout most of the long hours of the night. There seemed to be nothing, no fingerhold to which even his courage could fasten in the slimy mess of disastrous incompetence revealed in France, or in the cheerful inefficiency of our amateur attempts to cope with the grim reality of a robot war.

We had neither the machines we needed, nor the means of producing them. We were disastrously short of warships; the lack of destroyers was such as to chill the blood, so that when one thought of the Navy for comfort, pride did not give reassurance, for sailors, even our sailors, needed ships. Our aircraft shortage was such that it seemed an unrealisable hope that Lord Beaverbrook's rocket-like energy could produce what was needed in time.

Good will existed in the same abundant measure as inexperience; if we were short of weapons we were rich in bright ideas, but most of our Ministers were as ignorant of war as the eager recruits drilling everywhere with sticks.

And here sat the man on whom lay the responsibility of moulding this heterogeneous nation into a fighting machine, shaping a population largely composed of peace votaries, football fans, bus-catchers, stamp-lickers, fag-smokers and pub-crawlers into soldiers, sailors and airmen. On him lay the burden of selecting men to do all the work that needed doing, of filling the key posts, for in the last resort everything depends on the men chosen. The greatest genius at the head of affairs must fail if he is a bad chooser of men.

It was with a feeling not far removed from anguish that I watched the Prime Minister and sensed his unhappiness.

Bad news never ceased coming in. Every time the door opened it was certain that the paper in the secretary's hand told of some loss, some set-back, some sinking.

Confirmation had come of an earlier message that Italy would consider herself to be a belligerent as from 1 a.m. that night.

This was only depressing as proof that the carrion bird Mussolini thought the game was down. It would be true to say, I think, that the only relief that night was this declaration of war, for there was satisfaction in the certainty that, come what might, we should now quite soon have the chance of kicking someone where it hurt.

Looking at my watch, I listened for the single stroke of Big Ben at one o'clock, and heard the sound which echoed in the night, the gavel of fate striking the dome of time, announcing the inescapable verdict which would one day condemn the hyena aggressor. Winston Churchill had listened too. As the ripple of the echo died in the distance he looked across at me but said nothing. Presently he asked if I knew St. Valéry. Yes, I had driven through it. It was just a typical French Channel summer resort, a stretch of sand or shingle, with mean, scattered little bungalows dominated on either side by high chalk cliffs.

After a long interval he asked me about the French Navy. Did I know it? What were its reactions at the moment?

The seamen? Yes, I knew something of them, having done much sailing in Brittany as a boy. They were the salt of the earth, simple and unsophisticated. The Prime Minister smiled when I told him that the most flattering thing ever said to me was many years ago by a French lady we both knew, herself from Brittany, who averred that I looked like a sailor from her own stormy coast.

And the officers? he asked. I only knew what the Army said. A completely closed caste, a law unto themselves. If "Love God and hate the English" was not their motto, it ought to be. Dislike of Britain was a canker eating their collective souls; everyone in France knew this. And they were absorbed in their own affairs, hypnotised by their own hierarchy, but they were men "*de bonne éducation*". They had a complete hold over their men; I had found that out from sailors I had employed on my own little yacht in the days when I had one.

I went on to remind the Prime Minister that during the previous winter I had told him of some discontent in the larger French ships owing to the poor fare of the crews and the lavish mess of the officers, but this surely meant little, for to the French sailor his officers belonged to a higher species, possessed of great knowledge and redoubtable secrets of the sea and the stars.

"What will happen to the Navy if France drops out of the war?"

"I have no idea. It will follow the Admirals, I suppose, and the Admirals will follow Darlan. Why I can't imagine, save that he is a man of strong character." My mind went no further. I really could not imagine France out of the war, nor that her sailors with the gay little red pompoms on their caps should not always sail the seas in friendly co-operation with our own. They also belonged to a free race, were real sailors, not jack-booted soldiers from the Baltic rolling about the decks, like the German crews.

And I thought no more of the French Navy.

I did not take my eyes off the heavy hunched figure in black. The strong light under a green shade caused the pale face to look paler than usual. For the first time in my life I understood the Agony of Gethsemane, what it meant to carry absolutely alone an immeasurable burden.

Churchill was profoundly unhappy. For the first and only time in my experience I heard words akin to despair pass his lips. Several times, hands flat on the table, his eyes fixed on the blotting-paper between them, he said that we were losing everywhere, in every field, owing to lack of preparation and lack of planning.

It was heart-breaking to me that this load should have been laid on the very man who had prophesied the calamity and worked with all his soul to avert it. I longed to help, but knew I could do nothing, and that my only possible contribution was to sit without moving or speaking, hoping that somehow the intenseness of my sympathy and devotion would help. My one prayer was that, if the invasion came, I should be there, to stand in front of him and shield him.

CHAPTER X

Tuesday, June 11th

Corbin discusses Anglo-French friction—Lord Lloyd's impressions of Weygand and Reynaud—Reynaud's message to Roosevelt—Redman and Coleridge find Reynaud—Churchill and his colleagues fly to Briare—The Château du Muguet—The Supreme War Council meeting—First impression of de Gaulle—Reynaud asks, too late, for cancellation of the combined air and naval attack on Italy—Churchill on the military situation—Weygand's catastrophic report—At Churchill's request, Georges gives his account of the situation—Churchill endeavours to stiffen French resistance—He refuses the last British fighter reserve, but promises maximum air support—Reynaud pleads for squadrons to be based in France—Pétain supports Weygand —Reynaud continues to press for greater air support but Churchill maintains his decision—De Gaulle suggests an amalgamation of French and British armoured units— Weygand hints at a French surrender—Reynaud's anger— Churchill inquires as to the possibility of establishing Atlantic bridgeheads—Reynaud's answer—French irritation at Churchill's suggestions for guerrilla warfare—Churchill emphasises British determination to fight on—Reynaud deeply moved—Churchill asks about the French Navy— Reynaud says France will carry on the struggle—Weygand on an invasion of Britain—The discussion trails off and the Conference peters out—A night in the Presidential train.

EARLY on the morning of the 11th I telephoned to Corbin from my house. He asked me to come and see him. I found him as usual in the big corner room on the ground floor of the Embassy in Albert Gate. The Park seen through the windows looked pleasant and peaceful, but the Ambassador's face was drawn and his cheeks hollow. No time was wasted talking of the military situation. Neither of us could do anything about it. I told him I thought the Prime Minister would probably fly that afternoon to meet Reynaud somewhere south of Paris. I did not yet know the place of the rendezvous or indeed if one had been arranged. Did he? I asked. But he knew no more than I did.

I then spoke to him of the frequent and often unnecessary disputes between France and Britain. The Prime Minister and Reynaud did their best to prevent them. But others were involved; could they not be checked? I told him about Weygand, and he shrugged his shoulders slightly. He was as concerned as I was at the increasing friction, all too natural in the circumstances. We discussed a number of incidents which had caused irritation, the details of which I have no record, and he gave me the gist of a very good paper he had written to his Government on the subject. We were doing our best, but I think we both felt it was a complete waste of time. It was the last time I saw him.

I then saw Lord Lloyd. The impression he had brought back from his trip to Paris on the previous day was dismal. He had seen Weygand before Reynaud, and found him, to say the least of it, depressed.

Weygand had talked of the gaping wound, "*la plaie béante*", which had existed on the front of Altmayer's Tenth Army since the 8th. He said he had no reserves, and that if nothing was done the armies would simply break up. They were utterly exhausted by six days of fighting. Reliefs were impossible owing to lack of troops. He had, said Lloyd, put forward no plan, appeared to be entirely devoid of ideas, and had only two preoccupations: his haunting fear of revolution, and his dislike of Reynaud, expressed in waspish stings. He held that the *Réduit Breton* was silly—de Gaulle had put Reynaud up to the idea, just what you would expect from such a source; it was the conception of a theorist full of his own conceits and importance, but totally lacking in experience.

Weygand had then informed Lloyd that he had taken upon himself the decision to declare Paris an open town, and had written to Reynaud to tell him so. The politicians could not make up their minds, and he was not going to allow Paris to be destroyed for no purpose.

Lloyd was a man of gestures himself; as he acted the part of Weygand he threw up his arms, and his voice, imitating that of the

Commander-in-Chief, broke in high-pitched excitement. But the description Weygand had given of the troops was convincing. What could an army do with no air cover, especially against an enemy who used his air force as aggressively as did the Germans? What weapons were now left against German tanks? Had primitive man had to face dinosaurs, he would have felt much as did the modern soldier armed only with a rifle and faced with tanks against which his bullets were as unavailing as would have been a stone axe against the armour of a primeval monster.

Villers-Cotterets, the charming little town south of the Aisne and of Soissons, on the edge of Compiègne Forest, only 74 kilometres from Paris, was in enemy hands.

No wonder the Commander-in-Chief was dispirited. Lloyd said he responded to no kind of stimulus and either shrugged his shoulders or grimaced at any mention of continuing the war overseas. Weygand had not said so definitely, but Lloyd had gathered from what he saw that the Staff were on the point of packing up and moving south.

His drive from Vincennes to Paris had been a nightmare. The population, so listless when I had left, had been stricken with panic and was flying down the roads helter-skelter, pedestrians, bicycles, pushcarts and cars inextricably mixed.

He had found Reynaud alone, calm and seemingly very isolated, but he had asserted that the Government would not give way. He also was leaving Paris that night. Mandel, it appeared, was making sure no politicians likely to treat with the enemy were being left in the capital, and that remarkable man Dautry had been busy evacuating from the Paris region young workmen under 30. He had said that their morale was excellent. Again I felt a pang at not having been in Paris to lend what moral support I could, but it would have been a nightmare to be cut off from London, and no one could administer hope in convincing doses better than Lloyd.

He had brought back a copy of the message Reynaud had sent to Roosevelt before leaving Paris. It expressed a dream rather than the reality, a dream the Premier himself can hardly have believed in.

His was a normal Gallic reaction toward disaster, one which, being totally incomprehensible to the Anglo-Saxon temperament, has often caused the deepest misunderstandings between France and Britain. In France an oration at a state funeral attributing all the virtues everyone knows he was most glaringly deficient in to the deceased is considered not only normal, but necessary to satisfy good manners and public decency.

To say you will do a thing you know you cannot or will not do is to a Frenchman the next best thing to doing it, as our Army so often found in the First World War, when so many promises to attack never materialised. This does not of course mean that the French did not time and time again attack brilliantly or with the utmost gallantry according to the agreed plan. But when for some reason they did not intend doing so, they often thought it more polite to carry out the semblance of an operation rather than refuse participation. In the ability to distinguish between the reality of a body blow and the feints of shadow-boxing resides one of the more subtle gifts of the liaison officer.

Reynaud's message to Roosevelt said that the French divisions had been fighting for six days and six nights, without an hour's respite, against an enemy enormously superior in numbers and in material. The Germans were now almost at the gates of Paris.

"We shall fight before Paris," wrote Reynaud to Roosevelt, "we shall fight behind Paris." (The words "we shall fight in Paris", used by Clemenceau in the original sentence which he had coined, were omitted.)

"We shall hold one of our provinces, and if we are driven from it, we shall go to North Africa and, if need be, to our American possessions.

"Part of the Government has already left Paris. I myself am on the point of joining the Armies. It will be to intensify the struggle and not to abandon it. May I ask you, Mr. President, to explain this to your people, and to tell them that we are resolved to sacrifice ourselves in the struggle we are carrying on on behalf of all free men?"

Reynaud, when he wrote, may have evoked a picture of himself visiting the Armies, but he took no step to do so; indeed it would have been well-nigh impossible as no one knew where any headquarters were, and, moreover, it would have been quite useless.

That same evening (10th) Ismay had managed to telephone to Colonel Redman at Vincennes, no mean achievement, as the most improbable circuits had to be tried before one could be found that could be used, and told him to locate Reynaud and arrange for a meeting of the War Council next day.

Redman at once went to Paris, only to find that the Premier and
his entourage had vanished. Our Embassy was closed. No one
knew where they had gone. He had fortunately sent his extremely
able Number Two, the Naval member of his trinity, Commander
Coleridge, to find accommodation for his Mission in the neighbourhood of Briare, south-east of Orléans, where Weygand's Headquarters was to be set up. It took Redman until four in the morning
to get hold of Coleridge, who immediately set about tracking down
Reynaud. After a prolonged search he located him in a small hotel
in the neighbourhood and obtained his agreement to a meeting of the
War Council at Briare that afternoon. He managed to get the
information back to Redman, who passed it to London, no small feat
of persistency and initiative on the part of both officers.

After several changes in the time of our departure, we finally
took off at 2.30 p.m. in the Flamingo. It was escorted by twelve
Hurricanes. In the plane were Anthony Eden, General Dill, Pug
Ismay, Brigadier Lund, Captain Berkeley, Pug's assistant and
matchless translator, and myself.

Having no papers to study, and a role which would only take shape
as a result of the conference, I had leisure to enjoy watching the
escort planes, graceful and alert, and to wonder exactly what would
happen if we were attacked. It was curious to be engaged in this
semi-warlike operation while sitting in a most comfortable arm-
chair.

Presently other thoughts drove away all sense of pleasure and
exhilaration. The toyland unfolding beneath us had been amusing
to watch as I attempted to recognise localities, until suddenly I saw it
as a doll's house in the shop-front of a burning building, soon to be
engulfed in flames. Then there was my wife and her ambulance,
somewhere on the surface below, but far away and certainly very
near to, and perhaps in, the conflagration. I made an effort to
banish these weakening thoughts.

Winston brooded in his arm-chair, his eyes on the horizon.
Occasionally he beckoned to one of us to ask a question, then
relapsed into silence.

Most of the time, Eden and Dill, heads together, were discussing
endless tables and columns of figures. What pleasant well-bred faces
they had, I thought, in spite of their puckered brows.

Ismay, too, had an enormous number of folders in his dispatch-cases. He never took his eyes off them save when called by Churchill or Dill, when he would look up, wide-eyed, put his hand to his ear to hear through the vibrations of the machine, and smile as soon as he had grasped what was wanted of him.

We arrived at Briare late in the afternoon, having made a considerable detour. Aerodromes seldom give an impression of being overpopulated, but this one seemed particularly flat and deserted. Winston, in black, leaning on his stick, strolled about beaming as if he had left all his preoccupations in the plane and had reached the one spot in the world he most wished to visit at that particular moment. He conveyed the impression that the long journey had been well worth while since at last it was vouchsafed to him to walk about the aerodrome of Briare.

I, on the other hand, thought it a quite beastly place and hoped I should never see it again. The fact that my wishes have been fulfilled does not make me feel more kindly toward it.

Three or four cars drove up at intervals, and the Prime Minister left in the first with a French Colonel, who, from his expression, might have been welcoming poor relations at a funeral reception.

We drove a few kilometres to a hideous house, the sort of building the *nouveau riche* French *bourgeoisie* delight in, a villa expanded by successful business in groceries or indifferent champagne into a large monstrosity of red lobster-coloured brick, and stone the hue of unripe Camembert.

This was Weygand's abode, where the Prime Minister was to sleep.

The place, to which I took an instant dislike, had, I was glad to hear, a ridiculous name: *Le Château du Muguet*—Lily of the Valley Castle.

As soon as we walked into the building I felt that the impression conveyed by the Colonel on the aerodrome was but a projection of the attitude of our hosts. It was like walking into a house thinking one was expected, to find one had been invited for the following week. Our presence was not really desired.

It was a subtle feeling, and I may have been wrong, for every form of politeness was shown, even to the extent of giving us tea, but I do not think so. The strain caused by a situation which had greatly deteriorated since I had last seen our hosts had relaxed the bonds of friendship, even in the case of the staunchest of our French *vis-à-vis*.

Within a few minutes we all trooped into the large dining-room where the conference was to be held: Pétain, de Gaulle, de Margerie and Colonel de Villelume, followed Reynaud. I sat near the window between Ismay and de Gaulle. It was now 7 o'clock.

The Frenchmen sat with set white faces, their eyes on the table. They looked for all the world like prisoners hauled up from some deep dungeon to hear an inevitable verdict.

For relief I turned to de Gaulle, whose bearing alone among his compatriots matched the calm, healthy phlegm of the British. A strange-looking man, enormously tall; sitting at the table he dominated everyone else by his height, as he had done when walking into the room. No chin, a long, drooping, elephantine nose over a closely-cut moustache, a shadow over a small mouth whose thick lips tended to protrude as if in a pout before speaking, a high, receding forehead and pointed head surmounted by sparse black hair lying flat and neatly parted. His heavily-hooded eyes were very shrewd. When about to speak he oscillated his head slightly, like a pendulum, while searching for words. I at once remembered and understood the nickname of *"Le Connétable"* which Pétain said had been given him at St. Cyr. It was easy to imagine that head on a ruff, that secret face at Catherine de Medici's Council Chamber.

I studied him with great interest, little thinking that for a while we should both be bent with such complete concentration on the same task, nor that later we should be driven so far apart.

That afternoon he had a look of confidence and self-possession which was very appealing. He had, I thought, brought it from Abbeville, where he had fought a successful tank action (the only one). Fresh air had given his sallow skin a healthy colour. His cheeks were almost pink. That freshness of complexion I never saw on his face again, nor, I think, did I often see him smile as he did when he turned towards me then. It was a frank, confident smile that belied his usual expression and made me feel I should greatly like this man. I perceived that afternoon what was perhaps the real de Gaulle, or maybe that part of him which might have prevailed had he remained a soldier, straight, direct, even rather brutal.

After an awkward little pause, and before the actual conference started, Reynaud said there was a particular point he wished to raise. He evidently found considerable difficulty in doing so.

He wished, he said, to refer to the combined Anglo-French air and naval operation that was to take place that night against Genoa, Turin and Milan. To his great regret he had to ask that it should be countermanded. Lyons was completely unprotected, so were the great petrol depots near Marseilles. The Italians were sure to retaliate, with disastrous results.

This was the first I had heard of the plan: I looked at the Prime Minister, who was looking at Ismay, who was looking at his wrist-watch. His lips were pursed in a characteristic pout. Then he looked up beaming. Had he had a tail to wag it would have been wagging hard enough to break the back legs of his chair. His expression was that of a retriever coming up to master to tell him he has hidden his bone this time where it really could not be found. "The operation cannot be stopped," he said, "the planes left England a quarter of an hour ago." Margerie translated in cold, precise words that fell like silver coins on a counter.

Reynaud's eyebrows arched higher, but he made no comment. Weygand looked at Pug with faint distaste but said nothing either, nor did Pétain, in comparison with whom Lazarus would have looked skittish and high in colour. His face was as expressionless as a slab of marble. There was a rather awkward pause, then, after a few words of formal welcome, Reynaud turned towards Churchill with that stiff-necked movement of his, and again raising his eye-brows asked him, with a gesture of the hands and the slight facial twitch familiar to him, to address the conference.

The Prime Minister then spoke; the words came slowly, carefully selected but hammered together sharply into a vivid mosaic. He said, in substance, that he had come to France to consider with Monsieur Reynaud and his advisers the realities of a situation which must be faced without flinching. The matter for discussion was how best to carry on with the struggle which nothing could prevent the British from pursuing. His own impression was that as soon as the Germans had stabilised themselves on a front in France, they would turn on England. He hoped they would do so for two reasons. It would give France relief and enable the British to take a fuller and more equal share in the struggle, but, above all, it would give our R.A.F. the opportunity of smashing the German air power. He had complete confidence that they would do so. Every effort was being made in Great Britain to turn out arms and re-equip the armies. At this very moment the British were sending troops to France, and a British infantry division was deployed about Le Mans.

A Canadian division and 72 guns were landing that night, so that there were now four British divisions in France. Another division would arrive about June 20th. The dispatch of yet a further division would depend on the guns the French could provide. Then there were the troops from Narvik. If the French Army could hold out till the spring of 1941, the British would have from 20 to 25 divisions to place at the disposal of the French Command, to employ anywhere. They might, for example, be used to form continental bridgeheads. He realised, he said, that the numbers he had given were small in the face of the present emergency, but if the French could hold out, the British participation would grow rapidly. The whole problem was how to tide over the present period until the potential strength of the Allies materialised.

He stopped. Reynaud thanked him, but I felt his suppressed irritation and that of the other Frenchmen at the inadequacy of this trickle to halt a conflagration whose flames were fast spreading from the Channel to the Atlantic. Reynaud added no comment to his formal acknowledgement of Churchill's words, and asked Weygand to report on the military situation. No one expected good news, but what we were told by the Commander-in-Chief was so bad that the sweat poured off my face as I listened. There was inescapable reality in the tale he unfolded while the light of the June evening faded under gathering clouds in the sky outside. The story had not carried the same conviction when read in reports or listened to at second hand. He appeared more intent on persuading his listeners that all was lost than on considering with them means of continuing the struggle. There was not a single battalion in reserve. The totality of the French forces were engaged. The fighting from Abbeville to Reims had been going on for more than six days without inter-mission. "The troops fight all day then fall back to new positions during the night. The men have had neither food nor rest. They collapse into sleep when halted and have to be shaken in the morning to open fire."

In the last forty-eight hours fighting had spread eastwards to the Meuse. So far there had been no fighting on the Maginot Line, but a frontal attack was expected there. Nearly all the divisions that had been held in reserve behind it had been sent elsewhere.

The German attacks on the Montmédy front had been very violent, but the troops, without exception, had fought well.*

---

* On the 10th Weygand had informed Reynaud that the troops in General Frère's Army were no longer fighting, owing to exhaustion. (Baudouin, *Neuf Mois au Gouvernement*, p. 159.)

"There has not been the least breakdown, nor the least sign of failure either amongst the troops or in the Command," went on Weygand aggressively. (There was an almost perceptible stiffening of the British at this. Each could read in the others' minds: Corap, Dunkirk, and now the 51st Division cornered at St. Valéry). The French Command had hoped to hold the Somme–Aisne line, Weygand was saying, but although thanks to the R.A.F. heavy losses had been inflicted on the enemy's armour as well as on his Air Force, the overwhelming superiority of the Germans in aircraft, tanks and manpower had compelled a withdrawal. The result was that the French Armies were falling back to their last line of defence. This ran along the lower Seine and the Paris defence positions, followed the Oise and the Marne to join the north-west extremity of the Marne line, thence on to the Maginot forts. This line had been attacked at most points and broken on the lower Seine, and quite recently on the Marne. Up to this point Weygand's voice had been calm, expository; it now rose a note or two as he said: "The German mechanised columns get through our lines, curl round and blow up the bridges behind our troops, who, when they reach them, find themselves cut off. In other cases, as the enemy aircraft can spot French troop movements unhindered, they blow up from the air the bridges they are making for," and he told the story I had already heard of the German plane which, flying low, had blown up the French explosive charges on the Oise bridges, cutting off the troops from the positions they were withdrawing to. "It is," he said, "a race between the exhaustion of the French and the shortness of breath of the enemy divisions." That was why in an order of the day he had spoken of this being the last quarter of an hour.

Some divisions were, he said, reduced to three and even to two battalions. The best way to illustrate the position was perhaps to give the order of battle at the moment. The Seine sector of 135 kilometres was held by five divisions, two of which had only two regiments, and by the remnants of the Third Light Motorised Division. The Germans had two bridgeheads about Elbeuf and Vernon.

Two weak cavalry divisions were being reconstituted about Mantes and Melun. On the Oise, on a 35-kilometre front, there were two good divisions supported by three who were exhausted. Fortunately the enemy was not very aggressive here, he said. On the Oise and on the Ourcq front, covering 55 kilometres, there were five

TUESDAY, JUNE 11TH 143

divisions, but only one of these was good. Here also was the 4th Light Motorised Division, which had been thrown into the battle although its vehicles were not run in. The enemy here was threatening to advance on Paris via Senlis and Crépy. From the Ourcq to the Marne, on a front of 44 kilometres, there was only one division of two regiments and part of the 52nd Division. In this sector the enemy was threatening Meaux. "There is nothing to prevent the enemy reaching Paris. We are fighting on our last line and it has been breached." His tone now as dramatic as his words, he rapped out: "I am helpless, I cannot intervene for I have no reserves, there are no reserves. *C'est la dislocation*"—the break-up.

I looked round and read consternation on all the English faces. My own mouth was so dry I could not swallow. I wrote quickly to make up for lost time as I found I had stopped to listen, for the picture evoked was slow to take shape in my mind.

The account Weygand had given was probably that which he saw and believed to be true. But he may have thought he had administered too violent a shock, for after a moment's pause he resumed in a much calmer voice from which the high sibilant notes had been eliminated. If the enemy could be held for a few days longer, something might be attempted with the four divisions being reconstituted in Normandy, together with the British divisions and the contingent from Narvik. "But the fact remains that the battle has reached its last and most critical stage. The result is on a knife-edge balance. We may fall on either side at any moment." He was convinced that the enemy was also exhausted. Were a counter-attack possible, the advance would be stemmed.

The situation was this: "Either the Allied positions will fall, or the enemy will be constrained by the strength of the opposition he is encountering to call a halt to his advance. It is the God of Armies who will decide."

The Commander-in-Chief may now have thought that he had been too optimistic, for he added: "I cannot guarantee that our troops will hold out for another hour. If the last line of defence is broken I cannot see how a co-ordinated defence on French territory will be possible," and he repeated that the entire French Army had been engaged, was fighting *sans défaillance*, and that he could no longer intervene since he had no reserves.

I looked at Reynaud. Eyebrows raised, he was gazing at the middle of the table. Churchill, hunched over the table, his face flushed, was watching Weygand intently. His expression was not benevolent. But Weygand was now launched on his favourite theme, the folly of having embarked on the war at all. "I wish to place on record that I consider that those responsible embarked upon the war very lightly and without any conception of the power of German armaments. As it is, we have lost something like two-fifths of our initial strength."

It may be that the Prime Minister and Eden both felt the discussion was slipping on to ground where a conflict between politicians and soldiers would be difficult to avoid, or perhaps they concluded simply that the Commander-in-Chief was wandering too far from the subject under discussion; they both intervened together and once again spoke of the landing of the Canadians. Whatever their object, they were successful only in diverting the Commander-in-Chief back to his tale of woe. We were told we should be prepared for a German offensive north of Basle, a passage of the Rhine, and a push in the direction of Belfort. On the other hand, he thought the Alpine screen, although weak, could hold the Italians. He then summarised a detailed report which he had received at 5 p.m. that day. The gist of it was that the Army Group responsible for the line extending from the sea to Reims had re-established the situation on its front, but was so extended and so weak that the forces it disposed of could only provide the thinnest of screens against a hostile advance.

Weygand's voice and manner showed he had come to the end of his *exposé*. He closed by saying that he had already informed the Premier in writing that successful resistance might not be possible under such conditions as now prevailed, and that the deep penetration by enemy tank units might make it impossible to re-establish the line. He would repeat what he had already said on May 29th: "If the armies are disarticulated and cut off, I should consider it impossible to maintain a co-ordinated defence of the French territory. To say anything else would be untrue." And he added some words which might have been construed to mean that if it was deemed useful to the cause, he was prepared to withdraw. It was a gesture without significance, empty words without meaning, not intended to be taken seriously. Nor were they. Reynaud waved a casual hand and murmured: "*Il n'en est pas question.*" Churchill did not even speak, he just looked at the ceiling, crossly making the gesture of one brushing away a fly.

Weygand had finished. He was drained dry like a squeezed lemon.

Not an idea, not a suggestion was to be wrung out of him. This must have been Churchill's conclusion, for he put him no questions, did not even look at him again, and merely asked that General Georges should be summoned. During the short interval before Georges appeared, Churchill said nothing, but sat flushed and pre-occupied, playing with his ring. I looked at de Gaulle. I had noted that he had been ceaselessly smoking cigarettes, lighting one from another, his lips pursed and rounded in the characteristic movement I had already observed. Not a muscle of his face had moved. Nothing had been said that had caused his expression to change. The Prime Minister had looked at him several times. He was searching for something he had failed to find in the other French faces. The fact that he returned several times to a study of de Gaulle made me think he had detected in him the thing he was looking for.

When Georges came in he looked ghastly, but later his expression became more normal. The close similarity of his account to that already given by Weygand was very striking. They both told the same story in almost similar words. There were only differences of detail.

He told us that the Allies had lost a minimum of 35 divisions out of 105, as well as all the mechanised cavalry and a substantial pro-portion of the armoured divisions.

Furthermore, the best divisions were included amongst those lost, as well as the excellent British divisions. Twenty to twenty-five of the divisions at present engaged were completely dislocated. Although the troops were showing a fine spirit of self-sacrifice, the battle was proving extremely costly. Some divisions had only two battalions left. The French fighting forces were at the moment but a thin screen made up of weak units and tired men with no reserves behind them. Reims was threatened. There were signs that an attack in the direction of Châlons and the Argonne was imminent. Only from two to four infantry divisions were being reconstituted and they were made up of very mediocre elements.

Georges intended to speak up for the troops, and did so. He was proud of the way many of them were fighting and was determined that where heroism had been shown it should be recognised. There was no Englishman at that table who did not understand and appreciate his intention, and his sober words carried infinitely more weight and conviction than had Weygand's discourse, which had been larded with far too many exclamations about "*troupes sans défaillances*"—an Army that had fought magnificently without any exception. Such statements had exactly the contrary effect on British ears to that intended.

In his usual matter-of-fact, decided way Georges said: "The fact is that some divisions have ceased to exist, they are only numbers. The Army is not in a position to oppose a powerful thrust."

The Prime Minister interjected: "And the troops from Narvik?"

"They only represent a very small unit," answered Georges. I was watching Churchill, as we all were. It was evident that Georges' description had shaken him far more than had that of Weygand, for he trusted Georges and knew he would neither lie nor mislead. He was clearly horrified. But he would not surrender to the atmosphere of calamity that hung like a miasma in the room, and doggedly began to enumerate once more the forces we should soon send to France. Everything we had would be sent excepting a small force held back to deal with a possible invasion. Eden broke in to point out that this force, all we had to defend Britain, amounted to two brigades of regular troops and a few Territorial units.

Georges evidently now felt it his duty to remove any illusion that might have remained with his English listeners, for he intervened again to say that the Germans had a preponderance of three to one, and their strength was constantly increasing. Under these conditions a most dangerous situation might develop at any moment, all the more so that Italy's declaration of war had necessitated sending some fighter squadrons to that front. The French had only from 170 to 180 fighter aircraft left, with very tired pilots.

Reynaud chimed in as he had done at every meeting with: "If this battle is lost, it will be through lack of aviation," uttered in a resigned voice, as he might have said: "Well, the poor chap is dead but it was his own fault." This sentence, true as are most clichés, but as unenlightening, emphasised that we were getting nowhere. Not a single positive suggestion had been made, nor had the hint of a plan emerged.

The Prime Minister may have sensed this, and felt that it was time he intervened again. His mouth had been working, an indication that he was pouring an idea into the mould of words. His voice when he spoke was warm and deep, an admirable medium for giving utterance to his generous ideas. He wished, he said, to express his admiration for the heroic resistance of the French Armies, and Great Britain's grief at not being able to take a more effective part in the struggle. The inescapable fact was that the B.E.F. had come out of Flanders almost literally naked. It could only resume the struggle after it had been re-armed. Had it not been for events in the north, some thirteen or fourteen British divisions would now be fighting by the side of the French. This was the gist of his words, but they conveyed far more; the longing of the British people to help their friends in distress, their determination to do so the moment they could, and his evocation of the disaster in the north, whilst conveying no hint of reproach, nevertheless did recall facts that explained Britain's momentary helplessness.

Then, returning to his constant purpose of instilling the will to fight into the French, of demonstrating that, come what might, the struggle must continue, he evoked the past. We had been near disaster before in the last war, and had survived. Now, as then, we were losing sight of the war as a whole in the contemplation of our own immediate losses. We must not be hypnotised by our defeats, discouraged by our temporary weakness, or blind to the enemy's difficulties. The German Armies must now also be in a state of extreme exhaustion and feeling the strain of their immensely long lines of communication.

The pressure might diminish in forty-eight hours. Might it not be possible, while holding the main line, to mount a counter-attack with the help of the British forces that would then be in position in the region of Rouen?

If the front held for another three or four weeks, there would be a substantial British force available to attack the enemy's flank. He was convinced the enemy was feeling his losses acutely; there was a complete absence of exultation in Germany. Every hour, every day gained tended to retrieve our fortunes. Whereupon Weygand broke in to say discouragingly but truthfully that it was a question of hours, not of days and weeks. His voice was impatient, tinged with exasperation.

General Dill, grasping the Prime Minister's purpose, anxious to support him, and feeling that Weygand was the man he should particularly address himself to, attempted to placate him by saying that he was at liberty to use the British troops now in France as he thought fit. He was not even bound to use them as divisions.

"*Merci*," said Weygand, "I will note that." His tone was polite. Dill was a soldier and entitled to be courteously treated, not like one of these interfering politicians.

It seemed as if Dill's intervention had created a new atmosphere which Churchill at once took advantage of. He weighed in again like a ship of the line under full sail seizing the opportunity afforded by a change of wind to strike. His broadsides were formidable. The tide might turn at any moment. There had been just such complete changes of fortune during the last war, and he proceeded to paint word pictures of some of the most tragic moments of that period. He spoke of the Marne. He told of the days that had followed March 21st, 1918. Bowing courteously to Pétain, he said he recalled meeting the Marshal at Beauvais during that terrible time. I could see he was gathering his immense reserves of moral strength in an attempt to carry the French with him away and out of the slough of despond into which they had fallen.

I ceased taking notes and watched him, hypnotised. He found wonderful flashing words with which to express his fiery eloquence. They came in torrents, French and English phrases tumbling over each other like waves racing for the shore when driven by a storm. Something of the impression he then made comes back to me as I read his account of what occurred that afternoon. He wanted the French to fight in Paris, describing how a great city, if stubbornly defended, absorbed immense armies. And the pageant of history, the lurid glow of burning cities, some as beautiful as Paris, collapsing on garrisons who refused to accept defeat, arose before our eyes. The French perceptibly froze at this.*

Incongruously perhaps, but with a slight sense of personal scorn, a half-forgotten story took shape in my memory concerning 300 Spartans who on another summer day long ago sat "combing their long hair for death in the passes of Thermopylæ." If such men

---

* On this day Weygand, having decided to declare Paris an open town, issued orders in consequence. He states in his book that on the following day (12th) he confirmed this order by telephone to the Military Governor of Paris, General Héring, as follows:

(1) Paris open town.

(2) Neither the line of the old forts, nor the belt of fortifications, nor the town, will be defended.

(3) No destruction of bridges or any other destruction will be carried out. Fighting troops will not pass through the city but will follow the exterior boulevards. The police forces will act in consequence.

"To this decision, which is personal to myself, Paris, almost alone of the great European capitals, owes it that, in this first peril, it maintained its beauty intact. (*Rappelé au Service*, pp. 199–200.)

There may be amongst future generations of Frenchmen those who think that a few ruins in Paris would have been more becoming to her fame than her unscarred beauty.

existed in France, they were not in that room. Leonidas was there, but he was not French. But Churchill, if he had noticed the perceptible movement which had led all the French to sit back in their chairs with the tension of a motorist pressing hard on the brakes, save de Gaulle, and de Margerie who was completely absorbed in his work, did not heed it, or, if he did, it merely spurred him on, for he went straight on, now counter-attacking on the subject of the Royal Air Force. Weygand had asked that every British fighter plane should be sent to France as this was the decisive battle that would settle the fate of both nations. This, Churchill declared with great force, was not so, there was a wider horizon, a vaster field to be considered.

Today we had the battle of France, tomorrow we should have that of Britain, and it was on this field that the fate of the war would be decided. If we won that battle, all we had now lost would be retrieved. He looked very fierce, and it was quite evident that nothing would make him surrender the last air defence of Britain. And he said so. Although we were doing all we could in the air, the French could not expect us to destroy irretrievably our only hope in the present battle, the Air Arm. I remembered he had told me in London he would not compromise on this absolutely vital issue, and he was keeping faith with himself.

There was obvious relief amongst the English, who had been watching him intently and perhaps with some fear that French eloquence and the magnitude of the French disaster, which had so obviously awakened his deepest sympathy, might cause him to give way.

He now went on to say in a more expository tone that the British Government was considering daily how it could help. He must repeat that our fighter force had been completely disorganised by Dunkirk. Nevertheless, six to eight squadrons from England were taking part in the battle every day. This was in addition to Air Marshal Barratt's force, which was being kept up to full strength. But one difficulty should not be lost sight of: British fighters based in France suffered inordinate losses in aircraft destroyed on the ground. Nevertheless the B.A.A.F.* had done much great work and would continue to do so. It would of course remain at the complete disposal of the French High Command and comply with its every request. The British were not being selfish. He did not wish the

* British Advanced Air Force.

French to think that. They were acting in the deep belief that if their fighter defence was broken down they would be unable to continue the war.

The fighter force would, they believed, break up the attack on their island and cripple the might of Germany when it came, and it would surely come. But whatever happened we would fight on and on and on, *toujours*, all the time, everywhere, *partout, pas de grâce*, no mercy. *Puis la victoire!*

Reynaud, who had listened politely, easing his head in his collar now and then, said he fully accepted that the British fighter force should be kept in being, but he must assert that it was equally important to maintain the last line of defence in France. It was evident that British fighters operating from England must be less effective than those based in France. After all, where was the danger? If the worst befell, they could always regain their home bases. The French High Command was persuaded that a large-scale air attack on the advancing Germans might reverse the situation. The Air Force was the only weapon left to the Allies. Great Britain could therefore turn the scales of the present battle in favour of the Allies if she so wished. He stopped, looked at Georges, and made a movement· of the chin in his direction. He knew that the General had more influence on Churchill than any other Frenchman and had observed, quick as he was, how carefully the Prime Minister had listened to him. He wanted his support and got it. Very solemnly Georges said he fully agreed with Reynaud.

Weygand then said that there could be no comparison between the last and the present war. The fearful collaboration between air and armour did not exist in 1914–18. The enemy could not then make hops of from 40 to 50 kilometres.

He, the Commander-in-Chief, face to face with the troops, could tell them to get killed where they stood, but facing the Heads of the Governments he had to tell them the truth! He spoke dramatically, as if revealing some great secret. This struck an odd note; the English seemed puzzled and rather shocked. But there was no time for them to analyse their feeling, for Pétain was speaking. He was calm, detached, and took up what Churchill had said as if he had been an important member of the audience at a conference who wished to draw attention to one or two points omitted by the lecturer. He sat there very straight, very pale, looking at his hands spread on the table.

He wished, he said, to support General Weygand in his contention that the present war in no way resembled the last one. Nor were the incidents Mr. Churchill had recalled in any way comparable with those we were now living. When in 1918 General Gough's Army was driven back, he, as Commander-in-Chief of the French Army, had been able to send him 20 divisions forthwith. Later, at the very time when he had seen Mr. Churchill at Beauvais, he had sent 20 more. At Verdun the French divisions in line were relieved every three days.

He added, without the inflection of his voice changing: "In those days there were 60 British divisions in the line."

He then paused and said gravely, alluding to Churchill's advocacy of fighting in Paris: "To make Paris into a city of ruins will not affect the issue."

There was a rather painful pause brought to an end by Eden, who said that at the Cabinet Meeting that morning Lord Halifax had given some interesting information from a highly-placed neutral, who had stated that the German losses were very heavy and there was no enthusiasm for the war in the Reich. "That is the very reason," snapped Weygand, "why I informed the troops that this was 'the last quarter of an hour'."

"Let us not lose sight of the fact," said Reynaud, "that the enemy is at the gates of Paris, that the Seine and the Marne have been crossed, and that the troops are completely exhausted. The men have the impression of being utterly undefended from air attacks." England could afford greater air support than she was giving. The French Government, having given the British Government the fullest explanations in this connection, did not wish to add anything. But all those who had taken part in the fighting agreed in saying that were the German Air Force less powerful, the battle would assume a very different form.

Georges again said he fully concurred, and it was undeniable that British air squadrons based in France were far more effective than those based on England. He added that he doubted whether at this stage the German Air Force was in a position to launch a heavy attack against Britain, to which the Prime Minister retorted harshly that the Germans had four times the air strength of the British, and the main purpose of this great armada was exactly for the purpose of smashing Britain. But Georges went on as if he had not heard, that a massive attack by bombers on the Marne might yet turn the situation, and Reynaud chimed in to repeat that fresh aircraft was the only element that might possibly tip the balance in the Allies' favour.

It was quite plain from Churchill's expression that he had no intention of giving way. He diverted the discussion by saying that an attack on the United Kingdom would in all probability bring the United States into the war, since the whole British population would resist the attack with the utmost fierceness. The losses the German Air Force would sustain might well be the turning-point of the war. Generally speaking, the British pilots brought down four or five German machines for the loss of two of theirs. At Dunkirk the proportion had been four to seven. In England the proportion would probably be six to one.

It was of capital importance, he rapped out, to keep in existence the instrument on which depended the intervention of the United States in the conflict. It would be folly to ruin the only weapon capable of achieving this result. Moreover, it was far from certain that the contrary decision would reverse the position in France.

Reynaud dryly intervened to say that nothing was less desirable than the break-up of the British Air Force except that of the western front, and once more repeated that history would no doubt say that the battle of France had been lost because of weaknesses in the air.

Churchill evidently did not like this; he may also have been jarred by Reynaud's *leit motif*, for he added with a frown: "Thanks also to lack of tanks and to the numerical superiority of the enemy." But Reynaud was not to be deterred. "The depressing effect on morale caused by German air superiority, especially by their dive-bombers, must be taken into account." This drew from Eden the remark that the British could not help in that respect. Possessing no such machines, they could not inflict similar punishment on the Germans, to which Reynaud tartly replied that nothing of the sort was expected of us. All that was asked was that our fighters should keep the dive-bombers off.

As an approaching squall is heralded by choppy waters, so the rising tone of the French Premier's voice warned of impending trouble. Churchill perceived this, and in sentences warm and soothing, emphasising by a deeper tone the first syllable of key words, he moulded phrases rounded and smooth that fell like drops of oil flicked on a rising sea. He said infantry had always the impression of being unprotected from the air—the men in the line never saw a plane. It was already so in the last war. And he told how the men from Dunkirk back in England had booed the R.A.F. pilots to whose efforts they owed their safety.

The acerbity had gone from Reynaud's voice when he answered, but his theme was unchanged, for he repeated almost word for word Georges' plea that more and still more British fighters should be based in France. The Prime Minister, having got the discussion back into his own hands, was a trifle blunt as he repeated the arguments for not doing so. But, easing up a little, he said that the whole position would be reviewed on his return to England. "We are always thankful, but always famished," said Reynaud in a quite friendly tone. There was a pause, broken by de Gaulle, who said he wished to make a suggestion. General Evans' Armoured Division had tanks the armour of which was too light. The French tanks were heavy, but the French were very short of light armour for reconnaissance purposes. An association or amalgamation would be highly effective. The Prime Minister said the suggestion would be examined at once. I thought how little anybody seemed to know about the difficulty of combining and supplying French and British units. Quite apart from psychological difficulties, there were others the manager of any factory would have foreseen. But why worry? No one in that room in fact believed that at this stage anything of the kind would be done.

Now Weygand was speaking again: "We are at the last quarter of an hour." If he says that again, I thought, I shall do something foolish, and, by the look of my notes, I broke my pencil.

Thereupon fancy came to my rescue as it often does, and I saw Big Ben with a French General's cap on, marking time at the double, chiming the last quarter of an hour incessantly, at ever accelerating speed, while the dial of the clock became Weygand's face.

My mind wandered from the discussion, but I do not think I missed much; Weygand was saying that there was conceivably still a hope of winning through, and that was why any possible help was indispensable.

The Heads of Governments and the Generals had met to examine what would be the consequence of the eventual dislocation of the armies. The enemy already held bridgeheads across the Seine, and his armour was manœuvring to encircle Paris from both sides. If the present line was broken, there was no hope that it could be re-established, as there was nothing behind it. "Once this defensive battle has been lost," he said, "there is nothing to prevent the total invasion of France owing to the strength and power of penetration of the German panzer divisions." Not only Paris but every large town in France would be occupied. Doubtless the remainder of the French forces would fight on until not a man remained, but this would be uncoordinated warfare, and he himself, as Commander-in-Chief, would find himself completely powerless. He found it difficult to imagine how, if the worst happened, France could carry on with the war.

Well, now we had it. There was no mistaking the Commander-in-Chief's meaning.

I looked at Reynaud. He had bristled visibly. When he spoke, his voice was carefully controlled and modulated, but he was plainly very angry.

The Commander-in-Chief had given, he said in effect, the most competent view available on the military situation, but, and here he rapped out his words, the question of whether or not the war was to continue was the responsibility of the Government and of the Government alone.

The two men glared at each other. Reynaud's eyebrows were lifted so high that every wrinkle beneath them was ironed out. But if in consequence his face was blank, his eyes darted fury. Weygand opened and closed his mouth. His parchment skin, tightly stretched on his Mongolian face, looked as if it would crack under the strain of his moving jaw. But he said nothing for a few moments whilst all watched him. Then he recovered some control and, with the playful *bonhomie* of the dog who persists in having a last snap at the postman's trousers, repeated that he would be only too glad to serve under anyone who could escape from the consequences of the present situation. His clear intention was to indicate that he maintained his previous statement.

The Prime Minister had been watching the two speakers very attentively. I guessed he had learnt much from the glimpse he had been given of the off-stage relations of the principal actors in the tragedy. What he did was to ring the curtain down and ask the cast if an entirely fresh approach could not be attempted in the next act.

What were the possibilities, he enquired, of establishing one or more bridgeheads on the Atlantic? If these were established British divisions could be put in at ever-increasing pace. He felt certain also that the United States would soon be taking her share. This meant Brittany. I wondered whether the true attitude of each would now emerge.

Reynaud answered that the problem was being studied. General Altmayer (the younger) was on the spot taking stock of the situation. Certain measures in view of this eventuality had been taken on his instructions some time back. I felt, perhaps because his interest in the plan had not been apparent for some time, that Reynaud had lost faith in the idea. In any case he spoke without conviction and seemed anxious to hand over the discussion to Weygand. Nothing loth, the General proceeded finally to demolish the project. He said the problem presented two difficulties, the first strategic, the other concerning supplies.

It was difficult to fight to the last on a given position and at the same time to withdraw troops to another. Also, 70 per cent of the armies' needs were supplied from the Paris region. Brittany certainly offered the advantage of open communications with Great Britain, but it had neither fortifications nor resources. Everything should be done to hold it, but he did not think it could be long defended. The German Air Force could make things very difficult for all those in this restricted territory. Meanwhile, the Germans would systematically destroy every town, village and factory in occupied France.

Reynaud said he could not but concur with General Weygand's conclusions. The military difficulties of such a step were immense, nevertheless he fully appreciated the great political importance it might have; which meant exactly nothing.

The Prime Minister did not pursue the subject, and to my chagrin turned to his favourite hobby-horse, guerrilla warfare.

I should much have preferred it had he concentrated on trying to get the French to promise to go on fighting in North Africa. Reynaud and de Gaulle would certainly have backed him. But perhaps he hesitated to raise a subject which would have immediately divided the French into two camps.

The Prime Minister said he put forward his proposals with diffidence in the presence of the heads of the French Army, but if only some effective means of holding up the German tanks could be devised, the tactics he suggested might lead to some secure bridge-heads being held for a few months until Britain's great strength developed, which it was doing at a tremendous pace, and until American help came in full measure.

This offer of support when so little could be given, however generously meant, simply irritated the French.

I felt again the exasperation which had been perceptible earlier, when the French had measured the inadequacy of the contribution we proposed against the magnitude of their need, and I understood it and sympathised.

Weygand showed ill-concealed scorn at the Prime Minister's suggestion, and Pétain anger. Evidently determined the proposal should be at once squashed, "It would mean the destruction of the country," he growled. He was far more moved than he had been by anything so far. Real wrath rumbled behind his words. Reynaud evidently also believed the suggestion an impossible one, and his comment showed that at some points his thought did not diverge as widely from that of the Marshal as might have been expected. He also dwelt on the suffering it would impose on the country: towns would be destroyed. . . . All this is leading nowhere, I thought. It was becoming painfully clear to me that the battle of France was lost and that no one believed in miracles. The only reality consisted in planning the next stage of the war in Africa. But no one spoke of this. I became very depressed. Hope lay in planning campaigns for the future, in establishing a new base from which attacks could be launched. But the talk was only of make-believe operations in a prostrate country with armies that had ceased to exist. This much had been made clear: if matters were left where they were, faith and confidence would be allowed to vanish from the room, absorbed by the spirit of defeat as wavelets are by sand. Darkness rather than light was being shed from the now-lighted chandeliers. A miasma of despond had fallen on the conference like a fog. No one appeared able to see his way. Then Churchill reacted explosively. As a slap in the face is considered a remedy for hysteria or for a swoon, so he interjected violently that if the destruction of towns was an unpleasant perspective, that of falling a helpless prey to the enemy was a worse one. Britain was not only willing to suffer as France was suffering, she would gladly draw upon herself the full weight of Nazi ferocity. Meanwhile the main thing was to be able to hold out. A bridgehead on the Atlantic or some other form of resistance might achieve this. There was nothing Great Britain would not do for France except give up the struggle. She would fight on, of that he was certain, until Hitlerism was destroyed. She would never give in, never. She would fight on for years, she would fight in the air, she would fight with her Navy and impose on Europe the most severe blockade. England controlled the seas. Her Empire and that of France were intact, the Belgian and Dutch Colonies depended on them. This war might well soon become a war of continents. Although the collapse of France evoked the most distressing picture, yet he felt certain that, in spite of it, Germany could at last be brought to her knees. "It is possible that the Nazis may dominate Europe, but it will be a Europe in revolt, and in the end it is certain that a régime whose victories are in the main due to its machines will collapse. Machines will one day beat machines."

The fog had gone, blown away by the great gusts of Churchill's eloquence. All could see one thing clearly: the path England was following. It lay straight ahead, steep, jagged and dangerous, but leading upward to where, high up, shone a light. I felt this so strongly that I lifted my eyes, as in dedication, and, grateful as a thirsty man is for a glass of water, I heard Victor Hugo's tremendous line sing in my ears: *"L'espoir changea de camp, le combat changea d'âme."* Others than myself must, I think, have seen, as Churchill spoke, a dim vista of utter ruin, dust-clouds over collapsing cities, but in the far distance the sun of victory rising on a silent world of dead towns and rubble.

I was glad to see that Reynaud was moved and as much affected as the British perceptibly were. I saw him glancing at Pétain, whose face might have been a mask of white plaster. But if Weygand had been warmed and moved by that fire, he certainly did not show it.

Churchill had not quite finished. Should the French Armies be forced, in spite of their heroism, temporarily to suspend fighting in France, what would the French Navy do? He did not wait for an answer, did not want an answer, and I wondered if he had meant to raise the subject, for he added at once that these were nightmare questions. He hoped that the disaster of a French collapse would not occur.

I had been struck by Churchill's words about the French Navy. It must have been much in his mind, I thought, for he had asked me about it in London. And I wondered what the answer was. But Reynaud was saying that France's determination to carry on with the war was no less than Britain's. It was plucky to say so in the face of his colleagues, who certainly did not concur, and I wished I felt he himself really believed it was true.

Courteously, Churchill said that Great Britain had the utmost confidence in the French High Command, and reiterated every Englishman's grief that a greater measure of help could not be given to France in this tragic hour.

I have a memory, but a vague one, of an interlude in which Weygand said something about the Germans having a hundred divisions to spare to invade Britain. Churchill's answer (which he gives in his book) to Weygand's question "What would you do then?" was that he was no military expert; but his technical advisers were of opinion that the best method of dealing with the German invasion of the island of Britain was to drown as many as possible on the way over and knock the others on the head as they crawled ashore.

I remember more clearly than the words Winston's chuckle as he said it, and I have a clear memory of Weygand's answer: "I must admit you have a very good anti-tank ditch."

The discussion seemed to trail off. Churchill, evidently haunted and tortured at watching the martyrdom of the people he liked so well, and in whom we had placed such implicit military trust, was distressed over the meagre contribution which was all we were able to make. Churchill, being Churchill, was bound to say so. Years had been lost, but soon we should be able to garner what we had sown in the last few months, and he repeated his deep regrets that we were not able to have more fighting units alongside the French.

"It is like talking of rain to a man in the Sahara," said Reynaud, and he repeated that history would record that if this battle was lost, it would have been owing to lack of air forces. The Prime Minister did not take this up.

Reynaud, clearly referring back to his passage with Weygand, said that should the last line of defence be broken, a political question would arise, but meanwhile the French Government felt they could place their trust and hopes in the French Army.

Churchill then asked that this opportunity should be taken for the C.I.G.S. and Weygand to confer, particularly on the possibility of organising a counter-attack taking account of the troops from Narvik and the five or six good divisions soon to be provided by Great Britain. He also asked that the Brittany bridgehead be studied.

Reynaud repeated that General Altmayer had been appointed by Weygand to do this. Churchill nodded, and concluded by saying that even in this dark hour he reaffirmed his faith in victory. Even should the Germans occupy all France they would not win the war. The resolution of the British, American intervention, economic pressure, would break down German resistance in the end. The German régime was only kept in being by a small group of evil men.

The conference was in danger of ending in anticlimax, but it merely petered out on Reynaud's repeating in a toneless voice that he, like Mr. Churchill, had confidence in ultimate victory.

As we could not all be accommodated at The Lily of the Valley Castle I was taken to a mess some distance away, my hosts the pleasant French officers of the Mission to the British at G.Q.G.

It poured with rain on the way, which did not help raise anyone's spirits. This was one of the occasions when it was a genuine boon to have to do with well-bred men. These French officers, nearly all cavalrymen and *gens du monde*, were as sad as I, far more so since they were more involved; the homes of several were no doubt overrun by now; but although we were all very tired into the bargain, we managed to spend a reasonable evening, the war not being mentioned once.

Presently I was driven back to the train, where all but the Prime Minister, claimed by the Château du Muguet, were spending the night. It turned out to be the Presidential train, and very comfortable.

Pug and his assistants were drawing up minutes and sorting out papers generally. It looked as if he would have to spend most of the night at it.

In another compartment Eden and Dill were looking at more papers, heads together as usual. I went to bed after reading through my notes and filling in some gaps. But I was thinking of the French Navy.

CHAPTER XI

Wednesday, June 12th

(1)

Breakfast in the train at Briare—Thompson prevented from ministering to Churchill—"Uh ay ma bain?"—Churchill and the automatic—His wrath at General Vuillemin's behaviour— His instructions to me—Pétain's attitude—Anxieties about the French Fleet—The Conference resumes—Weygand repeats his dismal tale—Air Marshal Barratt reports— Churchill promises to consider additional air support— Eden and Dill on British reinforcements—Reynaud asks for no "unprovoked" attacks on Italy—Churchill's mild complaint of Vuillemin's sabotage—Reynaud apologises—A roving discussion — Crete — Suez — Cyprus — Churchill's questions on the defence of Paris—Weygand's answer—Hope of American help—Churchill's formal request for a meeting between the British and French Governments if the situation deteriorates—The Conference ends—A short discussion between Weygand and Dill—Weygand's hostility— Churchill's last words with Georges and Darlan.

WE were all up early. The storm overnight had cleared the air and the morning was fine and cool. Hospitality had been pushed so far as to provide an excellent English breakfast, served at a long table in the dining-car.

Dill and Eden sat at one end discussing something earnestly as they ate. No sign of Pug; he was no doubt at work again after two or three hours' sleep.

Not feeling sociable, I took a seat half-way down the table. Someone sat down opposite me. I did not look up for a while, and when I did was astonished to see the Prime Minister's detective, Thompson. I had known him for more than twenty years, for Scotland Yard very intelligently had kept the same excellent man on the job of guarding Churchill, which he did very well. He was part of the Churchill

160

household, and had no doubt taken his turn at wheeling the prams in days gone by. Cheerful and alert as he was, I always enjoyed chatting with him. On occasions such as these he condescended to act as a kind of stage gentleman's gentleman to the Prime Minister.

Surprised into tactlessness I said: "Why, Thompson, what are you doing here? Why aren't you with the Prime Minister? Surely he will need you?" His honest, high-coloured thin face looked offended. Perhaps he thought that I felt he ought not to be breakfasting with Cabinet Ministers, C.I.G.S.s and what nots. But I was only concerned about the Prime Minister's comfort and had a disturbing picture of him alone and unattended in the Castle of the Muguet, for I well knew the French would not provide the personal attendance he was used to. "I had to sleep here, and the French failed to realise I needed a car," said Thompson, stiffly. Really worried, and thinking that lack of fluency in the French language might have accounted for the fact that Thompson was conveyanceless, I set about getting him one. There was another conference planned, and the party for London was to leave as early as possible that morning, so it was important for the Prime Minister to be up and packed.

Later that day I heard that Thompson had indeed been missed. Two French officers were finishing their *café au lait* in the conference room, which was also the dining-room, when the big double door burst open and they beheld an astonishing sight. An apparition which they said resembled an angry Japanese genie, in long, flowing red silk kimono over other similar but white garments, girdled with a white belt of like material, stood there, sparse hair on end, and said with every sign of anger: "*Uh ay ma bain?*" They were not used to seeing the Prime Minister in his night attire, so their fright and astonishment may be excused. But as usual he made his meaning perfectly clear even in French, and his needs were attended to.*

I was only told of these happenings after the departure of the English party.

When I arrived at the château I went straight to the Prime Minister's bedroom and found him finishing dressing. He was very cross.

* Years later I reminded him of the incident one night after dinner. His expression was one of startled concern, as if an inaccurate quotation in a parliamentary debate had been alleged against him, and he said in a slightly guilty voice, in which rang a note of enquiry: "I suppose I ought to have said, '*Uh ay MONG bain?*' " and he chuckled.

"Don't point that revolver at me," he barked as I fumbled in strapping my revolver to my belt; then added with a half chuckle: "Do you remember when mine went off at Vimy?" and I remembered of course. He was then commanding a battalion and had come to visit me. He was always testing out new forms of trench clothing and weapons. On this occasion he had shown me before we started for the trenches a complicated automatic revolver with which he was very pleased. I was leading the way down a communication trench when I heard a burst of fire literally in my ear. I dived behind the next traverse thinking we had been surprised by a daylight raid. I peered round cautiously, revolver in hand. There was Winston, his patent automatic firing dangerously and continuously in the direction of his feet as it dangled at the end of its lanyard, which he held at arm's length. He danced like a cat on hot bricks in his attempts to get out of the unpredictable line of fire as the barrel pointed this way and that. I collapsed on the duckboards laughing until I could laugh no longer. My guest was only half amused then and later when reminded of the incident, but he never forgot. The marvellous archivist in his brain who always and instantly turns up, neatly filed and classified, all the facts concerning the person he is dealing with never failed to produce this story, tucked away under the more noteworthy records which come to Winston's mind when I am about.

I put down his ill-humour at first to his breakfast, which consisted of the usual French coffee-pot and a roll on a tiny metal tray, balanced precariously on the humps of his heavy ivory hair-brushes, which oscillated dangerously whenever he lifted the cup or attempted to butter his roll, for I knew he liked a good breakfast; but it was not that.

He told me a tale that horrified me. It appeared that during dinner the previous evening Air Marshal Barratt had telephoned to Ismay to say that the local French Air Command objected to our aircraft taking off from the airfields near Marseilles to join their fellows from England in the bombardment of Genoa and the industrial centres of Northern Italy. Dinner had been interrupted to discuss the matter. On strong British representations, it being urged again that the R.A.F. bombers from England must by then be on or near their targets, and on the promise that the British Government would make a public announcement that the operation was a reprisal for the bombing of Malta, Reynaud agreed that the French authorities should be ordered to withdraw their objection. But Barratt had reported later that night that General Vuillemin had had lorries driven on to the airfield just as our bombers were making ready to take off, and that they had been unable to leave the ground.

I asked Churchill if he was going to take up this unheard-of behaviour at the Council meeting, but he said he had decided not to do so. As our machines had been stopped nothing could be done now, and recriminations would not help in the frightful predicament we were in.

Our ground crews and staff had asked permission to shoot the obstructions off the airfield, but this was refused. Once upon a time at Crécy the French chivalry cut their way through the Genoese archers of their own army who obstructed them on their way to attack the English. Times had changed.

It had never occurred to any of us on the previous afternoon that the French had not agreed, when they had been told that the Wellingtons had left England, that the operation should proceed as planned.

It was my impression that the Prime Minister had a very frank word with Reynaud on the subject before the conference, at which the subject did come up, but in lenitive form.*

"Go on reiterating that we shall carry on, whatever they do," he told me. "If they have lost their faith in themselves let them develop faith in us and in our determination. We will carry them as well as everything else, or," he added characteristically, "we will carry those who will let themselves be carried. You are of course to stay on. I am sorry now you were not here these last few days."

He also told me Reynaud had said Pétain had prepared a paper to the effect that France must ask for an armistice, but that he was still as yet ashamed to hand it to him. This was my chance of bringing up the subject I had been thinking about ever since the conference of the previous evening.

"You mentioned the French Fleet at the conference yesterday," I said; "I can see you are worried about what may happen to it if the French ask for an armistice. It seems to me that in that case if their Fleet is still under complete French control, and the Germans occupy

---

*Churchill in his book (*The Second World War*, Vol. II, p. 139) seeks to minimise the incident by saying that "the French people near the airfields had dragged all kinds of country carts and lorries on to them . . ." The peasantry did not know we were going to bomb Genoa. If there were peasants' carts amongst the obstructions they had been ordered there by the French Air Command.

all France, they can force its surrender wherever it may be, if they so wish. With their methods they might say: Either you surrender the Fleet or we will burn down Amiens on Monday, Rouen on Tuesday, Nantes on Wednesday, and so on, ending with a threat to destroy Paris on Saturday in case of non-compliance. Is it conceivable that under such circumstances the French would not give way?

"You have seen the people who would have to decide. Others far more defeatist are in the background. Even if Reynaud—and I believe in his pluck and determination—were to accept such a monstrous responsibility, is it conceivable the others would allow him to let France be destroyed? No man should be put in such a frightful position."

I was following my own train of thought when I concluded: "The one thing I simply can neither face nor think about is that my wife should fall into German hands and be tortured to bring pressure on me."

Churchill said nothing as he went downstairs, but he looked very stern, with the expression of deep concentration he always wears when he is utterly absorbed in the contemplation of a problem. Thompson, who was at the door, walked in to pack his things.

The Frenchmen were standing about in the hall and conference room waiting for the Prime Minister; so was the British contingent, which had been joined by Air Marshal Barratt and Colonel Woodall. They both left soon after the conference opened. Woodall told me long afterwards that his most lasting impression of that morning had been the damp, limp hand Weygand extended to him.

Churchill took Reynaud aside for a few minutes. It was evident he was doing most of the talking. Then we trooped into the dining-room. It was about 8 o'clock. On the French side Pétain's absence left an obvious gap. It was difficult to avoid the impression that he had kept away because he disapproved of the proceedings of the night before. Georges was not there either. He had had his say and his continued absence from his headquarters could hardly have been justified, but General Koeltz attended, presumably to represent him. I was sorry to see that another absentee was de Gaulle. He had gone to Brittany to investigate how the matter of the bridgehead stood. Darlan had joined the party. Rubicund and nautical, he was complete with bulldog pipe, hands thrust in his monkey-jacket. If he looked ill-at-ease the impression conveyed was that this was because he was so far from the sea. And there was General Vuillemin.

How he had the face to attend after the events of the previous night baffled me. But there he was, larger than life, still bursting out of his straining jumper. His colourless eyes oscillated over his puffy cheeks, which occasionally shook with a tremor, like twin jellyfish gently responding to a wave's caress.

Neither Margerie nor Berkeley were there; presumably they were working at the minutes of the previous meeting, and I realised without enthusiasm that it would fall to me to translate both French into English and English into French. Weygand had already been to his headquarters at Vaugereau, two or three kilometres away. He opened the proceedings by saying that no special news had come in. Certainly no good news. Nothing had occurred to alter the *exposé* he had given the preceding evening. There was now nothing to prevent the Germans getting to Paris by advancing south of the Seine. Once more he described, with further emphasis and wealth of detail, the condition of his divisions, many of which had only three or four guns left. Four of them had no guns at all. His forces were dislocated. If there was no pause in the attack, resistance could only be carried out by isolated columns. "And Brittany?" interjected Churchill, who was then told that de Gaulle had gone to investigate the position there.

Weygand concluded his catastrophic *exposé* by saying: "It is I who read the armistice terms to the Germans twenty years ago, you can imagine what I feel." Those who heard felt that there was more of weakness than of tragedy in his words, and shuddered inwardly at the abyss of surrender they implied.

Churchill might not have heard, for he totally disregarded both the bathos and the clear implication of what Weygand had said. Acting as if he were answering a question put by someone else, he said blandly that the French attached, with every justification, much importance to the contribution made by the R.A.F. He had therefore sent for Air Marshal Barratt. He would like this opportunity to be taken of elucidating what support the French wished us to give them. We had at present in France under Air Marshal Barratt eleven squadrons, six of bombers and five of fighters. The British believed that their best and most real contribution was to keep these squadrons up to strength.

Barratt then said that at the moment he only had 50 to 60 fighters and 70 to 80 bombers fit for operations. Moreover, his bombers were all Battles, better suited for night than for day work.

"What I ask for," said Reynaud, "is that four squadrons of fighters should be based in France in addition to the five squadrons already here." He went on to develop the old theme we knew so well, and which was as true as it was irrelevant. French officers assured him that the morale of their troops would be very high but for the fact that they were dominated from the air.

Few things are more irritating in really important discussions than wails concerning the unattainable. It is as exasperating as to be told when standing on the deck of a sinking ship that it would have been better, all things considered, to have taken the land route as Aunt Jane had advised. It was perhaps because of this that everyone gave Weygand ungrudging, if secret, commendation, the more noteworthy because unusual, when, disregarding his Premier with marked brusqueness, he said he was in great need of day bombers which would to some extent make up for the lack of numbers of his fighting troops. Churchill broke in to explain that there were two bomber forces, those under Air Marshal Barratt and those that were operated by Bomber Command. "Yes," said the Air Marshal, "and those of Bomber Command are operating against objectives suggested by General Weygand, and," he went on, "a force of up to a hundred bombers of Bomber Command are by now attacking German communications." Churchill saw that the essential points concerning the R.A.F. had now emerged, and put an end to the discussion by saying that the moment he got back to England he would study very carefully whether it was possible to give the French additional air support. He would certainly do all he could to send Barratt some Blenheims. But, he repeated, looking his most determined, it would be a fatal act of folly to deprive the United Kingdom of the force essential to ensure its defence.

"Well," said Barratt, "if Blenheims are sent, I must have additional transport and additional aerodromes." He was shockingly badly off for transport, he added. The subject was now closed, and Barratt and Woodall left the meeting.

Eden and Dill then intervened to underline, each in turn, the speed with which British help was being made available. The 52nd Division was deployed about Le Mans, the landing of the Canadians had started the previous evening. If the French could help with American guns, quite large forces would soon be available, as there were actually 30 divisions in various stages of training now in England, but very few guns. General Dill again said that the French might engage the British forces unit by unit. A necessary gesture perhaps, but I hated the idea of their also becoming involved in the policy of the *pain à cacheter*.

The French listened to all this in silence. The fact that Reynaud was easing his head in his collar and blinking announced that he was about to broach a new subject. He generally spoke with decision and clarity, but these characteristics were absent when he said, as one pleading a bad cause, that at the last meeting of the Supreme War Council it had been decided to strike hard at Italy. Since then, General Vuillemin had urged that such operations would lead to reprisals, and as there was no French Air Force in the south, the consequences would be disastrous. General Vuillemin therefore requested that there should be no attacks on industrial Northern Italy unless the Italians first attacked similar objectives in France.

Then, evidently anxious to turn from a subject he felt he had had to mention but wished to leave as soon as possible, he plunged down the side-issue of fraternisation between French and Italians on their common frontier, notably near Barcelonette. There had been a good deal of this, he said, and then surprisingly added, adopting unconsciously perhaps Vuillemin's point of view, that it would not be wise to provoke the Italians too far. "But," he added, "this need not prevent Great Britain carrying out whatever attacks against Italy she wishes, provided they are carried out by aircraft based in England." He seemed to imply that he thought this fraternisation was a good thing; but Churchill did not, and said so. There might be some Fifth Column activities behind it, was his comment. "We do not want any more towns destroyed," broke in Weygand, "we must avoid the danger of our factories being smashed by air attack in reprisal. It is very bad for the morale of the population that they should be bombed without retaliation. But," he added, "we shall bomb the Italians if they bomb us!" What sort of war was he envisaging? What humbug it was! If he had bombers to bomb back in retaliation, why not use them now? I was later to learn how typical of his whole attitude this intervention had been.

Churchill now mentioned the air attack sabotaged by the French the previous night. His tone was mild. He had evidently decided that as the subject had been indirectly raised by Reynaud it could not be avoided, but reproaches must be eschewed. The operation Reynaud referred to was undertaken in accordance with a decision taken in common, he said; ground staff and the necessary units had been sent to the south of France so that the projected bombing operations against Northern Italy by combined squadrons from England and the south of France could be carried out. The date had been notified to the French Air Command well ahead of time. The aircraft from England had started before a French objection to the attack had been raised on the previous evening, and before Air Marshal Barratt had been informed of this. He would say no more, but in any announcement on the subject it would be made clear that the attack had been made by aircraft from England. I had been glad to observe that Eden was showing signs of indignation as the unpleasant tale unfolded. Dill also looked grave and stern. They had had no opportunity of discussion with the Prime Minister that morning, nor do I believe they had heard of the developments since dinner the previous evening. With a politeness that gave a very sharp edge to his words, Eden said, looking hard at him, that General Vuillemin had been aware of this operation since it was first mooted, and his agreement obtained to every measure taken in France. The necessity of hitting hard at Italy had been accepted as basic policy. When that decision was taken, the facts were not very different from what they were today, yet General Vuillemin had only raised objections at the very last moment. It was indeed regrettable that so much time and trouble had been wasted.

I translated with satisfaction, also looking straight at Vuillemin, but I could see no light in his eyes, nor could I fix those glaucous revolving protuberances.

Reynaud, evidently realising how deeply the British felt on the matter, and what a deplorable effect it would certainly have in England, did the best thing he could. He apologised. The French were completely wrong, he said, and he could only express deep regret. He said this with sincerity and was obviously deeply chagrined. The British were mollified. I looked at Vuillemin, but was still unable to detect any sign of comprehension on his face, or life in his eyes.*

---

* Reynaud writes: "I learnt with a sense of humiliation next morning (the 12th) during the second session of the Conference that the British had carried out the operation without us, and excused myself to the British Ministers." He is, as has been seen, mistaken in this. He heard of what had happened from Mr. Churchill before the conference, if he had not done so from his own people earlier. He adds that Vuillemin's attitude no doubt found favour in the eyes of Vichy as Pétain and Weygand conferred on him the highest distinction. (*La France a sauvé l'Europe*, Vol. II, p. 301.)

The discussion then began to roam. We would not occupy Crete, Churchill said, unless the Italians attacked Greece, and even then would only do so if Greek consent was given, a view with which Reynaud agreed on the grounds that we should not take the initiative in such an operation, as Mussolini had undertaken not to attack the Balkan States. He asked whether the Italians were likely to make a parachute or Fifth Column attack against Suez. Churchill reassured him that all precautions had been taken, and Eden added that four battalions had been sent from Palestine to Egypt to deal with security, and described the measures taken to make things uncomfortable for the Italians in Abyssinia. The French had, it seemed, taken similar steps, and were in touch with the British local authorities on the subject.

Weygand then returned to the Mediterranean. It was very important that Cyprus should not be lost to Italy. The Navy would make such a thing impossible, said Churchill, and Dill added that the island's garrison had been reinforced.

There was a pause, and then Churchill returned with great emphasis to his theme of the previous evening concerning Paris. He wished to put some quite definite questions. The first was to ask if the solid block represented by Paris and its suburbs, the centre of the railway system of the whole country, would not, if defended, present an obstacle to the enemy which would hinder and delay him as it had in 1914?

His second question was, if the answer to the first was in the affirmative, would not this enable a counter-stroke against the lower Seine to be launched? His third related to the idea he had so persistently clung to: would it not be possible, should the phase of co-ordinated warfare come to an end, to wage a war of mobile columns against the enemy's communications? Had the enemy sufficient forces to hold down all the countries he had overrun whilst at the same time fighting the French and British Armies?

His last question revealed his overriding preoccupation, could not the war be prolonged until the United States joined in the conflict?

Weygand, elbows on the table, had been listening with an expression of aggressive ill-will, tinged with exasperation. I could not tell if Reynaud had meant to answer his English opposite number, for I had not been looking at him but at the Commander-in-Chief, whose tenseness commanded attention. In any case Reynaud did not have a chance of doing so. Weygand pounced into the verbal arena, his jaws working as if he were masticating a bolt. The situation was in no way analogous to that of 1914, he snapped. It was not the intention to hold Paris. The "it" was imperative; I had never heard even Clemenceau or Lloyd George use the neuter pronoun so purposefully as meaning the personal one. "It" meant "I" much more emphatically than if he had just said "I". It was much as when a King says "We". It was so final that even Churchill said nothing. Orders had been given that if the outer defences fell, the city was to be declared an open town to avoid bloodshed and destruction. (This statement did not correspond with the orders he had given.)* Becoming sarcastic, he went on to say that he fully agreed with the Prime Minister's suggestion for a counter-attack on the lower Seine, if ten divisions, complete with artillery and provided of course with sufficient air support, were placed at his disposal.

Churchill was looking at the middle of the table, his lips slightly pursed. It was a pure guess, but it seemed to me that he had written off Weygand as a total loss in the grim balance sheet he was casting, and was working out a plan on a quite different set of values. But Weygand had not finished. He added a postscript. Answering Churchill's last question, he said he thought that Germany had ample forces to hold down all the subjugated nations and pursue the struggle against what was left of the Allied forces.

Chiming in to support Weygand's last point, Reynaud said that Germany had raised fifty-five divisions and built from four to five thousand tanks since the outbreak of the war. "Our only hope," he said, employing the expressive French gesture of raised shoulders, combined with open hands, palms upwards, the whole emphasised with a sigh, "is in the industrial resources of the U.S.A."

"We are in the closest touch with the United States," said Churchill, "and will continue to impress on their Government the gravity of the situation and the urgency of our needs, but there is a matter the importance of which overshadows all others, and which I must put to you. Should there be a fundamental change in the situation, I must request you, before coming to a final decision which may govern French action in the second phase of the war, to let the British Government know at once. They will come over immediately to meet the French Government at any convenient place which you choose to indicate to discuss the new circumstances with you." He

* See p. 148 footnote.

spoke very slowly. The only note I detected in his voice was one of emphasis. Tremendous, slow emphasis. But he wanted to make sure, so he repeated what he had said.

It dawned on me for the first time, as it did no doubt on the others, that we were within sight of a cross-roads at which the destinies of the two nations might divide. As I translated for a second time the same sentences, I found myself imitating the measured cadence of Churchill's words. ·

Then he said, and there was a different note in his voice, one of warning perhaps, or of solemn admonition, that this request was a formal one put by the British Government to the French Government.

Reynaud at once answered that he quite understood this request, which Mr. Churchill was entitled to make. He undertook that it would be complied with.

The conference was over. I was hoping to have a word with the Prime Minister before he left, but as I hurried out after him I was stopped by the C.I.G.S., who wanted to clear up some points with Weygand and would I translate? So, to my chagrin, I had to sit down again. My notes on this conversation are short. Dill told Weygand that Brooke, the G.O.C. of the new force, was the best officer of his rank we had got, that he was to be under the Group Commander, but would keep in very close touch with Altmayer, the Army Commander. A few matters of details were also dealt with, troop movements, landings, and the like, but what I did underline in my notes that afternoon was the strain of finding myself so close to Weygand and being forced to understand and render his ideas.

His own hostility to me, and, I felt certain, to the British point of view, was as perceptible as is sulphuric acid, and I, on my side, was as loth to be near him as to someone suffering from a virulent disease. I need not have worried; a thirst to surrender is not a contagious complaint.

I found the Prime Minister in the hall, talking to Georges, who had come over to say good-bye. On the steps, just before he got into his car, Churchill told me that Georges had said it was all but over with the French Army, and that in his opinion an armistice would soon be inevitable. He had had a word with Darlan, who had told him positively that, whatever happened, the French Fleet would not fall into German hands.

CHAPTER XII

Wednesday, June 12th

(2)

At the Château du Muguet after Churchill's departure—A long and depressing discussion with Georges—Barratt's disturbing news—I borrow a car—Last talk with Pétain— Unsuccessful efforts to locate the British Embassy—Bad feeling between Weygand and de Gaulle—The telephone at the Château du Muguet—An uncomfortable luncheon party —My French driver—The refugees—The Embassy at the Château de Champchevrier—The Ambassador and his Staff.

WHEN the English party left the Château du Muguet, I did not accompany them but turned back into the big hall where lay my suitcase. In and out bustled officers, few of whom I knew. Never have I felt more utterly lost. No immigrant landed on a strange shore, unmet, without money, ignorant of his destination and of the language, can ever have been more disconsolate than I was. Until I could locate our Embassy, which was "somewhere in Touraine", I was useless, since I had no means of communication and no codes, supposing telegraphs to be functioning, which was doubtful. Moreover I had no transport, which added to my preoccupations. The news that Churchill's party had to leave without fighter escort, owing to the weather, made me feel no happier. I stood there a long time. The hall was a big one; it had either several large windows or was glazed like a conservatory, I forget which. At the far end was a large gallery or ballroom, the long arm of the L of which the hall was the short one. It was there that Reynaud spent most of the morning. I could see him sitting on a sofa talking now with Weygand, now with Georges, now with Pétain, who had appeared from nowhere. I did not go in, there was nothing for me to say.

Several times Reynaud walked through the hall, his expression set and strained. I do not think he said anything more important than to ask me to lunch. I was glad he did. There was nowhere else to go.

Presently Georges came along and we had a long talk. At his own headquarters at one end of Briare there was nothing he could do but wait for such news as came in. He no longer had any means of intervening in the battle since he had no reserves.

He repeated what he had told the Prime Minister. The Army was at the end of its powers of resistance, and he drew a most vivid picture of the agony the fighting had been. The scenes he conjured up became as living as if I had witnessed them myself; they took shape in my mind as the continuation of events I had myself witnessed in the last war. They are all there, those pictures in the volumes on war which take up so much space on the shelves of my life. The crash of exploding shells, the machine-guns chattering like teeth in skulls thrown up and resuscitated into jittering frenzy by earth-splitting noise, are no worse in one war than in another. The battlefields where armies meet head-on each hold the maximum of horror and terror the human mind can register; but Georges described battle scenes worse than anything I had witnessed. The shooting from the air of all horse transport, the concentrated effort of the remnants of a whole division to man-haul three or four guns by night to a new position, the attempt to dig-in in readiness for the battle that must last the whole long June day, and so the next night and the night after that. He spoke of troops straining every nerve to reach the protection of a river, only to find German armour waiting for them on the far side, and always the merciless air attack.

I looked into his strong, tired face, which betrayed no emotion, feeling even deeper regard and affection for him than ever before, now that this terrible burden lay on his shoulders. I asked about the Fourth Army, where I imagined my wife to be. He knew her well. I did not want to introduce personal matters, he also had children with the armies. I remembered his son who, at the age of five, had discovered the earth was round, having observed that the sun went down in one place always to reappear in the opposite direction.

I gathered that Réquin was preparing to defend the "Mountain of Reims", the high, wooded hills south of the town, the Aisne having been lost long since, but I do not think Georges knew much more. He left me to join Reynaud.

Then Barratt called me up. He wanted to know if anything had been decided on the subject of bombing Italy. "Nothing," I said. He then told me he had just heard the French Navy had run out on the joint operation of bombarding Genoa the night before.

Had Darlan known this when he spoke to the Prime Minister? It was hardly credible that he had not. It was, in fact, highly probable that he had himself issued the counter-order. This information did not make me feel more comfortable, nor increase my faith in the bluff Admiral.

Then I began to consider the question of my own transport, but did not feel justified, unless all other means failed, in bothering Reynaud about it. Fortunately a charming reserve officer came to my rescue. He spoke perfect English and knew as much about hunting in the Midlands as I did. I pointed out that it was a French responsibility to provide me with a car. I had no means of transport and could not procure any.

He said there was a great shortage of cars, but presently came back, having, I am certain, taken great trouble to get me a conveyance which would be available after luncheon. He begged me to send it back as soon as possible.

I told him I would, but the sheer impossibility of finding any replacement led to my keeping it until I left for England six days later. I sent a message explaining my predicament, but doubt if it ever reached its destination.

I was standing in the middle of the hall when Marshal Pétain came up to me. He talked for a long time, moving presently to the wall, against which he leaned.

He said bluntly that it was murder to keep the Army fighting on in present conditions, and told me tales of the hopeless odds the French were contending against. "An armistice is inevitable," he said, "and it is sheer pusillanimity to shirk the issue. Whilst Ministers hesitate and think of their reputations, soldiers are being killed and the land of France is being ruined (*saccagée*). We must pay now, and pay dearly, for the anarchy we have indulged in for so long. Where now are the Deputies who sought popularity by voting against any measure of rearmament? And the *Front Populaire*, where are its leaders now that the poor deluded chaps who went about with clenched fists have nothing but clenched fists to shake at the German tanks?"

"But," I objected, "*Monsieur le Maréchal*, France cannot be allowed to become absorbed into the German stomach and there quietly digested. You know we shall fight on. You must fight on in Africa or elsewhere until we have developed our strength and we can make a *retour offensif* together."

"Africa?" said Pétain, "What is the use of sending recruits to Africa, as Reynaud wishes? There are no rifles there to arm them with. In any case, the disorganisation of the Ministry of War is such that they could never get the men to the harbours, still less to sea, and if they could, Italian submarines would undoubtedly drown them."

But I went on obstinately. "You cannot leave us to fight on alone in what will still be our common struggle."

"You have left us to fight alone," he said, and there was an edge of subdued anger to his words. "That hardly tallies with the appeals we constantly hear for British air support," I answered. I was not angry, I saw all too clearly the picture Georges had drawn of the retreating armies.

"I had not meant it that way," said the Marshal in a gentler tone. "Your people are doing the best they can, as we are. I was thinking of between the wars."

We had both been very blind, I said. And we must now pay for it. "*Que voulez vous?*" Then after a slight pause he said that as France could not continue the struggle, wisdom dictated that England should also seek peace, for she certainly could not carry on alone. "You have no army," he went on. "What could you achieve where the French Army has failed?"

"But you heard the Prime Minister?" I said. "Words are very fine," he replied, "but you cannot beat Hitler with words." And he repeated that it was just a cruel self-deception to think we could stand up to the Germans alone for more than a month, the time it would take them to organise the invasion and the bombing of England. Then, in the tone of putting someone in his place for being insufferably presumptuous, he returned to the theme of the French Army. It was sheer folly to think we could succeed where it had failed.

Still I felt no anger, only cold fear as I realised that this conviction of our inevitable destruction in a short time presented a deadly danger. If the French could but be made to believe we could fight on successfully, then many of them would stand by us. I also realised, knowing them, that they would not be able to bear the thought that we had carried the war to a successful conclusion after they had withdrawn from it.

They would wish us to win, or some of them would, but their pride would be torn to ribbons, and a feeling of injury would prevail. I realised much better than before the Prime Minister's insight when, from the first, he had told me to insist on our determination and our faith.

I tried it on the old Marshal with complete lack of success. I gave him my word that Churchill had stated a fact when he said the entire population would fight to the last. I had just been to England and been left in no doubt of that. The Germans were not in England yet. They would have to beat the Navy as well as the Air Force. Was it conceivable that the Navy would be driven off the sea?

"Your Government would quite calmly allow France to be destroyed under the pretence you can defy Germany and even beat her, which shows its ignorance, and it would then sue for peace too late. Meanwhile it would have been the end of France.

"The indifference of your Government is proved by the fact that you are withholding the greater part of your Air Force in this decisive battle."*

It was no good, but I was nettled, and after enumerating our aircraft fighting in France, telling him the figures given at the conference, I said that it was surely obvious that our retaining a minimum force of fighters in England was a complete proof of our determination to go on with the war. "If we really felt the struggle would end in France, we should send our last machine to fight there."

The conversation was leading nowhere, and I began to feel not only irritation but estrangement towards the Marshal, whose attitude, for the first time in our relationship, savoured of hostility.

"*Vous verrez, Monsieur le Maréchal, vous verrez*," I terminated. "You will see. I know in my soul we shall win. If not, England will be a heap of rubble. This will not be the case if you go on fighting with us. Churchill estimates the resources of our joint Empires, backed by the production of America, better than you do in France."

The old Marshal may have heard, but he was not listening, for returning to his own train of thought he said: "*C'est la catastrophe, c'est la débandade.*" His tone astonished me. That afternoon,

* Churchill, in *The Second World War*, Vol. II, p. 139, says that Pétain should "have been ashamed to support even tacitly Weygand's demand for our last 25 squadrons of fighters, when he had made up his mind that all was lost and that France should give in." But, in fairness, ought not Weygand to have been included in the same condemnation? He had made up his mind on the subject of an armistice as clearly as had the Marshal.

reconstituting the conversation word for word, I noted that his voice had sounded satisfied, almost as if he accepted defeat joyfully. I was so taken aback that I saluted but did not shake hands as I broke away.

That was the last time I ever spoke to Marshal Pétain privately. I never sought another interview, it would have been a pure waste of time.

As I still stood in the hall, more people I knew came in and I spoke to several. It was then I was told the story of the Prime Minister's bath by one of the officers to whom he had put his problem. As he told it to one and the other, the tale improved in the telling. This I could see as he went from group to group, observing from his gestures and expressions that the Japanese genie he had depicted Winston as resembling assumed ever larger shape and an ever fiercer expression. It was the only light relief that morning. Then someone told me Pétain was keeping in close touch with the Spanish Ambassador, Lequerica, that he had seen him and intended seeing him again. I could form my own conclusions. I did.

My main personal preoccupation of getting into touch with the British Mission, which must be in the neighbourhood, and of locating our Embassy, remained. No one had an idea where either of them were, so I set out in search of a telephone. A lift was offered me to Georges' headquarters, where the few lines available were in constant use. Meanwhile I spoke to this one and that, gathering up the threads broken when I left Paris. It appeared that Weygand and de Gaulle were at daggers drawn. Before leaving Paris, at a conference at which both Reynaud and Weygand were present, de Gaulle had told Baudouin, who was advocating an armistice on the ground that the situation was getting worse and worse, that the situation was, it was true, getting worse, but only because it was being allowed to get worse.

This had not endeared him to the Commander-in-Chief.

In return Weygand vented his spleen against de Gaulle by describing him as utterly blinded by vanity. He was *outrecuidant*, insufferable, and had more of the journalist than the officer in his make-up. It was just what I should have expected Weygand to say, and I disliked him the more for these spiteful jabs at the man who wanted to fight. "*Le dernier quart d'heure*"—it suddenly occurred to me that he really did consider the position in the light of that expression. The last quarter of an hour during which he still must fight, the last bad quarter of an hour to be got through as quickly as possible.

An officer told me that the system of *points d'appui* adopted never really had a chance of succeeding, for they were too far apart to lend each other mutual support, and there were not sufficient reserves to counter-attack the enemy whilst he was engaged in reducing them.

Then I heard that already on the 9th (Sunday), some German reconnaissance units had reached l'Isle-Adam, only 37 kilometres from Paris. A reconnaissance is not an army; but in London we had had no idea that the Germans had penetrated so close to the capital by Sunday.

As I could not worry people concerning my anxiety to locate the British in this pandemonium, I returned to Lily of the Valley Castle, still in search of a telephone. It may seem incredible, but the only line in this, the Commander-in-Chief's, house was the ordinary civilian rural service connected with the village, where the operator, a young woman, went off duty for two hours in the middle of the day and closed down at six p.m. True, the Castle was not Headquarters, but nevertheless it was here that the Commander-in-Chief spent, if not most, at least a great deal of his time. Here were the Premier and swarms of officers, but no attempt had been made to lay a telephone line. This made me realise, as much as anything else, the hopeless state of deliquescence of the French Army, the defeatism of the Staff, and Services that were not even trying.

My mind flew back to a scene in 1914, before the Marne, when French and British were in full retreat. General Joffre and Field-Marshal Sir John French met in the palace of Compiègne; signallers were laying lines everywhere from picture to picture in the galleries. The noise of the hammering was such they had to be told to stop. It was purposeful, intent and businesslike. They were the soldiers of an army which, though beaten, meant to fight on. Nothing else even occurred to them, though they were less than 80 kilometres from Paris.

The difference between the two situations nearly made me cry out in anguish as I looked at the old-fashioned telephone, a wooden box fastened inconveniently on the wall of the butler's pantry. The usual French contraption like an ear-trumpet into which you spoke hung at its side on a hook.

A peculiarity of this pantry was that access to what was apparently the sole W.C. in the château could only be gained through it.

As I stood by that telephone for a very long time, I ended by having a fair idea of how many and who were the temporary inhabitants of the Lily of the Valley.

I wiled away the time talking to the young lady in the village post office.

It always pays in France to be on good terms with the telephone operator, and my memory of places I have spent some time in is spangled with little flirtations with a series of girls I have never seen but whose pleasant voices I remember. After the First War this used to be the only compensating feature of a hopelessly inefficient service. Misguided indeed were those who adopted a bullying attitude towards the anonymous tormentors these girls could be if they chose. I knew the American wife of a Minister of Posts and Telegraphs who, infuriated by endless delays and wrong numbers, snapped out at last: "I shall report you, I am the Minister's wife." "Do not get so excited, *ma petite*," came the answer. "*Ça tombe bien*, it so happens that I am his mistress."

My conversation was on other lines. I soon knew the age of my young lady, and of her brother at the front. "*On est bien inquiète*." Had I by any chance any news of him? And she told me his regiment.

Regretfully I had to say I could not help. Then there was a sigh. Would the war soon be over? Between her efforts to call up this village or that, the young lady informed me that the tourist season would soon be on in Briare, and this war, if it continued interfering with travel, would mean a serious loss to the inhabitants. "*Fera beaucoup de tort au pays*". This information took me aback. The idea that anybody would ever wish to do anything but shun Briare came as a shock. A wide detour would be the ordinary person's reaction after the first visit, I thought. But the talk went on, interrupted only by the voices of other operators saying they knew of no British Mission. This was annoying, as I was hoping to contact Colonel Count de Salis of the Irish Guards, attached to the British Mission to French Headquarters. He would, I knew, be helpful if I failed to get in touch with Redman and his team.

I had espied, some time back, out of the corner of my eye a slice of Weygand revealed in the slit of the slightly open door. His one eye which I could see gazed beyond me at the W.C., then rested on me with cold malevolence as he closed the door. I realised I was in an immensely strong strategic position. I was guarding the Thermopylæ that led to the lavatory. I considered abandoning the field.

But why should I lose the chance of gaining touch with British officers, to satisfy the Commander-in-Chief's exaggerated sense of propriety? So I remained.

Meanwhile my knowledge of Briare was increasing. There were two hotels, l'Hôtel de la Poste and l'Hôtel du Cerf. The latter had a really good cuisine, a fact generally held to be more important than that Napoleon had once slept at the former. Here there were prolonged interruptions. My little informant, warming to her task, got involved in some disputes in which the words sped over the wires at the tempo of a bumble-bee's wing beats. *"Non, ça va décidément mal ce matin,"* she confided. "The *'Central'* won't answer now."

Then we got back to the Cerf. There had been a *repas de noces* there lately at which she had been. Wonderful! The *specialité* was the *confit d'oie.* "I assure you, *vraiment, vraiment exquis.*"

The door opened slightly wider to reveal Weygand, whose face now wore an expression of pain, superimposed on the previous one of active hostility.

"And the wine, *Mademoiselle,* tell me of the wine," I asked.

Weygand hesitated, but dislike of England prevailed. One hand closed the unbuttoned tunic, the other slammed the door.

A little later, although I was looking at the door, I was startled by the violence of its opening, still more so by the figure of Weygand which charged past me and disappeared. The door of the W.C. slammed. I wondered if I could explain over the telephone to my young friend the story of Alice in Wonderland. It would be news to her. I wanted to say I had just seen the white rabbit scuttle by, in an awful hurry, then dive into his hole.

There was a horrified cry in my ear. *"Mais il est midi passé,* it is gone twelve, and I have been gossiping and forgot the time. *Je me ferai gronder,* I shall be scolded for being late for lunch. Good-bye, *Monsieur,* I shall be back at two." So I never got de Salis, and the Ambassador was still somewhere in Touraine, lost in a territory as wide as Kent and Sussex combined.

There were more conversations in the hall. One with Captain Estonnier, Weygand's A.D.C., a pleasant, courteous and efficient man, reinforced an impression I had already formed, that the French, or some of them, did really believe that if they stopped fighting they could just pay up and settle down with the loss of a province or so until the time came to recover them.

Several very likeable French officers I knew walked in. Talking to them seemed to relieve the atmosphere. Then Georges appeared again for a moment. The news was far worse. General Frère, who last night still clung to a measure of optimism, now declared he could not hold out. Reims had fallen. Then Georges was gone, and it was years before I saw him again at Algiers. As he disappeared I realised the danger that the fall of Reims meant for my wife, and felt sick with apprehension.

Then lunch-time came. It turned out to be even worse than I had anticipated, and was certainly one of the most unpleasant meals I ever assisted at. Weygand sat on Reynaud's right, I on his left. Pétain sat opposite. An Admiral sat on my left. My attempts to engage him in conversation were a complete failure. How different had been my hosts of the night before! They had certainly not been happy, but good manners had come to the rescue and had prevented the meal from degenerating into an insufferable exchange of reproaches and bad feeling, which, even if not uttered, found expression in looks or behaviour. But then we had had common interests unconnected with the war, common friends too, an endless resource.

I was wondering if perhaps the hostility between Weygand and myself might not be a major factor in the lack of conviviality of the occasion when, observing Weygand and Reynaud sitting side by side, it seemed to me that our mutual dislike was the very milk of human kindness compared with the murderous hostility those two felt for each other.

On occasions such as this, a survival of boyish curiosity overcomes me, as when I had to find out what my Aunt Cecilia's cat would do if the goldfish bowl were poured over it as it sat glaring at me. So I threw a few pebbles, based on the fund of local knowledge so recently acquired from the nice telephone girl, at the walls of the glass-house in which we found ourselves.

My remarks fell on a morose and suspicious silence, and it dawned on me that the intimate knowledge of the locality I was displaying was confirming several of my fellow-guests in the belief that I was certainly a member "*de l'Intelligence Service*", whose knowledge of all things is, as everyone knows, minute. Briare had evidently not escaped the scrutiny of that omniscient, all-pervading spy organisation. Discouraged, I gave up all attempts at geniality.

After a long interval, Pétain suddenly spoke. It was as if an idea he had been following suddenly broke into words, as the fin of a fish might emerge unaccountably above the surface of the water, for he began in the middle of a sentence, or so it seemed to me. He was visualising himself as a young officer of Chasseurs Alpins in the high Alps. For a moment I saw him as he was seeing himself, young, vigorous, his lungs full of wonderful crystal air, a sarcastic quip on his lips; then his words died off as his thoughts slipped back into the shadows of his memory. I imagined that he must have been thinking of the Italian declaration of war when his train of thought broke, and pictures of the distant days when he had looked at Italy from a French peak substituted themselves for an idea that his mind had lost track of.

I took my leave as soon as I could and said good-bye to Reynaud. He was a changed man. It was as if those determined to capitulate had been wrapping him up all the morning in the crêpe bands of their defeatism and he had emerged looking like a mummy. I had seen him like this before, and he had shaken himself free. I hoped he would do so again.

I told him I would try to see him next day after I had located the Ambassador. "Do not forget the aviation," he said, and repeated for the nth time that if this battle was lost it would be because of lack of aviation. "It will not have been only because of that," I said, and left.

The pleasant English-speaking officer put me in the car he had provided. The driver, in civil life a Paris factory worker, was jovial, simple and willing.

I have always liked Frenchmen of this type. When they escape from politics, as they do in the Army, and have to deal with officers whom they see are exposed to the same dangers as themselves, they not only accept but welcome leadership. They are trustful, friendly and faithful. It was evident that the chauffeur and I were unlikely to take part in any battles together, but the *camaraderie* of war soon prevailed and we were presently on excellent terms. I was told all about my new friend's family affairs, in which I took a genuine, though fleeting, interest.

I decided to make for Tours, hoping to find out there where the Ambassador was. We followed small roads, hoping, with partial success, to avoid the flow of refugees. Things were only really difficult where our way crossed the north–south roads, which were packed with lines of cars head to tail, three abreast.

To cut across this solid mass required some firmness. These

Paris.   French Refugees in the Place de la Concorde

French Refugees

refugees, who represented the motorised advance-guard of the flood, bore no resemblance to those I had known in the last war: the great wagons drawn by six oxen, loaded with the entire infant population of a village, the footsore women carrying babies and dragging tired children, the sick in wheelbarrows, were not there. The processions were made up in the main of small cars, and the vans used in minute family businesses. The big limousines were no doubt by now at Nice or Biarritz. The streams of modest cars were packed with people, and nearly all had bedding and many had bicycles tied to the roof. From this altitude, as well as from the sides, hung the most extraordinary assortment of belongings, ranging from bird-cages to pots and pans. If by mischance a car broke down, it looked as if its passengers would be able to establish in the nearest field a home bearing some likeness to the one they had left. Some indeed were doing so, having presumably come to the end of their petrol. For that is what they were doing, going as far as their petrol would take them. How most of them kept going was a mystery, for the fuel consumption of cars driven perforce most of the time in first or second gear must have been high. Many cars, which had presumably broken down, had been pushed into the ditches, the mattresses on top sagging over on to the hedges like dead things, and I was reminded of the dead that had hung for months on the barbed wire during the last war.

In some cases a family was grouped in a field so that the children might be fed, in others, the children sat alone with frightened faces, but very quiet. The parents had evidently gone to forage for food. In all villages there were endless queues at the butchers and bakers, as there were at the rare petrol stations. Patient, hopeless queues. Many people were also waiting to draw water wherever there was a well or pump. What struck me was the calmness of all these people. There was no fussing, no gesticulating, and the drivers were careful, well aware that a mishap would leave them stranded.

I looked intently at the occupants of car after car. Many were old people. The French would never leave an aged relative behind, and it was good to see the family unit proving so strong; on no face did I see a trace of panic, on the contrary I was struck by what seemed to be a look of unconcern, of resignation and acceptance of the inevitable. There must have been almost as many dramas as there were cars, faced bravely, even stoically. And the adventures must have been innumerable. I heard of one after the war. A well-to-do couple were driving two cars. To save petrol, the smaller one, the husband at the wheel, was towed by the larger, in which sat his wife driven by the chauffeur. The towing-rope broke; just then the column moved farther and faster than usual. Other cars wormed their way past the stranded one. When the owner decided to abandon his car and walk, he could not catch up. He eventually made his way back to Paris and did not see his wife again for four years.

I found it singularly unpleasant to be displaying a British uniform so far from the front—not that one in a thousand had any idea, or cared, what army I belonged to. My driver had, however, no inhibitions; he blew his horn importantly and mercilessly, unaware that by making such a frightful noise he was forfeiting some of the esteem I had felt for him.

The frequent halts served one useful purpose. I wrote up my notes on my knees when we were stopped or going dead slow. I was to do much scribbling in this way during the next few days; this has resulted in much that I wrote being exasperatingly difficult to decipher.

At Tours I found out at the post office that the Embassy was only a few kilometres from the town, and having covered nearly 250 kilometres, which said much for the driver's skill and determination, I arrived in time for dinner at the very beautiful Château de Champ-chevrier where the Embassy was installed.

It was a vast and magnificent building, a real château, as unlike Lily of the Valley Castle as Longleat is to one of Mr. Bevan's temporary utility hutches. Its great seventeenth-century stone front rested on a high, wide terrace reached by a fine flight of steps. Beyond this was a large open space to the side of which extended vast and monumental stables of the same period as the main building, where I noticed a number of our military police. From the terrace, beyond lawns, were woods, bisected by a wide grass avenue.

The place belonged to a Baroness of the same name. In the big dining-room the family, a numerous body of women young and old, and children, sat at one table, the Embassy staff at another, some distance away.

It was striking how the good breeding of our hosts, who did not seem to be in the least embarrassed or put out by the influx of so many strangers, or, indeed, to notice their existence, made an anomalous occasion seem quite normal. The place was so vast that an entire Embassy plus policemen and wireless operators, chauffeurs and servants, seemed to inconvenience no one, although the family was evidently swollen by relatives from Paris and the north.

Perfect taste and good manners dictated the attitude of leaving us entirely to ourselves.

They knew none of us could impart such information as we had. They must have presumed that the diplomats had news. They could not have guessed the complete ignorance of events from which the entire Embassy staff suffered, but they never at any time asked to be informed, vitally though they were affected, and vanished after the meal to their own part of the house as if they were ghosts.

After dinner I gave the Ambassador an account of the conference at Briare and my impressions. He told me he had seen Baudouin, who was in a neighbouring château 15 kilometres away, twice during the day in the hope of news, but he had known nothing, and it was the Ambassador who had told him of the meeting at Briare. There had been a Cabinet meeting at Tours, called by Chautemps, at which, since no one knew anything, nothing had been decided. Baudouin was envious of the Ambassador's field wireless, for his only means of communication was the village telephone. So I told Campbell of the similar situation at Briare. We decided to see Reynaud next day, and then went to the immense room where the staff were working under the indefatigable Henry Mack, the First Secretary. A remarkable man this, urbane, cheerful, the soul of efficiency and a veritable diplomatic stakhanovite for work. Nothing ever rattled him or diminished the warm charm of his manner. No sleepless night, however deeply it might line his face, dimmed his perception or slowed down his industry. I can hear the warmth of his brogue as I write, and respond over the years to its charm and remember with admiration the example he set. He is himself an Ambassador today, which is fortunate for us, for wherever he represents Britain, she will be held in special esteem.

The Foreign Office is a curious institution to one trained in the fighting services. Unlike the Army it does not turn men out of a mould which forms them morally and physically, cutting to a sealed pattern their hair and their prejudices. In the Foreign Service men differ widely in appearance, taste and interests. Nothing could be more different in the Embassy team, for instance, than the Minister, Oliver Harvey, pale, correct, obviously hatched out in a chancery, "*La Carrière*" stamped on every seam, and the rather untidy Mack, who might have been anything from a member of the Kildare Street

Club to a pleasant young gardener in his Sunday best, or the rather noisy young man described as a Secretary in His Majesty's Foreign Service, who had arrived at the château on a bicycle, owing to a mishap to one of the Embassy cars on the way from Paris, and, when the Ambassador refused to allow the machine to be strapped on to his beautiful shining Rolls-Royce, jumped on it again and rode it to Bordeaux. Nobody seemed to mind the fact that the prolonged ride would deprive the Embassy of his services for some time.

CHAPTER XIII

Thursday, June 13th

(1)

The Champchevrier family—The Ambassador and I drive to Chissay—The refugees again—Châteaux on the Loire—A memory of Amboise—A tribute to the women of France—Reynaud at Chissay—Madame de Portes as traffic controller—Margerie blows away the cobwebs—Costa de Beauregard—A heroic girl secretary—Enter Ève Curie—De Gaulle's frustration—His strictures on Weygand—Reynaud's firmness His account of the Cabinet meeting—Weygand's demand for an armistice—Reynaud's gratifying reaction—His colleagues support him—Campinchi's fine attitude on the French Navy—A missing telegram located—Madame de Portes' hatred—Luncheon with the Ambassador at the Bon Laboureur—*Return to Chissay—Churchill expected at Tours.*

THE first impression of pleasure at waking up in my nice room in the Château de Champchevrier and seeing the fine vista it overlooked yielded to feelings of the deepest sorrow, as I realised the Germans would very soon be here, stamping about the corridors, occupying this very room, and lording it over the owners, who were so much a part of the place that they shared its name.

Breakfast was as dinner had been. The family talking away about their own affairs at their distant table seemed much more at ease than the British interlopers, who moved awkwardly from table to sideboard to fetch the coffee, obviously feeling they had no business to be there.

I remember speaking a few words to Madame de Champchevrier and to one of her daughters, whom I met on the doorstep, about a pack of staghounds belonging to her son-in-law, who hunted forests I knew well in Poitou. Then, having investigated the condition of my car and chauffeur, matters of great moment, for motors were now as important and rare as were horses on the battlefield of Bosworth, I passed the time of day with some military policemen who were standing about. It is extraordinary how reassuring British soldiers can be. This small group, perfectly turned out, their belts pipe-clayed and trousers creased, were the very embodiment of confident, unquestioning strength and discipline. They stood for a reality one clutched at in a nightmare world where everything collapsed and everyone ran away.

We were as isolated at Champchevrier as we might have been on an atoll in the South Seas. The telephone was not working. Its way of expressing its feelings was to splutter, squawk or buzz when you took off the receiver, and the wireless also refused to function. The different members of the French Government were evidently marooned as we were in what were no doubt equally splendid châteaux, and sat in them *incommunicado*. Better start off to see Reynaud as soon as possible, the Ambassador and I thought, and we left, each in our own car, following different routes. The Minister, Oliver Harvey, accompanied Sir Ronald.

The weather had been cloudy. Rain now began to fall steadily, and continued most of the morning.

As overflowing water at first spreads in trickles, then gathers momentum as it progresses along well-defined channels, so the floods of refugees were greater on the main roads and less on the side roads than the day before. The procession in the rain was un-utterably depressing, but it was evident that the mass of the fleeing population was yet to come.

I joined the main Saumur–Tours road at Langeais, where the magnificent medieval castle looked greyer than usual in the down-pour. It was there that Ann of Brittany married King Charles VIII of France. We passed below the château of Cinq-Mars, which I remembered had so struck Churchill's imagination, for Richelieu had razed it "*à hauteur de l'infamie*", that is, demolished everything above the first floor as a mark of infamy, when he had the head of its owner, the Marquis de Cinq-Mars, chopped off, either for duelling, which he disapproved of, or for plotting, I forget which. Then on our left appeared the beautiful and high Château de Luynes, with its great round towers and pointed roofs, and so to Tours.

There had been something very painful in reading as I drove, in the light of today's miseries, the imposing stone catalogue of France's past grandeur.

What a proud, rich country France must have been at the time when great nobles could put up such magnificent piles every few miles.

But, I reflected, it was only a few generations before that period of wealth and power that the English were besieging Orléans, and the King of France's dominions were reduced to a small island within his own realm. France had a way of emerging greater from her worst tribulations. There was consolation in the thought.

As columns from several roads were joining into a solid pack of cars making for the bridge at Tours, I decided to keep north of the Loire as far as Amboise, though it was farther, and cut across the river there.

I was not as clever as I thought, for though Amboise was a smaller place than Tours, it was closer to Paris, and I had ample leisure to contemplate yet one more fine royal château as we progressed towards it over the bridge, yard by yard, jammed between refugee cars surmounted by dripping mattresses. A personal sadness was added to my thoughts by memories of the time when, after the First War, I had introduced my wife to Touraine, and we had thought of taking on lease the lovely château of Azay-le-Rideau, a Renaissance dream building lost in trees and water which the French Government was then prepared to let. The dream had remained a dream, like so many others. More precise was the memory of a lunch at a restaurant taken two years earlier on the quayside at this same Amboise. How pleasant it had been to watch the great sunlit river from the shade of trees and awning.

I remembered the big, good-looking waitress seeing to the needs of twenty parties with indefatigable efficiency, and my French companion saying that her accent made it clear she was from Poitou. So we asked her, and she was. Such a small thing, but a bitter-sweet memory today. Where were they now, all the good-looking girls of France I remembered in two wars? The *"patissière d'Epernay"* must be old now. She had been lovely in 1914. Then . there had been that very pretty *boulangère*, wearing such a becoming *Vendée* cap, at the Ile d'Aix, whom I had watched saying good-bye to the young sailor who had been called up when war threatened, perhaps at the time of Munich. She had been rather casual about it, and did not allow this affair of the heart to interfere with the selling of her beautiful golden loaves. The waitress from Poitou would not waste tears over anybody either.

Were they hard-hearted, these women of France, too intent on accumulating *sous* to have much time left for sentimentality; or had the shadow of war always been so near the land that each generation accepted it as something inevitable, that had to be put up with? *"Que voulez vous, c'est la guerre,"* they would say with a shrug.

No, they were just practical, I thought, not expecting too much of life, but allocating to each of its carefully segregated aspects its due share of whole-hearted attention. Food is important in life, so they concentrated on that with excellent results; in the matter of love, when more important material interests did not intervene, they were more ardent, gay and light-hearted than our girls.

In business, in the earning of money, admitted by the entire population to hold pride of place over every other inclination or occupation, they could give points to an ant or an adding machine in hard work, application, concentration and efficiency.

What an advantage this gave them, I thought, over their Anglo-Saxon counterparts, who slopped over from one thing into the other, neither entirely sentimental nor whole-heartedly practical, too shy to be the one, too indolent to be the other, indecisive and neutral like the English weather, disappointing on the whole. And the proof? Think what çooks they make!

So I jotted down my impressions on the bridge at Amboise in an attempt to slink out for a few moments from the darkness of a shadow from which there was no escaping.

Reynaud was installed at the Château of Chissay, perched high above the River Cher. It was a handsome pile, of medium size as buildings of the Renaissance go, and was rendered the more attractive in that a page of architectural history had been added by every generation or so to the original structure. Mercifully, the urge to build had ceased in the seventeenth century.

The inner courtyard was reached by a long and narrow drive rising steeply from the porter's lodge on the fringe of the village. Numerous cars with military drivers were trying to ascend and descend and finding it difficult to avoid collisions. In the courtyard itself I saw to my utter astonishment Madame de Portes in a dressing-gown over red pyjamas, directing the traffic from the steps of the main entrance. She was shouting to the drivers where to park. I had not seen red trousers on French legs since 1914. This evocation of the past was depressing, and enhanced the general air of unreality I had been struggling against since my return.

I did my own parking so as to avoid the lady I had never spoken to, and stepped into an open gallery at the side of the courtyard.

The impression I received there was that of a mad-house, a stage mad-house about which walked sane actors whilst, backstage, supers rehearsed their lunatic parts.

It was the circumstances that were hallucinatory, not the people.

At the end of the gallery farthest from the house was a small room, evidently the owner's den. Everything there was dusty and rather dirty. The walls were hung with pictures which had long lost all meaning, together with small antlers, trophies of a minor Nimrod. Hooked on to these were a couple of French hunting-horns, black with grime. From another stag's point hung a depressed and ancient fez, grey with the same dust that lay thick on the table. On this, small piles of ancient bills and letters were held in position by hideous Victorian bronze paper-weights, a dog that looked like a sheep, and a shepherdess that might have been fashioned out of melting chocolate.

In the middle of this cobweb-haunted room stood Margerie, who had annexed the place for his own. His vigorous personality gave the impression of a rapidly revolving ventilator in that depressing room. Dust and cobwebs were being blown away.

Once or twice whilst we talked, an ancient man with a white moustache peeped in, then, bewildered and scared, withdrew, only to return, drawn back to his lair by instinct, his previous visit perhaps forgotten, or seeking refuge there as he found every other room in the house occupied. This was its owner, Monsieur Costa de Beauregard. Margerie kept disappearing, being constantly called away or summoned to answer the telephone which never stopped ringing at the other end of the gallery. There may have been other officials in the place, but I only remember him and Reynaud's secretary, Leca. Margerie's sole assistant was the most hard-working, cheerful girl secretary I have ever met. At one moment she was answering the telephone in the narrow room at the other end of the gallery which was her domain, then running, a pretty, plump streak of lightning, looking for someone, then back to her typewriter, which forthwith emitted sounds as of a heavy hailstorm on a tin roof. These two, Margerie and the girl, between them were receiving or trying to pass on telephone messages from the score of châteaux housing the Ministers of the Third Republic, getting off a message to Roosevelt, deciphering a pile of telegrams, and dealing with casual callers such as myself. The confusion was indescribable. No theatrical producer ever achieved such an impression of Bedlam. What would, I suppose, have delighted an audience was the contrast between the calmness of the actors and the insane circumstances which provided the background of their action.

The mind boggled at the thought that this was the heart of France, the brain centre from which every impulse must emanate, the place of decision conjured up by the imagination of the exhausted and beaten armies in their anguish, the spot on which centred the hopes of the flying population, the authority to which turned the terror-stricken cities. By the mercy of Providence none could see it. They would not have believed their eyes if they had.

But strangely enough I have one charming memory associated with that morning. Into that gallery out of nowhere walked Ève Curie. Dark hair in a tress round her head, fresh, pretty, animated, obviously very intelligent and completely self-possessed, in her blue and white print summer frock, she brought with her a sanity which the place had hitherto lacked. She was in charge of American propaganda, or of American correspondents, or something of the kind, and was at once immersed in discussion with Margerie. The next moment she was gone. The sun, which had peeped out for a moment, disappeared too, and I remembered some old lines written in Touraine a long time ago:

> "*Plus oblige et peut d'avantage*
> *Un beau visage*
> *Qu'un homme armé.*"

A ray of light on a cloudy summer day and Ève Curie remained associated in my mind during all the years of the war.

Beyond the pandemonium of the secretary's small room (by now I had ascertained she could speak and type in several languages), there was a big drawing-room where I found de Gaulle seated on a circular Victorian sofa, so contrived that three people could sit on it in comfort provided they turned their backs on each other. If on the other hand conversation was desired, it could only be achieved at the expense of a crick in the neck. I joined him for a few minutes. With heads twisted round after the fashion of parrots, we obtained a painful view of each other's profiles as we spoke.

There were other officers in the room whom I do not remember.

De Gaulle was angry. He had been in Brittany the day before, had seen General Altmayer, and was convinced Brittany could be held. It was evident from the way he spoke that his hope of defending the peninsula was meeting with much opposition.

He was suffering from frustration and exasperation. His criticism of Weygand was devastating. I was glad to feel I was supported in such a quarter.

"Do you not think," I said, "that his method of engaging such troops as he has, piecemeal, is disastrous? That is how he will employ the fresh troops from England."

"*Exactement, c'est bien ça,*" he said with great emphasis, repeating the phrase I had heard from Reynaud: "*C'est la tactique du pain à cacheter,*" and he used the words I had heard attributed to him. "The defeated are those who accept defeat."

He was very impressive even on that ridiculous sofa, which, low though it was, could not detract from his great height. Furthermore, he radiated a confidence which found its source in the vision of a hope as yet scarcely perceptible, like the light before dawn on a stormy night, but as certain of realisation as the rising sun.

He stood for the real core of France, I thought, and out-balanced the defeatists in the other scale. His courage was keen and clear, born of love of, and inspired by, his country. Those who hated him because of these qualities were ghouls born of political putrefaction. Such was the picture I drew of him in my mind when someone came to say Reynaud wanted me. I found him with the Ambassador, who had been there for about ten minutes.

To my intense satisfaction and relief Reynaud showed every sign of resolution and firmness. Although he could not have had much sleep he looked fresh and rested. A very different person from the one I had left at Briare. He said that although some weakness in the Cabinet had emerged at the meeting of the previous evening at Cangé, he could rely on very solid support in his resolution to fight on. As far as he was concerned, his mind was made up. He would fight on in Africa.

His answers to my questions made me realise, as de Gaulle had already done, that there was now little chance of the Government moving to Brittany. Weygand, who had attended the meeting, had demanded that an immediate armistice be requested of the enemy. He had said that the soldiers were no longer fighting and were throwing their weapons away. He had developed the theme we were to hear so much of from now on: the danger of anarchy. The French Army was the only element of order left in the country: it must be saved from total decomposition. What the Government and the Command were now faced with, according to him, was a headlong flight of soldiers and refugees inextricably mixed.

He had foreseen such a dislocation of the forces and had prepared orders to meet the contingency. These orders had now been issued. He repeated again and again that the Government should seek an armistice. If its terms were unacceptable they could reject it. This was the first I heard of a proposal that was to be the undoing of France. Then, it seemed, Pétain had read a written document he had prepared in support of Weygand's views. It was probably the same paper Churchill had heard about at Briare.

Reynaud had reacted violently against the armistice proposals and ridiculed the idea of asking for these "on approval", to be returned if not entirely satisfactory. Hitler was not Kaiser Wilhelm but Genghis Khan, he had said. I was full of admiration for Reynaud. To have stood up to the Commander-in-Chief and Marshal Pétain, the only soldiers present, and refused to be browbeaten by their technical arguments, was no small proof of courage. He had evidently given a clear lead which the more steadfast of his colleagues had gladly followed.

It was gratifying to hear that in that terrible hour many Ministers had been more concerned about the honour of France than with any other consideration and had felt that to seek an armistice otherwise than with Britain's consent was unthinkable. This had not been the attitude of all, but the majority had supported the Premier.

Reverting to the question of the *Réduit Breton* I observed that it seemed quite true that none of the troops in the armies now engaged could possibly be withdrawn to form an effective garrison. The opportunity for doing that was gone. But what of the troops in the Maginot Line? What was the use of part of the shell once the egg was broken? They would surely be trapped. Although so late, was it not still possible to transfer them to Brittany? The static troops of the forts, perfectly fresh, could hold a line if they could be got there.

The Premier thought it was perhaps too late, but would I raise the question with de Gaulle?

I then asked if the question of the Fleet had been considered. Here again Reynaud's answer was eminently satisfactory.

Campinchi had been splendid. The idea of allowing the Fleet to fall into Hitler's hands to be used against England was unthinkable. He had declared that as the Fleet must be involved in the question of an armistice, that consideration alone put the proposal out of court. Reynaud was evidently very pleased with his friend, and I thought what a fine little chap that Corsican was.

Having heard what seemed to be the essentials, and wishing to catch the elusive de Gaulle, who had a remarkable knack of disappearing without trace, in spite of his size, I asked to be excused and set off in search of him. But de Gaulle had vanished, so I returned to Margerie. I had asked him to let me see a telegram from the French Embassy in London referred to in a most secret and immediate one we had received at Champchevrier. It presumably contained a text which should have been repeated to us but had not arrived. As soon as I told him what it was about, Margerie said yes, he had seen it, now where could it be? He and the secretary had had bouts of searching for it as they ran, all in vain. The last thing he had said when I left him to see de Gaulle was that he would look again, he had had an idea. I found him in the secretary's room, where the Ambassador joined us. Margerie had the telephone to one ear, and was at the same time dictating to the secretary the draft of a message from Reynaud to President Roosevelt. With his free hand he gave us a crumpled copy of the missing telegram. "But where was it?" I asked. Margerie put his hand over the receiver and said, with a look at the secretary which was the equivalent of pushing her out of earshot: "Chut! It was in Madame de Portes' bed."

For a little while we remained in the secretary's room looking at some telegrams and reports Margerie had given us to read. Madame de Portes herself appeared three or four times, this time in normal female garb, whispering mysteriously to one or the other. Of course never a word to the Ambassador or myself, but if I have ever seen hate in a woman's eyes, it was in her glances as they swept across us like the strokes of a scythe. What a very unattractive woman, I thought, apart from the ugly expression the presence of Englishmen called forth. She was certainly not pretty and quite as certainly untidy, and her voice even in an undertone made one think of a corncrake, a corncrake muffled under an eiderdown. The story of the Princess who dispelled all doubts concerning her origin when she complained that she had not slept a wink owing to the discomfort caused by a rose petal put under the mattress to test her royal sensibility, came to my mind. By those standards Madame de Portes was no princess. An official telegram under a sheet had not interfered with her slumbers. But no banshee could damp my rising spirits.

The Ambassador too was feeling encouraged by his talk with Reynaud. I asked him and Harvey to lunch at the inn of the *Bon Laboureur* at Chenonceaux, renowned for its good cooking. As the place was on an east–west road, we met no traffic on the way.

We ate in a large inner room deserted save for the family of the millionaire chocolate maker, Menier, the owner of the great Château of Chenonceaux. In the group was beautiful blonde Madame Menier whom I had often admired in Paris. She was almost as beautiful as ever and her pearls were superb.

The Ambassador said that several times during his interview with Reynaud, Madame de Portes had popped her head round the door. We had all been told that as soon as any of us left the Premier she dashed in, asking exactly what had been said and assailing him with reproaches. "What did he say? What is the sense in going on? Thousands of men are being killed while you hesitate to stop the war. Delay will only mean harsher German terms." We readily believed the story. The lady's every action bore it out.

The meal and the 1929 Vouvray were excellent, and together with the good impression Reynaud had made on us, and the encouraging account he had given of the attitude of the majority of the Cabinet, led to our feeling that, in spite of all indications to the contrary, there must be a silver lining to our cloud. But that silver lining was not, we knew, overhead in France. There could be little hope that anything beyond delaying the German advance could now be achieved there. As proof of this I had been told that the First Corps had not a single gun left.

We compared notes about people and found the impression we had both gathered was that Baudouin had dropped the mask and was now openly on the side of Weygand and Pétain.

Poor Reynaud, he was certainly not fortunate in his appointments —or rather, in those Madame de Portes had suggested to him.

After lunch the Ambassador and Harvey made for Tours and Champchevrier. I returned to Chissay. There were some further points needing elucidation by Reynaud, amongst others the question of the *Réduit Breton* and his own movements.

I also hoped de Gaulle might have returned.

When my valiant chauffeur had battled his way past many cars up the steep and narrow drive which led to the château, I was told that Reynaud had gone to Tours, where Churchill was expected. This was astonishing news. Worried lest I should arrive too late, we turned about and speeded regardless of consequences. I feared that the Ambassador, as much in the dark as I concerning the Prime Minister's visit, would drive straight through Tours and miss him. I decided, once I had located Churchill, to send the chauffeur to Champchevrier with a note.

But why this journey? What did it portend? Only a matter of the greatest moment could have brought the Prime Minister across those dangerous skies on two successive days. Had he news of American intervention?

The real explanation did not even occur to me. It was that the French Government, acting through their Embassy in London, or more probably using military signals, had invited Churchill to come to Tours as a sequel to the Cabinet meeting of the previous evening (the 12th). Why neither the Ambassador nor I had been told this was, and remains, a mystery. It was of course not known whether Churchill would or could come, or even if he had received the invitation, and he landed unheralded and unmet. But still I should have imagined the matter would somehow have come out in the course of our talks with such a variety of people during the morning. It is extraordinary that Reynaud himself did not mention it. My only guess is that, in the general confusion, everyone thought someone else had told us and that it was assumed we knew. I imagine that the absence of a reply from Churchill deprived the question of the priority it would otherwise have had and that it was consequently overshadowed by other matters of moment.

CHAPTER XIV

Thursday, June 13th

(2)

Churchill and his party at the Préfecture at Tours—The last meeting of the Supreme War Council—The contrast between Tours and Briare—Churchill's attitude—I translate for Reynaud—His account of the Cabinet meeting—Decision to appeal for American help—He asks what would be the British attitude if the French asked for an armistice— Halifax—Beaverbrook—Cadogan—Churchill's reply to Reynaud—He speaks to the French nation—Margerie takes over as interpreter—Reynaud repeats his question— Churchill refuses to consider it and proposes to await Roosevelt's reply—Reynaud agrees—Churchill on the danger to Anglo-French relations—The French trance—Reynaud taken aback by Churchill's determination—His further appeal to Britain—We adjourn to the garden—Beaverbrook's common-sense proposal—Reynaud's talk with Jeanneney and Herriot —We return to the Préfecture—Churchill sums up— Reynaud's renewed firmness—The Conference decides to await Roosevelt's answer—Churchill asks for the captured German pilots—The Conference ends—Churchill sees Jeanneney and Herriot—De Gaulle tells me of Baudouin's misrepresentation of Churchill—I obtain Churchill's denial— The Flamingo flies off.

MY chauffeur, exhilarated by the ceaseless screech of his klaxon, drove towards Tours as one inspired. This time we took the southern route via Bléré, and found that, from that place on, the skiddy, wet road was full of refugee cars. They were fortunately seldom double-banked, and I only just caught glimpses of the resigned, frozen faces of the occupants. Columns of cars two or three miles long were waiting at the petrol stations. The broad avenue leading into Tours from the south had become a camp. Refugees from the cars spread wide in search of food. Some were washing themselves or their clothes in buckets.

An intelligent gendarme told me official cars had been making for the *Préfecture* close by, so I went there. The first thing I saw was the Ambassador's Rolls. Sir Ronald fortunately had seen Reynaud driving in, and been told by him that Churchill had arrived. He told me that he, like myself, had had no idea the Prime Minister was coming, was expected, or had been asked to come.

In the building I found the English party. It consisted of Churchill, Halifax, Beaverbrook, Cadogan, Ismay and Berkeley. On our way upstairs I had time to gather that they had had great difficulty in obtaining a meagre and bad lunch at the Grand Hotel, and Winston, hanging back, asked me about Baudouin, who had appeared while he was at lunch. I told him he was now doing his damnedest to persuade Reynaud to throw up the sponge. "He is working on behalf of Weygand and Pétain." Churchill growled that he had gathered as much, and that Baudouin had ruined an already inadequate meal by seasoning it with an outpouring of oily defeatism. The Prime Minister looked extremely stern and concentrated. His likeness to the elder Napoleon when in deep thought struck me. He looked down as he walked, making no effort, as he had when he arrived at Briare, to seem detached and cheerful. He was evidently deeply preoccupied. Halifax, immensely tall, debonair, thin and loose-limbed, seemed interested in things happening above our heads; he was closer to heaven than any of us. This was not the impression Beaverbrook gave. Evidently concerned, he was fiddling with his change as if feeling for a coin with which to tip someone. From the way he looked at Baudouin, one could only infer that if he gave him half a crown it would be in the hope of inducing him to go away. He looked tough, as indeed he is, the lips on his wide mouth were clamped together. Ismay, whose expression would, I hoped, give me guidance, looked very stern. Cadogan, dapper and cool, stuck close to Halifax.

We presently found ourselves in a smallish room on the first floor, furnished inconveniently with a few deep, light-coloured leather arm-chairs and some straight chairs. This was presumably the *Préfet's* study. There was no table, but a desk at which sat Georges Mandel. Before him on a tray was a chicken which he was eating with his fingers as best he could while answering the telephone.

A gleam of pleasure came over Churchill's face as he saw him, then his gaze rested for a moment, rather wistfully I thought, on the chicken. After a few words of greeting, Mandel left the room, carrying his tray, and Reynaud replaced him at the desk.

There were nine Englishmen in the room to two Frenchmen, Reynaud and Baudouin. But it was not the fact that they were more numerous that was striking. They were a solid mass, a steel buoy firmly moored in the eddying, whirling, dark flood sweeping over France.

The impression was the stronger in that we were all aware that the two Frenchmen represented two totally different points of view. Baudouin throughout, his keen intelligent face intent and alert, never said a word but never took his eyes off Reynaud even when Churchill was speaking, except to make notes.

It was evident that Reynaud was being closely observed by a hostile witness, and I thought that he was aware of this. Whatever the reason, he had radically changed since the morning. His colour, his manner, his whole attitude, were different. My notes say that I was horrified at the alteration.

The atmosphere was completely dissimilar from that at Briare. There we had had from Churchill an outpouring of good will, of sympathy, of sorrow. The dark scene had been illuminated, fiercely at times, by the burning torch of Britain's determination, which he held high, using it to show the French the way he was urging them to follow.

Today was more like a business meeting, and I do not think anyone quite took in that this was the Supreme War Council of Britain and France. Certainly it occurred to no one that it was the last in the series of the all-powerful and solemn gatherings held until so lately in the subdued pomp of historical buildings.

Churchill's attitude had undergone a subtle change. He was as sympathetic as ever, kindly and understanding, but alert, keen to detect shades of meaning in Reynaud's phrases and gestures, intent on weighing his words, on measuring the repercussions they might have. The other Englishmen sat easily, listening. None spoke in answer to the glances Churchill shot in the direction of one or the other. They were assessors, forming their own conclusions, not unsympathetic to Reynaud, far from it, but keenly appraising the situation from the British point of view. This was the great difference from previous meetings. There was now a British and a French point of view, sharply divided. There was no longer, as there had always been, a solid central core of understanding, the common ground to both countries, a kernel of identical interests which might be chipped, but could not be fractured by events. It came to me that I had witnessed similar scenes before, in politics and business, when the representatives of interests hitherto in partnership find that circumstances impose upon them a dissociation as painful to the spirit as the tearing off of an adhesive bandage is to the body, as dangerous to the survival of good understanding as the uprooting of a flower in bloom is to the plant. On such occasions most men's endeavour is to avoid hurting the feelings of those now on the other side of the table, who are still their friends and whom they want to keep as such. I have never known such well-meant efforts to be entirely successful.

Churchill let himself down into one of the deep leather armchairs and, on a sign, I sat next to him. Then at once arose the question of interpreting.

Berkeley was there to translate into English, but there was no sign of Margerie, who always acted as the other interpreter, translating English into French. Reynaud therefore asked me to take his place and translate the remarks of my compatriots. I hate translating. It is a very difficult thing to do adequately, requiring qualifications beyond a mere knowledge of French and English. Furthermore it demands meticulous attention. Notes must be made of a long statement, and I, no more than Margerie, knew shorthand, yet not a single word must be missed. It is especially difficult to interpret and also get an impression of the proceedings, for the interpreter must sink his personality in that of the person whose ideas he is rendering. Moreover, when translating before an audience completely conversant with both languages, the task seems the more difficult in that you are conscious that most of them will have thought of the word you are searching for before you have found it.

Interpreters could, in fact, have been dispensed with on this as on other occasions, but translations were, nevertheless, and I think rightly, insisted upon, for when every word mattered they gave time to consider what had been said. Also to speak a language well does not necessarily mean having the power of grasping all its finer shades of meaning.

It came to me with a sinking feeling that it was my misfortune to have to translate at what promised to be the most momentous and probably the gravest of the meetings so far held between the Governments.

Reynaud opened the proceedings. He said that at a Cabinet meeting held on the preceding evening General Weygand had declared the situation of the French Army to be desperate. It was at its last gasp and it was necessary to ask for an armistice forthwith.

Some military formations had lost all cohesion and were robbing passers-by in the forests near Paris. We were then told that the Commander-in-Chief, abandoning the purely military sphere which was his concern, had insistently demanded an armistice on the ground that this offered the only means of escaping a complete occupation of France, which would damage the very soul and structure of the country.

The majority of the Cabinet had not endorsed this point of view. Some Ministers had held that public opinion was not prepared for such news. The General nevertheless persisted that hostilities must be brought to an end. The matter went no further, "but," went on Reynaud, "if Paris is taken, and it is difficult to see how this will not happen, the question will inevitably be raised again."

In spite of what Weygand had said, Reynaud did not consider the situation to be desperate yet. Heavy losses had been inflicted on the enemy. The French Army had succeeded in greatly weakening the common foe. It was true, as Weygand and others had pointed out, that France had already sacrificed everything to the common cause, and now had nothing left; but he felt that if in spite of its plight the Army could fight on a little while longer, help would soon be forthcoming from Great Britain and the United States of America.

One thing was imperative, he declared, and that was that American support should be available in time and in sufficient measure. He gathered hope from the fact that Roosevelt had suggested that the message he had sent him on June 10th should be made public. This was encouraging, as was the promise of aircraft and guns.

Reynaud said he proposed sending a further message to President Roosevelt that day, telling him that the last hour had come and that the Allied cause lay in his hands.

Reynaud's voice lost its firmness as he went on to say that his Government—meaning, I thought, his colleagues rather than himself—would not continue the struggle unless Roosevelt's reply conveyed a firm assurance of immediate aid. It became clear that he was talking of the other Ministers when he added: "They will say: 'Why carry on when the certain result will be the occupation of the whole of France and the systematic debasement of its people by Hitler?' " The Government might leave the country, but the people could not. The Nazis would corrupt them and France would cease to exist. That was the dreadful prospect. The alternative was an armistice or peace.

There was a pause after these appalling words, as each one gazed at the picture conjured up in his mind. Then Reynaud, perhaps having intended that all should have had time to take in the implications of what he had said, went on in an even flatter voice:

The Government had not lost sight of the fact that a solemn pledge had been entered into that no separate peace would be concluded. But what was the British Government's attitude in view of the present situation? France, as General Weygand had said, had been completely sacrificed. She had nothing left. This being the plain and terrible truth, it would come as a shock to the French Government and people if Britain failed to understand and did not concede that France was physically incapable of carrying on. Was France, under these circumstances, still expected to fight on with the only result of delivering up her people to German despotism and Nazi corruption? Was she to be handed over to specialists in bringing conquered people to heel?

Would Great Britain realise the hard facts now facing France?

Churchill, during the latter part of Reynaud's remarks, had looked at no one. He appeared to be at his fiercest. I had often seen the same expression on his face while he thought out his retort when an opponent in the House of Commons said something that aroused his ire. But I do not think he was angry. He was probably weighing the words he would use, measuring the terms he would employ as he contemplated the picture of fallen France painted by Reynaud, a picture which had failed to convey the impression of heroic self-sacrifice on the battlefield, but evoked the pathetic, rather sordid police photograph of a murder. Churchill was also no doubt assessing what Reynaud's statement meant to Britain.

Although he had been prepared by the Briare meeting to hear that resistance in Metropolitan France was all but over, the final words must nevertheless have come as a shock, for Reynaud had given no hint of an intention to continue the war outside France. Exclamation marks on my notes denote the shock and horror I felt. I was certainly more surprised than anyone save perhaps the Ambassador, for no one else had had the encouraging talk with Reynaud we had been so cheered by that morning. I wondered what had occurred to change him in so short a time. I am still unenlightened today.

Halifax, his long figure curled like a question mark, reclined in his chair. He had never taken his eyes off Reynaud. His good hand, clasping his artificial one, the legacy of a war wound, was under his chin, his mouth slightly open, his head a little bent to one side. His general attitude conveyed, as it always does, an impression of extreme courteousness and attention. His expression seemed slightly tinged with scepticism. I thought that perhaps this was how this High Anglican would listen to a sermon on modern miracles in a Roman Catholic Church.

Beaverbrook did not hide his feelings as he sat well forward in his chair, his hands clamped between his knees encased in the narrow trousers he affected. He was flushed, his sparse hair untidy, his eyebrows close together, and the long upper lip of his Irish type of face pushed forward as he watched Reynaud intently but without perceptible approval. His round head looked like a cannon-ball that might be projected at any moment at Reynaud by the powerful spring his small, tense body provided.

Cadogan was politely and alertly attentive. The juxtaposition of Cadogan and Churchill, as I looked from one to the other, recalled, perhaps because it was the first time I had seen them together, a story once told me by Jack Churchill, Winston's elder brother.

On the eve of one of Marlborough's great battles in Flanders, Marlborough, followed by his staff, and its chief, his friend and colleague, that splendid soldier Cadogan, was reconnoitring the position. Cantering to a slight rise, he looked about him intently. As he did so, he dropped his glove, then turning to Cadogan he said harshly: "Pick up my glove, Cadogan." The staff drew their breath in amazement, wondering how this proud man would react to the insult. Would he refuse? But the heavily-booted General obeyed, dismounted and, bowing low, handed the glove to the Duke.

That night Marlborough sent for Cadogan and said: "Do you remember the place where I dropped my glove? I want the main battery to be set up there."

"It is there now," answered Cadogan. Cadogan had realised that Marlborough wished to impress an exact spot on his mind, and, being a fine tactician, had understood why. A supremely good example of perfect understanding.

Now here were the descendants of the two great leaders, brought together as their forebears had been, by virtue of the services their Houses have rendered, generation after generation, to the country. Later, recalling this scene, I thought how fortunate England has been to be served through the centuries by such men, and by others imbued with the same transcendent loyalty, though bearing lesser names. At the moment it was only the old story of the Flanders battlefield that flashed in my mind, a vivid picture, as I watched the two men in that small room at Tours.

Reynaud had stopped. Churchill now began to speak. It was my turn to translate.

He said that Great Britain realised what France had endured and was still suffering. He did not underestimate the bitterness of the ordeal. Our turn in England would soon come and England was ready. She grieved that her contribution to the present land struggle was so small.

Then, addressing himself more directly to Reynaud, and speaking in the first person, he went on:

"If our Army had not been lost in the north, you might perhaps have resisted, for we should then have played an important part in the present defensive battle which opened on June 5th. But we could not be at your side because of reverses suffered owing to our having accepted the strategy of the Command in the north." (Well, I thought, the plain truth is out at last.)

Then his tone changed, he was no longer talking to Reynaud, but to the French nation.

"The British people have not yet felt the German lash, but they do not underestimate its force. This in no way deters them; far from being cowed, they are looking forward to thrashing Hitler. They have but one thought, to win the war and destroy Hitlerism."

Winston was gathering momentum as he went, his eyes flashed, his hands were clenched as if grasping a double-handed sword. The picture he was drawing made him splutter with rage as he contemplated it.

"Everything is subordinated to the British determination to destroy Hitler and his gang," he rasped. "No risk, however formidable, will hinder us. Everything, absolutely everything, will be subordinated to that aim. To win the war is our single thought.

Every hour of every day we shall rehearse our pledge. It will be our last thought at night and our first thought in the morning. We all think alike, every one of us. I know the British people, their endless capacity for enduring and persisting and for striking back. And they will strike until the foe is beaten.

"We must fight, we will fight, and that is why we must ask our friends to fight on."

At this point the door opened and Margerie appeared. He sat down and made me a sign that as soon as I had finished translating the last group of sentences he was prepared to carry on. This was relief indeed, for to do justice in French to Winston's torrent of boiling, bubbling eloquence, was a difficult, not to say an impossible, task. Margerie quite rightly did not attempt to do so. He was content to give, as far as possible, an exact translation of the words used, leaving the audience to appreciate, from Churchill's own delivery in English, the emphasis he intended.

Churchill, with but a fractional halt as Margerie sat down, went on: "You must give us time. We ask you to fight on as long as possible, if not in Paris, at least behind Paris, in the provinces, down to the sea, then, if need be, in North Africa. At all costs time must be gained. The period we are asking you to endure is not limitless. A pledge from the United States would make it quite short.

"And what is the alternative? The alternative is the destruction of France, more certain than if she fights on, for Hitler will abide by no pledges.

"We have no illusions as to German strength. We know it to be immense. It is possible that for a while Hitler will be the absolute master of Europe. But this will not last. It cannot last. All his victories cannot destroy the natural forces of resistance of the nations, great or small, that may temporarily find themselves under his heel.

"France must fight on. She still has her fine Navy, her great Empire. With what remains of her Army she can pursue guerrilla warfare on a grand scale and wage war on the enemy's communications.

"If Germany fails in her attack against England, the destruction of which is indispensable to Hitler, if within two or three months his assault on our island has not succeeded, if the power of his Air Force is curbed or destroyed, then after months of suffering the whole hateful edifice of Nazidom will topple over. Should the United

States give immediate help to the Allies, and perhaps even declare war, then victory may not be so far off as it seems today."

With ever-increasing emphasis and vehemence, he said that in any case, and in any eventuality, Britain would fight on. Nothing would shake her resolution. She would accept no terms, no surrender. "We shall listen to no peace proposals emanating from Hitler—to do so would merely be to court another Munich followed by another occupation of Prague.

"The war will continue, and can but end in our destruction or our victory." He stopped, then said, looking hard at Reynaud: "That is my answer to your question."

This magnificent declaration of faith, this challenge, had been delivered for the benefit of two Frenchmen. One, Baudouin, was, we all knew, one of the defeatists. If he was moved, he did not show it. Latterly he appeared to have been entirely absorbed by the task of taking notes. Reynaud, who generally responded to Churchill's words, simply looked intent, even impatient. He might have been thinking: 'I have heard that already,' and that was practically what he said when he spoke.

His voice had a slight undertone of irritability, a flavour of irony I had not detected before when he addressed Churchill. "The question I put just now," he said, "was not what England would do. Mr. Churchill has always told me that he will never give in, and that the resolution of the British nation is indomitable." Then, with a slight gesture of the hands, the irony in his voice now quite perceptible, he said he was personally convinced that Great Britain would not give way until she had known sufferings equal to those now endured by the French people.

I sat up sharply at this. Reynaud was implying that we would behave as the French were behaving if submitted to a similar ordeal, and that we would under similar circumstances throw up the sponge as the French intended doing.

A feeling of near-hostility crept over me. I was convinced Reynaud did not believe a word he was saying. He knew the British well enough to realise that Churchill's speech, eloquent as it was, was but a plain statement of fact. Even allowing for national pride, he surely was aware that we would not behave as the French were doing today.

So far he had not even mentioned fighting on in Africa as he had that morning. Was that coming later? Was this a piece of special pleading on behalf of some of his colleagues? Was he going to put the Weygand–Pétain case once more and then dramatically dissociate himself from it? We must wait and see. Meanwhile he was a very different man from the cheerful, determined little chap of a few hours ago. For a moment I saw him as a ventriloquist's dummy voicing the views—of whom? Pétain? Weygand? Could it be Madame de Portes?

He was now saying: "The question I have asked is this: Suppose a French Government, which would not include me, said to the British Government: 'We know that you will continue the war. We also would continue it if we had any hope of a sufficiently early victory that would re-establish France as she deserves to be re-established. In such a case we would be at your side to continue the struggle, if need be in North Africa. But we see no sufficient hope of an early victory. There is no chance of the United States joining in the conflict in the months before the Presidential election. It is also possible that Mr. Roosevelt might die. It is quite natural that Great Britain should go on with the war, in view of the fact that she has not suffered as we have; in fact, she has suffered little, but we, the French Government, do not think we can abandon our people without their being able to perceive a light at the end of the tunnel. We cannot abandon our people to German domination. We must come to terms. We have no choice. This would be a most grave decision for the French Government to take, but it might be the only one. Our problem is this. Should we persist in a war without hope and should we leave the land of France? It is now too late to organise the *Réduit Breton*, and the French Government could not remain there; nor is there a hope of finding any place in France where a genuine French Government might escape capture. If we left, the position would then be that Hitler would in all probability set up a puppet Government with so-called legal powers which would at once set about its task of corruption.' In the hypothetical case of a French Government reasoning as I have just done, and coming to the conclusion that it had not got the right thus to abandon France to Germany, would not the British Government then agree that France, having sacrificed what was finest and best of her youth, could do no more? Would Great Britain not agree that, France having nothing further to contribute to the common cause, she would release her from the agreement concluded three months ago and allow her to conclude a separate peace? Could this not be conceded whilst maintaining Anglo-French solidarity?"

If Reynaud had been able to indicate that Churchill had in fact not answered his earlier question, Churchill might now address the same reproach to Reynaud.

Churchill had spoken of the French fighting on in their Empire. Reynaud had not even referred to this possibility.

I also saw a trap. I did not think then or later that Reynaud intended to lay one, but it was nevertheless a trap to ask us to bind ourselves to solidarity with France if that country concluded a separate peace with Hitler and her territory became a base for enemy action against us. To accept such a bargain would be to deprive ourselves of the power to strike at the Germans in France. I felt no sympathy for Reynaud just then or indeed for France either. If she dropped out of the war she must take the consequences. It was perhaps from that moment that there grew in my mind a feeling that gathered strength with every day that went by. "Those who are not for us are against us"; there are no half tones in war. And I remembered a French line:

> "*Mieux vaut un franc ennemi*
> *Qu'un bon ami qui m'égratigne.*"

I looked at Winston sharply, stupidly thinking for an instant that his tenderness for France, his sympathy for her suffering, might conceal the danger from him. But of course he saw it; he was only thinking of England now. Perhaps he even felt resentment, long held back, for the appalling French blunders which had landed us in our present predicament. What he had said concerning the disaster in the north indicated this.

He began to speak, and it was evident from his first words that he refused to consider Reynaud's suggestion. Characteristically, his method of avoiding the dilemma was to rise above it.

"Under no circumstances," said Churchill, "will Great Britain waste time in reproaches and recriminations. But that is a very different matter from becoming a consenting party to a peace made in contravention of the agreement so recently concluded."

So that was that. Nothing could be plainer, more crystal-clear.

All the Englishmen present quite perceptibly closed round him, forming an even more solid phalanx than before. Other Englishmen, those of the fields and factories, would have growled their approbation. The men in that room did nothing obvious, they had had a different training, but it came to the same thing. Even Halifax, like the dove in spring, assumed a livelier hue.

Churchill went on that he thought the first thing to do was to inform President Roosevelt of the situation and await his answer before considering anything else. Let Monsieur Reynaud put the position to the President in the strongest terms. He himself would send that night a supporting message which would follow the other dispatches pleading for France. "Things," he said, "move fast in America. Electoral considerations may play in favour of intervention as they may against it.

"Before posing ourselves decisive questions, we must appeal to Roosevelt. Let the French Government undertake to do this and we will support them by telegram. That is the first thing to do, and it must be done before an answer is given to the extremely grave question put by Monsieur Reynaud.

"I have already said we would refrain from reproaches and recriminations. The cause of France will always be dear to us, and if we win the war we will one day restore her to all her power and dignity. But that is a very different thing"—and his eyes flashed with anger—"from asking Great Britain to consent to a departure from the solemn undertaking binding the two countries." He stopped, but went on looking at Reynaud with the utmost sternness, awaiting his answer.

Reynaud, in a smooth, flat voice said: "The declaration Mr. Churchill has just made is very moving and has deeply stirred me. I shall therefore telegraph to Monsieur Roosevelt telling him of the deterioration in the situation. I shall tell him the truth, and I shall say that the French Army which was the advance-guard of democracy has been destroyed holding the first line. Will the main forces of democracy follow? The U.S.A. are involved as well as Great Britain. If America does not intervene, or does not intervene in time, it will be the story of the Horatii and the Curiatii all over again."

I was interested to hear Reynaud use the same simile as I had when talking to him not so long ago in Paris. He, of course, knew his classics better than I did, but he must have thought the example appropriate or he would not have used it.

"Many faults have been committed, we French can well admit it. If we had all been ready together, the situation would be better today. Hitler kills France today, he will then attack England, then will come the turn of the United States. The peril which threatens us all is both moral and material.

"The proposal is now to draw up a telegram to Monsieur Roosevelt and to await his answer. I earnestly hope that Mr. Churchill will feel he can identify himself with my message and tell the President it is his message also, the message of Great Britain as well as of France.

"I also wish to thank Mr. Churchill personally."

Churchill spoke again. A firm promise from America would introduce a tremendous new factor, he said. In that case the situation would need re-examining. "On other points which do not concern the British Government, the French Government will have to come to its own decisions. But there are, nevertheless, a certain number of questions which we shall have to examine together, for, whatever happens, the war will continue ever grimmer, ever fiercer, ever more terrible.

"We are fast approaching a universal blockade, a blockade of the whole of Europe which will become increasingly effective, while at the same time the Nazis will be seizing everything they need for their own supplies. Famine and desperate suffering will certainly ensue. These are terrible but inescapable prospects. Do not let us attempt to ignore them.

"France, if she is occupied by the Germans, cannot hope to be spared. The lifting of the blockade could only mean that England was defeated.

"If we fight on with success, if we can see the winter through, the struggle will then develop with full fury. France cannot hope to elude the consequences of this duel. As a result there may well develop a bitter antagonism between the French and English people. There will, in fact, be many questions to be considered if the President's reply is of a negative character."

He then said that all these problems required examination and consideration. Meanwhile he was anxious to know how long France could hold out before Weygand felt himself obliged to sue for an armistice. Was another week possible—or less?

Reynaud did not answer this question. But his voice, though not his face, more apt to register amusement than distress, revealed deep concern and indeed alarm. The childish conception in which his mind had found refuge of France bowing herself out of the war whilst remaining on good terms with us was blown sky-high. Had he not considered that the enemy would use French harbours as bases against us? Would fly their planes from French aerodromes to attack us? Would draw sustenance from the soil of France for their armies? Did he think France could escape the consequences of this? and that, out of tenderness for France, we would abstain from smashing at the enemy on French soil, or would hesitate to starve him even if it meant starving France as well? The French, from Reynaud down, were in a trance. To an increasing degree the war seemed to have become to them something unreal, a nightmare which could be brought to an end by the simple method of waking up into peace.

To them Churchill's speeches were but the overtones of a frantic ballet, a witches' sabbath, his words the magnificent evocation of a dead past which, to his listeners, conveyed no more reality than would have done a reading of *The Cid* on the wireless to a brawling audience in a Montmartre café, hardly conscious of it except as a noise which they would willingly have turned off.

Weygand, Pétain and others wished at all costs to stop a game they had ceased to understand.

The troops, weary supers, had ceased to take any part in a play they felt they had been brought into under false pretences, and were moving off-stage. It was to have been a war fought behind unassailable defences, active only in the verbal exchange of insults over the radio; and now they were being chased across their own country, with no one giving any indication of how soon the end would come. So they trudged on, throwing away as they went their inadequate weapons, the symbols of the outmoded war theories of their chiefs.

To the troops streaming back to the Loire, or to Ministers in Touraine, there was something shocking, out of place and in bad taste, in these Englishmen's rude talk of continuing the war. Instead of agreeing to wake up to an unpleasant but livable reality, the British persisted in their hallucination, determined to enact its most unpleasant and impossible features. It seemed as foolish as the sheep announcing it was going to cut the butcher's throat. But there it was. Never had the mad English seemed more maddeningly mad. Helpless, their troops in flight, they spoke as if they had their hands round Hitler's throat and were feeling for his windpipe with their thumbs.

They even seemed to believe what they said. It was the realisation of their purpose and faith that had taken Reynaud aback. Churchill's

words, which made it plain that in our grim and implacable determination we would destroy everything, even the French, if they stood
between us and our enemy, had startled him out of the aberration
into which he had so recently drifted. His voice and manner clearly
showed this. He said that he viewed with horror the prospect that,
supposing the war should continue (what else?), Great Britain would
inflict the immense suffering of a blockade upon the French people.
It would be an indescribable disaster if France and Great Britain
separated. They could not hope for independence apart from each
other. (An absurd tune sang in my ears: "Here we go gathering nuts
in May".) So we were to ensure our joint independence by a
collective surrender . . . nuts, just nuts, nuts in June.

But Reynaud was speaking on: Even if it were to turn out that
Roosevelt could only offer us insufficient hope, if he, Reynaud, had
to abandon his hold of that to which he was desperately clinging
(presumably the hope that the United States would join in the war),
he trusted that Great Britain would, in recognition of the sacrifices of
France, make some gesture to avoid an antagonism that would, he
felt, be fatal. "If France continued to suffer without England's
making a gesture, recognising what we have endured, I should be
very preoccupied for the future," he said. "This might result in a
new and very grave situation in Europe."

I was more and more bewildered. If it was a question of gestures
or phrases, no one could have been more generous, more understanding towards France than Churchill had been. He had been
careful to hide from the British public the miserable shortcomings
and often dubious actions of our allies. What more was Reynaud
asking? That we should not hit the Germans so long as they skulked
behind France's skirts? What had he really meant? It sounded
uncommonly as if he were hinting that, should we not give some
impossible promise not to injure France, she would consider joining
the enemy. What else could he mean? I was horrified. This was
what had taken the place of fighting on in North Africa, which had
been his theme that very morning. It was as disquieting as it was
incomprehensible.

No possible good could come of going on talking on these lines.
Remembering how, when confronted with a difficult situation at the
Peace Conference, Lloyd George often asked for an adjournment to
consult his colleagues, I scribbled a note to Churchill suggesting he
should do likewise, and leant over and handed it to him as he was

speaking. He stopped, read it, nodded and went on with what he had been saying, which was in fact a repetition. "We shall have to consider the whole position after the receipt of the American answer. We shall have to examine many things if France decides to ask for an armistice and a treaty. The American answer can be expected within twenty-four hours. For the moment the only move open to us is to put the situation to the American President with the greatest frankness."

Churchill then said he hoped Reynaud would not mind his conferring with his colleagues. Turning round he looked out of the window at the now sunny garden, and feeling no doubt that this was the most likely place where it would be possible to talk quietly without being overheard, he said: "*Dans le jardin.*" So to the garden we went.

It was a hideous rectangle surrounded by laurel bushes with a single path running parallel to them. The centre was filled with tufty, ill-kept grass. A drab, official garden, as unimaginative, as lacking in beauty as the republican form of Government it typified. The leaves were dripping water and we had to avoid them and the numerous puddles in the muddy path. Walking three abreast was a squeeze, and one or other dropped back every few steps, driven out of line by a wet branch or a puddle. Nevertheless, the pack kept close together, walking fast round and round that beastly patch of grass. Beaverbrook and Halifax at once expressed complete support of Churchill. The diplomats tended to form a bunch round Halifax a little way behind, though the Ambassador drew up to the Prime Minister several times to answer questions. I believe that everyone was too stunned to speak. I certainly was. I felt completely at sea, rather savage and greatly bewildered as well as frustrated and useless, being unable to cast any light on Reynaud's mood, or even guess at an explanation of what seemed a new and defeatist policy on his part. All I could say was that Reynaud had been completely different that morning when he had described how at the Cabinet meeting the night before he had resisted the "armisticers" and been supported by most of his colleagues in opposing Weygand's peace offensive.

It was possible, I thought, that he had been playing the devil's advocate just now, putting the case of the defeatists and of Weygand and Pétain to see how Churchill would react. But in any case I had not liked the last bit, the piece about the grave situation that would arise if we did not make "a gesture". I note my own remarks because I wrote them down and remember them, although they were surely the least important. But the fact was that little of any moment was said by anybody.

Churchill was thinking, putting an occasional question to this one or that. He asked me about de Gaulle, and I told him I was certain he was completely staunch, and I went on to summarise my talks with Pétain and Georges at Briare after Churchill had left. I said that Weygand looked upon anyone wishing to fight on as an enemy.

There followed some speculation as to what Reynaud had meant to imply. Would he finally decide to go to North Africa? Had he got it in him to brave Pétain and Weygand, or would he slide out, do a Pontius Pilate and leave the way clear for someone else to make peace?

I was asked for my view, and said I thought he was fundamentally in favour of fighting on, that the whole of what there was of him was with us, but that he could not be bigger than God had made him, and he was subjected to terrible strains and stresses. He had so far failed to form and lead a phalanx of the stronger Ministers who wished to fight on. It must be realised how very difficult was the task of civilians assailed by doubts as to their competence in face of the strong, the violent, opinion of the soldiers in favour of peace.

And so on we went, in a formation imposed by wet leaves and puddles, down the garden path.

Then suddenly Beaverbrook spoke. His dynamism was immediately felt. "There is nothing to do but to repeat what you have already said, Winston. Telegraph to Roosevelt and await the answer. Tell Reynaud that we have nothing to say or discuss until Roosevelt's answer is received. Don't commit yourself to anything. We shall gain a little time and see how those Frenchmen sort themselves out. We are doing no good here. In fact, listening to these declarations of Reynaud's only does harm. Let's get along home." It was as simple as that, but it was what everyone felt to be the voice of common sense, and so, up the garden path, back we went to the *Préfecture*. The promenade had taken about twenty minutes.

We had, of course, no idea of what had been going on on the French side during the interval. Baudouin has given his version of what occurred. He writes:

"During the suspension of the meeting, while the three members of the War Cabinet were taking a few steps in the garden, the President of the Council (Reynaud) and I went into the adjoining room where the Presidents of the two Assemblies (Senate and

Chamber), MM. Jeanneney and Herriot, and M. Mandel were waiting. M. Paul Reynaud gave a brief outline of the talk that had taken place. He was subjected to the violent reproaches of MM. Jeanneney and Herriot, who will not accept that the President of the Council (Reynaud) should have allowed it to be understood that one day France would sue for a separate armistice. They are all three violently opposed to the armistice and they reproach M. Reynaud for his weakness. President Herriot is very moved. His face is ravaged and tears are on his cheeks. M. Mandel declares he must see Churchill."

I believe this account to be truthful, all the more so that the scene he describes is contrary to the thesis he was defending.

We trooped back into the *Préfet's* study, and as is always the case, responding to some primeval squatters' instinct, returned to the places each one had lately occupied. So true is this that anyone finding his seat taken on such an occasion feels mildly aggrieved. This general observation found its immediate application when Sir Alexander Cadogan found himself in the necessity of selecting a straight chair, as General de Gaulle, who had now joined the party, lowered his immense frame into the arm-chair lately occupied by the Permanent Under-Secretary of State at the Foreign Office.

Churchill resumed the conversation. He said that nothing in the discussion he had just had with his colleagues had led any of them to change their views. Lord Halifax and Lord Beaverbrook had expressed their approbation of what he had said just now, and it could therefore be assumed that the Cabinet would also agree. "We think that President Roosevelt should be approached without delay. We are returning to England this evening and will send him an appeal that will be identical with yours."

The tone of Reynaud's voice when he answered arrested my attention. It was more natural, easier, more confident. His attitude had changed again, it was more alert. He thanked Churchill for his declaration. He was convinced that the American President would take a step forward, and that he could then discuss with the British Government the conditions under which the French could continue the war. This is extraordinary, I thought. This is the old Reynaud. I must have been right in thinking he was putting the case of the defeatists to get Churchill's reaction. Having found him completely firm, he is building on that.

His every word confirmed that view. He was now saying that "the two Governments can meet again after President Roosevelt's answer has been received, with the object of putting all their forces in a common pool. This is my deep conviction," he said, "even after telling you all that the Cabinet requested me to say." He was going to prepare his message to the President. He would tell him frankly what the situation was and how much it had deteriorated. He would explain how, under these conditions, it was indispensable to give the French Government and people some hope. He would endeavour to obtain from him the declaration of war that he had already asked for, which could not mean the dispatch of an expeditionary force, but that America would lend the support of her Navy and Air Force to the Allies, and send them American arms. These would indeed be important factors. He asked Churchill if he had anything to add. "No," said Churchill. He also would put the position bluntly to President Roosevelt. As regards what M. Reynaud had said concerning a separate peace, no reply to that question could be given until the President's answer had been received. Then he and M. Reynaud could meet and consider what decisions were called for. If America joined them, then victory was certain. "It will be a war of continents fought across the oceans, and the enslaved nations will be freed one by one as they were in the last war." If America stood aloof, then the French people might have to suffer Nazi domination for a while, but he knew this would not break their spirit, nor would Nazi propaganda, however clever, make them love Hitler or what he stood for.

Reynaud said he agreed with Churchill and that, when they met again, he hoped it would be to discuss ways and means of continuing their joint war.

Churchill had one more point to make: he did not wish to leave, he said, before putting it, for he attached great importance to it. There were in France several hundred German pilots held as prisoners. Many of them had been brought down by the R.A.F. They constituted a great danger. He asked Reynaud to agree to their being sent to England forthwith, where they would be out of harm's way. He considered the matter urgent. He would like orders to be given that very evening to put his request into effect.

Reynaud at once agreed, and said he would issue the necessary instructions forthwith.

Churchill thanked him, and said that during the next forty-eight hours, while the President's answer was awaited, the British disembarkation in France would continue.

Reynaud expressed gratitude at this. He said that the point of view he had put forward earlier was purely hypothetical. The case would only arise if the President's answer was unfavourable. In that eventuality, however, a new situation would have arisen which would involve grave consequences. He had wished the Prime Minister to be informed of this at once.

Churchill's comment was that this would perhaps prove to be the Allies' darkest hour. "Whether or not this be so," he said, "my conviction that Hitler and all that he stands for will be smashed, and that Nazism will not reign over Europe, remains entire." Reynaud, showing emotion for the first time, said rather pathetically that he also maintained complete faith in the future, for otherwise life would not be worth living.

And that was the end of the conference.

Everyone got up, watches were consulted, people moved to the window to look at the sky, exchanging views on the weather. It was 5.50 p.m.

We walked downstairs. In the courtyard was a small crowd, perhaps a hundred persons, some in uniform, others, journalists, in plain clothes. They were a sad-faced, sombre little gathering, anxious for a word, for a crumb of comfort.

Churchill had disappeared. I learnt presently that he had gone into a room on the ground floor and there seen Jeanneney and Herriot. I have little doubt they told him of their resolve to throw all the weight of their great positions and personalities into the scales in favour of continued resistance. I very soon had reason to regret not having been there, for within the next few days statements which I am sure Churchill never made during that interview were attributed to him. He reappeared in less than ten minutes and got into the Ambassador's car. I thought I had better remain at the *Préfecture* and ascertain what the next move was to be.

As I stood in the doorway, de Gaulle appeared. He had, as I have noted, joined the conference late, but had taken no part in the discussion. He called me aside and said that Baudouin was putting it about to all and sundry, notably to the journalists, that Churchill had shown complete comprehension of the French situation and would understand if France concluded an armistice and a separate peace. I noted his words: "... *que l'Angleterre comprendrait si la*

France faisait un armistice et une paix séparée." Had Churchill really said that? de Gaulle asked. It would be most unfortunate if he had, for it would give the defeatists the right to say: "What is the good of fighting on when even the English do not expect us to?" And also it would deeply affect others who were not prepared to break unilaterally France's pledge to England not to make a separate peace.

I asserted that the Prime Minister could not have made anything approaching such a statement after the conference, for at it he had clearly indicated the contrary. What he had said in French, when the idea was indicated by Reynaud, was "*Je comprends*" (I understand) in the sense of "I understand what you say," not in the sense of "I agree".* "Have you been with him the whole time?" asked de Gaulle. "Yes, excepting at lunch when Baudouin joined him. He would never have made an important statement to him, quite apart from the fact he was going to see Reynaud in a few moments. I was not in the room when he saw Jeanneney and Herriot. But I have every reason to believe he was even less likely to have made such a declaration then than earlier, for he had in the meantime had the opportunity of consulting his colleagues, who were as opposed to the idea as he was. Furthermore, the two Presidents would not only not have made such a suggestion to him, they would have been, I am sure, opposed to his making it."

"Well, that's what Baudouin is saying. He is putting it about that France is now released from her engagement to England. It is unfortunate."

"I will see if I can catch the Prime Minister before he leaves," I said and, running out, I found my car and pelted after the English party. At the aerodrome all the planes were revving up against the dismal background of smashed hangars and a bomb-pitted runway.

I told Churchill of Baudouin's effort, and got from him absolute and categorical confirmation that at no time had he given to anyone the least indication of his consenting to the French concluding a separate armistice. "When I said '*Je comprends*', that meant I understand. *Comprendre* means understand in French, doesn't it? Well," said Winston, "when for once I use exactly the right word in their own language, it is going rather far to assume that I intended it

---

* Several times while Reynaud was speaking the Prime Minister had nodded or said "*Je comprends*," indicating his understanding of the words before they were translated.

to mean something quite different. Tell them my French is not so bad as that."*

He beamed. "Shay——" But I did not hear the rest, lost in the roar of the engine. He clutched his hat, bent his head to the draught of the propellers, waved his stick, and the precious, lovable man was off. I gazed upward, in a moment the Flamingo and its escort had disappeared. I prayed for his safe return with total fervour.

---

* The importance of this incident, and the use Baudouin made of the Prime Minister's phrase "*Je comprends*" is illustrated by the following telegram sent by Admiral Darlan:

"All (French) warships from (French) Admiralty. Secret. 5124 to 5127. 17.45.23/6 (5.45 p.m. 23rd June 1940)."

(1) *Since from imperative reasons the legal* [(*sic*) i.e. the legal government] (my italics) of France has begun armistice negotiations with Germany and Italy a violent campaign has been undertaken over the wireless, and even by foreign agents, to bring about confusion and disunion amongst Frenchmen. . . .

(6) It should not be forgotten that the British Prime Minister, informed on June 11th (*sic*) of the necessity in which France found herself of bringing the struggle to an end, declared that *he understood* (my italics) that necessity and accepted it without withdrawing his sympathy from our country. He is therefore not qualified to speak otherwise.

CHAPTER XV

Thursday, June 13th

(3)

*Mandel's account of the French Cabinet meeting that evening
—Weygand's outburst—The Cabinet meeting on the 12th—
The French Ministers wish to meet Churchill—Their
astonishment at his departure without seeing them—and
their reproach of Reynaud — The mystery of Reynaud's
failure to inform Churchill—A terrible mistake—Campinchi remains firm about the Fleet—Pétain supports
Weygand's demand for an armistice—A Cabinet majority in
favour of surrender—The effect of Churchill's absence—
Reynaud's ghastly appearance—Mandel on Madame de
Portes—The* mous *and the* durs—My renewed admiration of
Mandel—I report to the Ambassador—We prepare to move
to Bordeaux—The consequences of Reynaud's failure to
arrange a meeting between Churchill and the French
Ministers—A misleading impression given to the British of
the French Cabinet's attitude—Reynaud's diminished
authority.*

AFTER seeing the English party off, I returned to the *Préfecture* at
Tours. Everyone had gone, and as usual there was no one to say
whither the participants in the late conference had betaken themselves. Thinking Reynaud had probably returned to Chissay, I
battled my way there through the sinister refugee columns, which
presently froze into immobility as darkness fell. When I arrived at
Chissay it was only to be told by Margerie that the Premier was
attending a Cabinet meeting at the President of the Republic's
château at Cangé, near Tours. Margerie believed the main question
to be decided was whether the Government was to leave next day.

So back I went after a short and nasty meal at Chenonceaux. The
long-suffering chauffeur had lost his buoyancy as he once more
wound his way through the ghostly refugee columns, but we found

the château without much difficulty. There were no sentries at the gate, not even a policeman at the door. It was sinister. In the vast gloomy hall a forlorn *huissier* (usher) went to find someone. An individual, presumably a member of the President's household, appeared and told me that the Ministers had left and the President had retired.

To my enquiries as to whom I could get into touch with to find out what had occurred, he told me that Mandel was at Tours, at the *Préfecture*. So I went there, to find him sitting at the *Préfet's* desk, cold and precise as usual. He was so detached that when he spoke he might have been a biologist informing a colleague of the strange antics of some lower form of animal when submitted to an unusual test. He began by telling me that Weygand had tried to panic the Cabinet that evening by asserting that the Communists had taken charge in Paris, that Maurice Thorez was installed at the Élysée, that the mob had disarmed the police and the Republican Guard, and that telephone communications with Paris were severed. He was, said Mandel, beside himself with excitement.

Mandel knew this to be absurd as he had been speaking to the *Préfet de Police* in Paris half an hour earlier, so he adopted the simple course of calling up the *Préfet* and asking Weygand to come over to the telephone. He was put through at once and said to the Prefect that General Weygand, who was standing beside him, had been informed that the Communists had assumed control in Paris and that mob rule prevailed. "I am handing the receiver to General Weygand, will you please tell him the position." There was a curious gleam in Mandel's glaucous eyes as he described Weygand's obvious discomfiture as he listened to the *Préfet*.

But it appeared that the rebuff had only affected Weygand temporarily, for a moment later he informed the Ministers that the Government should have remained in Paris, taking example from the Roman Senate which had awaited the Barbarians in Rome.

"What good would that have done?" I asked in amazement. "They would have been collected by the Germans, put in a Black Maria and driven to an unknown destination."

"Exactly," said Mandel. "Weygand revealed by that sentence his desire to be rid of them.

"Weygand went on to say that the Government, having lacked the courage to remain in Paris, should at least have the pluck to declare it would not leave France under any circumstances."

"It sounds as if he had been rather rude," I said. "He was," answered Mandel, "either of deliberate purpose or because he was hysterical." "Do you mean no one put him in his place?" "No," said Mandel, "nor when he said he intended to place General de Gaulle under arrest for having taken steps to send men and material to North Africa without consulting him. After all," commented Mandel, "de Gaulle is a Minister—not that Weygand worries about Ministers. He accused us of being incapable of coming to a decision, and said that those amongst us who were die-hards were only covering our lack of courage by verbal bravery."

"This is fantastic," I exclaimed. "Do you mean no one said anything, not even the President of the Republic?"

"I did something," said Mandel, "I smiled, whereupon Weygand said he was being insulted, gathered up his skirts like a furious prima donna and, without even a bow before the curtain, flounced out. He was so beside himself that he remarked before my private secretary that the Ministers were mad and ought to be arrested."

It was my turn to smile. It took no great effort to picture the scene. "But surely there was more to it than that. He must have said something besides hurling insults at the Government?"

Mandel then told me what had occurred at the Cabinet meeting of the previous evening (the 12th). Weygand had described the situation much in the same terms as he had at Briare, but I pricked up my ears when I heard that he had informed the Cabinet that Churchill had refused fighter support.*

Otherwise all he had added to his general *exposé* was the statement that the situation had worsened. The Seine was crossed at many points. The panzers were moving across the open country of Champagne. There were no reserves. He had raised the spectre of anarchy and drawn a terrible picture of refugees and troops inextricably mixed and without food, uncontrolled and famished, ravaging the countryside, and had concluded by requesting the Government to sue for an armistice.

His general thesis, said Mandel, was that if the French found the

* On the night of the 13th General Weygand's Chief of Staff had seen Air Marshal Barratt, bearer of a message from Churchill to Reynaud. The message stated that in addition to the 6 bomber and 5 fighter squadrons of the R.A.F. in France, the French would dispose of 60 Blenheims and 10 fighter squadrons based on England which would intervene as far as their range of action would allow, and of 180 night bombers. (Weygand, *Rappelé au Service*, p. 221.)

armistice terms of the Germans too unpleasant, all they had to do
was reject them.

"How can anybody seriously make such a statement?" I exclaimed. "After Czechoslovakia and at the time of Munich I read, at
meeting after meeting in my constituency, extracts from Hitler's *Mein
Kampf* dealing with exactly that point. Common sense, historical
experience and what has happened of late in Europe proves the
Führer right when he says that 'a country that has laid down its
arms will not under any circumstances take them up again.' Was
there no one to tell Weygand that?" "No," Mandel answered, and
went on to say that a majority of the Cabinet had undoubtedly
supported Reynaud, who was emphatically in favour of continuing
the war from North Africa.* There was opposition to this, but he
finally satisfied everybody by saying he would ask Churchill to return
as soon as possible.

"Why were we not told?" I asked, my sense of grievance returning.
"Weren't you?" said Mandel. "One of the disadvantages of this
situation is that no one knows what anybody else knows or doesn't

* M. Bouthillier, the Minister of Finance, who was a supporter of Weygand,
has noted what Reynaud said on the subject of an armistice at this meeting.
"The German conditions are already fixed. . . . Be certain they include the
occupation of all our harbours and the use of our Fleet against England.
Such will be the answer of the Reich to our request for an armistice. We
shall have committed a cowardly action for no purpose. Think of England.
We have signed the undertaking not to conclude a separate peace. We cannot
speak to the enemy without our ally's agreement. We have an immense interest
in respecting this pact. Today it is not burdensome, for England expects
nothing of us beyond that we should keep our pledged word. We on the other
hand expect everything of England, and it is impossible to conceive the future
of France without the friendship or the support of the Anglo-Saxon world."
(*Le Drame de Vichy*, Vol. I, p. 58.)

Edouard Herriot in *Épisodes*, 1940–1944, (p. 61) writes that Dautry produced
that night (12th), at a meeting at Reynaud's residence at Chissay, a note he
had written at 2 p.m. that afternoon. It ran:

"The armistice would have as a consequence a rupture between Anglo-
Saxon democracy and ourselves. It would lead to the dismemberment of the
nation and for many generations the enslavement of the parcel of territory to
which France would be reduced. Franco-British naval power, with the support
of America, assures us in default of liberty of manœuvre on our invaded soil
freedom of action in the world. This liberty may allow the reconstruction
around the nucleus of the present Anglo-French Army of an immense army
which will later be in a position to disembark along the long ribbon of the
French shores under the protection of a formidable aviation. Thus in 1943, or
in 1944 or 1945, we shall be powerful enough to crush Germany and to rebuild
on the ruins and misery of our country a new France, if we have saved her
soul."

know. In fact no one was aware Churchill had even received the invitation till he arrived at Tours."

The *Réduit Breton* had received short shrift, it seemed, Weygand asserting there were no troops whatever to defend it. He added amiably that the *réduit* had never existed save in the *Président du Conseil's* imagination. "So," went on Mandel, "instead of going to Nantes, the Government will move to Bordeaux. It is going there tomorrow. By the way, will you tell the Ambassador the Embassy staff must leave for Bordeaux not later than ten tomorrow morning?"

The meeting that evening had started badly. He had driven to Cangé with Reynaud. They had found the members of the Government walking about in the park in a drizzle. When they heard that Reynaud had seen Churchill, who had just left for England, some were taken aback, others were aggrieved, none were pleased.

Some Ministers told Reynaud they had been tricked, reminding him, several forcibly, that he had told them he would ask Churchill to discuss the situation with them.

"Did he?" I asked, a horrible cold feeling creeping over me. "He certainly did," answered Mandel.*

"But he never gave Churchill the least indication of this," I exclaimed, feeling something disastrous had occurred.

With growing indignation I said: "Why did *you* not tell Churchill; *you* knew?"

"As you are aware, I was not present at the Supreme Council

---

* The President of the Republic writes (*Témoignage*, p. 77): "A great disappointment found expression in the Council. M. Chautemps used bitter words; other Ministers echoed his expressions. They would have been glad to obtain contact with the British statesmen at the critical moment when France was in mortal peril. Perhaps, in fact, their presence would have reaffirmed a resistance to which they attached so high a price."

Reynaud himself writes of the Cabinet meeting held on the 12th . . . "and it was decided that Churchill be invited to appear before the Cabinet next day." (*La France a sauvé l'Europe*, Vol. II, p. 316.) And the President of the Republic, M. Lebrun: "The Cabinet dispersed, expressing the wish to hear the British Prime Minister at the next meeting." (*Témoignage*, p. 76).

Baudouin writes under date the 12th: "M. Paul Reynaud will ask Mr. Churchill to come to France tomorrow. He will ask him to give his views to the French Ministers." (*Neuf Mois au Gouvernement*, p. 50.)

Weygand writes: "In conclusion, the President of the Council stated that he had promised Mr. Churchill not to decide anything without having seen him again. He would ask him to come to France next day and would ask him to lay before the French Ministers his war programme. No decision would be taken until this was done." (*Rappelé au Service*, p. 150.)

meeting," answered Mandel coldly. "I naturally thought the two Prime Ministers had discussed the matter and that it had been found that Churchill could not spare the time. After all, if he had not left when he did, he could not have reached England before dark." I told him I was certain that, had the Prime Minister had the faintest idea that the French Ministers wished to see him, he would have grasped the vital importance of meeting them and stayed on. "Why did Reynaud not mention this?"   "I don't know," said Mandel. "Perhaps he just forgot. Perhaps he felt Churchill could only have told the others what he had told him, so considered the meeting unnecessary." I knew that if this was true a terrible mistake had been made. I sensed that all these Frenchmen were looking to Churchill for a lead. I knew the formidable impact his eloquence and will always had on his auditors. I felt he might have carried them with him in his determination to fight on. He was the leader they really recognised and looked to. They would have feared his scorn and been glad to lay some at least of the responsibility they found so irksome on his broad shoulders.

Something perhaps irreparable had happened. An opportunity that might not recur had been missed.

I was so depressed by this news that I carried on the rest of the conversation rather perfunctorily, putting my questions with no great zest.

Had the Fleet been discussed?

Yes, for quite half an hour, and Campinchi had been very firm on the subject. Yesterday already he had made the point that the question of the Fleet alone made an armistice impossible, for it was inconceivable that it should pass into German hands and be used against the British. When the question came up again this evening he was strongly supported by Monnet and Marin, who argued that there was no point in asking for an armistice unless the Government was prepared to hand over the Fleet to the enemy. An armistice would inevitably end in the Germans controlling the Fleet, they declared. They had used the word infamous in describing such a transaction.

Weygand had answered that he would oppose any such idea, and was in favour of the Fleet sailing for North Africa, but the others had countered by saying that this would not prevent the Germans from insisting as part of the armistice terms that the Fleet should be surrendered.

"So no conclusion was reached?" "No, none," answered Mandel, "beyond deciding to await Roosevelt's answer.

"I gathered the impression," went on Mandel, "that the Cabinet might finally decide to scuttle the Fleet before asking for an armistice."

Mandel also told me that Pétain had read a statement in which he fully supported Weygand's demand for an armistice. He had declared that the Government must remain in France whatever happened. If they failed to do so they ran the risk of being repudiated. A very clear threat. There had also been a lot about killing the soul of France by running away to Africa.

Well, there was nothing unexpected in Pétain's attitude. Mandel made it clear that Reynaud on the other hand had stoutly maintained that an armistice would drive a fatal wedge between France and Britain, and consequently alienate the United States, on which the only hope of recovery rested.

I gathered that one way or another much heat had been generated.

Mandel's conclusion was that, although a vote for continuing the war would probably have been obtained yesterday, today, had one been taken, it would in all probability have been in favour of surrender.

The immense prestige Pétain had in the country had weighed heavily with Ministers who the day before were for fighting on. They hesitated to pit their authority against his popularity. This weighed more with them than Weygand's hysteria and scolding.

The bad impression and the ill-temper caused by the disappointment of not seeing Churchill had been the background of the discussion and undoubtedly played its part in swaying the majority of the Cabinet towards surrender. To these bewildered men the picture of Churchill flying off to his own country without seeing them gave them a feeling of being abandoned. Churchill would not confer with them, left them to their own devices? What could they do, when there was nothing left to fight with in France, and their most eminent soldiers advised surrender? It took a stout heart to opt for continued resistance now that the impression had been gained that Britain was cutting adrift. To be responsible, yet to be in flight, the forerunners of a flying army, with nothing solid on which to build either a plan or a hope, was dreadful indeed.

Mandel had been silent for a while, and I had been brooding over what he had said, when the door opened and Reynaud himself appeared. I presumed that he had just given the broadcast I had heard he was to deliver.* What he had said did not seem to matter under the circumstances. I certainly did not care, nor, I think, did Mandel. Reynaud looked ghastly, with a completely unnatural expression, still and white. He said nothing, just stood there in the dim light by the door. "Have you any news?" he finally asked Mandel. "No." "And Paris?" "No."

Thinking he might wish to speak to Mandel privately, I offered to go, but he shook his head and looked at the telephone on the desk. If he had wanted to telephone he changed his mind, turned on his heels and walked out. He had not been gone five minutes when Madame de Portes threw the door open.

Mandel and I stared in astonishment. We were so taken aback that neither of us got up. We hardly had time to. She wore the only expression I have ever seen on her face, hostile and aggressive. She looked round quickly, evidently seeking Reynaud. Her swift glance searched every corner, it darted under the table as if the Premier might have been hiding there. She then stepped back into the shadowy corridor, fixing us after the manner of a burglar covering householders as he retreats. As the door closed Mandel said: "Her influence has been sinister this day." Answering his thought, I said how horrified I had been at the change in Reynaud since the morning, to which Mandel replied: "He is very subject to influence."

Had he driven with her from Chissay to Tours? Had she had lunch alone with him? I do not know.

Mandel gave me the list of Ministers he described as "*mous*", defeatists, and of those prepared to fight on, the "*durs*". Starting with the *mous* he named Delbos, my opposite number on the Parliamentary Anglo-French Committee. I would not believe it. "Well," said Mandel, "that is my impression." But in the days to come Delbos' actions proved me right.

To my further amazement he then named Ybarnegaray, a gallant Basque who had fought with distinction in the First War and had

---

* In this broadcast Reynaud had made an appeal to the United States. He asked America to give France, even from afar, the hope of victory, necessary for every fighting man. To the French he said that the power of the democracies, in spite of their reverses, remained immense . . . "the French will have to suffer, let them be worthy of the nation's past." He had a sentence aimed at Pétain, Weygand, and the defeatist Ministers: "In the course of the great trials of our history our people have known days when counsels of weakness may have troubled her. It is because they never abdicated that they remained great."

been anti-Munich. "But he was a good soldier," I said. "Well, he is too much of a soldier now," said Mandel. "After listening to Pétain he sat back in his chair and declared: 'I am a soldier, my Chiefs have spoken, I obey'."

"This is unbelievable."

But Mandel was going on with his *mous*. "Chautemps is particularly dangerous. In that wonderful voice of his he depicts the misery of the refugees in their cars. He always ends by giving a heart-rending account of the poor old grandmother in the back seat weighed down with babies and a cage full of canaries. The old lady he elects to tell us about always has '*très mal au ventre*'—a bad pain in her inside. The account invariably affects our colleagues deeply." In Bordeaux I was to hear the story from Chautemps himself. Mandel proved to have been word for word accurate.

He then proceeded to develop the theme of Chautemps' action on the Cabinet. He was influential with the Left, and had been loyal to Reynaud until now but seemed unable to stand the strain. He had taken up a definite position in opposition to Reynaud that afternoon. Bouthillier was another.

Prouvost was a sinister influence. In the main he was plain scared. For the moment he was more frightened at the idea of leaving France than at any other. He had too much wealth to like the idea of abandoning it. Then Baudouin of course, "*cela va sans dire*." That made up the de Portes team. Pomaret was for an armistice. Queuille and Chichery were weak, hesitant and therefore *mous*.*

The *durs* included that splendid old conservative, Louis Marin, and of course Campinchi. Georges Monnet would not hear of allowing Great Britain to stand and fight alone. Rollin, the Minister of the Colonies, was also firm, as was Rio, and the simple, straightforward Dautry, who went on insisting that the young men should be sent to North Africa. Sérol, the Socialist, had kept a cool head and calmly argued against an armistice.

I left Mandel more impressed by him than ever. His detachment and objectivity in all this confusion was indeed astonishing. A very curious man. One side of his mind was watching the antics of his colleagues with ironical amusement. The spectacle of all this weakness fascinated him, while the problem of unravelling the motives of each one absorbed him, for it was a game he had become

* Pomaret and Chichery joined Pétain's Government, as did Ybarnegaray.

expert in long ago when serving Clemenceau, and had practised ever since. The other side of his mind was watching events through those eyes that were like thimbles full of sea water, behind which lay the cold alertness of a barracuda always ready to pounce with startling rapidity on anything that passed within its vision. If it was possible to be fond of a fish I should have been fond of Mandel. For he was like a fish if you could imagine one with the straight damp locks of black hair hanging like seaweed over its gills. I expected him to pounce on the defeatists at any moment. But the opportunity did not come in time, or, perhaps, the fear that his religion might weaken his authority held him back.*

On my return to Champchevrier at about midnight, I told the Ambassador about the move to Bordeaux and he gave orders accordingly. He also sent out warning messages to George Vanier, the Canadian Minister, and Colin Bain Marais, the South African, who were at some distance from the château. This was the first intimation the Embassy had had of so early a move, for the telephone had again given out. A great bustle ensued. I told him what Mandel had said. We discussed the possibilities of the situation, as was inevitable, but we knew there was nothing we could do. I thought it would be prudent to ask for a destroyer to be sent to the mouth of the Gironde, and he agreed to my making the suggestion to the Prime Minister.

When I told Mack about this, a twinkle in his eye warned me that he thought a soldier was readier to see to his retreat than a diplomat, but presently we were glad enough that the destroyer was sent; that, however, is another story. We explained in the telegram that if we left we should have to evacuate some fifty people, including the Canadian and South African Legations.

Mack told me that the first indication the Embassy had received of Churchill's visit to Tours was when he heard Commander Thompson his A.D.C's voice on the telephone, saying "We're here." "Where?" the astonished Mack asked. When told, he gave Thompson some indications as to where the various French authorities were to be found. He tried but failed to get through to Chissay to warn the Ambassador. He could not have guessed his *patron* was

* Baudouin thus describes Mandel at the Cabinet meeting that evening: "M. Mandel, silent today as he was yesterday, a fortress of contempt whose eyes of ice are amused to observe in his colleagues fear and a mediocrity which exceeded even his most pessimistic expectation." (*Neuf Mois au Gouvernement*, p. 163).

enjoying at that moment an excellent meal at the *Bon Laboureur*.

I worked late on a long telegram reporting to the Prime Minister what had occurred since he had left that afternoon. Mack and I worked alongside, each at our own tasks, but shared a remarkably good bottle of brandy he had unearthed from somewhere. It kept us awake and provided, as I remember it, if not a silver lining, at least a golden aroma to the black cloud encompassing us.

I cannot pretend that I appreciated to the full at the time the extremely serious consequences of Reynaud's failure to arrange a meeting between the Prime Minister and the French Cabinet. The circumstances succeeding each other were too catastrophic for it to be possible to analyse the effects of either recent or past events. Every hour as it sped by went into the discard, all attention being riveted on the next, certain to bring its own evil tidings. It was not unlike sitting in a trench under a bombardment. Each shell that hurtled past was forgotten while the ear strained for the sound of the next.

The evidence of the disappointment, even dismay, of the French Cabinet, when they heard Churchill had been literally round the corner from where they were collected to meet him, is overwhelming. Their amazement that he should have left without seeing them is entirely comprehensible.*

Why did Reynaud act as he did? It is difficult to believe, but it is not impossible, that, as Mandel said, he forgot his promise to his colleagues. He may have thought that his seeing Churchill amounted to the same thing as Churchill meeting the Cabinet. If that is so, it was a grave mistake. To repeat Churchill's views meant little to them. They had already been told what he had said at Briare. What they required was that the doubts of each should be dealt with, their

---

* "Those French Ministers who had remained at Tours saw the British Ministers get into cars and hastened to the Château of Cangé, not doubting that Mr. Churchill and his colleagues were going there also. On arriving there they found the majority of the members of the Government in the park, together with General Weygand, who had been waiting there for the end of the Supreme Council Meeting. They learned, a few moments later, on the arrival of the President of the Council and M. Mandel, that the British Premier, having left for London, would not be present at the Cabinet meeting specially convened to meet him. This led to something more than astonishment. There was surprise, disappointment on all faces, when the Ministers found that Mr. Churchill was not there. M. Camille Chautemps expressed his disapprobation loudly in angry terms. The Council of Ministers opened in a glacial atmosphere." (Baudouin, *Neuf Mois au Gouvernement*, p. 169).

questions answered. Reynaud certainly could not do that. The Ministers would not accept him as a substitute for Churchill, or believe he was in a position to deal with their queries concerning the potential of England's effort and her determination. They naturally believed that a defenceless Britain could not succeed where their Army, which they had thought so strong, had failed. Only Churchill could have persuaded them that Britain not only had a chance but genuinely believed in ultimate victory.*

Had the French Cabinet and Weygand met Churchill at Tours it is unlikely that Weygand would have said at Bordeaux a few days later: "England's neck will be wrung like a chicken's"; or that, if he had said it, he would have been believed.

Did Reynaud fear Weygand's explosions, or to expose to Churchill his lack of grip on his own Government? That is scarcely likely; he had held Weygand in check at Briare in Churchill's presence. Weygand would hardly have dared behave in the presence of the British Prime Minister as he had at the Cabinet meeting on the 13th.

A touch of vanity perhaps led Reynaud to desire to handle the situation himself. Till then he had dealt with Churchill; would it not be an abdication to surrender this position? Could he not best interpret the French Cabinet to the Prime Minister and the Prime Minister to them? How could he acknowledge even to himself that his own Cabinet looked more to the Englishman than to him? Did he not feel, though he would not admit it, that had Churchill appeared in person he would have been effaced?

No one will ever know why Reynaud acted as he did. It is unlikely that he himself is quite sure.

Of one thing only can one be certain: Reynaud miscalculated his own position and the mentality of his colleagues. He did not realise on the 12th that they only supported him conditionally because he promised to produce Churchill next day. Or perhaps he did realise it as an afterthought, and resented the implication of the

---

* Reynaud's own explanation is very unconvincing; he writes: "In fact, this conference took time and he (Churchill) had to return to London without having expressed to me the desire to see my colleagues." (*La France a sauvé l'Europe*, Vol. II, p. 319). It is impossible to imagine Churchill's suggesting he should meet the French Cabinet without being invited to do so. Had he done so, French Ministers at the time and French historians of the future would have been very indignant; they would have averred Churchill had attempted to dominate and bully the French Government.

request, whilst failing to appreciate the violence of the reaction disappointment would engender and the fury of Weygand's onslaught or the cold determination of Pétain.

What is even more strange is that Reynaud should have conveyed to the British Ministers so inaccurate an account of the attitude of his own Cabinet.

The impression he gave during the meeting was that, unless the Americans declared war forthwith, France must sue for peace.

It is true that he indicated that he would not be a member of the Government that did so. But that was a small matter in no way affecting the issue.

There is no record in his own account of the meeting on the 12th or in that of any other person who was present of the Cabinet having decided to ask him to take this line. All they had decided was that they wanted to hear Churchill. Reynaud may have concluded that the Ministers would in fact tell the Prime Minister that France could not carry on the war, but that is not what they had decided on the evening before his meeting with Churchill. On the contrary, as he had told the Ambassador and myself, he had himself strongly urged the case for continuing the war and been supported by a majority of his colleagues in saying so.*

Perhaps he thought that by taking the line he did, he would ensure

---

* Bouthillier quotes Weygand's testimony at the Pétain trial on July 31st, 1945. Referring to the Cabinet meeting of July 13th, he said: "Two Ministers, M. Bouthillier and M. Chautemps, noted one after the other two facts: The fact that, the *Président du Conseil* having promised that M. Winston Churchill should be heard by the Council, M. Winston Churchill left without having been heard. The second and by far the more important point was that *M. le Président du Conseil* told M. Winston Churchill that the Government had taken the decision not to conclude an armistice and to continue the war, whereas, the day before, the Government had declared it would take no decision." (*Le Drame de Vichy*, p. 66).

Lebrun (*Témoignage*, p. 78): "M. Bouthillier . . . concluded by saying that the Cabinet had not decided on the previous day against an armistice. I was forced to make a contrary assertion, invoking the testimony of General Weygand himself."

Herriot (*Épisodes*, p. 63): "On an observation by Bouthillier, President Lebrun, I was told, underlined the fact that the Cabinet had, the previous day, rejected an armistice."

Baudouin (*Neuf Mois au Gouvernement*, p. 160): "(Chautemps and Bouthillier) . . . declared that on the previous day the Cabinet had not decided against asking for an armistice, but simply asked for the advice of the British Government on this question. It had even been agreed that Mr. Churchill would explain—of course if he accepted to do so—his views to the members of the French Government."

Churchill's putting the maximum pressure on Roosevelt. If such was his idea it was as unnecessary as it was dangerous.

It was only after seeing Jeanneney and Herriot that Reynaud had said at the Tours conference that the point of view he had previously put forward was that which his Cabinet had asked him to state.

It may be that Reynaud merely played his cards badly at Tours, or failed to express his meaning, or perhaps those whom he had seen between the time the Ambassador and I left him in the morning and the meeting at the *Préfecture* in the afternoon had confused him as to where his duty lay.

All this is guessing. I do not know. By the time he was settled at Bordeaux he had recovered something of his equipoise.

What is now obvious is that by the night of Thursday, June 13th, the possibility of France remaining in the war had almost disappeared.

The British Ministers had left Tours with no great hopes. The subsequent meeting of the French Cabinet had made more tenuous an already slender chance. Reynaud's authority over his colleagues had been greatly diminished. Weygand had been openly rude to him and' had insulted the whole Cabinet without being called to book, and, as a result of it all, the question that affected the history of France for all time, the question which if wrongly resolved might tarnish her past as well as cast a shadow over her future for centuries, was made to depend not upon her own will and determination, but upon the decision of another nation, the United States, and the final word rested not with her own leaders, her Cabinet, her Prime Minister or her President, but with President Roosevelt.

CHAPTER XVI

Friday, June 14th

The journey to Bordeaux—Refugees block the roads— French Air Force convoys in retreat—Idle troops in the villages—The contrast with the First World War—Clemenceau and the troops in 1918—A sad leave-taking at Niort— Changed attitude of French civilians to a British uniform— Arrival in Bordeaux—Mandel provides us with rooms at the Hotel Montré—The German entry into Paris—Dinner at the Chapon Fin—Mandel's advice to the Ambassador—We decide to send joint dispatches—Churchill's moving message to the French Government—Mackenzie King's telegram— Reynaud's office in the rue Vital-Carles—His reaction to Churchill's message—His disappointment at Roosevelt's answer to his message of June 10th—His hopes of continuing the struggle from North Africa—The Ambassador and I report our impression of Reynaud—The defeatists swarm into Bordeaux.

THE night had been a short one. I cannot remember if we slept at all. The work done was no doubt largely wasted, as it is doubtful whether many of the messages we sent got through to London, for we were dependent on the French telegraph, Air Commodore Colyer's wireless being still out of order. The French telegraph service gave proof that it was working with great devotion to duty under impossible conditions, for now and then quite useless bundles of telegrams forwarded from Paris, and days old, were received at Champchevrier. Many dealt with routine matters that were part of a world that had ceased to exist.

We moved off by contingents at the time indicated. Madame de Champchevrier and one of her daughters were at the door; dressed in black, they might have been farmer folk, so simple were they. But a stout heart beat under the old lady's cotton blouse. She was not going to run away and abandon her place and people whatever

235

diplomats and soldiers with red tabs might do. *"On ne lâche pas,"* she said, speaking of herself and her family.

It was a lovely morning. The Ambassador took me in his car as far as Tours. We intended to find out if there was any news at the *Préfecture*, but the place was deserted.

The drive to within a mile of Tours along the pleasant country roads was easy and we gained much by approaching the town along the northern river-bank from the west; but within a mile of the bridge over the Loire we became engulfed in the flow of refugees, and were surrounded by cars with boiling radiators which the occupants at every halt took the opportunity of cooling down with cold water from cans they all seemed to carry. Progressing by foot-long jerks, the Ambassador's Rolls superbly driven with the authority of a chauffeur used to having the way cleared for him by the whistles of Paris policemen, we at last got over, and at the *Préfecture* I got into my car, which had been faithfully following in the wake of Sir Ronald's splendid machine. Gendarmes on motor-cycles cleared a way for us out of the town. As the road I had to follow ran very near the property of friends I knew well and stayed with most summers, I decided to lunch there, for I was anxious to know how they had fared so far.

There were many traffic jams, but by manœuvring round towns and villages I at last reached my destination. To my disappointment I found that the son of the house was alone in charge, a handsome fair little boy whom I had known the whole length of the years that made up his decade. Undismayed by the departure of his mother, who was mobilised and had left to rejoin her medical unit that morning, he presided at the enormous table at which sat some 20 or 30 refugee relatives from Belgium and the north. It was some satisfaction to find that my revolver and uniform impressed my small host, to whom hitherto I had been a sort of joke called "Uncle Smackchild", but the great and beautiful castle overlooking a sweeping valley seemed a sad and lonely place that day, full of the shadows of gay, very civilised parties and people.

The relatives from the north were full of their adventures and of strange and surprising tales of Fifth Columnists.

I tried to borrow a map of the country to the south, but in vain. Maps were the most precious things one could possess in those days, as my wife was to find during her flight across France. After bidding good-bye to the servants, who were old friends, to my boy host and his British governess, I went on my way, feeling I was closing a book that would never again be opened.

On we went, haunted by fear of a breakdown. I wrote as best I could on my knees. A word or so every minute, as the jolting allowed, but listening to the sound of the engine all the time.

By now the roads were clear, but every town and village swarmed with people.

I passed several long French Air Force convoys, their planes on enormous floats. Well-fed officers in touring cars led the way. In most of the convoys I saw there were also cars in which sat ladies whose ample proportions and commanding looks proclaimed them to be wives of senior officers.

These processions, which I had met with everywhere on my rare journeyings, the advance-guard of the flying armies, filled me with anger and contempt. Why was the French Air Force on the ground instead of in the air with our lads, trying to beat the swarming Luftwaffe off the helpless infantry?

Another strange fact: nearly all the towns and villages I passed through were full of gaping, idle soldiers. They were not in formations, just individuals in uniform, hanging about, evidently having been put down there and then forgotten. On the long run I must have seen many hundreds, perhaps several thousands. How came it then that we were constantly told that all resources in man-power had been exhausted; that every available man had been thrown into the battle? The answer seemed clear, the machinery of the Army had completely broken down.

During this horrible, depressing journey I endured the kind of sorrow that withers faith. All that I had believed in, worked and hoped for during so many years, could not now be recalled without pain. The finger of memory touching the past hurt as if probing a wound. What would all the brave and gallant French airmen I had known in the first war, de Rose, Guynemer, and so many others, think of these fat convoys and their sleek personnel ambulating like a herd of cows towards Bordeaux?

I thought of the book I had planned to write after *Prelude to Victory* published at the beginning of the war. It was to have been the story of the French mutinies in 1917. A fine and sad story of which the French Army had no reason to be ashamed. The book was to have ended on an incident in 1918, when the French forces, fully recovered, were awaiting the long-planned Ludendorff attack in Champagne. They had left a large zone in front of their main line of resistance, garrisoned by small bodies of troops only. It was hoped, and the hope was justified, that the Germans, believing this zone to be the main French position, would deploy to attack it and be exhausted and their *élan* and formations broken by the time they reached the real French line. The orders to the troops in this forward area were that they must not under any circumstances fall back. They were to hold out and be killed where they stood.

Clemenceau had gone one day to visit the doomed troops and had spoken to them in his gruff way, not minimising the sacrifice that was being asked of them. Their fate would have been his had he had his way, and the men knew it. They said nothing, but some of them went off and presently came back with a bouquet of such wild flowers as grow on the parapets of trenches, then, having formed a sort of deputation, presented him with their posy without saying anything. Clemenceau, who was the toughest, the hardest, and perhaps the most cruel man I have ever met, who had but one love, France, sobbed.

He did not say another word, but his huge shoulders shook now and then as he walked back to the rear, never turning his head as he went.

When he died, the faded posy was found in his desk with the instruction that when he was buried standing, as was his wish, it should be placed over his heart.

What would the terrible old "Tiger" have thought and felt had he stood on the Bordeaux road that day?

I stopped to see other friends near Niort. This also was a sad leave-taking. They had longed for a little good news but I had none to give them. Some were members of a scientific formation, important enough to justify my promising to help them reach England, where their work would contribute its quota to the winning of the war, but they felt they must stay where they were. They could not move without orders, even though they knew orders were unlikely to reach them.

Included in the group was a woman who had done much good in the world, whom I greatly admired and respected, a friend of my younger years. Her friendship had been precious to me for decades. Before I got into my car she walked away with bowed head and did not look back. I watched her, realising that she was going one way, I another. The signposts showed clearly that we were starting on widely divergent roads that were unlikely to meet again. Suddenly I

General de Gaulle

The German Entry into Paris

had a sense of loneliness and loss that epitomised everything I had so far felt. As I looked out of the back window of the moving car at the figure that still did not look back, I knew that the last tie that bound me to the France of my youth was severed.

Presently I noticed that the attitude of the people to the sight of an English uniform had changed. It was unmistakable. Individuals were morose if not hostile, their faces blank. My gay chauffeur felt it too, and was worried on behalf of his English charge, who was a friend by now, and whose feelings he did not wish to see offended. Finding it too difficult to express his emotions, he shrugged his shoulders and said: *"C'est la guerre,"* adding vindictively, *"une sale guerre, une saloperie de guerre, ah oui, pour ça, c'est une saloperie de guerre,"* feeling like all simple people the world over whose vocabulary is small, that reiteration of the same words in a different tone and with added expletives emphasises and amplifies the original thought.

On the outskirts of the dreary suburbs of Bordeaux we were stopped by a post of gendarmes. No one was to be allowed in, all traffic was being diverted. It took no great oratorical effort to explain to its rather sceptical commander that I was entitled to enter. When I presently ascertained the quality and variety of the individuals of both sexes who had found their way into the city, presumably past that very post, I felt rather foolish at having taken the trouble to justify my business.

I found the Embassy at the Consulate, superimposed on the original staff and horribly cramped for space. They had been allocated a château, the Château Filhot, 50 kilometres from Bordeaux. It was out of the question that we should be so far away when vital questions had to be dealt with hour by hour and even minute by minute, so Mandel had again come to the rescue and got us rooms at the Hotel Montré, close to the Consulate and across the road from the *Chapon Fin*, where we had all our meals. The Ambassador had kindly kept me the room next to his.

I was told the Germans had entered Paris that morning. What a jab of pain that expected news gave!* I put calls through to the

* When notified that Paris was an open town, the Germans had demanded that no resistance be offered either by troops or by the population, either in Paris or north of the line St. Germain, Versailles, Juvisy, St. Maur and Meaux, otherwise the city would be treated as being in the war zone.

General Weygand telegraphed his acceptance of this condition. (*Rappelé au Service*, p. 221.)

Préfets in a number of towns to ask if by any chance there was any news of my wife's unit. Answers came from some during the night. None had heard anything of it.

During dinner at the *Chapon Fin*, discreetly supervised at a distance by the white-bearded proprietor of that remarkable establishment, where the best food in Europe is served in a room imitating a rockery, the Ambassador told me he had seen Mandel, who thought it extremely important that no opportunity should be lost of emphasising to Reynaud and to any other member of the French Government we came in contact with that the British Government had no intention of condoning a separate peace by France. This would, in Mandel's view, both strengthen Reynaud's own attitude and provide him with a powerful argument in the Cabinet.

Campbell said he would emphasise this to Baudouin, who was, thank goodness, his special responsibility, next day. He also told me that Mandel had informed Reynaud that I had been profoundly shocked by his attitude at Tours. He had thought it would do him good to know this. I wondered what the effect on Reynaud would be. I was soon to find out.

The Ambassador suggested that from now on we should work in even closer touch than heretofore. He proposed that, as he had to be in constant touch with Reynaud as Head of the French Government, and I had to keep similar contact with him in his capacity as Minister of Defence, we should, so far as possible, see him together and report by joint telegram. This arrangement might, he said, be extended to interviews with other persons whenever appropriate and practicable. I readily agreed.

We were both of one mind, and in the situation in which we found ourselves it was our evident duty to tender common advice and information to the Government at home. This new arrangement would relieve them from the necessity of comparing parallel reports and lighten the task of the overworked enciphering staff, who were labouring under greater difficulties than ever.

The first result of this joint enterprise was that we decided to see the Premier at once. There was a good reason for doing so. A telegram had been received from the Prime Minister for the French Government. It was a magnificent message but its purpose was unmistakable: by renewing Britain's undertaking to France it clearly demanded a similar assurance from France to Britain.

It paid homage to the constancy and courage of the French Army
in the face of common adversity and went on: "We seize this
opportunity to proclaim the indissoluble union of our two peoples
and of our two Empires . . . the ordeal by fire will only fuse
them together into one unconquerable whole. We renew to the
French Republic our pledge and resolve to continue the struggle at
all costs in France, in this Island, upon the oceans and in the air,
wherever it may lead us, using all our resources up to the utmost
limit, and sharing together the burden of repairing the ravages of
war. We shall never turn from the conflict until France stands safe
and erect in all her grandeur . . ."

Very moving messages had been sent to Reynaud by the
Dominions. Notably Mackenzie King had telegraphed in the name
of Canada: "We have followed, with the pride of blood, the heroic
action of your soldiers. Canada swears to France, as she has to Great
Britain, her complete support to the extreme limit of her forces and
resources. I have read your appeal to the United States. You may
rest assured that the peoples of North America are fully conscious of
the needs of the hour. I am certain that the support which, with the
full weight of its economic and material power, this continent is
affording the French Republic for the defence of the sacred cause for
which she is fighting, will be accelerated to a rhythm as yet unknown.
The sacrifices and the devotion of France are an example to free men
the world over."

We tried but failed to get any answer from Reynaud's office, so
went there at 11 p.m. It was in the rue Vital-Carles, a few hundred
yards from our hotel, at the residence of the General Commanding
the Bordeaux Region. It was a very dark night. Seeing a sentry at the
gate we asked if this was where the Premier lived. He did not know.
We crossed a courtyard and reached a dimly-lit hall. There were tall
columns supporting part of the upper floor on the sides of the hall,
and a broad staircase. We walked up this. No one on the landing,
so we started down a passage whose darkness seemed compact of
futility and desolation. Hearing voices, we opened a door, and there
were Reynaud, Margerie and a couple of secretaries eating poached
eggs. It looked a convivial little gathering; the participants appeared
to have banished the war for the moment, and as we entered the
faces of all at that table reflected clearly that we had brought a
spectre with us into the brightly-lit little room. We were, in fact, an
awful bore. On being asked, but not pressed, to share the picnic

meal, we sat down. Campbell slowly translated word for word Churchill's telegram. Reynaud was evidently too exhausted for consecutive thought, but his native wit had not abandoned him.

Grasping the implication of the telegram, he showed some ill-humour. The thesis he had developed at Tours had failed, the British were determined to hold France to her pledge. Had he not realised this, the Ambassador's remarks would have removed any lingering doubts he might have had, for Campbell said in so many words that His Majesty's Government would not willingly accept that France should abandon the struggle. Evidently following the same line of thought as myself, Reynaud exclaimed: "It is all very well for Mandel to talk, but I have to face the possible resignations of Pétain and Weygand." Then, half-crossly, half-smiling, he said to the Ambassador but pointing at me: *"Ce Général devrait comprendre qu'hier j'avais à faire une communication de la part du Cabinet."**

I was not displeased at this, for it showed he had been roused by what I had told Mandel. Even a flick might help, and it was important he should realise that he could not avoid responsibility by invoking his colleagues.

As if we had been carrying on a conversation without words, Reynaud went on to say that the point of view he had expressed at Tours did not necessarily represent his own attitude. Unconsciously perhaps, and also because he was very tired, he was giving a different slant to his declaration of the day before, for he repeated that he had been speaking for others rather than for himself when he had asked the British Ministers what England would do if France renounced the struggle, which did not quite correspond with the facts.

He then told us that he had only received a fragmentary version of President Roosevelt's answer to his message of the 10th. As far as he could make out, it was disappointing, for it contained no promise of a declaration of war, which was what France so badly needed to encourage her to continue the struggle. Reynaud added that he had that morning sent the American President a telegram in still stronger terms than that of the 10th. (This latter telegram was the one he had decided to send after the Tours meeting.)

Then he harked back to Roosevelt's telegram, naturally attaching more importance to the President's answer than to his own com-

* "This General ought to understand that yesterday I had to make a communication on behalf of the Cabinet."

munication. Roosevelt had, it seemed, referred with satisfaction to Reynaud's previous statement that the French Government would continue the struggle from North Africa, and he cheered us up by indicating that this was still his intention. He gave real substance to this assurance by telling us that he had sent de Gaulle to London to see what we could afford in the way of transport for troops and war material to North African harbours.

This was distinctly hopeful.

But the man was worn out. He began to talk of his colleagues who had nothing better to do than constantly press for Cabinet meetings. Again he seemed forlorn and undecided.

We took our leave, and, at the hotel, drew up our first joint telegram, giving a faithful account of what had occurred. We gave it as our opinion that Reynaud was swaying backwards and forwards under the impact of the defeatist Ministers, who were bent on forcing him to abandon his own inclination to fight on. We both felt that he had that evening been too tired and bewildered to be rational, and that what we had extracted from a turgid and disconnected flow of words could not be taken to express a policy or even a point of view. We strongly recommended that His Majesty's Government should make it perfectly clear that they would not in any way condone a separate peace by France, arguing that this was the best way of strengthening Reynaud against his defeatist colleagues.

As far as I was concerned I persisted in believing that this was the kind of message that would be most welcome to the real Reynaud.

That night I heard of the stream of new arrivals who were pouring into Bordeaux. The mistresses of Ministers who boasted such attachments, and most of them apparently did, were here *au grand complet*.

Mandel, with his lady, was at the *Préfecture*, Laval was at the Town Hall, guest of the defeatist Maire of Bordeaux, Marquet.

Another influential visitor was Reibel, a senator working for Weygand. He was, we were told, already intriguing hard for his *patron*. Thank goodness, Jeanneney was also here. But he and those who thought as he did were evidently outnumbered, for the moment at least, and I felt that night as if all the sewers in France had burst and that their nauseating mess was seeping into the beautiful city like a rising flood of abomination.

CHAPTER XVII

Saturday, June 15th

In the morning the Ambassador and I went to Reynaud's offices at
the *Quartier Général*, rue Vital-Carles, where we were shown the
full text of Roosevelt's telegram of the 13th.

We could find in it no grounds for the disappointment Reynaud had expressed the night before. The fragmentary text he had then seen must have omitted the most important and encouraging parts of the message.

Roosevelt said that the United States Government were not only doing everything in their power to send the Allies all the material they required, but were redoubling their efforts in this direction, and this because of American faith in and support for the ideals for which they were fighting.

It was gratifying to us that the President had seized upon and underlined Reynaud's declaration that France would go on fighting even if this meant withdrawing to North Africa and the Atlantic.

Particularly opportune was his reference to the fleets: the French and British Fleets retained the mastery of the seas; this, combined with the continued resistance of the British Empire, which he understood to be the attitude of the French Empire as well, still carried the lesson history attributes to naval power.

In our talk with Reynaud the Ambassador and I did not fail to point out that the President's promise of unlimited aid did amount to a form of belligerency.

It was difficult to believe that the United States, following the road indicated by Roosevelt, would not soon find itself involved in the war.

We also emphasised the President's obvious satisfaction at and support of the determination expressed by Reynaud to fight on outside France.

The impression Reynaud gave me that morning was one of lassitude. He still appeared to cling to his avowed determination of fighting on, but lacked the vigour I had often seen him display previously when rehearsing his battles with the defeatists. It was difficult not to feel he was weakening.

"Everything," he kept on repeating, "depends upon Roosevelt's answer to my last telegram." But I thought, perhaps because I did not believe the President's answer would come up to French hopes, that at heart he knew these hopes were an illusion which served no other purpose than to postpone decision. It was not an exhilarating interview.

The Ambassador left to get into touch with the French Foreign Office, and I remained on to see Margerie, for I knew General Brooke was to have seen Weygand and Georges the previous day, and

I wanted to know what had been decided as regards the employment of our troops.

Margerie had temporarily disappeared.

As I waited in a smallish room upstairs, Chautemps walked in. There were two other people there, whose names I do not remember. Chautemps sat down, and at once, in a musical, rhythmical wail, began to describe the sufferings of the refugees. It sounded like one of the more lachrymose psalms.

I was to remember that voice later at funerals in the Middle East when the paid mourners raised their voices in lament.

Chautemps would have made a stone weep. He evoked in tear-drenched words the hungry people searching the countryside for food long since devoured by others, the exposure of children in fields, the despair of the family whose car had run out of petrol, the motors thrown into ditches to clear the roads. It was very sad and very true. But when he came to describing the grandmother in the back of the car with *mal au ventre*, and used the very words I had heard attributed to him a day or two before, I suddenly felt exasperated by the sob-impregnated voice. I remembered all too well the demoralising effect pathetic or horrible incidents could have on the decisions of responsible men in war, so I interrupted him to say I had witnessed far worse incidents in the First War, but that the men who had won it had steeled themselves against them. How could the present peaceful, if uncomfortable, exodus compare, for instance, with such horrors as when the Germans drove women in front of them in Artois, and French troops had to shoot at them or be overrun? "They did it," I said, "and because they did they beat the Germans in the end." Then, getting angrier as I went on, I added that the grandmother might have *mal au ventre* today, but that, if France gave in, many Frenchmen would soon have *mal au derrière*, sore behinds, where the German boot kicked them; exasperated, I strode out of the room into a dusty gravelled courtyard, and was cooling off there when Ève Curie walked quickly towards me. My mood changed instantly as I saw her, moving gracefully and rapidly, hatless, and in the same blue and white dress she had worn at Chissay. I felt pleasure, then concern, when I saw her expression. It was strained and unhappy. "May I talk to you?" she said. "It is important, very important."

Then suddenly and passionately: "This place is full of defeatists. And, don't you see it, they are all double-crossing you, don't you realise that? There is a neat little plan for a French Government to stay and surrender while Paul Reynaud, just to save his face, slinks off. He will have made a gesture, the man who signed the Treaty with you will not repudiate it, he will go, but the others will remain and come to terms with the Germans. They will argue that someone had to negotiate on behalf of France, and better they than an imaginary Communist Government—as if the Germans would tolerate such a thing! These poltroons will say that they will reject anything but reasonable terms, but they know perfectly well that once they have begun to negotiate they will have to do the Germans' bidding whatever that may be. So you see, you are being fooled, fooled!" There was a touch of exasperation in her voice now. "You will all say in England in your silly way 'Good sport, Reynaud, he stuck to us,' and not see that what matters is that he should stand by the Alliance and see that it is kept in the spirit as well as in the letter, which means fighting on at your side, at all costs, yes, at all costs, and to the end. And you will say in England of all these politicians who think in terms of constituencies and can't think in terms of France, 'Give them fair play, don't be too hard on them, it must be very uncomfortable to be a French Minister.' "

I had been listening spellbound to the torrent of words. The pain in those upturned dark eyes frightened me and made me feel as if I had been wakened by this lovely creature on the edge of an abyss. The strain was almost too much, so, catching for relief at the comic form of words she had used and the picture conjured up of the uncomfortable French Ministers, some of whom I had seen having most comfortable meals and who were staying, I knew, at most comfortable hotels with comfortable ladies, I smiled. But there was such disappointment and disillusion depicted on her face as she noted it, she so evidently considered that I was incapable of understanding, that I felt first contrite, then silly, then just a brute; but I could not explain. I could not tell her of my stupid thought, and that it had come to me as a means of escape from the vision she had evoked, simply because I could not bear what she was saying. She was crying now, not really crying, but tears welled out of her eyes and slowly followed each other down her cheeks as her hands twisted a handkerchief. "You see, I am thinking of France really," there was a wail in her voice, but what a different one from Chautemps'; it was the plaint of a beautiful, gentle animal wounded to death. "England is of course important in the war, I know she will one day win the war, but England is important to me because she is the partner by whom France pledged herself to stand to the end. They must not dishonour France. That is the only thing that would really kill France. France can survive if she is not dishonoured. We cannot betray England."

I was deeply moved, and wondered if it had not been given to me to see one of the strange manifestations of the spirit of France which, in great emergencies, so often expresses itself through a woman, pointing the way to noble solutions, simple in themselves, but beyond the grasp and the courage of her contemporaries.

I have only seen Ève Curie once since then and that was several years later, in banal circumstances. I do not think it was given to her to do anything particularly striking in the war. I do not suppose a great cathedral will ever be dedicated to her like Notre Dame of Paris to Sainte Geneviève, or that a statue will be put up to her as to Jeanne Hachette at Beauvais, or that she will be beatified like the maid Joan, but I do believe that in her heart burnt that day the same pure flame of love of her country that enabled other women in other ages to lead France from darkness into light.

The conversation suddenly fell to an ordinary level, in ordinary tones. I noticed Margerie at the far end of the terrace in earnest conversation with his wife. "Well, I believe in Reynaud," I said, "I believe he is fighting hard to carry the Government with him. If he fails I still believe he will go to Africa and carry on the war at our side with those Ministers who will stand by him."

"He has already lost his hold on the Government," said Ève Curie, "and he will resign and Pétain will succeed him, unless the English force France to stand by the Alliance. Reynaud in his heart knows this, he knows Roosevelt will not declare war, and so, to that extent, he is deceiving you. They are all, or very nearly all, deceiving you, playing with words."

"Not Mandel," I said.

"No, not Mandel, nor the Socialists. They are turning out to be good Frenchmen."

"Louis Marin is not a Socialist," I said.

"No, he is the exception, but he is a Lorrainer, he knows the Germans."

"That one is not double-crossing us," and I nodded in the direction of Margerie. "I trust him."

"He has a very rich wife," said Ève Curie, "she is talking to him now, and is surely telling him not to be foolish and not to do anything that will endanger their fortune. He will take her advice, he is an official, he will serve the Government that remains in France."

A slight inclination of the head, and Ève Curie was gone. No postscript thoughts, no smile as a concession to convention or of farewell to the unknown man she had chosen to confide in. Later that day, when besieged by appeals for help to leave France, it occurred to me she had made no such request; I believe no thought of her own safety or future crossed her mind. For a moment next day I thought of finding her to make sure she got away somehow. Then I realised I would be doing this more because she was lovely and appealing than for any other reason, and I had no right, at that terrible time, even in gratitude, to devote a single minute to anything but my job.

Ève Curie turned out to be right as regards Margerie, who was to serve the Pétain Government as Vichy Consul-General at Shanghai, where, however, he showed what friendliness he could towards Britain, and was less than half-hearted in carrying out instructions hostile to de Gaulle. But he could not, he felt, break the tradition of service of his family. He had followed his father and he wished his sons to follow him. But Ève Curie was wrong as regards Madame de Margerie. On her way through London to China, she told her English friends, who believed her, that she had been much opposed to her husband serving Vichy.

When Ève Curie had gone I went into the building, where I was soon followed by Margerie. I said I wished to speak to him. Sitting in his small office, I told him that there were a number of things that, quite apart from the situation, were disturbing me deeply.

In the first place, where were the German pilots who were to be handed over to us? We must know so as to make arrangements to take them over. He said he would enquire, but the confusion was extreme, the different departments, even in Bordeaux, could not reach each other by telephone. Then I said bluntly that I had now serious misgivings as to Reynaud's real intentions. Was his purpose weakening? If he really meant to go on fighting in Africa why were not more serious steps taken to make this possible? To this Margerie answered that de Gaulle was now in London to ask for shipping to transport troops and material, and that that morning the Premier had sent for Darlan to tell him he wished the maximum amount of shipping collected for this purpose.

I answered dryly that it was perhaps rather late in the day to carry out a measure which had been so long contemplated but concerning which nothing had yet been done. Margerie then said, what I already knew, that General Noguès, the Commander-in-Chief in North Africa, had been very much opposed to receiving troops or recruits, on the ground that there was insufficient accommodation for them; he had no cadres to provide instructors and no spare weapons, and he thought the climate was rather warm for young Frenchmen at this season; there was moreover a shortage of doctors in North Africa.

I jumped at this. It was monstrous, I said. If it was warm, that meant buildings were not needed. As for the rest, it only exposed lack of firmness on the Premier's part. Why did he not sack this obstructionist General together with a few others I could name?

It was the same thing with the *Réduit Breton*, I went on. That was a reality; something could have been done about it. British troops together with the French could have held for some time a zone close to England, and hard fighting there would have enhanced the chances of getting men and material away to North Africa. The Mediterranean harbours could have been covered by holding the Plateau Central, and I went on to say that the people of Brittany were very fine. They would have proved staunch in the ordeal that fighting in the *réduit* would have meant for them. (I was mistaken in this, as in so many other things. I later learnt that in Brittany villages the women walked out to meet retreating troops and took their rifles from them in their opposition to what they deemed to be a useless resistance.)

Margerie thought that the *Réduit Breton* or the Cherbourg Peninsula might yet be held. As he knew as little on the subject as I, I did not pursue the matter. What use to talk of defending one corner of France when the General in charge was determined to surrender the whole?

And this brought me to my main point. "If Reynaud is really determined to fight on, why does he not sack Weygand who never ceases proclaiming his determination to stop fighting? He did not know the answer when he took over, he never has known it. He has felt defeated from the beginning.

"How can a Government proclaim its determination to fight and hope to be believed when it maintains in office such a Commander-in-Chief?"

"The people think him the best General we have got," said Margerie, which was true, "and he has Pétain's full backing, and the Marshal's influence is enormous. It is growing in the Cabinet," which was also true. "The greater the danger, the greater also the desire of weak men to shelter behind some personality ready to give a lead," he went on. "In a military disaster it is but natural that civilians should plead ignorance and take refuge behind the professional soldier. The risk in doing so is far less than in challenging the wisdom of the military man on professional matters, for if the civilian opposes the General and he turns out to be wrong and the General right, he will be deemed to be a fool, a clown and a knave."

Margerie was right as regards Pétain's influence. Bouthillier has since written of him in his book: "His prestige was such in my eyes that his words seemed to me to be those of an oracle."*

With Ève Curie's voice ringing in my ears, I persisted in trying to elucidate Reynaud's point of view from Margerie, who was still his closest collaborator.

"If," I asked, "the Premier is really determined to go on with the war, why make his decision dependent upon a declaration by Roosevelt, all the more so that neither you, nor I, nor Reynaud really think the United States will declare war—how can she? Is Reynaud not deceiving himself and incidentally us by subordinating his decision to something so uncertain and so unlikely? Is it not in reality just a device for postponing a decision for a few hours?"

And I went on: "Surely your prosecution of the war has nothing to do with Roosevelt, or the United States; either you go on with the war as we are doing, simply because we prefer annihilation to defeat, or you decide only to fight if there is a fair chance of your winning. Nothing Roosevelt may say or do will save France from occupation now. He has promised all the arms and supplies the United States can produce. If he declared war he could hardly do more. It seems to me that Reynaud should face up to the fact that he must either continue the war with France occupied, as the Dutch are doing, or accept defeat and surrender. But if he intends fighting on, then surely he must get rid of Weygand and re-form his Government without Pétain. Would President Lebrun not accept his resignation on the understanding he would entrust him with the formation of a new Government from which the defeatists would be excluded?"

"I do not know," said Margerie. "I imagine Reynaud has thought

* Yves Bouthillier, *Le Drame de Vichy*, Vol. I, p. 22.

of getting rid of Weygand," he went on, but I noticed he said
nothing about Pétain. "If, as I do not doubt," I persisted, "Reynaud
would prefer France to remain our ally, he should take the steps
necessary to that end. It is not playing fair to us to protest his
determination to fight and yet not to do everything circumstances
dictate to make this possible."

Margerie answered that Reynaud was withholding nothing from
us, that he was endeavouring so to manœuvre as to induce the
majority of the Government to support him and remain in the war.
He then said that if the Government went to Africa some Ministers
would have to remain to negotiate and prevent anarchy. I contested
this point of view, which I thought completely mistaken. The
Germans would see to it that there was no anarchy, and a delegation
of the Government remaining in France would only provide the
enemy with hostages he would know how to make good use of.
"You are presuming," I said, "that Hitler will not occupy all France.
Why? If he does not it will only be because it does not suit him to do
so; he will not refrain out of kindheartedness."

Margerie's view was that if Roosevelt's answer was favourable
practically the whole Government would go to Africa; if not, then
Reynaud and only a very few would leave France.

This struck me as a most unfortunate solution. In the latter case
Reynaud and his companions would be refugees, the real Government would be at the mercy of the Germans, under whose orders
they would issue ukases to the French Empire. Why not dismiss the
defeatist Ministers, I pleaded again, and form a Government of
resolute men? If the ex-Ministers formed a Government under the
Germans they would then be mere Quislings. If Reynaud and only a
few Ministers went to Africa, could he and they give orders to the
Fleet? The finest gesture Reynaud could make in favour of solidarity
was to order the Fleet to British harbours. To which Margerie said,
as Reynaud had said before, that it was silly to send the Fleet to
England when we were talking of defending North Africa. But, I
explained, British harbours meant Gibraltar, Alexandria. Surely the
important thing was that the Germans should not be in a position
to force the French to hand over the Fleet. I knew, however, all this
was leading nowhere, it was just talk, Margerie could not affect the
issue, nor did he commit himself. I went away as unhappy and
disturbed as when I began the conversation.

This colloquy left me with the impression that Reynaud was still clinging to the idea of fighting on in Africa, but as a vague idea, something to talk about, not a clear plan that must be carried out and to which everything must be subordinated.

Margerie had given me the text of Reynaud's last telegram to the American President. With it in my pocket I went in search of the Ambassador. The crowd of distressed and frightened people outside the British Consulate had grown. I had to elbow and push through them as they struggled to force their way in past a couple of military policemen. Another crowd, that of the more privileged, almost as large as the one outside, packed the stairs and waiting-rooms. My sleeve was constantly plucked by people I knew, as I forced my way through.

The Ambassador was in the Consul-General's room; it was suffocating, because of a fire on which documents were burning. I told Sir Ronald everything I had heard since I saw him, including what Ève Curie had said.

We sent off a short telegram dealing with Reynaud's message to Roosevelt, explaining that what it amounted to was that France's decision to fight on virtually depended on an assurance by the President that the United States would enter the war at an early date.

We gave it as our opinion that failing such an assurance the decision to ask for an armistice would follow rapidly, in which case the Ambassador and I would do our utmost to obtain the scuttling of the Fleet (we both thought at the time that it might be easier to obtain this than its sailing for British harbours) and added, summarising our joint conclusion on the situation: "We have little confidence in anything now."

I went into another room where an attempt was being made to deal with the milling crowd of would-be refugees, which included a number of distinguished Frenchmen, anxious to leave France.

We had already heard at Champchevrier that the Germans were reported to have dropped mines in the Gironde, and that the French said that their mine-sweeping equipment could not deal with the type of mine the enemy had laid. This report was now confirmed and assumed great importance, as very valuable equipment was being loaded on ships bound for England. The problem of embarking refugees was further complicated by this circumstance. An Englishman who knew about these things ascertained that the right mine-sweeping equipment had been delivered at Bordeaux. He was sent to investigate, but was told that, if that was so, no one knew where it was or would know how to use it if it were located.

It was, therefore, a question of getting the people out to Le Verdon at the extreme end of the southern peninsula of the Gironde estuary and embarking them there, on such ships as we could lay our hands on, practically in the open sea. My only contribution was that, remembering a most pleasant shipowner of La Rochelle, up the coast, whom I had met when yachting there a couple of years earlier, I suggested that, as he had a fleet of deep-sea fishing-vessels, he might be asked to help. This was agreed to with alacrity. By luck I got him on the telephone and he promised to send a couple of boats, each capable of carrying 300 people. These were, however, as it turned out, not needed.

The confusion and general helplessness were put to an end by the appearance of the Naval Attaché, Pleydell-Bouverie. It was admirable to see the ability of this officer and the ease with which he improvised a plan. I do not think there is an Englishman born who does not derive a sense of inner satisfaction when he is given yet another proof of the Navy's competence.

It was in this general faith that the Ambassador and I sent a further telegram to London renewing my previous request for a warship. We felt that the Navy always got through. We said that as there was now no organised resistance to the German advance, Bordeaux might well be the next objective of the enemy, and that a ship, preferably a small cruiser, would be very useful to evacuate the Embassy staff, the Polish and Belgian Governments and our Missions to them, as well as the Dominion Legations. In the improbable event of the warship arriving before it was needed for this purpose, we should be very glad to have it for the dispatch of telegrams, as we were far from certain that those we were sending were reaching London. At best they were apt to be much delayed.

The Ambassador added that if the French Government decided to continue the struggle overseas, he and a few of his staff would go with them unless contrary instructions were received. We were then summoned by Reynaud.

At the entrance to the rue Vital-Carles, which was closed by a police barrier, we were cheered by a small crowd. As the position of Britain was well known, it was nice to feel that part of the public at least favoured resistance. The Premier told us that Pétain was determined to demand an armistice. He had been clamouring for a

Cabinet meeting since early morning. Reynaud had finally fixed one for 6 p.m., whereupon the Marshal had come in person to request that it be held earlier. Reynaud had given way to the extent of advancing the time to 4 p.m. He told us that the Marshal had evidently made up his mind to resign unless an armistice was asked for or the United States declared war.

Reynaud was sticking to his guns but appeared uncertain at whom to point them; moreover he did not seem convinced they were loaded with the kind of ammunition that would hold off the Pétain–Weygand attack.

Typical of the way in which we were all ready to grasp at any straw that drifted by in the spate of disaster, Reynaud eagerly seized on an idea I suggested to him. "Why don't you, *Monsieur le Président*, impose your will at the Cabinet meeting this afternoon, let who will resign, and then declare that you and those of your colleagues who have held by you will leave France tonight. You would then, if you accept this suggestion, make a declaration to that effect over the wireless, accompanied by the most solemn warning that any brutality, any abuse of power on the part of the Germans in France, would be immediately followed by heavy air bombardment of German towns." Reynaud was delighted by the suggestion, and brightened up considerably.

"That is not only a very good idea," he said, "but an important suggestion too. But only England could make it possible. Would she?" I said I guaranteed she would, I was certain the Prime Minister would agree.

Returning to the theme I had broached earlier with Margerie, I suggested that the British forces, by no means unimportant in numbers, should no longer be dispersed according to the usual Weygand method, but be concentrated and fall back on Brest or Cherbourg to cover such evacuation as was possible, while all the troops that could be got out of the Maginot Line were sent south, their right resting on the fine Army of the Alps, their left on the difficult Cevennes Mountains, thus covering Marseilles and Toulon so that a really serious attempt at evacuation to North Africa could be made.*

---

* What had occurred was this. General Brooke, now in command of the B.E.F. in France, met Generals Weygand and Georges on the 14th. He was told the two Governments had agreed to create a bridgehead in Brittany and that he was to deploy his forces north and south of Rennes. Brooke pointed

Continued on p. 256

It was so important to keep up the urge to fight, to counteract the miasma of defeatism, to indicate that we only thought in terms of ways and means of continuing the struggle, that the Ambassador and I returned to the Consulate feeling something, however little, had been accomplished. But on arriving there we heard that our troops were falling back to the coast anyway.

Soon after leaving Reynaud we received a message from London giving us news that would be shattering to French hopes: President Roosevelt had telegraphed to Churchill that he could not agree to the publication of his message of the 13th to Reynaud.*

This communication, the President stated, was in no sense intended to commit, and did not commit, the Government of the U.S. to military participation.

No more information was given, nor did we need any. We knew that the flimsy grounds on which Reynaud had taken his stand had

---

out that this line was 150 kilometres long and required at least 15 divisions. He was told that the instructions he was receiving must be regarded as an order. (Churchill, *The Second World War*, Vol. II, p. 169.)

It should be remembered in this connection that at Cangé, on June 12th, Weygand had declared the *Réduit Breton* only existed in the imagination of M. Reynaud. When asked by General Brooke whether the disembarkation of British troops should not cease, General Weygand answered that "This would not be a good way of supporting the morale of the French Armies which are fighting until the last extremity."

Yet when it was announced on the 17th that the Pétain Government had asked for an armistice, these British troops had not even been informed of that fact. (*Op. cit.* Vol. II, p. 171.)

But General Brooke had realised the position was hopeless and sought and obtained permission, on the night of the 14th, to re-embark. He was released from French command. (*Ibid.*)

As a result of this timely decision, 136,000 British troops, 310 guns and 20,000 Polish troops were saved.

General Weygand, however, considered he had been ill-used. He states (*Rappelé au Service*, p. 231) that on June 18th (the French Government having on the night of the 16th asked for an armistice largely at his instigation) he telegraphed through the French Military Attaché in London a message for the C.I.G.S. saying he failed to understand how General Brooke could have reported on the 14th that French resistance had ceased. On the contrary General Brooke was informed that this resistance was continuing, "is still continuing today, the 18th . . ."

Baudouin notes in his diary, under this same date of June 18th (*Neuf Mois au Gouvernement*, p. 133), that "at the Cabinet Meeting held at 11 a.m. General Weygand gave dramatic details on the state of the Army, which is not only dislocated but dissociated. If some remnants are still fighting heroically, disorder is gaining pretty well everywhere."

* This was the message referred to on pp. 242–3, Chapter XVI, and on pp. 244–5, Chapter XVII.

been disrupted and that it would mean an immense access of strength to the defeatists.

No instruction was sent from London to inform the French of this message, and we did not do so. The news might ruin Reynaud's chance of maintaining his position at that afternoon's Cabinet meeting, and, after all, the French had their own Ambassador in Washington.

Churchill in his book has described this telegram as disappointing, and so it was—inevitable no doubt from the President's point of view, but nevertheless very, very disappointing. In fact at Bordeaux it was more than that, it was much as if another fall of rock had closed almost the last of the channels giving air to entombed men.

The Ambassador and I were summoned by Reynaud once more before lunch. He read us a very good paper he had prepared for the afternoon Cabinet meeting. Its purpose was to prove the futility of asking for an armistice.

It declared that, whatever terms the Germans might offer and whatever promises they might make, the fate of France was sealed if she accepted them. If France was false to her ally and made a dishonourable peace, she would inevitably share the fate of all countries which had fallen under Nazi domination. France would, if she made peace under such conditions, fall into servitude for many years and be reduced to the status of Slovakia. This was excellent. The Presidents of the two Chambers had visited him, and we concluded that they had, as always, encouraged him.*

But, having told us what he intended saying at the Cabinet meeting, he went on to describe the position as he saw it, and it was not encouraging.

He could not, he said, withstand any longer the constant and unceasing pressure that was being brought on him, and he now felt the time had come when he must reach a clear understanding with his colleagues. If he could not obtain sufficient support he would resign. If things went well, and if on the whole the Cabinet supported him,

* Reynaud (*La France a sauvé l'Europe*, Vol. II, p. 335) refers to this interview as follows: "President Jeanneney testified (concerning this interview) as follows at the Riom Trial. 'President Paul Reynaud told us of his extreme alarm at the rapid advance of the German Armies. He repeated to us what he had said at Tours, his irritation concerning the High Command, which was extremely indocile to the instructions of the Government, and we felt that dissensions within the Government were extremely likely. He informed us at that time of his very firm intention never to give up the struggle. On which we firmly approved of his decisions and we encouraged him.' "

there would be four or five resignations, including that of Marshal Pétain. He would never go back on England, though others would. This led me to ask him specifically about the Fleet. He said he could not guarantee what others would do if he were no longer in power. He asserted, very emphatically, that under no circumstances would he ever be a party to surrendering the French Fleet and allowing it to be used against a loyal ally. From which the Ambassador and I concluded that Reynaud must have thought some of his colleagues, or their probable successors, would be capable of such an act of treachery.

As we left, thinking the remark might prove useful if quoted at the Cabinet, I said: "We expect France to do no less than Poland, Norway and Holland."

A hurried word, after this meeting, with Mandel, who was in a better position to judge the position than we were and who was completely staunch and reliable, led us to telegraph that the mood in which the Cabinet would begin its deliberations would be in favour of establishing two Governments, one in France to negotiate, the other in Africa to continue the struggle, Reynaud to be head of the latter and Pétain of the former.

Although we went on pressing for the continuation of the war in Africa, we were fast losing faith in the realisation of that hope. We expressed the opinion in our telegram that the plan was unlikely to materialise, and that in any event Reynaud, Mandel and only a very few others would leave France. They would exercise but a doubtful authority, for Pétain and Weygand would control the armed forces. It was unlikely that under these circumstances the latter would delegate to Reynaud authority over the Army in Africa, or that if they did the Germans would not force them to withdraw it.

Anxious not to neglect even small things, we begged the Government to encourage the French by offering as much tonnage as possible for the transport of French troops both from the western and southern harbours.

We finally sat down at the *Chapon Fin* to the usual remarkable meal ordered by Oliver Harvey, but I could not eat it, nor, I think, could the Ambassador. Our appetites would in any case have been spoilt by the nausea induced by the sight of Laval, who, unlike us, was evidently enjoying a succulent meal. He sat some distance away with a companion, and I was amazed at his appearance. The nut-meg-brown friendly little man I had known years before, whose hair had been as sleek and black as that of a Red Indian, was now gross, flabby and high in colour. That I knew him to be an enemy may have influenced my impression, but I thought him a revolting sight and he made me feel sick.

That afternoon, sitting in my room at the Hotel Montré wondering if we might not learn at any moment that German paratroops had landed or that a fast mechanised column was making for the city, I wrote: "This is certainly one of the worst days I have ever lived. I do not believe anything could possibly be worse. My personal conclusion is that Reynaud is terrified of Pétain's resigning as he cannot face the prospect of governing in the face of the Marshal's and the Commander-in-Chief's combined and violent opposition." Concerning Reynaud himself I wrote that I thought he was beaten by events. These had overcome him, and what wonder? He had put up and was still putting up a brave fight, using against the defeatists, a little intermittently perhaps, the total strength God had given him. And I wondered whether the apprehension of being described as a refugee, a man who had fled to save his skin, would influence him against going to Africa? But I concluded that this was not so. He had made and was making mistakes, but they were not dictated by self-interest or fear. He was, I wrote, doing the very best he could according to his lights and powers. But then what of the Fleet? Did he realise in his bones that the chance of survival of both our countries was small if it fell into German hands? Did he feel it to be a fundamental question, something like the ocean drying up? To Britain it was as simple as that. It should have meant as much to France.

No, I thought, Reynaud does not see this question as we do. He would never hand over the Fleet or agree to its being handed over, but he can contemplate others doing so. Laval is in the wings. His past gives likelihood to the whispered suggestion that he is scheming to draw France into a German alliance. These things are politics to Reynaud, to us they are matters of national survival. He must be made to realise this.

Our long and trying wait was broken at intervals by the arrival of a British officer or civilian, each telling of some fresh aspect of the complete demoralisation of the French troops and officials.

They all said that no attempt whatsoever was being made to destroy machinery that could be of use to the Germans. Fleets of cars and carriers were left ready for their use. No one had heard of any of the immense stores of petrol being destroyed. Aircraft engines still in their crates had been seen lying about at many places. A few men with hammers at the arms depots could have smashed the lot, or burnt them.

We had other visitors. Fear is a horrible thing when it gets the better of a man. We saw that day some men turned into jellies by fear. As Georges Mandel, easily the bravest man in Bordeaux, was a Jew, I can say that some of his co-religionists, with every justification for apprehension as to their fate at the hands of the Nazis, were so transfigured by fear as to be totally unrecognisable. I saw two large flabby white fellows I knew whom I described to Campbell as looking like a couple of blancmanges pursued by a Sunday-school treat. Some arrogant, aggressive men I had never thought were Jews came to beg for passages, proclaiming themselves as such, having ceased to be either arrogant or aggressive. Everything was done to try to ensure the escape of those most justified in their fear of falling into Nazi hands, but the shipping space was far short of the demand.

Behind this nightmare scene lay the horrible feeling of being trapped. There was nothing between us and the Germans. This was accentuated when yet another report came in that the Germans had dropped more mines in the Gironde below Bordeaux. The sensation of helplessness, of feeling as an insect might feel in the path of an oncoming spate, aware of the danger yet incapable of avoiding it, led me to worry more than ever about my wife just because I was so hemmed in, so unable to offer help or advice, above all so totally unaware of where she might be. Had she made for the Mediterranean? I devoutly hoped she had.

I went to see Yves Delbos at his hotel, and told him bluntly I had been informed he was a *mou*. Was this so? He indignantly denied it and I believed him. As he did in fact sail in the *Massiglia* with Mandel, the latter had been wrong concerning him at Tours.

We were told by one of our visitors that shortly before the Cabinet meeting there had been a violent dispute between Reynaud and Weygand. We only learned the details later. What occurred, according to Reynaud's account, was that he told the Commander-in-Chief he would not alter his decision to go to North Africa and that it would be necessary for Weygand himself to give the order to cease fighting as the Dutch Commander-in-Chief had done when he felt the moment had come.

"The Government cannot leave France," said Weygand. "Algeria consists of three French departments," answered Reynaud. "It is not the same thing," retorted Weygand. He argued that to seek an armistice was a Governmental responsibility, whereas to order a cease fire was ·a military one which he would not take; to which Reynaud answered that if this was what worried him he would himself assume full responsibility for the decision and give him a written order to that effect. Weygand refused to accept this solution, declaring that the "honour of the Army" was involved, on which Reynaud makes the justifiable comment that this was indeed a strange remark, since it drew a distinction between the honour of France and that of her Army.

In his book Reynaud quotes Weygand's evidence at the Riom Trial in regard to this interview, which he says was in the main accurate.* The General stated that the Premier felt his choice lay between following the example of either the King of the Belgians or that of the Queen of Holland, who went to England leaving the Chief of Staff to surrender. Reynaud had made up his mind: he would not ask for an armistice and would if necessary leave France.

Reynaud writes that he decided, after this altercation, to dismiss Weygand after the Cabinet meeting. Unfortunately he did not do so.

Endeavouring to make sure we had not left anything undone that might have been of any help or use to the cause we were working for, it occurred to the Ambassador and to me that it might be as well not to rely solely on our verbal reminder to Reynaud concerning the German air pilots. He had much on his mind, and, further, we were by now convinced there were those at Bordeaux who if they could would prevent these enemy pilots being handed over as prisoners to the British. So we wrote Reynaud an urgent and insistent note asking him to inform us as soon as possible to what port they were being taken for embarkation. We did not believe he had any intention of evading his undertaking but were determined he should not be allowed to forget his promise.

We waited on through the dreadful afternoon, occasionally going down to see this person or that who asked for us. Then back to our bedrooms, where we worked at our reports, often walking across the small lobby that separated us to compare drafts or reassure each other that no point had been overlooked, but in the main, I think, just for company's sake. Bordeaux was by now a quicksand, and it was more reassuring than either of us would have admitted to hear

* *La France a sauvé l'Europe*, Vol. II, pp. 337–8.

an English voice and to look at an English face, however worried its expression. We got out a map and, knowing our troops were falling back to the coast, wondered when the retreat had begun and where they had got to by now. We hoped and prayed that another Dunkirk did not lie ahead. If, as seemed likely, our troops were no longer under French command, the chances of such a calamity were considerably reduced.

That map emphasised in the most unpleasant way the thought at the back of our minds: there were probably by now no military formations on which we could place the slightest reliance between Bordeaux and the enemy.

The thought of the French Government a few hundred yards away arguing and certainly quarrelling over a matter of vital importance to us, while we sat helplessly in our hotel bedrooms, gave a sharp edge to my spleen. There was a picture in my mind of an imp, invisible to all but me, grafting white feathers on to the defeatists, which I knew with certainty would grow, and grow again, however carefully they were plucked out of their skins in the years to come, and would eventually sprout out of their tombs. I could hear the cowards trying to involve the stalwarts in their poltroonery, spinning words, politicians' words, enunciating aphorisms, mouthing clichés: "The sacred soil of France"—"You cannot abandon the people"—"Do not forget the grandmothers"—"We must not be divided, a formula uniting the Government must be found"—"A Governmental crisis must be avoided at all costs". I visualised the weakness of the waverers turning to livid panic under the blast of Weygand's strident cries of doom, while he himself, demented by his fear of standing alone before history as the General who failed and had to surrender, was frantically determined to force the Government to shoulder the responsibility he had not the courage to assume. Would the stout-hearted ones, Mandel, Louis Marin, the Socialists, manage to win the day? With all the fervour of which I was capable I prayed that they would.

Why did this wretched Government not just pack up and go to Africa? I thought of all the brave Frenchmen I had known in the First War, soldiers and politicians. They would not have hesitated. After all, Africa was but another base from which to fight. The French had fought a war in 1914–18 with whole provinces in German occupation, bravely disregarding the plight of their fellow country-men left at the enemy's mercy; to have the whole of France occupied was evidently much worse but only a question of degree. The thing that mattered was to fight on. And I put myself the question: If Britain were occupied by the Germans, would any of those of us still able to do so cease fighting so long as we had ground to stand on anywhere in the world? Of course we would not, and there was no heroism about it, it was a simple question of the personal preference of a multitude of British people who agreed, each one making his personal decision, that there was really no argument about it, since, although he disliked both fighting and dying, he disliked the idea of surrender still more.

If France were held down, every yard of her, by Nazi troopers, then she could not fight, but if the will to fight was there, if every man who could escape joined us, then she would be truly one with us and our sister still.

A feeling of frustration overcame me, I was desperate at being able to do nothing to tip the scales in so vitally important a cause, and I wrote in my notes that Churchill's presence at Bordeaux that afternoon would have been worth more than millions in gold could buy. It was impossible to project his personality. Only he could do his own work of infusing courage and hope. Out of this emerged an idea. Could he be brought over next day? I spoke of this to the Ambassador, who, though not wholly in favour of the idea, agreed to keep it in mind.

Time passed, excruciatingly. We tried to hope, but not with much conviction, that Roosevelt would respond to Reynaud's last desperate appeal. We could not move from the hotel during the latter part of the afternoon, as a summons to see Reynaud might come at any moment. Much as we should have liked to call on the Presidents of the Chambers we could not do so, we just had to wait.

The Cabinet meeting started at 4 p.m. It went on till after 7 p.m., when we were sent for.

Reynaud looked pale, washed-out would be the right description, a starched collar that had fallen back into the tub. The Ambassador and I sat down, as had become our routine, on the left of the Premier's desk, an imitation ebony table with inferior ormolu. It was at the back of the room and he sat facing the windows. The Ambassador sat beside him on his left, I next to Campbell at the side of the table.

Reynaud said he would like to tell us what the Government had decided; I interrupted to ask if, as it was so important, he would mind my taking down what he said, and seizing a large sheet of foolscap headed *République Française*, one of many strewn on the table, I began to write. I had not got ten words down when I heard him say: "As Mr. Churchill stated at Tours he would agree that France should sue for an armistice . . ." I put down my pencil and said, probably sharply: "I cannot take that down, for it is untrue."

"But," said the Premier, not so much surprised as aggrieved, "Baudouin asserted at the Council meeting that he did say so and that he had made a note of it at the time he said it." I was growing very indignant indeed. "This is a curious conversation," I said, "in view of the fact that we were all three of us at the conference; we were not absent for a moment, and therefore know, all three of us, that the Prime Minister never said anything of the sort." The Ambassador now chimed in. He was quite as angry as I was, more so perhaps, since he had a special reason of his own for feeling exasperated. What he said took me completely aback, as it apparently did Reynaud. This question had come up that very morning in a conversation he had had with Baudouin. The Ambassador had asked Baudouin if he could throw any light on the source of rumours to the effect that Churchill had said Britain would consent to France suing for an armistice. Baudouin had declared that this was indeed strange, for he knew the Prime Minister had said nothing of the sort, and he himself was prepared to say so explicitly.

This piece of information, on top of what Reynaud had just told us, threw our meeting *à trois*, into confusion. "In any case you, *Monsieur le Président*, know quite well—*vous savez parfaitement*—that Mr. Churchill said nothing of the sort," I reiterated.

During the rather confused discussion which followed, someone suggested that Margerie should be asked to produce his notes. He appeared the moment the Premier's bell had ceased ringing, and was back with his minutes of the Tours meeting in less than a minute. He read these from beginning to end, standing at the table facing the Premier. They were the verbatim report of the words he and Berkeley had used in their translations at Tours.

There was not a word in them that could conceivably be twisted into the statement Baudouin now asserted Churchill had made.

Margerie, having finished, looked at Reynaud, who said "*Merci*." He withdrew.

Without saying another word Reynaud leant forward, took a sheet of paper and began to write a message to the Prime Minister. We got it through in code by telephone at 1.20 a.m. on the 16th. Its sense was as follows:

"At the meeting of the Cabinet this afternoon it was held that at a moment when the enemy is on the point of occupying the entire country, which will mean inflicting cruel privations and suffering on the French nation, the departure of the Government would be considered by the people as desertion. This might give rise to violent reactions on the part of the public unless it had been established that the peace conditions imposed by Herr Hitler and Signor Mussolini were unacceptable as being contrary to the vital and honourable interests of France.

The Cabinet Council does not doubt that these conditions will in any event be unacceptable, but have decided that it is indispensable that this should be proved beyond doubt. If this course is not adopted the Government will break up, as many of its members would, in that case, refuse to leave the soil of France.

With a view to ascertaining German and Italian conditions, the Cabinet decided to seek leave of the British Government to enquire through the United States Government what armistice terms would be offered to France by the German and Italian Governments.

"The President of the Council is authorised, if the British Government will agree to the French Government's taking this step, to declare to the British Government that the surrender of the French Fleet to Germany would be held to be an unacceptable condition.

"Should the British Government withhold its consent to this step, it seems likely, in view of the opinions expressed at the Cabinet meeting, that the President of the Council would have no alternative but to resign."

At this point Roosevelt's reply to Reynaud's last message of the 14th was handed to him. As he read it he grew still paler, his face contracted, his eyes became just slits, an *accent grave* and an *accent aigu* to either side of his nose. "Our appeal has failed," he said in a small toneless voice, "the Americans will not declare war."

This was the President's answer:

Confidential.   Washington, June 15th.
                                              11 a.m.

"I am sending you this answer to your message of yesterday, which, I am sure you realise, has been the object on our part of the most serious and friendly examination.

"Allow me, in the first place, to reiterate to you the expression of the ever increasing admiration with which the American people and its Government pay tribute to the brilliant courage displayed by the French Armies on French soil in their resistance to the invader. I must also repeat in the most solemn terms that, neglecting no possible effort under present conditions, the Government of the United States has allowed the Allied Armies to order in this country, during the last few weeks, aeroplanes, artillery and ammunition of all kinds, and that, so long as the Allied Governments pursue their resistance, it will redouble its efforts in the same sense. I think it possible to say that, with each passing week, an ever increasing amount of war material will be placed at the disposal of the Allied Armies.

"In conformity with its policy of non-recognition of the aequisition of gains achieved by force of arms, the Government of the United States will refuse to recognise the validity of any attempt of a nature to impair the independence of France and its territorial integrity.

"In these hours, so heart-rending for the French people and for yourself, I assure you of my deepest sympathy, and I can furthermore assure you that, as long as the French Nation continues to defend its liberty, and in so doing the cause of democratic institutions in the world, it can rely upon receiving from the United States in ever increasing quantities material and supplies of all kinds.

"I know you will understand that these declarations imply no military commitments. Congress alone can undertake such engagements."

Reynaud gave us the telegram to read and resumed his writing. The blow had been not the less painful for being expected. He took it well.

The next paragraph of his telegram to Mr. Churchill referred to Tours. "It was agreed there last Thursday at your suggestion," he wrote, "that the question of authorising a request for an armistice would be reconsidered if President Roosevelt's reply was negative. This eventuality having materialised, I think the question must now be put afresh."

This he was certainly entitled to say.

He gave us the message, asking us to transmit it with the utmost speed and to insist that it conveyed a formal decision of the Cabinet at a meeting presided over by the President of the Republic. He asked for an answer early next morning, Sunday.

I have no clear recollection of how we sent this highest-priority telegram to the Consulate, but we did so and remained on for some time with the Premier, obtaining from him some further details, which we embodied in a message to the Prime Minister which was also sent over the telephone in code. It was received in London at 4 a.m. on the 16th. The gist of it was that at the Cabinet meeting Chautemps had rallied the majority of the Ministers to the thesis that the Government would be accused of having taken flight if they went to North Africa unless they had previously ascertained that the terms of the armistice were unacceptable. Chautemps' argument was that if the Government left France without finding out what were the German terms for an armistice it would have forfeited its claim to exert any authority over the French people. His reasoning was very subtle. He affected to believe that the German terms would be unacceptable, but how could one be certain of this if they had not been asked for? Once these outrageous terms were known, he declared, then the French nation would rally and resist as never before.

Reynaud gave us that evening yet one more version of Chautemps' description of the plight of the refugees; this by now had the same excruciating effect on me as the sound of a nail scratching on a slate. We were not spared the stories of the cars running out of petrol, nor were the grandmothers' pains passed over in silence. I felt that thanks to Chautemps I should never really like French grandmothers again. He described the French soldiers as being shot like rabbits in an enclosure.

Reynaud said he had put up a good fight but had been beaten by numbers. He also said that if His Majesty's Government withheld the authorisation to ask for the enemy's terms, he would resign, for he insisted that he would under no circumstances repudiate the document undertaking not to conclude a separate peace, which he himself had signed. But he added that if he did resign he could not guarantee that his successor would maintain the decision reached at the Cabinet meeting that the surrender of the Fleet would be considered an unacceptable condition to the conclusion of an armistice. *

The Ambassador and I took strong objection to this. It was, we said, an attempt to use the Fleet as a means of forcing the British Government to condone the repudiation of the Anglo-French agreement which his Government was now asking for. He had agreed on a previous occasion that the Fleet was the one thing the Germans wanted, and I reminded him of a point I had made to him previously, namely that they would not hesitate to burn a town a day until they got it, if it was within the power of the French Government to hand it over.

We also argued that it was impossible to believe that reasonable men could place the least trust in Hitler's word. As soon as France held out her hands to be manacled and was helpless, the Germans would break every undertaking they might have given to obtain surrender, and then turn on Britain without delay.

How could anyone believe that the lot of the French people would be improved by accepting the German yoke now? Could any fate be more dreadful than that of accepting German terms in the hope of obtaining some concessions from an utterly untrustworthy and ruthless enemy, only to find, as the French would surely find if the Government adhered to its present plan, that once defeat had been accepted there would be no limit to the humiliating conditions Hitler would exact from a helpless France? He would tear the country and its empire to pieces. If France ever survived such a blow, how would the French nation regard the man who had placed the yoke on their necks when there was an alternative, that of fighting on?

The Ambassador and I fired these arguments at Reynaud in relays, but to our double assault he answered that he had used the very same arguments to his colleagues, and they had remained absolutely adamant. Nothing would move them. They insisted that the enemy's terms must be ascertained before the Government could decide whether it would go to North Africa or remain in France.

---

* "I was convinced that Germany, whose vital interest it was to invade Great Britain, whose soldiers had escaped practically naked from Dunkirk, would insist on the surrender of our Fleet to attack the British Isles immediately." (*La France a sauvé l'Europe*, p. 36.)

This was written in explanation of why he favoured Pétain as his successor, for the Marshal had, he says, declared at the Cabinet meeting that it would be dishonourable to hand over the Fleet to the Germans.

He then told us that Weygand, who had been present during the first part of the meeting only, exercised great pressure in favour of an armistice and had asserted that the Army might break up at any moment. Reynaud's comment was that if the Commander-in-Chief was right, the German armoured divisions might reach Bordeaux in a very short time, thus making the removal of the Government difficult, if not impossible. We had thought of this ourselves.

We asked Reynaud why, if he could not carry the Cabinet, he did not resign on the understanding that the President would entrust him with the formation of a new Government from which the defeatists would be excluded. He shrugged his shoulders at this, only saying, "And Pétain?", meaning that in his opinion no Government could stand in the face of the Marshal's opposition. I could not accept this. He was thinking in peace-time terms of a noisy press and parliamentary opposition, but at the moment he could do what he liked, for he held control. The only danger I could see was that of a military *coup* by Weygand. This was certainly possible, and I mentioned it in a telephone talk to the Prime Minister.*

The last question I put the Premier was to ask if he would go to

---

* Reynaud writes : "On my return to Paris in May 1945 I learnt that when Weygand left the second Cabinet Meeting held at Cangé, that of the 13th June, he stated in the presence of M. Max Brusset, Georges Mandel's *Chef de Cabinet*, 'They are mad! They have understood nothing! It will be necessary to arrest them . . .!' " (This was in effect what Mandel had told me at Tours.)

As soon as he reached Bordeaux on June 15th, Weygand took steps to put this plan into effect.

M. Christian Foucher, Secretary in the diplomatic service, published under the title 'The Plot' in the newspaper *La Marseillaise* on June 15th, 1943, an article in which he tells how the Aviation Cadets of the Mérignac Camp, near Bordeaux, of whom he was one, were assembled by their officer instructors, who told them in substance this: "Marshal Pétain and General Weygand are determined to carry on with the war by all means, but the civilians wish to capitulate. It is very possible that they will have the Marshal and General Weygand arrested with the help of a Senegalese Regiment stationed near Bordeaux. You will be entrusted with the glorious duty to watch over the safety of the great leaders." On that day M. Foucher saw General Weygand at Mérignac.

These Cadets were formed into sections and distributed over Bordeaux. They were given automatic weapons, some of which were mounted. On the evening of the 16th it was learnt that Marshal Pétain had assumed power to ask for an armistice. An officer declared loudly: "I wonder if we have not been fooled," and M. Reynaud adds: "I have not heard that the trustworthiness of this witness has been questioned. If his testimony is accurate it is obvious that General Weygand had prepared a *coup d'état* against the Government to be carried out if I had not been overthrown." (Reynaud, *La Francé a sauvé l'Europe*, Vol. II, p. 457.)

England if he could not hold the present Government together.
"No," he said, "it must be North Africa or nothing."

Our meeting ended with a reiterated request by Reynaud for a
prompt answer to his message to the Prime Minister, if possible by
telephone next morning (Sunday).

We drove straight to the *Préfecture* to see Mandel, who gave us an
account of the all-important Cabinet meeting that differed considerably from that given us by Reynaud. He asserted that the
majority of the Ministers had not really been in favour of asking for
an armistice, but determined leadership had been lacking and that
was why they had drifted towards the Chautemps solution. Had
Reynaud been the leader of a political party to which most of the
Ministers belonged, they would have rallied to him, but he was not.
The Premier had, according to Mandel, done his best and had put up
a better fight than we had gathered from his own account. We had, it
seemed, gained a wrong impression, no doubt due to his having
started with the untrue allegation concerning what Churchill had
said at Tours, following it with the Chautemps scheme, and bracket-
ing with this the request that Great Britain should release France
from her engagement.

Reynaud had practically convinced the Cabinet (Mandel said
Pétain had seemed to be convinced also) in favour of adopting the
Dutch solution of the Army's laying down its arms without the
Government asking for an armistice. The argument that had seemed
to carry great weight with the Marshal was that by this plan fighting
would cease forthwith, whereas an armistice would require at least
four days to negotiate. As this largely met his main point he had
been silenced. Then Reynaud had made a strange mistake. No
doubt influenced by the fact that Weygand had proved both
hysterical and rude when present at Cabinet meetings and knowing
by now he could not silence him, he had balked at calling him in but
hit on the unfortunate solution of asking Pétain to go to the next
room, where Weygand was waiting, to persuade him to accept the
"Dutch" solution.

It was during the Marshal's absence that Chautemps had disclosed
his plan with the greatest eloquence and persuasiveness. The Marshal
had returned in a quarter of an hour, not only having failed in his
mission but completely reconverted to the Weygand thesis.*

---

* Reynaud writes of this incident: "What occurred between the two men?
Did Weygand change Pétain's opinion on the question of the honour of the

The B.E.F. leaving France. British Infantry on the march

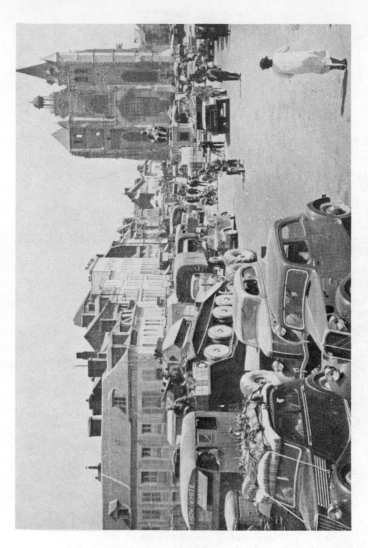

British Units passing through the market square at Le Neubourg

It was clear from what Mandel said that the lure Chautemps had dangled before the Cabinet, and to which most of them had succumbed, had been that of procrastination. Gaining time had proved an irresistible bait. And there was another point in favour of his crafty proposal: it meant casting a share of responsibility on the British Government; either they agreed and the French were covered, or they disagreed, when the French would have a grievance.

None can really have believed that an armistice once asked for could be rejected; if they imagined that the Germans would not insist on dictating armistice terms, using exactly the same formula the French had imposed on them in 1918, then they were fools, and blind ones at that. But they were not stupid.

They must have foreseen that they would have to accept the German terms in the very railway carriage at Rethondes in the forest of Compiègne where Foch had dictated his, twenty-two years ago. Marin, Monnet, Sérol, Dautry, Campinchi, Thellier, and especially Rio, had strongly opposed Chautemps' proposal; it had been supported by Pétain, Ybarnegaray, Pomaret, Bouthillier, Prouvost, Baudouin and, of course, Chautemps himself.

Mandel said he had done his best to make the defeatists realise what they were doing, but had not prevailed against Chautemps' grandmothers. When I made a grimace he said: "So now you have heard at first hand about the Grandmother?" and a wry smile tilted his thin lips for a second.

That was his way of showing his feelings. I was boiling with rage at the thought of Chautemps, the subtle dialectician, who did not for a moment believe in the thesis he defended with so much eloquence, but understood so well the weakness of his colleagues. If ever a man knowingly and of malice aforethought sold his colleagues and his country it was Chautemps. Why? He was not venal. Had he been there would have been an explanation; he was just yellow, frenzied with fear. Neither the future of his country nor honour counted, so long as fighting stopped. A pathological case. Like Judas, I thought,

---

French Army differing from that of France, or did he argue that if fighting ceased, they would forfeit the advantage of the argument they had based on the suffering of the soldiers, which they had used at the Cabinet Meetings at Cangé? Only they knew and they have preferred to keep silence." (Reynaud, *La France a sauvé l'Europe*, Vol. II, p. 339–40.)

Weygand does not in his book mention the incident, which is, however, referred to by many other witnesses.

preferring Judas. In the sequel Judas hanged himself; Chautemps went to America.

Mandel had not finished. "We were then treated," he said, "to a dissertation by Frossard on the theme that 'Armistice does not mean capitulation'."

Mandel was as usual facing facts coldly, dispassionately, objectively; it was therefore the more arresting that he should say there was still one hope and one only. This was that the British Government should refuse to release France from her obligation. He believed that if our Government were completely uncompromising it might yet shock those of his colleagues who were still wavering into a more virile, a more realistic frame of mind. "Though of course Weygand is not making this easy, he is giving it out that in three weeks' time England's neck will be wrung like a chicken's."

He also told us that the military had neglected nothing in their endeavour to panic the Ministers and had staged a dramatic little incident.

The General Commanding the Bordeaux Region had asked to be received by the Cabinet, and in melodramatic tones had announced further disaster. This occurred whilst Weygand was still being heard. Play had also been made with the fact that the B.E.F. no longer considered itself under French command.*

We told Mandel the gist of Roosevelt's telegram, which he had of course not yet heard of. We also told him of our anxiety concerning the Fleet. Mandel understood perfectly. No one, he said, was in favour of allowing the Fleet to fall into German hands, though few Ministers had thought the matter out or would face the logical issue of the course the majority inclined to. Nothing revealed Weygand's muddle-headedness more than his views concerning the Fleet, he added. At Cangé he had declared that no French ship should fall into German hands and that the Fleet should sail to North African harbours for safety, yet he had done nothing to apply this principle to his own troops by sending them to North Africa.

Mandel concluded by begging us most earnestly to point out to the French Government that neither Poland, Norway, nor Holland had given up the struggle under similar circumstances and that we expected no less from France. "To condone the request for an armistice is to make an abject surrender inevitable."

We did as he asked in a telegram received in London at 4 a.m. on

* See footnote, p. 256.

the 16th, adding that we had heard from several sources that Darlan had declared the Navy would not, under any circumstances, submit to surrender.

When we returned to the hotel I telephoned to the Prime Minister, who never seemed to sleep. As the Ambassador always communicated with the Foreign Office by telegram, telephoning gained time, while relieving to some small extent Mullard and Cunningham, who never stopped enciphering and deciphering day and night. No two men ever worked harder or with more devotion. I still cannot understand how they managed to work without sleep for so long a period.

In my talk with Churchill I summarised the position, painting it in very sombre colours, and told him practically word for word what Mandel had said, for I knew he trusted him and placed great weight on his views. I also asked if there was a possibility of his meeting Reynaud next day. He said he would consider this.

He asked some questions; his voice was incisive and sharp, and I thought that the great Duke of Marlborough must have spoken with the same decision and clarity at Oudenarde and Malplaquet.

There was another Weygand–Reynaud incident that evening which Mandel did not mention.

Weygand's version is as follows:

"At 7.55 p.m. the Cabinet meeting came to an end without the military leaders having been recalled. Most of the Ministers walked out, the President of the Council amongst the last. Reynaud came straight up to me. 'The Ministers,' he said, 'are in favour of a capitulation of the land forces only, and this capitulation must be asked for by the Commander-in-Chief.' He further implied that I had assented to this solution. Thus the Head of the Government believed, or feigned to believe, that I had accepted such dishonour. Our conversation without witness amounted to a manœuvre to make me a consenting party to this plan. I was determined that the conversation which followed should be heard, and witnesses were not lacking in the hall. I therefore stepped back and, raising my voice, I gave him the most categoric denial, in terms which might not have been in accordance with the protocol but which were at least impossible to misunderstand. I affirmed I had not said what he maintained I had said and that nobody could compel me to take an action of which I disapproved. The silence which followed added resonance to my words. Reynaud, obviously *gené* by my reaction, answered that he had perhaps misunderstood me, and invited me to calm myself. These words exacerbated my indignation. Certainly not, I declared, I would not calm myself, nor would I hold my tongue, if need be let me be dismissed, but I would never accept such an infamy. Never would I inflict such shame on our colours. The President of the Council was mistaken if, having sent for me from so far to assume command, he thought he would find in me a man ready to accept any job. And furthermore the cessation of hostilities, like the declaration of war, was a question of the general conduct of the war, which was a matter for the Government. Let it take its responsibilities. Reynaud left the room affirming he would.

"Matters could not be allowed to remain there. It was necessary to get out of this equivocal situation and to put an end to an indescribable manœuvre. I therefore went into the room where the Cabinet meeting had taken place so as to inform the President of the Republic, who was speaking to MM. Bouthillier and Mandel. When I wished to give him an account of what had occurred, he refused to hear me excepting in the presence of the President of the Council. I was about to leave, wondering as to the best means of conveying my meaning, when the latter, informed by my A.D.C., entered the room.

"I was then able to relate to the Head of the State what had occurred and my determination not to capitulate. Did they take me for a child? Was it to decoy me into this ambush that I had been sent for from Beirut? I had been far too long informed of the business of the country to be ignorant as to where the responsibilities for the present drama lay.

"The President of the Republic reproached me for my intemperance and tried to silence me, whereupon I reminded him that when I was Commander-in-Chief in 1933, I had appealed to him, as Supreme Head of the Armed Forces of the National Defence, concerning certain measures taken against the national interest. He had refused to hear me then. This painful scene closed on my reiterated affirmation that no one could compel me to undertake a dishonourable action which I refused to carry out."[*]

* * *

* *Rappelé au Service*, p. 227. Reynaud's comment on this is as follows: "Was Weygand's object to provoke a violent incident which would have enabled him to carry out the *coup de force* prepared by him against the Government, which I was to be informed of five years later and which, according to a reliable witness, had been laid on the day before?" (*La France a sauvé l'Europe*, Vol. II, p. 344.)

This self-portrait by General Weygand will describe him better to British readers than any picture I could attempt to paint.

One is left with a sense of sympathy and pity for the French Army, which, in the hour when it was expiating faults certainly not committed by its troops, was so unfortunate as to be commanded by a hysterical, egocentric old man. It was this same General Weygand, who on June 15th screamed and raved that nothing would ever make him order his troops to surrender, who nevertheless on June 22nd ordered the three French Armies still resisting in Eastern France, those commanded by Generals Condé, Bourret and Laure, to lay down their arms.

CHAPTER XVIII

Sunday, June 16th

(1)

The Ambassador and I compare notes and find no grounds for optimism—Our argument with Reynaud—Madame de Portes again—The Consulate besieged by refugees—Two brave men, Lord Suffolk and M. Labarthe—H.M.S. Berkeley *arrives in the Gironde—News of my wife—Churchill's reply to Reynaud: leave given to ask German armistice conditions if the Fleet sails for British harbours—We consult Jeanneney —We deliver the message to Reynaud—His unfavourable reaction—Churchill suggests a meeting with Reynaud—The morning meeting of the French Cabinet—The atmosphere at the* Chapon Fin—*A second telegram from London about the armistice and the Fleet—Further argument with Reynaud— interrupted by a telephone call from de Gaulle—The magical effect on Reynaud of the British offer of a Declaration of Union—Madame de Portes in the secretaries' room— Churchill telephones to Reynaud—We withdraw the two telegrams about the Fleet—An agonising wait for the French Cabinet's decision.*

IN the early hours of the morning, before going to bed, I noted the conclusions the Ambassador and I had come to after going over the events of the day. We endeavoured to assess what resources were left to Reynaud in the conflict of wills with Weygand in which he had fared so badly, and the chances of his retrieving the ground already lost. We concluded he had just about reached the end of his tether. He was losing, if he had not already lost, control of his Cabinet. The President of the Republic meant well but was weak. He might have lent support to a strong man, but was incapable of giving fresh inspiration to an exhausted one. Mandel was too aloof, too cutting, almost too inhuman to provide that faith which was the quality in shortest supply, after courage, at Bordeaux. We were convinced that once the French asked for an armistice they would not fight again, and the Chautemps proposal to examine the German conditions and reject them if too harsh was just a trick to obtain the agreement of weak Ministers to a surrender. In any case, they were being subjected to every form of pressure by the defeatists, as were the Deputies and Senators present at Bordeaux.*

Metropolitan France had obviously to be written off for the moment, whether Reynaud or Pétain and Weygand prevailed, since the Army was no longer fighting. That was not the question. The conflict in the Government concerned the Empire and the Fleet. Reynaud wished the Empire to remain in the war, whereas the *Capitulards*, the cravens whose cowardice had become courage in reverse through being led by such eminent soldiers, were determined to remain in France and to drag down everything French into the quicksand of defeat.

We tried without much success to analyse the motives of the defeatist party. A surrender of the Army meant that if the whole Army capitulated every soldier might be made a prisoner, and the whole of France might be occupied, but would this be avoided by asking for armistice terms? If the Germans intended to take the French Army into captivity, they would do so. The French Army and people, once they had given up resistance, could not, it was evident, oppose any terms the Germans might force upon them, however dreadful these might be. But it might be argued that if the German terms were barbarous, the French Empire might rebel against them, although France could not do otherwise than submit. We concluded that the German terms would probably not be too harsh, in the first instance at least, as they would certainly wish to induce the surrender of the Empire. This of course did not mean that once France had surrendered the Germans would observe whatever terms they had granted. Further exactions would certainly follow, as recent European history clearly showed.†

It never occurred to us, nor, I think, to anyone else, that Hitler

---

* The President of the Republic writes: "The atmosphere of the town is bad. The uncertainty of the news, the German advance, the influx of refugees, all these things have created a great malaise, an obvious troubling of the minds, of which the members of the Fifth Column will take advantage to activate their deadly propaganda. The Parliamentarians who have arrived from the different provinces are surrounded, isolated, lectured. The uselessness of the struggle is demonstrated. An end must be made." (*Témoignage*,p. 80.)

† "As soon as Hitler received the request for an armistice transmitted by Spain, he called Mussolini to Munich.

Continued on p. 278

would hit on the fiendish plan of dividing France. Had he occupied the whole country he would have united it against him. His plan was intended to create conditions which would divide France against herself.

Before going to bed, after 4 a.m. on the 16th, we resolved to strain every nerve to prevent the French Government from asking for an armistice, so as to gain time for the British Government to make its influence felt and put forward further proposals. The telephone conversations we had had with London, guarded hints for the most part, had left us with the impression that the Government's view coincided with the advice we had been tendering, which was that a stiff attitude would yield far better results than an over-sympathetic one. We had by now had ample opportunity to realise that sympathy tended to be translated into condonation, and concessions to be taken as proof that we were following the same path as France. Our last conversation with Mandel had reinforced this point of view. It was a relief to find, from a Foreign Office telephone call to Campbell two or three hours after he had gone to bed, that opinion in London was hardening in this sense.

It was still early in the morning when Reynaud asked to see us. He was nervously exhausted and his depression took the form of being hardly able to wait for the British Cabinet's and Churchill's reaction to his message of the night before. We told him we had not yet heard, there had not been time for it to be considered, but that he need be in no doubt as to the impression it had made. France had engaged herself by a most solemn undertaking not to conclude a separate peace, and Great Britain had done the same; now, although it was

---

"The Duce brought his programme: occupation of France east of the Rhône, of Corsica and Tunisia, and surrender of the French Fleet and aviation.

"This programme was set aside by Hitler, who explained his hopes of an early peace with Great Britain, and his desire not to bring the French into too violent an opposition to him. The report of the Italian General Staff dated June 18th, 1940 (*Graziani Papers*) states: 'In the matter of the French Fleet the Führer declared that the best thing would be that it should be sunk by the French. The worst solution would be that it should join the British Navy, for the large number of light units which the French possess would allow the two Navies, if united, to develop the convoy system considerably. Under these conditions Great Britain could supply herself without difficulty, and transport considerable forces in all directions, maintaining or creating a series of theatres of operations, which would prolong the war and prevent the enemy being struck decisively. . . . It seems prudent to leave France with the hope of regaining her Fleet once peace is signed. When we have beaten England and when we make peace, we shall see.' " (*Amiral Docteur, Darlan*, p. 78.)

British Troops on Transport leaving Cherbourg

Cherbourg.   British Motor Transport burning near the Quayside

The Evacuation of the B.E.F.   Scenes on board a Troopship

perfectly possible for France to fight on in her Empire, and none knew this better than he did, she asked us to relieve her of her binding promise.

What did he suppose the British Government and people would think?

We pointed out that the agreement not to make a separate peace had been concluded to meet just such a contingency as had now arisen. It had not been drawn up as a polite formula, but was intended to bind the two countries to each other in the gravest contingencies, so that it would not be possible, whatever the temptation, however attractive the bait offered by the enemy, however terrible the conditions to which each might be subjected, for either country to abandon its ally or shake itself free of its pledge.

We argued, and argued again, that those who drew up the agreement and signed it, and he was one of them, knowing they could not foresee the future, had taken this step intending to bind the two countries to a common fate.

Unaware that this was Reynaud's own argument against Weygand, we pointed out with considerable force that a military commander might sue for an armistice without dishonour if he had fought to the end, but that this was certainly not the case of a Government which was in a position to carry on with the war considerably more effectively than could the Norwegians or the Dutch. We reminded Reynaud that no one had criticised the King of the Belgians more bitterly than he, and on what grounds? Because the King had allowed himself to fall into enemy hands and had not followed the example of the Queen of Holland by going to England, there to symbolise the spirit of Dutch resistance. The Queen was reported to have said when she left that where there was no liberty there was no place for the House of Orange. A proud declaration applicable with still greater force to a French Government, heirs of the Revolution. And I put it to him again that Pétain, since he would not leave, should be left as a kind of Stadthalter to negotiate the surrender of the forces while the Government left for North Africa.

The question of Pétain's resignation was raised. Once more Reynaud expressed his doubts and fears concerning the effect this might have on public opinion. What would the reaction be if he accepted it? The Ambassador and I pointed out that there could be none amongst the public at large as there were no longer any newspapers in the peace-time sense, and the only news was what the

Government chose to give out. It was difficult to see, we insisted, how he could carry out his policy of fighting on unless he accepted the Marshal's resignation. It seemed from Reynaud's attitude that he agreed.

Madame de Portes opened the door several times during this conversation. We had seen her in the secretaries' room while we were waiting to be taken in to Reynaud: she was talking at the top of her voice, going from one to the other, but of course pretending not to see us.

Now, when she appeared, she showed her impatience at finding us still with the Premier by stamping her foot and closing the door none too gently. At her next intrusion she made faces at Reynaud as if she had vital news to impart. The Ambassador and I looked at each other, irritated and shocked almost beyond endurance, but we managed to hold our tongues. When I left, I went into Margerie's office to complain. He could only reiterate his little saying about her: "She is ugly, *mal soignée*, dirty, nasty and half-demented, and a sore trial to me." Anyway, I got sympathy.

As we drove away, I thought once more that Helène de Portes had done Paul Reynaud more harm than anyone, for it was she who had imposed on him as collaborators the men who were now his bitterest opponents.

Yet presumably she loved him, unless she was merely infatuated with the power her hold over him gave her.

At the Consulate the pandemonium outside and on the stairs was worse than ever. It was an appalling sight. The anxiety of people desperately anxious to get away was very comprehensible. It was natural that they should clutch at all who went by, claiming acquaintanceship, mutual friends, asking for news, begging to be given the means of returning to England. Many were absolutely terrified. Some concealed their apprehension with commendable courage, as did Count H., a Pole, who had good reasons for not wishing to fall into German hands. M. R., on the other hand, was so revolting that his genuine and explicable fear aroused no pity.

Going in and out of the Consulate had become a real ordeal. Pleydell-Bouverie was handling the question of transport with cheerful efficiency. If there were ships to be had he would get them, but it was no joke trying to deal with the 2,000 refugees who had gathered at Bordeaux and were increasing at the rate of 100 an hour. Two brave men, an Englishman, Lord Suffolk, and a Frenchman, Labarthe, were each in his own sphere trying to get on board ship some invaluable machinery, rare metals and substances they had been collecting at considerable risk from all over France.

Two more different types could hardly have been imagined. The Frenchman thin, sallow, ascetic, the product of overheated rooms and difficult examinations, was said to be very much to the Left politically, but he was a fighter and was endeavouring to collect skilled men and to secure passages for them. The Englishman, big, burly, in riding-boots and swinging a loaded hunting-crop, affected the looks of Jorrocks, save that he sported a moustache. He might have been driving cattle to Bordeaux instead of invaluable instruments and bushels of commercial diamonds. They confirmed the lamentable news of the indifference, the lethargy, that prevented any destruction of war material certain to be of immediate use to the Germans.

Presently came the unexpected and cheering news that a destroyer, H.M.S. *Berkeley*, had arrived in the Gironde, but the estuary was still mined. The French sweepers were unwilling to go so far as to test whether their gear was effective against these supposed magnetic mines.

Then, at last, while I was still at the Consulate, a message came from my wife, via the Consul-General at Lyons, asking me to send word to her at the *Préfecture* at Nevers that night to tell her where to make for. This was bad news. She was still evidently in the very centre of France, more than 300 miles from Bordeaux, and the Germans were reported to be on the Loire a few miles to the north of Nevers. I guessed that she had not got farther south because she had stuck to her Army, which turned out to be the fact. I consoled myself with the thought that she evidently knew I was at Bordeaux and so would try to get there; this she eventually did, with her whole unit, after really epic adventures. I managed to get a message through to Nevers, but she never reached the place. It was occupied by the Germans that day.

Shortly before lunch the following message came through from London:

"Foreign Office to Sir Ronald Campbell.

"Please give M. Reynaud the following message, which has been approved by the Cabinet:

"Mr. Churchill to M. Reynaud.   16th June, 1940.
                                                  12.35 p.m.

"Our agreement forbidding separate negotiations, whether for armistice or peace, was made with the French Republic, and not with any particular French Administration or statesman. It therefore involves the honour of France. Nevertheless, provided, *but only provided, that the French Fleet is sailed forthwith for British harbours pending negotiations*, His Majesty's Government give their full consent to an inquiry by the French Government to ascertain the terms of an armistice for France. His Majesty's Government, being resolved to continue the war, wholly exclude themselves from all part in the above-mentioned inquiry concerning an armistice."

I told the Ambassador I was very perturbed by this message. I felt it a mistake to do anything in the nature of releasing the French from their agreement. The door once opened would never be closed again, and I quoted Mandel. I offered to telephone the Prime Minister and put him this point of view. He would no doubt bite my head off, but what was the point of my being where I was if I did not say what I thought? I had not agreed with Churchill in all things over the years, and it was perhaps because I was not a "yes man" that I found myself at Bordeaux today.

There was another aspect to this message. Might not the French, especially the Navy, feel insulted by the peremptory condition that they should sail forthwith to British harbours? Would this not be taken as proof of distrust or at least lack of confidence (which it was) and afford them a pretext for refusing any proposal aimed at achieving the same result which we might subsequently make?

"After all," I argued, "we are in the last resort dependent on the decision of the French themselves, and if they get it into their heads that we wish to hold their Fleet as hostage, the outcry concerning the honour of the flag raised yesterday by Weygand may be renewed with greater stridency by Darlan today."

But the Ambassador wisely pointed out that the Cabinet had known of Mandel's point of view before they sent the message, and it was a Cabinet decision. It was his duty to carry out his instructions.

He did, however, concede that there was force in my last point, and that if there was a new factor, such as a violent French reaction to the clause concerning the Navy, then we should be justified in referring back to London before informing Reynaud.

I suggested we should obtain Darlan's reaction, but neither of us trusted him, so on second thoughts I proposed we should try out the idea on Jeanneney, in whose loyalty and courage we placed complete faith. We drove off immediately to call on the President of the Senate, who was staying with his son-in-law, a Bordeaux doctor, at his simple bourgeois flat. Jeanneney seemed frail and thin, he had some difficulty in getting to his feet and swayed a little as he stood on the highly-polished waxed floor of the doctor's study, but his voice was calm. The strain and his age were telling on his physical condition, but had not in the least affected his mind. I looked at him with admiration and respect, for he was the soul of honour and rectitude, the embodiment of the finest qualities of heart and head which for so long distinguished the French middle and professional classes. The Ambassador with great tact put him our query as a hypothetical case. Would it not be wise, if the French Government did finally ask for an armistice, to send the French Fleet to British harbours before doing so? There it would be beyond enemy reach and the Germans could not make its surrender a condition. It was surely a proposal that should be welcomed, since if the Fleet were in French North African harbours, the Germans, once France was at their mercy, might impose the most dreadful pressure on the Government to surrender it. This would be true whether the Government remained in France or went to North Africa. The only way of ensuring the Fleet's safety was to place it out of the jurisdiction of the French Government itself. If the Germans, using Metropolitan France as a hostage, tortured the country so as to obtain control of the Fleet, what would happen? It was conceivable that it might then be thought that the only way out was to scuttle it. Were it in British harbours it would be safe for France.

It might sail for Canada if this was preferred, I added.

Jeanneney saw the point, and it was evident that the proposal presented with so much sympathy and tact by the Ambassador did not offend him, but he did not commit himself to advocating it.

He told us before we left that he and Herriot had seen Reynaud at his (Reynaud's) request earlier in the morning. Reynaud had said that constitutionally they should be consulted before the seat of the

Government was moved, and would they agree to its going to North Africa? They had readily and enthusiastically done so. The Premier had then asked if they would be prepared to repeat the statement to the Cabinet. They agreed again, and later did so.

In view of Jeanneney's reaction there was neither reason nor excuse for not delivering the Prime Minister's message to Reynaud. We were received without delay, for the Cabinet meeting was over. Sir Ronald read the message to him. His reaction was anything but favourable; he was annoyed and took no pains to disguise it.

Returning to his earlier arguments on the subject he said: "What a very silly thing to do, to ask that the French Fleet should go to British harbours when it is in fact at this very moment protecting Algeria and the Western Mediterranean. And you ask us to do this at the moment you are inviting us to go to North Africa: *non, vraiment, c'est trop bête*."

At this moment the door opened and Madame de Portes' head appeared round the corner. Had proof been needed that the Premier was really cross we had it then, for instead of the polite and questioning raising of the eyebrows which was his usual response to these intrusions, he just glared, and the door closed with unwonted celerity.

Reynaud then said: "This suggestion means offering all French North African harbours to the Italian Fleet as targets," and repeated: "It is really too silly. For one thing, the French Fleet is relieving the British in the Mediterranean. To send ours away would place a fresh strain on yours."

We produced the arguments which had convinced Jeanneney earlier, not omitting to point out that there were British harbours in the Mediterranean from which North Africa could be protected, but these did not affect Reynaud.

Returning to my first impression, I now felt definitely that Churchill's message was a mistake and that we had opened a dangerous door to the defeatists. Several times that day men who had placed their every hope in continuing the war from Africa said: "You would have done much better to have stood by the letter of the bargain and insisted that the French Government should do likewise." My personal opinion was that Reynaud thought so too. That feeling was reinforced when years later I read his book and compared my notes of the time with his text, for he writes that when later in the day, in circumstances I am about to relate, we withdrew this telegram, he was delighted and did not mention it to his colleagues, basing his opposition to those who clamoured for an armistice on the fact that France had pledged her word to Britain, and could not break it by unilateral action.

It is evident that this line of argument would have been valueless had the Ministers known the British Government had conceded that an armistice might be asked for; on the other hand it may equally be advanced that the Cabinet might have accepted the British stipulation had they known of it, though Reynaud's own reaction would seem to show that this was unlikely. None can tell. After considering the events of that terrible day everyone is entitled to his own opinion of what might have happened had Reynaud presented his case differently, but it is most unlikely that Weygand and his backers would have accepted the British proposal, for the question of the Fleet was not new. It had been discussed at Cangé, where the danger of the Germans demanding its surrender had been raised, yet the solution now proposed had occurred to no one, or had not been considered worth pursuing if it had.

It is difficult not to conclude that Weygand, Pétain and some at least of those determined to treat with the Germans would have refused to prejudice their negotiations by infuriating Hitler, as they would have done had the French Fleet been beyond his grasp.

Reynaud then told us the Prime Minister had spoken to him on the telephone. The line had not been too good, and the conversation short, but Churchill had suggested meeting him that night or next day somewhere in Brittany. Would I arrange this? It was finally settled that the meeting should take place off Concarneau, at sea, next day, the 17th. Churchill offered Reynaud H.M.S. *Berkeley* for the trip, but he naturally preferred a French ship, which, however, never materialised.

As we were about to leave, Reynaud said somewhat peevishly, addressing the ceiling, that he understood he had been described to London as being rather soft—*mou*. The meeting with Churchill would give him an opportunity to show him that he had been misinformed. This was a dig at me, and I realised Mandel had been using me as a goad to his Leader. If it could help I did not mind, however much I liked Reynaud personally.

This conversation took place, as I have noted, after the Cabinet meeting, of which the only echo we had had was from Jeanneney. I do not remember Reynaud alluding to it beyond mentioning that Pétain's attitude was becoming more and more intransigent, and that the meeting was to be resumed at five that afternoon.

In his account of the morning Cabinet meeting, after telling of the intervention of Jeanneney and Herriot and saying that the President of the Republic attended, Reynaud relates that, before any discussion started, Pétain read a letter of resignation, the pretext for which was the delay in asking for an armistice. Having read it he rose and made as if to leave the room. The President of the Republic showed strong emotion: "Ah, but you cannot do that to us at such a moment." "Then," Reynaud writes, "I said coldly to the Marshal that, since this letter was addressed to me, I requested him to await my reply. He consented, adding that he would not sit down, and he remained standing, his letter of resignation in his hand. I drew his attention to the fact that, when one has put so grave a question to one's ally—that is, to be relieved of one's pledged word—it was usual to await his answer, which I should be in a position to give the Cabinet in the afternoon. Rather shamefacedly the Marshal put his letter in his pocket and returned to his seat."*

Bouthillier gives a different account. He refers to the visit of the Presidents of the two Assemblies, but elects not to give their declarations in favour of moving the seat of the Government to North Africa.†

He then says Reynaud made two communications to the Cabinet. The first was to read Roosevelt's telegram, the second was, he comments, more of a shock. It was that: "The British Cabinet had not ratified the position taken at Tours by Mr. Churchill and his two colleagues. Whilst the French Government asked the British Government's consent to enquire of the enemy the conditions for an eventual armistice, the British Government appeared to have adopted an intransigent attitude, which foreshadowed a refusal."

Bouthillier goes on to say that these two pieces of information provoked consternation, and that then "M. Baudouin, who had been present at the meeting of the Supreme Council at Tours, indicated that the engagements taken by Mr. Churchill had been made without

* *La France a sauvé l'Europe*, Vol. II, p. 343.

† The President of the Republic writes that the Presidents of the two Assemblies made it clear that in their view the decision to move the seat of the Government to North Africa implied the continuation of the struggle. (*Témoignage*, p. 82.)

reservation and safeguarded completely the future of the Alliance. M. Paul Reynaud contested this."*

Here we have an echo, in an exaggerated form, of the conversation the Ambassador and I had had with Reynaud before the Cabinet meeting.

Bouthillier then says that misfortune had thus reached its nadir, for the two doors, the one which led to North Africa, and the other to negotiations with the Germans, remained closed. The only hope was, he thought, that the French communication sent after the Cabinet meeting the evening before, to which the news given by M. Reynaud evidently did not provide an answer, would lead the British Government to revise its position.†

We gathered for lunch at our usual large table in the centre of the room at the *Chapon Fin* where the senior members of the Embassy staff joined us when their work allowed. Some had finished their meal, others had not yet arrived.

The place was full; there were more Deputies and Senators than the day before. The Ambassador and I knew many. When we left we each spoke to a few we were acquainted with in the lobby, and I went

* Bouthillier, *Le Drame de Vichy*, pp. 81–2.

† Baudouin's account steers a course which hardly keeps truth within sight. "This morning," he writes, "Sir Ronald Campbell indicated that the British Cabinet did not ratify the point of view expressed by Mr. Churchill at the last Supreme Council held at Tours. The British Cabinet considers France to be bound by her undertaking not to negotiate separately with Germany and that she cannot be relieved of this pledge." He goes on to say, as does Bouthillier, that Reynaud was to go to Nantes immediately to meet Churchill at 1.30 or 2 p.m. that day. (As they note it was then noon, this was already an unlikely contingency, quite apart from the fact that no time or place for a meeting had yet been fixed.) The only explanation which can give any colour to this statement is that Reynaud was trying to gain time and indicated he intended meeting the Prime Minister as soon as possible, possibly at Nantes, in the hope that no decision would be arrived at before then. (Churchill's conversation on the telephone with Reynaud took place after the Cabinet meeting.)

Baudouin says that he himself then "emphasised how surprising and painful it was that the British Government should have gone back on the undertaking to relieve France of her promise and not to overwhelm an unfortunate associate, which was given by Mr. Churchill at Tours and afterwards confirmed by his two War Cabinet colleagues, Lord Halifax and Lord Beaverbrook. M. Reynaud answered, awkward and sad, that these three members of the British Cabinet had not bound the Cabinet as a whole, and that therefore the only thing to do was to accept its decision." (Baudouin, *Neuf Mois au Gouvernement*, pp. 171–2.)

There is no indication in this account, as there is in that of Bouthillier, that Reynaud refuted or contested this statement.

off to the Hotel Splendide, the largest hotel in the town, now full to bursting point. I hoped to glean there some impression of what the more important people, especially the politicians, were thinking. It was a discouraging experience. Deputies and Senators were fully aware that the question now being debated by the Government was whether the war should be continued from Africa, but few seemed in favour of this solution. They were not thinking in terms of France and her honour, but of their constituencies and their jobs. Surrender rather than sacrifice was the theme of their thoughts and conversations. The tide of defeat had swamped even the gestures of defiance. The lack of a virile reaction which had been so marked throughout all classes in France since the German break-through had now become a cloying helplessness.

Some made me think of birds caught in bird-lime, others of rabbits fascinated by a stoat, their eyes fixed on the Germans as on an inevitable doom. To such as these, talk of British resistance was as embarrassing as finding yourself in the wrong clothes at the wrong party, as tactless as a challenge to run to a legless man, as out of place as a bugle call in a mortuary.

My British uniform struck a false note. Men who hitherto would have rushed up, hands extended, exclaiming: "*Cher ami, quel bon vent vous amène!*" or "*Tiens, vous voilà, quelle chance!*" or again "*Mais c'est Spears! il va nous expliquer . . .*" varied by "*Mon Général, dites moi,*" or "*Puis-je vous demander?*" knew what I had to say and avoided me, that is, all but a few business men, anxious to leave the country. The exceptions, the *durs*, were, I noted with some annoyance as a Conservative, in the main Socialists.

I returned to the Hotel Montré with the clear impression that there would be no reaction amongst politicians against surrender. They might follow a bold lead, though this was doubtful, but would not welcome it. They would certainly not rise in anger against a Government that adopted defeat as its policy, and were more likely to gather round a leading figure who remained in France than to lend support to a Government that sailed for Africa to fight on.

It seemed to me that this would be true even without Pétain to head the defeatists. The white flag of the Kings of France on which the fleurs-de-lis were emblazoned symbolised the exact opposite conception of the one the Marshal was so anxious to hoist. The white flag stood now, not for a whole past of glory, but for abject surrender, and the bewildered, the hesitant, the faint-hearted, who together formed an undoubted majority at Bordeaux, would, I was convinced, rally to the emblem of submission. Who would resist when the great Marshal preached resignation? Who would fight when that redoubtable warrior Weygand proclaimed fighting to be folly? Who was the civilian so foolhardy as to challenge the soldiers in their own sphere when no military leader did so, none save the obscure de Gaulle, of whom no one had heard?

Henry of Navarre told his knights to rally to the white plumes on his helmet—*ralliez vous à mon panache blanc*. Now the white plumes of chivalry had become the white feathers of defeatism.

Democracy is a splendid conception, but has the disadvantage on occasions of placing in the lead men who will sap the strength of a country over a period of years, disrupt an empire in a matter of months, and encompass the defeat of a great nation in the space of a few days.

I found the Ambassador's conversations had led him to conclusions not very different from mine as regards the politicians. I sat in my room and wrote in the margin of my notes some names: Bayard, Du Guesclin, d'Assas, *les trois frères* Aymon, Amadis of Gaul, heroes of Ancient France, who had been my heroes too in the days of my childhood when my mother, brought up in France, and dearly loving it, its history and its legends, had told me of them with all the ardour of her Irish romanticism, warmed by the sunshine of Latin skies.

With a sharper pang, memory recalled that in the First War these names were often on the lips of General de Maud'huy, of whom I noted that he could not conceive of defeat so long as a single Frenchman remained alive.

A message from London, soon after 3.30, asked when the next French Cabinet meeting was to be held. Five that afternoon was the answer. About 4 p.m. a second telegram from the Foreign Office to the Ambassador was received. It ran:

"Foreign Office to Sir Ronald Campbell.

"You should inform M. Reynaud as follows:

"We expect to be consulted as soon as any armistice terms are received. This is necessary not merely in virtue of treaty forbidding separate peace or armistice, but also in view of vital consequences of any armistice to ourselves, having regard especially to the fact that British troops are fighting with French Army. You should impress on French Government that in stipulating for removal of French Fleet to British ports we have in mind French interests as well as our own, and are convinced that it will strengthen the hands of the French Government in any armistice discussions if they can show that the French Navy is out of reach of the German forces. As regards the French Air Force, we assume that every effort will be made to fly it to North Africa, unless indeed the French Government would prefer to send it to this country.

"We count on the French Government doing all they can both before and during any armistice discussions to extricate the Polish, Belgian, and Czech troops at present in France, and to send them to North Africa. Arrangements are being made to receive Polish and Belgian Governments in this country."

In five minutes we were with Reynaud again. The Ambassador read him the text, translating it slowly. Reynaud reacted as he had done to the first message; he invoked the same arguments and so did we.

He was perhaps more tired; he was certainly more difficult and petulant than at our earlier interview. But we were more determined, for we saw clearly that London expected us somehow to get the French Fleet out of the clutches of the Germans. It was the only thing left to fight for on the Bordeaux front now that the Cabinet had accepted the idea of an armistice.

Nevertheless I think it quite possible that Reynaud nursed the illusion he might still carry the day with his colleagues. I like to think he did, for he was plucky. But if he was dreaming that dream and had told us of it we would not have shared it, for he was so evidently at the end of his tether that it was unlikely he could overcome the implacable opposition facing him. He was gallant to the extreme limit of his capacity, which was not, however, unlimited, and he counted perhaps overmuch on his own cleverness and subtlety. That is why I think it possible that he hoped, having discharged what he conceived to be his duty in informing the British Government of his Cabinet's view, that Churchill and his colleagues would still hold France to her pledge. He hoped that, by playing the card of British intransigence, he could sway the Cabinet to his thesis. The way events unfolded lends probability to this hypothesis. If this was really his innermost thought, it would have been wiser to drop us a hint of it.

But we in Bordeaux and the Cabinet in London knew only one thing: that the French Government had asked British permission to sue for an armistice, and that the request had been made by Reynaud himself without qualifications. Moreover, he had asked us to insist, as we had in our telegram of the night before, that this request was the result of a formal Cabinet decision taken at a meeting presided over by the President of the Republic.

As the Ambassador and I argued with Reynaud more acrimoniously than ever on the subject of the Fleet, the telephone rang. Reynaud took up the receiver. The next moment his eyebrows went up so far they became indistinguishable from his neatly brushed hair; one eyebrow to either side of the parting. "One moment," he said, "I must take it down," and grasping a sheet of foolscap on the slippery table, he began to write, using a short gold pencil with an enormous lead. He repeated each word as he wrote it, and listening I became transfixed with amazement. I was so absorbed I did not even look at the Ambassador to see if he shared my feelings. Reynaud was taking down in French, from de Gaulle's dictation in London, the text of the Declaration of Union proposed by the British Government. On he wrote in a frightful scrawl, getting more excited as the message unfolded. The paper skidded on the smooth surface of the table. I held it. As each sheet was covered I handed him a fresh one. His pencil gave out; I handed him mine.

Finally he stopped and said into the telephone: "Does he agree to this? Did Churchill give you this personally?" There was a moment's pause and now he was speaking in English. It was evident that de Gaulle had handed the receiver to Churchill, who was assuring him that the document was a decision of the Cabinet. If there were alterations, they would be merely verbal.

Reynaud put the receiver down. He was transfigured with joy, and my old friendship for him surged out in a wave of appreciation at his response, for he was happy with a great happiness in the belief that France would now remain in the war. This was his thought as it was ours, and in those first moments this was all that mattered. The sense of the generosity of the offer was overwhelming, the sincerity of the gesture completely convincing.

I was as moved as when I used to hear at some Battalion Headquarters in Flanders of a great feat of bravery and self-sacrifice; of a

man who, exhausted, wet and tired, struggled back through the mud
under heavy fire to rescue a friend. For that was it. Britain, having
escaped so far, now turned back to help her stricken comrade,
offering to share with her everything she possessed. The one-
sided sacrifice of France seemed balanced in a moment by this
gesture of absolute solidarity.

The text of the proposed joint declaration was as follows:

"At this most fateful moment in the history of the modern
world the Governments of the United Kingdom and the French
Republic make this declaration of indissoluble union and un-
yielding resolution in their common defence of justice and freedom
against subjection to a system which reduces mankind to a life of
robots and slaves.

"The two Governments declare that France and Great Britain
shall no longer be two nations, but one Franco-British Union.

"The constitution of the Union will provide for joint organs of
defence, foreign, financial, and economic policies.

"Every citizen of France will enjoy immediately citizenship of
Great Britain; every British subject will become a citizen of France.

"Both countries will share responsibility for the repair of the
devastation of war, wherever it occurs in their territories, and the
resources of both shall be equally, and as one, applied to that
purpose.

"During the war there shall be a single War Cabinet, and all the
forces of Britain and France, whether on land, sea, or in the air,
will be placed under its direction. It will govern from wherever it
best can. The two Parliaments will be formally associated. The
nations of the British Empire are already forming new armies.
France will keep her available forces in the field, on the sea, and in
the air. The Union appeals to the United States to fortify the
economic resources of the Allies, and to bring her powerful
material aid to the common cause.

"The Union will concentrate its whole energy against the power
of the enemy, no matter where the battle may be.

"And thus we shall conquer."

"This must be typed at once so that you can have it for the Cabinet
meeting," I said, and gathering Reynaud's script I dashed off to the

secretaries' room. This re-found familiarity and enthusiasm which led me to snatch Reynaud's transcript and instruct his secretaries to have it typed denotes better than anything else the zest, the relief, the light-headedness induced by the new situation the British proposal created. It did not occur to us that it might not be accepted.

In the secretaries' room stood the inevitable Madame de Portes. As I handed a secretary the paper she stepped behind him and read over his shoulder, holding his arm to prevent his turning the pages too fast for her to read them. It was difficult to tell from her expression whether rage or amazement prevailed. But both feelings were apparent. As she went on delaying the secretary to read herself, I told him curtly the message must be typed without a moment's delay.

Reynaud writes that he was being spied upon at this period, and that the defeatists were made aware of the British proposal before the Cabinet meeting.

The above incident may suffice to explain how the information reached them. Madame de Portes was in constant communication with Baudouin and Prouvost.

When I returned to Reynaud's office, his exultation had if anything increased. "I will die defending these proposals," he exclaimed. The Ambassador, always cool, cautious and reserved, was beaming too. It was wonderful.

I recognised the voices of Ministers I knew in the adjoining room. They were collecting for the Cabinet to be held in the house next door. Mandel and Marin looked in for a moment. They were hurriedly told of the British proposals and were obviously both relieved and pleased. Then the telephone rang again. It was Churchill, who had got through a wonderfully-timed call. Reynaud's renewed hopes and courage must have been perceptible to the Prime Minister at the other end of the line. Yes, he accepted, said Reynaud, he was delighted, it was a splendid gesture of solidarity. Then came a few words about the meeting next day. Yes, Concarneau, that was settled. The time must be fixed later. He was just off to a Cabinet meeting when he would tell his colleagues. He was full of confidence.

As he put down the receiver he turned to us and said he presumed this offer superseded the two telegrams on the subject of the Fleet. The Ambassador and I both said we were convinced it did. It could not be otherwise. The proposal, if accepted, meant that France would go on in the war united with Great Britain. The disposal of the Fleet would then be a question of strategy to be settled by the joint staffs.

In this we were not mistaken, for on returning to the hotel we found a telegram from the Foreign Office: "Please suspend action," so we sent a message to Reynaud at the Cabinet meeting to say that he and we had been right in our surmise and that the two telegrams should be considered as cancelled.*

It was a difficult afternoon to live through. The Ambassador and I waited at the hotel. We walked into each other's rooms at intervals to compare notes, discuss ideas and impressions that occurred to one or the other. When Sir Ronald asked me several times what I thought Reynaud's chances were of carrying the day, I must confess to having been completely optimistic. The picture I kept recalling of Reynaud setting off with a light step to read the proposal to the President of the Republic made for cheerfulness. The Ambassador, more cautious, had doubts on the subject; I had none, declared I had a hunch all would be well and that it was inconceivable the most generous offer one country had ever made to another would be turned down. I have never trusted in a hunch since then, nor placed much faith in my prescience.

We speculated as to how the proposal could be worked out in practice. It would certainly be complicated. An Anglo-French Government was hard enough to imagine, but the picture evoked by an Anglo-French Parliament was irresistibly funny, for their only common denominator would be abysmal ignorance of each other's language. One of us used the French expression: "It would be a basketful of crabs."

I told the Ambassador that my pro-French tendencies had led sarcastically-minded journalists to dub me "the Member for Paris". Under this scheme this might come true.

The most convincing reason for optimism over the outcome of the French Cabinet's deliberations was, we reminded each other, the

* Churchill, referring to this incident, writes: "A messenger was therefore sent after him to say that the two earlier messages should be considered as 'cancelled'. 'Suspended' would have been a better word." (*The Second World War*, Vol. II, p. 185.) As Churchill has used the word 'cancelled' I have repeated it, for I have no copy of the message. I am, however, astonished that we did not repeat the word used by the Foreign Office, as obviously the endeavour in such circumstances is to render the exact shade of meaning of the authority at home. In this case, in the great hurry, it may have been that in the attempt to paraphrase the text of the telegram, as was always done for security reasons, a less appropriate word was used than that employed by the sender.

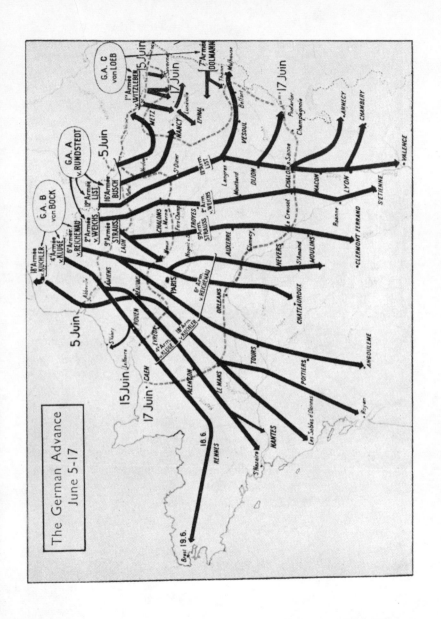

The German Advance
June 5-17

obvious one we had already used with Reynaud: How could it come about that, of the countries fighting Germany, France should be the only one to give up the struggle, when she possessed an intact Empire second only to our own and a Fleet whole and entire, the strongest after ours in Europe? No, it was unthinkable.

By 6.30 my optimism had suffered a set-back. If the Cabinet had accepted the British offer they would have done so enthusiastically, quickly, and we should have been told. The long delay portended no good, that was a fact. But still I went on thinking and saying that it was bound to come out all right, anything else was impossible.

CHAPTER XIX

Sunday, June 16th

(2)

The British arrangements for a meeting with Reynaud—We are summoned to hear the French Cabinet's decision—Margerie tells us Reynaud is going to resign—Reynaud on the Cabinet proceedings—We beg him to postpone his resignation—Churchill's account of the cancelled meeting—Mandel's cold rage—We appeal to Jeanneney—The attitude of M. Lebrun—We call again on Reynaud—De Gaulle's urgent appeal—Reynaud tells us that Pétain is forming a Government—and gives us its composition—His relief at giving up office—I dash his hopes of a meeting with Churchill—Farewell to Reynaud—De Gaulle fears Weygand will prevent his carrying on resistance—He asks for sanctuary on a British warship—He joins us at the Hotel Montré—His desire to go to England—I telephone Churchill and obtain leave to bring de Gaulle by plane next day—My last talk with Mandel—The end of a great man—Sir Ronald Campbell's calm courage.

IT was now seven. The Cabinet meeting had been going on for two hours when a telephone message from London came through saying the Prime Minister, Attlee, Sinclair, the three Chiefs of Staff and others would arrive in a warship off Concarneau at noon next day to meet Reynaud.

De Gaulle had been consulted and agreed to the time and place.*

At 7.30 we were sent for.

The rue Vital-Carles was barred by troops holding back the

---

* Baudouin's account of the day's events includes this passage: "I went to see the President of the Council at 4 p.m. with Bouthillier. I then learned that the meeting with Mr. Churchill was not to take place, he having refused to come and confer with the President (M. Reynaud)." (*Neuf Mois au Gouvernement*, p. 172.)

biggest crowd assembled there so far. Again they cheered the British car. An excellent omen; this was surely the voice of the people expressing their desire to fight on. A moment later we were in the bare, gloomy, dark-columned hall, empty but for a couple of orderlies idling by the window. Margerie stepped forward and said incisively, as one making a statement of fact that could not be discussed: "The President of the Council is going to tell you he is going to resign." "What's that, what did you say?" I exclaimed, surprise and anger fighting for precedence in my mind. Margerie repeated coldly but even more incisively than before: "The President of the Council is going to tell you he is going to resign," and he opened the door of a room on the ground floor which was not that in which Reynaud had hitherto received us.

So this was the end. Reynaud was beaten, he had not made the grade; France was leaving us to fight alone. I felt stunned and suffocated; I had great difficulty in making the physical effort of overcoming the nausea which rose like acid from my stomach to my throat. I do not know what the Ambassador felt. His pain and disappointment cannot have had the personal quality of mine. He probably thought of his great responsibility and how to discharge it. My feeling was one of intimate horror. I had never fully realised how much love of France was a part of myself till that moment. It was as if, as I gazed at the reflection of a beautiful, always beloved being in a familiar pool, two horrible hands had stretched out of the shadow and strangled her, whilst I, the onlooker, could neither move nor even cry out.

Realising in a moment that personal feeling mattered not at all and that if anything was to be retrieved from this catastrophe it must be reclaimed now, I got hold of myself, determined not to show what I felt. A flash of anger, an ill-judged word, might send Reynaud off on the side-track of recriminations, protests, explanations. What we wanted to know was whether there was still a spark of hope; it was necessary to listen to what he said, assess the situation calmly, then come to a decision.

Reynaud's appearance and demeanour were so different from what I expected that amazement changed my mood again. It was as if, walking into a room to condole with a widower, one was confronted by a bridegroom. Astonishment baffled me. If he was not gay, gaiety rippled under the surface of his manner; if he was not exactly detached, he spoke as an expert giving evidence at a trial.

It was obvious that he was immensely relieved but at some pains not to show it.

Later, in an attempt to describe my impression of him, I reported that his attitude had made me think of a man receiving the condolences of friends at the funeral of a rich uncle.

He proceeded to give us some account of the Cabinet meeting. He had read the British offer of union twice over to the Cabinet without obtaining any favourable reaction from his colleagues. "I then commented upon it, but it was no good. Some were astonished, others taken aback, more were hostile. 'What the proposal amounts to is that we should become a British Dominion', said one, and this statement reflected the reaction of most," Reynaud told us.* He went on to explain that he had been confronted by a stubborn majority absolutely determined to carry out what he described as the incredible folly of asking Hitler for his proposals, pretending to themselves they could reject them if they did not like them. Thinking of the electors, they hoped their wisdom in seeking to stop the conflict would be applauded, whilst their avowed readiness to renew it if the Germans were too exigent would be admired as a proof of bravery.

What nonsense, I thought. What chance will the French elector have of expressing an opinion after the German steam-roller has passed over him? Will he even be allowed to hear, much less discuss, what is afoot?

What lunatic could imagine a population under Nazi domination rejecting Nazi terms?

Reynaud told us that care had been taken to see that bad news from the front should reach the Cabinet at the psychological moment.

A telegram from General Georges had been read out saying that German armour was advancing on La Charité-sur-Loire and that it was absolutely essential to take a decision.†

"Was the Cabinet informed that Churchill proposes to meet you tomorrow and may even have started?" we asked. "Yes," answered Reynaud, "but it made no difference, they had made up their minds."

---

* Weygand writes that for France to have accepted these proposals, under the circumstances, would have placed her in a state of vassalage impossible to conceive of. (*Rappelé au Service*, p. 233.)

† "To fully appreciate the atmosphere prevailing at these successive meetings, it is necessary to note that whilst they were proceeding we were shown telegrams from the Army describing an ever more alarming situation." (Lebrun, *Témoignage*, p. 83).

Feeling it was still just possible that the President might entrust Reynaud with the formation of a new Government provided a successor had not yet been appointed, I asked with considerable emphasis whether he had resigned or not. He said he had not, but intended doing so, as the majority of the Cabinet was against him.

The Ambassador and I had like reactions. Putting the same idea forward each in our own way we begged Reynaud to renounce or at least postpone this irretrievable step until there had been time to consider all its implications. It was a matter of immense moment to England; to act thus without consulting her within a few hours of receiving at her hands the most fraternal offer one country had ever made to another was unthinkable. It was like stabbing a friend bent over you in grief and affection. Surely the matter could be left over until he had seen Churchill next day?

As we reported later to London, we worked on him for half an hour, doing our best to encourage him to try to get rid of the evil influences among his colleagues. Realising that we were making little impression, we told him we knew he was tired and overwrought by a terrible day of struggle. Let him rest awhile, take some food. He had said the British offer represented salvation; the Cabinet must have time to consider its implications.

We declared that we simply refused to accept what he had told us as a final decision. We would return at ten in the confident hope that he would by then have changed his mind.

The first thing to do was to get a message through to London to hold up the Prime Minister's journey, so, dashing through the crowd, who cheered us again, poor people, quite unaware of their fate and still hoping, we sent our message from the hotel.

Churchill in his book tells what happened in London as a result. "Our War Cabinet sat until six o'clock on the 16th, and thereafter I set out on my mission. I took with me the Leaders of the Labour and Liberal Parties, the three Chiefs of Staff, and various important officers and officials. A special train was waiting at Waterloo. We could reach Southampton in two hours, and a night of steaming at thirty knots in the cruiser would bring us to the rendezvous by noon on the 17th. We had taken our seats in the train. My wife had come to see me off. There was an odd delay in starting. Evidently some hitch had occurred. Presently my private secretary arrived from Downing Street breathless with the following message from Campbell at Bordeaux:

" 'Ministerial crisis has opened. . . . Hope to have news by midnight. Meanwhile meeting arranged for tomorrow impossible.'
"On this I returned to Downing Street with a heavy heart."

The Ambassador agreed that the best thing we could do was to see Jeanneney.

On our way we stopped to see Mandel. He was in a cold rage. "*Il n'y a rien à faire avec ces gens là,*" he said. "I called Chautemps a coward, and so did Rio. When there were protests I distributed the same diploma to his supporters, but it was no use. When you are dealing with panic-ridden troops only shooting will stop them. The only thing Reynaud has shot is his bolt," and describing the Premier he said that he had spoken without heat or fire, like a lawyer defending a cause he did not believe in and for which he had been promised an inadequate fee.

"No, Reynaud has lost all authority," he went on, and as for the President: "*C'est un pauvre homme* who just can't make up his mind to leave France." Rather sadly he added: "You should have held France to her signature. Churchill has been too nice. His kindness, his chivalry and loyalty may sometimes be a fault; they have been in this case." We had heard enough. It was all-important to catch Jeanneney before he saw the President. As Herriot worked in the most complete accord with him and, in matters constitutional, was inclined to accept his lead, a visit to him was the equivalent of seeing the Presidents of both the Assemblies.

Jeanneney seemed even frailer than earlier in the day, he steadied himself with one hand on his desk as he rose to greet us, but was if anything clearer-minded and calmer than ever. We showed him the British proposal. It was the first he had heard of it. He immediately grasped the nobility and generosity of the gesture and was deeply moved. Although the most meticulous and intransigent guardian of the constitution of which he was the highest exponent, he failed to detect in it a plot to subordinate France to England and make of his country a Dominion, as lesser men had done. It was, he said, a document of lofty purpose, inspired by the finest, the most exalted feelings. It was good to hear him say so.

When we gave him Reynaud's account of the Cabinet meeting, of which he had as yet heard nothing, a look of pain came over his face.

Could he do anything? He could not yet tell. He would see. We asked whether the President of the Republic could not be induced to entrust the formation of a new Government to Reynaud, who could then form an Administration from which the defeatists would be eliminated. And what about Mandel as an alternative? The President would probably not think that Mandel could form a Government, said Jeanneney, and he himself doubted whether he could, but, he went on, this was not a question for him; even in so grave an hour, perhaps because the situation was so desperately serious, he must conform to his constitutional position with particular care.

He could not advise the President until the President sought his advice and that of the President of the Chamber. He would consult Herriot.

He did not commit himself; he indicated that he would observe the law whatever happened. We could but agree, but begged him nevertheless in a matter of such supreme importance, involving as it did the Alliance, to find means of influencing the President of the Republic in favour of asking Reynaud to form a new Government. It should be made clear to M. Lebrun, we suggested, that the offer contained in the Prime Minister's message would of course not be extended to a Government which entered into negotiations with the enemy.

We left this fine old man, a monument of rectitude, with a slight feeling of comfort; he had given us a little ease in our distress. We knew he felt as we did and were certain that he and Herriot would do all in their power to keep France in the war.

He was as good as or better than his word. When soon afterwards the President of the Republic consulted him together with Herriot, they both declared together that they advised him to reappoint Reynaud.*

---

* President Lebrun says he consulted the Presidents of the Senate and Chamber and informed them of his intentions, but does not say what their reaction was. (*Témoignage*, p. 85.)

Jeanneney, giving evidence on July 26th, 1945, stated:

"M.Reynaud declared: 'In any case if the armistice is asked for, it will not be by me,' upon which M. Albert Lebrun said: 'Then who, tomorrow?' and M. Herriot and I at once, and I think together, answered: 'Paul Reynaud.' "

M. Herriot giving evidence on July 30th stated:

"M. Reynaud had said he would not act against his political conscience and ask for an armistice. The President of the Republic invited us to tell him, as custom demands, whom we suggested to succeed him. We answered 'Paul Reynaud.' We mentioned no other name. Let it be clearly understood that neither M. Jeanneney nor I put forward the name of Marshal Pétain."

During the years of the war I sometimes wondered if Sir Ronald Campbell and I, in our search for some means of stopping the rot, should not have asked to see Monsieur Lebrun. I had, of course, nothing to do with him officially and had only met him at receptions in pre-war days. The Ambassador was accredited to him as Head of the State but naturally never transacted business with him.

If either of us had thought it would do the slightest good I am sure we would have sought an audience with him, regardless of precedent, but we were persuaded it would be worse than useless.

Those purporting to be in close touch with the President may have done him a wrong in describing him as so demoralised that it was a waste of time to speak to him. That very afternoon Mandel had described him to me as stretched out on a sofa sobbing, incapable of taking anything in. This does not appear to have been true, for such witnesses as have since written of these events describe him as taking a quite active part in the deliberations. But we need not, I think, have any regrets, for nothing we could have said would have made the slightest difference. It is clear that the President had made up his mind that France was free of her obligations to Britain, and was at liberty to ask for an armistice if she deemed it to be in her interests to do so.

Much later, when the stresses and strains no longer existed, when the nightmare of Bordeaux was a thing of the past, M. Lebrun stated at the Pétain Trial that, as Britain had retained in her island part of her air strength (which he then recognised had proved to be in the ultimate interest of the coalition), it was his considered opinion that "from the moment when one nation signatory to a convention like that of March 28th, 1940, retains a part of its forces for its own defence instead of risking them in battle as does its partner, it is entitled to go through the form of producing a paper recalling the obligations of the agreement; but it has no longer the moral authority to say: 'I cannot free you from your obligations'."

In neither incarnation, that of collapsed despair or juridical argumentation, would the President of the French Republic have been of any help to us in our last endeavour to find someone at Bordeaux willing to make an ultimate effort to keep France in the war.

We tried to see Darlan but found it impossible; he was not to be traced, but we did have a word with a high-ranking French Naval officer who may have been his Chief of Staff, though I am not sure of this. We met him in the street. He was, to say the least, reserved, but did indicate that the Admiral had no intention of allowing the Fleet to fall into enemy hands.

Of all the· good dinners served us at the *Chapon Fin*, the one placed before us that night was the hardest to face. It was like a fairy tale; day after day meals were served to be dreamed of for a lifetime, but as difficult to eat as if the dishes were of cardboard served in sauces of sand; yet they had to be eaten for the sake of the scores of keen observers ready to draw deductions, to be at once disseminated, from the demeanour of the Ambassador and his companions. A glimpse of Laval, dark, bloated and satisfied, at a table not very far from ours, did little to stimulate our appetites.

I do not know whether the Ambassador felt the same reluctance to make our promised call on Reynaud as I did. A cowardly desire to put off the inevitable made me wish to gain a little time, any minute that meant postponement was welcome, and I thought that a condemned man must feel like that.

"Well, I suppose we ought to be going?" said Sir Ronald. "It is just on 10 o'clock." He was looking at his watch, betraying no emotion.

I faced up to the inevitable.

There was still a group of people at the entrance of the rue Vital Carles. They gave us a small friendly cheer.

The large hall of the Premier's residence was dark; just enough light for the columns and the wide stairs to throw out deep shadows. An historical building would have seemed ghostly under the circumstances, but this product of the Third Republic's architecture only created the atmosphere of an ill-lit furniture repository where every instinct is concentrated on not barking one's shins. There was absolutely no one about. The Ambassador remained in the hall while I climbed the stairs in search of someone.*

Meeting with no success I came down and on the last step was confronted by a French major. He was very excited and in great

---

* Writing of the following night, the 17th, Herriot describes a scene which differed in no wise from that of the 16th: "At the Ministry of War, as at the Presidency of the Council, there was no one on duty; no office was working, not a lamp was lit. A few men, a subaltern asleep, an N.C.O., two soldiers, two '*gardes mobiles*', were there to watch the building. Two busts (perhaps those of Marshals of bygone days) are the most living things in this cemetery. I have the impression the country is lost, that it is already dead." (*Épisodes*, pp. 79–80.)

distress. He explained that he was in command of a bombing formation and had heard France was giving up the struggle. He would never accept this, he shouted, never. "We fly to England tomorrow to fight on with you. Rendezvous in England," and he held out his hand. I felt deep sympathy for him, he was obviously sincere and in great anguish of mind, but he never came. I often wondered what form of persuasion or pressure had been put on him and others like him not to do so.

I could now see two or three orderlies who had emerged from nowhere, or perhaps my eyes had become used to the gloom. Margerie was talking to the Ambassador in the corner near the study where we had seen Reynaud earlier. I went to join them. Passing by a large column I was startled to see a tall figure flat against it, shrouded in its shadow. It called me by name in a loud whisper. I stopped and looked up at de Gaulle. "I must speak to you," he said, "it is extremely urgent." "But I can't now, the Ambassador and I are just going in to see the Premier." "You must," he insisted. "I have very good reason to believe Weygand intends arresting me."

I looked round. Margerie had opened the door of Reynaud's study; the Ambassador, about to enter, had stopped, waiting for me.

"We shan't be long, I think," I said to de Gaulle. "If you stay exactly where you are until we come out it should be all right. In any case I must go now, I really must. It is very, very important."

It certainly was.

Reynaud was standing when we came in, and we all three remained standing for the first part of the interview.

Reynaud was more reserved than usual; evidently the last thing he wished was to be questioned as to what had happened since we saw him last. He was going through a necessary formality, a producer giving an account of the last disastrous performance of a play to its backers. The curtain had been rung down, it was over, he must think of his own plans. The occasion was one which no longer concerned him, and the details did not greatly matter. He was at pains to underline his detachment. The obvious relief he had shown earlier was no longer apparent. If he still felt it, he concealed it. He told us, speaking easily in sentences that dovetailed neatly, that the President had asked the Marshal to form a Government. Pétain had had his list of Ministers ready in his pocket and forthwith obtained the President's approval to it. It was composed entirely of abject defeatists.

Reynaud gave us the principal names. Baudouin was Minister for Foreign Affairs. "So Italy has not made a bad investment," I said bitterly. Laval had been asked to join but had refused. We thought this was because he did not yet consider it safe to do so, but we were wrong.*

Weygand was to be Minister of Defence. This was certainly to have been expected, but I ground my teeth with rage. I expected Reynaud to make some comment, but no, he pronounced the name of the man with whom he had had his bitterest conflict, who was more responsible than any other for his downfall, with indifference, as if the acrimonious struggle raging a few hours ago had happened in the dim and almost forgotten past.

My friend General Colson was to be Minister of War. Now I understood why he had blushed scarlet when I ran into him in a village on the Loire.

He was an honest man. But even then he must have stood for surrender, and doubtless felt embarrassed when he met an old friend who could only think in terms of fighting on, and who he knew attributed the same feelings to him. The shortcomings of his department may also have helped to make him feel awkward. Well, Pétain did not hold that against him. The artisans of defeat now came together in the Government. 'What more natural,' I thought. 'They will now gather what they have sown'; and, much as I had liked him, I wrote Colson off the precious list of my friends.

There was for the first time a tone of sarcasm in Reynaud's voice as he gave us the next name, Bouthillier, the new Minister of Finance, the man he had created and who had turned on him.

More interesting, Darlan was to be Minister of Marine. The Ambassador and I looked at each other. The same thought occurred to us as we saw a new danger. Darlan as Pétain's Minister was

---

* Lebrun writes that he dissuaded Pétain from including Laval for fear of further complications on the British side. (*Témoignage*, p. 85.) On the other hand Weygand and Baudouin both state that Pétain had offered Laval the Ministry of Justice, which he refused, demanding the Foreign Office. Pétain gave way, but Charles-Roux and Weygand protested, inducing the Marshal to change his mind again, whereupon Laval withdrew in a huff. (Baudouin, *Neuf Mois au Gouvernement*, pp. 195–6. Weygand, *Rappelé au Service*, p. 237.) Marquet, Laval's *alter ego*, whose activities we had been observing with disgust ever since we arrived at Bordeaux, also refused to join the Government. (Bouthillier, *Le Drame de Vichy*, p. 92.)

Eight days later Laval was Vice-President of the Council and Marquet Minister of the Interior.

identifying himself with defeat. He was no longer the Naval Commander-in-Chief, the sailor who placed the fate of the Fleet above all political considerations. Now he was to be a member of a Government suing for an armistice, and, unless he resigned, would be bound by its verdict. Unless he felt at one with Pétain he would not be taking office in his Ministry.*

Prouvost was to be High Commissioner of Information. The team would hardly have been complete had it not included the principal poltroon of the last Administration; its undertaker, Chautemps, the bard of the grandmother with a pain, was to be Vice-President.

* Churchill writes: "His (Admiral Darlan's) authority over the Fleet was for all practical purposes absolute. He had only to order the ships to British, American, or French colonial harbours—some had already started—to be obeyed. In the morning of June 17, after the fall of M. Reynaud's Cabinet, he declared to General Georges that he had resolved to give the order. The next day Georges met him in the afternoon and asked him what had happened. Darlan replied that he had changed his mind. When asked why, he answered simply: 'I am now Minister of Marine.' This did not mean that he had changed his mind in order to become Minister of Marine, but that being Minister of Marine he had a different point of view." (*The Second World War*, Vol. II, p. 202.)

And Reynaud writes that Darlan often said at Vichy: "I did not create a Fleet to offer it to the British." (*La France a sauvé l'Europe*, p. 369.)

This was the man who, on June 3rd, had said to Jules Moch, ex-Minister in the Blum Government: "The Generals will no longer fight and the soldiers run away. If one day an armistice is sought I shall finish my career by an act of splendid indiscipline. I shall leave with the Fleet." (*La France a sauvé l'Europe*, p. 424.)

The lure of office certainly greatly influenced Darlan. Herriot is the most honest of men. He writes (in *Épisodes*, pp. 64–5) that he went to see Darlan on the morning of Saturday the 15th, hoping to obtain places for the ever increasing number of Deputies in a passenger ship. Darlan said this was impossible as he was preparing a large-scale operation for which he would need all his tonnage (presumably the transport of troops to Africa), "and he," writes Herriot, "drew me into the embrasure of a window and said brusquely: 'Is it true that those b——s Pétain and Weygand wish to conclude an armistice? If this is so, do you hear, I am leaving with the Fleet.' "

Next day (the 16th), after the fall of the Reynaud Government, Herriot says he met Darlan and, remembering the previous day's conversation, went up to him, hand extended, and said: "Admiral, you are doubtless taking steps for the departure of the Government" (to North Africa). "No," he answered. "A Government that leaves never returns"; and Herriot comments: "This Admiral knows how to swim" (*Épisodes*, p. 75).

Darlan at least does not deny the facts, however much they might run counter to his earlier declarations. Writing to Churchill on December 4th, 1942, he said: "If I did not consent to the French ships sailing for British harbours, it was because I knew this decision would lead to the total occupation of France and of North Africa." (Bouthillier, *Le Drame de Vichy*, p. 99.)

Reynaud has pointed out in his book that all the Ministers who were Deputies, including Chautemps, although they had enabled Pétain to achieve power, were later thrown out after they had been compromised in the overthrow of the Republic. Herriot has since written that this was a time when men held office for the identical reasons for which they would have been executed under Clemenceau, and that Bolo, had he lived under Vichy, would have been hoisted to power instead of being tied to a post and shot.*

We were also told that Paul Faure, the pacifist Socialist and Blum's opponent in the Party, was to have been included in the Government, but was later excluded because Pétain had discovered he was a pacifist! This was funny, or as funny as anything could be in this dreary, rotten, collapsing world of Bordeaux. What was the new Government but a pack of miserable pacifists?

Reynaud said that even Jeanneney and Herriot had come to the conclusion that as the whole Government were determined to support Pétain the only thing to do, although they thought it folly, was to permit the experiment of asking for an armistice to be tried, and "open the abscess". This does not appear to be an accurate account of their attitude.

The Ambassador and I stared at Reynaud. There was a silence. All words were useless now. I searched my mind to think of anything that was worth saying or doing and found nothing, only a growing realisation that there were two worlds in that room and Reynaud had left ours. The impression grew on me that he was dead, since he was not fighting any more. The last verse of *"Malbrouck s'en va t'en guerre"* sang in my memory. *"L'on vit partir son âme"* . . . There is not much one can say to a departing soul, so all I said to Reynaud's body, though with no great conviction, was "Will you come to England?" I did not believe he would, and was not surprised when he said no. He went on to explain, as if I had given him a cue he

* The other members of the Government were:
General Pujo—Air Minister
M. Frémicourt—Justice
M. Pomaret—Interior
M. Albert Rivière—Colonies
M. Albert Rivaud—Education
M. Frossard—Works and Transmissions
M. Chichery—Agriculture and Supplies
M. Février—Labour
M. Ybarnegaray—Ex-service men and families
M. R. Schuman—Under-Secretary refugees.

was anticipating, that if the Chautemps' *démarche* failed and the French Government, recognising their error, rejected the German terms, he might be recalled to office. I wondered if he had really made himself believe this; perhaps the Ambassador's impression was the same. Our views were not very different that day.

Reynaud was, I feel sure, quite aware that we thought he had failed. We knew and sympathised with his difficulties, but we assessed the opportunities he had missed, how he had allowed Pétain to dominate the situation and Weygand to bully him. He would no doubt have liked us to leave him at this our last interview with him as Prime Minister with a good impression so that we would pass it on, nothing was more natural, but he probably realised we had been too intimately concerned with events not to be disappointed in him, for we had but one measure by which to appraise men: the degree to which they stood up to defeatism.

The interview was turning into a mere conversation, the instinct of politeness led to the formation of phrases of doubtful significance. As the talk dragged on I saw a picture of Reynaud's Cabinet, composed in the main of frightened, bewildered men, subjected to blasts of bad news carefully timed to induce the maximum of discouragement, while the spectre of revolution was waved before their eyes, terrifying to their bourgeois mentalities. I could see the group of defeatists working for the surrender that was their victory, playing into each other's hands, producing this bogey or that as opportunity offered, while the others, the resisters, the *durs*, sat frustrated, angry and thwarted for lack of leadership.

Reynaud seemed to gain solace from just talking, but triviality reached its climax and the steadily growing distance separating us assumed the dimensions of light-years when he told us that his colleagues had been quite nice to him, especially the Marshal, who had assured him in the warmest tones that he hoped they would remain friends. The President of the Republic had asked him to remain at hand. He told us all this with satisfaction.

The impression he had given us earlier of a man relieved of a great burden returned. The idea he conveyed of the conversations he had had since his last Cabinet meeting was of a series of amiable talks among friends. He referred to Baudouin and others of his opponents in not unfriendly terms. But it was the attitude of the President of the Republic towards himself he wished to impress on us, for he referred to it again. "The President thought he might resort to me once more." This was of course, and quite naturally, what he wished Churchill to be told. It gave him stature, explained his decision to remain. He was the man of the day after tomorrow. But to us what the President of the Republic thought or did not think mattered very little. In any case, Lebrun may just have desired to show politeness, to ease the situation. His words probably meant nothing.

Talk, talk, the conversation we were engaged in was only a string of words on which any of us could place the interpretation he wished. Of only one thing can I be absolutely certain, and that is that not one of us, least of all Reynaud, guessed that on September 6th, forty-two days after this conversation, he would be arrested by Pétain; that, together with Mandel, he would be dragged from prison to prison in justifiable fear of his life (the Socialist Senator, Marx Dormoy, was murdered in July 1941 by Vichy by means of a time bomb placed under his pillow); and in November 1942 be handed over to the Germans in this same Bordeaux, put in an unwarmed cell where one bowl served for food and washing, and sent thence to a prison in Germany.

As he spoke on, the impression grew on me that, out of lassitude or reaction, he had taken refuge in escapism and had slipped into a world of unreality from which our activities appeared as a purposeless agitation which he was now able to observe objectively from afar.

He dissertated vaguely on this and that, hoped the matter of the Fleet would be settled to our satisfaction, an observation which I found trying, and then, suddenly remembering the projected meeting at Concarneau for the next day, asked at what time Churchill planned to arrive there. He would be glad to talk things over with him. He must ask the Marshal for a 'plane.

This made me angry. The idea that the Prime Minister should risk his invaluable life and others our nation could not spare, that at such a moment the direction of the war might be suspended, for what in fact would have been a chat with Reynaud, was more than I could bear.

The suggestion made it plain that the ex-Premier had lost all sense of reality. It was incompatible with any conception of what was at stake. For a moment I was overwhelmed with a sense of his being only a playboy.

A memory of the last war flashed into my mind. In place of Reynaud stood General Lanrezac in command of a fast retreating Army, and the long-forgotten voice was reciting, as I heard it recite long ago at Craonne, the verses of Horace: "Oh how much wiser is he who rather than go to war stays at home, caressing the breast of his mistress". So I said, as Churchill records: "Tomorrow there will be another Government and you will no longer speak for anyone. The meeting has been cancelled." This was perhaps unduly brutal, but I felt it necessary to underline the reality that we were fighting on and fighting alone now.*

The Ambassador made a sign. The interview was over. He and I shook hands with Reynaud; we had nothing more to say. I have not seen him since. A few days later, in London, Margerie told me that on leaving us Reynaud went into a drawing-room where Madame de Portes and their very beautiful friend, the Comtesse de Montgomery, were sitting. Reynaud sat down. He was tired but showed intense relief at being free of his burdens. After a moment he said, addressing the ladies: "I have prepared a really fine telegram for President Roosevelt." Then a pause, and: "I really must read you my telegram to President Roosevelt." Asking a secretary to fetch it, he read out his message with some complacency. I suppose it was the one that has been published, which ran:

"At the moment when I am giving up my post, I wish to tell you, Mr. President, that I know that the answer you gave to my last message went to the extreme limit of what was possible in present circumstances. I wish to express to you my extreme gratitude for this.

"In the immense misfortune which overwhelms us, France knows that, because America exists, the form of the civilisation which is hers will not die, and that one day freedom will live again in ancient Europe."

I was bitterly disappointed in Reynaud when I left him, but realised later that I had perhaps been unfair. He had always been quite straight with us, had never "double crossed" us and had fought for the Alliance to the best of his ability, against stronger men than he and bitter opposition in his most intimate circle.

* "In the evening I received the British Ambassador and General Spears and gave them an account of the conditions under which I had been overthrown. I was so convinced at that moment that I would resume power that I put the question as to whether I could keep the rendezvous with Churchill next day. But Spears objected with reason that this was not possible as I was no longer Prime Minister. One can judge (from this) whether I was 'discouraged' or 'down' as certain romanticised accounts of the armistice have made out." (*La France a sauvé l'Europe*, p. 366.)

True, he himself had placed these enemies where they could do him most harm, but that only proved he was a bad picker of men—and women—not that his heart was in the wrong place or that he lacked nobility and, courage. He did what he could, and, France having no Churchill, he was probably the best political leader she had.

On leaving Reynaud's study I at once looked for de Gaulle. He was standing bolt upright where we had left him, his back to the same column, in such a position as not to be seen from the entrance. The wait had evidently strained him still further. He was very white.

He repeated in a whisper that he had good reason to believe Weygand meant to have him arrested. He understood there was a British warship in the river. It was essential he should spend the night on board as it was the only place in Bordeaux where he would be safe. He wished to return to England as soon as possible.

The Ambassador had moved a few steps away. I made a sign and he joined us. We had a hurried conference and concluded that nothing could be decided in this sinister, shadowy hall where it was impossible to be certain we were not watched or overheard. In any case, to anyone entering the hall or indeed even to any passer-by the sight of the Ambassador and myself apparently addressing a column, our heads turned upwards like devotees of some invisible Simon Stylites as we spoke to the enormously tall de Gaulle, would be bound to attract the very attention we were seeking to avoid. The only place where we could talk was at the hotel, but how was de Gaulle to get there? Sir Ronald and I both thought it unwise to take him in the Ambassador's car as this would give a clue to the keen watchers we knew were about. The Hotel Montré was but five minutes away on foot, he must take his chance of getting there.

De Gaulle joined us quite soon, although he took longer than if he had walked straight there. In the Ambassador's room he repeated that Weygand intended either to arrest him or to order him to some distant place which would make it impossible for him to return to England.

But he was determined to go there, and it was essential that he should do so without delay. The fate of the French Empire was at stake. There was no one in France who would or could rally it now that Pétain and a team of defeatists had taken over. The call to continued resistance must be made at once before an appeal in the contrary sense was sent out from Bordeaux. If North Africa and the French Empire were to be saved, they could only be saved from England. A challenge to the defeatists could be sent out from there which he was certain would be heeded. He would give that call himself, let anyone join him who would.

The immediate problem was how to get away. The 'plane he had come in was at my disposal. He would like to return in it. He had been told that I would send the pilot his orders. He had thought it right to give provisional instructions that the aircraft should not fly back to England before 9 a.m. next day, unless the pilot heard from me.

De Gaulle was plainly overwrought. The shock of the news that an armistice was to be asked for, which he heard on landing, when only a few hours before he had been in the virile atmosphere of London and in contact with the indomitable Prime Minister, had been very great. He had arrived believing that his task would be to discuss the application of the British offer he had himself heard Reynaud welcome so fervently, and now he was met by this!

Then the question of his own security was extremely preoccupying. He must remain at liberty or his plans would be killed at birth. Clearly every effort must be made to help the solitary man prepared and willing to take the only steps likely to rally French opinion in favour of resistance.

As I listened to de Gaulle's short statement, I made up my mind. To help de Gaulle in his purpose was, I saw clearly, the only way of pursuing the mission the Prime Minister had entrusted to me. I believed passionately in the importance of continued French resistance, and here in Bordeaux there was nothing but the nauseating stench of defeat. With every hour that went by the tide of hope receded, revealing the unpleasant mud that the souls of slaves are made of.

I would return to England with de Gaulle and help him carry out his plan. He was right. It was essential that without a moment's delay, as an instant retort to Pétain's appeal for an armistice, the call of French resistance should be raised in England. It was obviously the only place from which this could be done. It was impossible to foretell what the attitude of the French authorities in North Africa or elsewhere would be. Now that Reynaud had resigned, de Gaulle, having ceased to be a Minister, would be merely the youngest Brigadier in the French Army, junior to all the regional authorities.

It was impossible to conceive of his successfully challenging Pétain's authority, from any part of the French Empire. If he attempted to do so he would, on grounds of seniority alone, excite the immediate antagonism of the entire French military hierarchy, which would suppress him.

I had a momentary qualm at the idea of leaving the Ambassador, who had shown himself so straight, so staunch and so kindly. But he was a diplomat, it was his job to deal with such situations. He would doubtless get away in his own good time. If I could have helped him it would have been different, but I could not. My work now lay in another direction. So, saying I had decided to ask the Prime Minister to allow me to bring de Gaulle to England, I went into Mack's room to try to get Churchill on the telephone. As I sat there the telephone rang. Unhooking the ear-trumpet-like receiver from over the bed, Mack answered. Astonishingly, it was the Duke of Windsor speaking from Nice. He was marooned there with the Duchess. Could a warship be sent to pick them up?

Mack knew this to be out of the question. There was not a chance of it, and he said so with suave but firm politeness. He was sorry to hear there was only a collier in the harbour. But was not the road to Spain open to motor-cars? I believe this was the means of escape the Duke adopted. We were all glad to hear later that he had reached safety.

In an incredibly short time my own call came through, and I took Mack's place, lying on the bed the better to manipulate the ear-trumpet on its short flex. I explained the latest events to the Prime Minister in guarded language, said I felt I was no longer useful where I was and that I wished to bring de Gaulle back to London with me next day. He was convinced he would be arrested if he remained and I thought so too. We were at that moment engaged in seeking a place where he could spend the night in safety. De Gaulle in England could do much to counteract the evil effects of the step the new régime was about to take. From there he could certainly help to keep the spirit of resistance alive.

Winston understood perfectly. The line was good, he only asked me to repeat one or two words. I could feel him hesitate. I think he saw at once de Gaulle's danger and the advantage of getting him out of France, but he did not see so clearly why I should come home. One or two questions made it plain that he was inclined to think I should stay on. I became insistent, pointing out that since I had been accredited to Reynaud in his capacity as Minister of Defence, as he was now eliminated and as there was no further defence, I had no longer any standing. What work remained to be done was exclusively within Campbell's sphere. I added that I could not trust myself to keep a civil tongue in my head if I met either Pétain or Weygand, nor could I see why I should at this stage. I was now free, I considered, to say what I pleased. I was emphatic on this score in my endeavour to make him realise that I should do more harm than good if I remained at Bordeaux.

"I am not sure," said the voice at the other end. "There is much to be done yet. There are some important matters to be settled," and I knew he was thinking of the Fleet. But I persisted: "Let me bring de Gaulle back and report to you, there is much to say, and if you wish me to return of course I will, but I want to come home tomorrow. I am now going to see our friend Georges Mandel, and I shall try to bring him over too." "All right," said the voice after another short pause, in not too pleased a tone, and I heard the receiver being put down.

I walked into the other room and told the Ambassador and de Gaulle that I had fixed it with the Prime Minister. When should we start?

It was decided that de Gaulle would come to the hotel at 7 a.m. and would go to the aerodrome with me in my car. I then said I would go to see Mandel, and left de Gaulle and the Ambassador whilst they waited for the emissaries who had been sent to scour the town in search of any officer of H.M.S. *Berkeley* they might find, so that de Gaulle could spend the night in the ship, safe from Weygand. The hotel, even if there had been room, was obviously not safe.

As I started for the *Préfecture* the dimmed street lights went out, which the driver took to mean there was an air-raid alarm. There were no sirens, probably none were installed. The drive through the heart of Bordeaux was difficult, for some streets were under repair and there were crowds milling in every direction. When we were stopped by an obstruction or a knot of people, I peered out in the hope of reading something of their thoughts, but, to my surprise, the faces I scanned in the dim light of the car's side-lamps showed only unconcern. There was hardly any sound save of footsteps. Citizens and refugees were just seeking news, driven hither and thither by rumour and curiosity.

The *Préfecture* was in complete darkness. I felt my way up the stairs until I reached a landing where two *sergents-de-ville* had just lighted a candle they were busy fixing in an inkwell. With this they showed me the way. A door was opened and I found myself in what seemed the largest, or rather the longest, room I had ever seen. It was, perhaps, a gallery, I could not tell, for the only light was a single candle at the far end on a very small table on the window side. At this sat Georges Mandel, his face a small white dab in the distance.

As I approached and his features became discernible, his usual pallor stood out eerily against the dense mass of shadows. These made me feel uncomfortable. They seemed to be solid yet impalpable objects with a strange quality of watchfulness. They were compact, tall and still, but alert; they advanced without moving, stealing on me as I proceeded down the immense room, freezing into immobility as soon as I paused to observe them.

I sat down by Mandel. He told me again that Reynaud had read the British proposal twice to the Cabinet, but without fire, without conviction, as a lawyer reading a document. It had fallen flat, had dropped out of the discussion almost unobserved.

"But," I interjected, "Reynaud was bursting with enthusiasm when it was made to him." "Well," answered Mandel, "when he felt that it evoked no enthusiasm, even from his friends, he became discouraged. It was like pressing the trigger and the cartridge not going off. When that happened he felt disarmed. He then picked up the old points, the old arguments he had used before, but he knew they were ineffective.

"He showed lassitude after that except when Baudouin riled him by claiming more than once that Churchill had given France leave to ask for an armistice. He retorted that he had lately refreshed his memory and looked at Margerie's notes of the Tours Conference. These showed that Churchill had said nothing of the sort.

"The defeatists formed a solid block, lending each other support. Chautemps, seeing his opportunity, renewed his proposal of the day before to ask the German conditions for an armistice.

"I had said nothing up to then," said Mandel, "but I felt that now was the time to speak. Not only was I exasperated, but I thought that I might obtain a reaction by forcing my colleagues, by a violent intervention, to face the realities of the situation, so I told them the position was simple, there were, sitting round the table, brave men and cowards. Feeling the cap fitted him, Chautemps picked it up and drew it down over his ears. Using the scraps of bad news that had of course been continuously passed in to us, notably the information that Blois had been bombed, he said furiously that the only question before us was whether we should go on making ourselves responsible for the massacre of the French nation. That clinched it." I was listening to a story I now knew by heart.

"What is the next move?" I asked him, and volunteered my own view that, as there was nothing more to be done in Bordeaux, the sooner the voice of French resistance was heard elsewhere the better. Obviously it could not be raised in a France governed by Pétain. Nothing but praise of the armistice would now be tolerated. North Africa? It was under Pétain's control. Would the authorities there throw him over? They would not, save in answer to a powerful appeal, and that appeal to all Frenchmen of good will to pursue the struggle could only be made from England, since she alone was fighting on. From England it would be possible to communicate with the high authorities in North Africa and elsewhere in an endeavour to make them throw in their lot with ours. Someone whose name was known and carried weight must make them see the shame of accepting defeat while they were undefeated and it was still possible to fight for France. So I begged Mandel either to fly over with de Gaulle and me next morning or to go in the destroyer. As he said nothing, and remembering the lady to whom he was known to be deeply attached, I said there would be two places for him, although we would be hard-pressed to take our own compatriots.

As he still did not answer, I said I had spoken to the Prime Minister within the half-hour and told him that I was going to ask him to come. "Reynaud has refused," I went on, and I repeated doggedly: "There must be an authorised French voice, not pledged to surrender, to guide the French Empire."

"I will consider it," answered Mandel. I persisted that I wanted to make all arrangements before I left, and then suddenly remembered he was a Jew. I recalled the fear I had seen in other Jews that day, and this made me realise he ran a special danger, the more so that the Germans had proclaimed their hatred of him. They rightly assessed his value as a clever and implacable enemy. I felt too that no act however vile would come as a surprise from some of the defeatists now in charge. Would a man who betrayed the honour of his country stop at betraying a colleague?

As if he read my thoughts he said: "You fear for me because I am a Jew. Well, it is just because I am a Jew that I will not go tomorrow; it would look as if I was afraid, as if I was running away. Wednesday, perhaps."

"It may be too late."

"I will not go tomorrow."

Just then a small door level with us on the other side of the hall opened. There must have been several candles in the room thus suddenly revealed, and their light played on a woman's fair hair. I guessed rather than recognised Mademoiselle Bretty's plump, pleasant features. She was peeping round the door. She looked at us both, then I heard her voice for the first and last time, a pleasant, gay, friendly voice which I have not forgotten. Its tone had an inflection of slight urgency and pleading, like that of a child asking with arms upheld to be picked up. "*Les malles sont faites, Georges,*" it said.—"The trunks are packed." Whether she had heard an echo of our voices in the great silent chamber and hoped Mandel would accept my offer and was thus hinting she would like him to agree to it, I do not know. The door closed. I rose. "*À bientôt, à très bientôt à Londres, j'espère,*" I said. "In London soon." I never saw him again. He was murdered by Vichy on July 7th, 1944. He had been handed over to the Germans together with Reynaud in November 1942, then was returned by them to the Vichy Government. The poor opinion I formed of the Vichy gang at its inception was amply justified.*

Mademoiselle Bretty stuck to Mandel, I was told, with the utmost courage and devotion and, I think, married him.

He was a great man. His intelligence struck all who came in contact with him. His memory was prodigious, his courage astounding. The story of how he forced Pétain to apologise to him for his arrest at Bordeaux not long after I left, and how, not thinking the terms used by the Marshal sufficiently comprehensive, he himself dictated to him a new formula, is a gem which is, however, outside the frame of my story. Men of his religion may well be proud of him. I purposely do not say "race", for he was French and nothing else, his

---

* "The death of Mandel, on the subject of which I questioned Laval during my false liberation in August 1944, was a revolting murder. Laval declared to me that Hitler had returned Mandel to France to serve as hostage when the Algiers Government was taking severe measures against the traitors. Sent to Paris and locked up in the Santé prison, the Governor of that establishment was said to have sent him by road without instruction or authorisation . . ." (Edouard Herriot, *Épisodes*, 1940–1944, p. 61.)

qualities were French, and he possessed the finer of these in more abundant measure and in higher degree than most of his contemporaries.

After leaving Mandel I returned to the hotel. The crowds on the way were noticeably less dense. De Gaulle had gone. As no officer of the *Berkeley* had been located and time was passing, he had thought it not over-safe to prolong his stay with us. He had not said where he was going, but had confirmed his appointment with me for next morning.

I had a talk with the Ambassador and Oliver Harvey. I regretted leaving them and felt I was running away, though I still thought my decision was right. They thought so too. We did not realise that as we spoke the machinery prepared to serve defeat was working with an efficiency unknown to the organs which had favoured resistance. According to Baudouin, two men were waiting at St. Jean de Luz for the telephone message asking Spain to transmit France's request for an armistice. They were to jump into a car, drive over the frontier to Irun and thence telephone the news to Madrid.

Campbell and I worked on at dispatches till 2.30 a.m., and at 3.30, whilst I was packing, he came in to read me some further ones of his own. During these interchanges he conveyed to me that he was really sorry I was leaving, and this, coming from so reserved and shy a man, greatly touched me. We had faced together a great ordeal in complete harmony, misfortune had drawn us together instead of driving us apart as it so often does. The slight difficulty and awkwardness due to my anomalous position when I had first come to Paris had long since disappeared.

I shall always feel the same about Ronny Campbell. It was only in great emergencies that he revealed himself in the full measure of his courage and calmness. There was no acid and no explosive capable of eating into or denting the solid steel of his integrity. It was only under great stress that the inner sweetness and kindliness of the man flowed out, like juice squeezed from a fruit under strong pressure. The exquisite tact he often displayed was born of delicate feelings generally encased in rather frigid manners, but the least appeal to his heart caused these to thaw, melted in the smile of his clear blue eyes.

CHAPTER XX

Monday, June 17th

A trying wait for de Gaulle—British officers' picture of the French collapse—De Gaulle and de Courcel arrive at last—A comedy of red herrings—The scene at the airport—De Gaulle and I rehearse our parts—The ordeal of the missing length of string—I haul de Gaulle into the 'plane—The sinking of the Champlain—*The British dumps on fire—We refuel at Jersey—De Gaulle's martyrdom begins—Churchill welcomes him at Number* 10.

I WAS up at six, waiting for de Gaulle in the empty, stuffy hall of the hotel. Two British officers walked in as I sat watching the door. They had come to Bordeaux hoping to obtain transport for some British wounded in a French hospital, and wanted to know where to make for when they had obtained it. They were disgusted and bewildered by what they had seen on the way and could hardly believe their eyes. There were plenty of ambulances on the roads, but these had been commandeered by drunken troops and inebriated women. Many lorries were loaded with the same unsavoury cargoes, but what they simply could not understand was that the officers seemed everywhere to have disappeared. They had seen none in the villages, where the men stood about in morose groups, nor had they observed any with the rare columns of troops on the march.

There must of course have been cases when officers did remain with their men, and this was certainly so with many armoured formations,* but these were the exceptions, and all the information presently received in England confirmed this distressing account. It was hardly credible, but then would anyone have believed that

---

* Evidence of Commandant Ragaine at the Riom Trial: "He was evacuated from Dunkirk to England with his armoured unit, whose morale was very high. On return to France they were not given tanks, not even rifles or machine-guns. At Bazas, south of Bordeaux, his men came to him in tears saying: 'Come and see!' They led him to a place where a whole battalion of R-40 brand-new tanks, complete in every way and which had never been employed, were burning. The men cried: 'If only we had had these tanks at Evreux!'—these tanks were of the most recent 'B' type."

in this same Bordeaux we were now in, a few days later, the shops would refuse to sell food to the English nurses who had looked after their wounded?

It was now 7 o'clock, the time at which de Gaulle was to have appeared, but there was no sign of him. By a quarter past I was concerned, by half past really worried. I sent up to call the Air Attaché, hoping we could concoct some scheme to find out if de Gaulle had been arrested. If he had, we should have to find some means of releasing him at least for long enough to get him to the aerodrome and on to the 'plane. I do not think Air Commodore Colyer had appeared before de Gaulle arrived with his A.D.C. This was Lieutenant de Courcel, a tall, thin, young man who was a diplomat by profession. He was reserved, well-bred, and turned out to be very long-suffering. He was pleasant-looking, although he would have had no difficulty in holding a walnut between the tips of his nose and chin. I do not know where they had spent the night.

They had brought quite a lot of luggage, which was stowed away in my car, and then, at de Gaulle's request, a curious little comedy was played. It was intended to mislead as to his true intentions, which, if suspected, might, and probably would, have started a hue and cry after him. The stratagem consisted in conveying the impression that he was quietly driving about Bordeaux on his lawful occasions.

If his intended departure was not suspected, it was unlikely that any immediate step would be taken to arrest him even if this was Weygand's intention. He had more important matters to deal with at the moment. On the other hand, if it was reported that de Gaulle was on the way to the aerodrome, a telephone call to the Commandant would have brought the adventure to an end before it started. So we drove to the two separate buildings where what there was of the Ministry of War was lodged, and de Gaulle, without leaving the car, the engine of which the chauffeur was ordered to keep running so as to be able to make a dash for it if necessary, told officials whom he sent for at both places to make a series of appointments for him with people he named, at specific times later in the morning. I do not think they yet knew the Government had fallen or that de Gaulle was no longer their chief. By this time I was enacting the part I had often seen on the films, of the individual who suddenly finds himself involved in unpredictable adventure. This may have been the reason why I thought that an official at one of our halts looked at me with suspicious and wide-awake curiosity, evidently wondering what I was doing in that car. Happily someone had thought of covering the baggage with overcoats, or that man, whose expression I can still recall, would have guessed what was afoot. I glanced at de Gaulle. He showed neither strain nor anxiety.

The last bogus appointment made, the chauffeur was told to step on it and we drove to the aerodrome at speed. It was quite a long way.

Getting past the guard at the entrance was, to me at least, a moment of acute anxiety, but there was no trouble. Beyond the hangars we beheld an extraordinary and unforgettable scene. The aerodrome was filled with more flying-machines than I have ever seen in one place either before or since, packed wing to wing as far as one could see. It was evident that every machine capable of taking the air had been collected, presumably in readiness to fly to Morocco. It was shocking to see them offering such a fabulous target. Since when had they left their armies? Why were they not taking off for Africa? How long had they been collected there like a great herd of flying sheep? There was no sign whatever of any machine making ready to leave. So this was the French counterpart to the R.A.F. at Dunkirk, I thought bitterly.

We found the British 'plane without too much difficulty; it was more tricky getting the car to it owing to the congestion, but it had to be done so as not to draw attention to the luggage. The pilot and his crew were pleasant, efficient men, as in my experience they always are; furthermore, they radiated a post-breakfast cheerfulness which aroused echoes of hunger in the emptiness of my own inside.

The pilot's only preoccupation was how to find space to take off, so closely were the 'planes packed together. Many had landed since he had arrived the previous evening.

Whilst he was cogitating and reconnoitring, de Gaulle and I discussed a little act. He would behave as if he had come to see me off, and at the last moment I was to haul him on board. It was quite possible that amongst the many officers standing about there might be someone watching him, ready to prevent his leaving.

Then suddenly a new difficulty arose. The pilot declared it was essential that de Gaulle's luggage, some of which was heavy, should be lashed. He had, I think, sent ahead a particularly heavy trunk. There was neither cord nor string on the 'plane, so the crew began to work with a will to release from the wooden wheel-blocks the stiff ropes used to pull them away before the machine starts, but do what they would, tearing their nails in a way painful to behold, they could not manage it. There was nothing for it, a ball of string must be found. Courcel set off at the double and soon disappeared in the shoal of 'planes. He was probably not gone for more than ten minutes, but I remember them as holding quite a high priority among the unpleasant periods of waiting I have experienced. De Gaulle showed little and said less, but I noted later in the 'plane that he must have found the tension excruciating. I chatted with the chauffeur, I chatted with de Gaulle, with the crew, then climbed on board to see if, like Sister Ann, I could see anyone coming. It was very trying. There could evidently be no question of leaving the boxes behind to be investigated by Weygand's men. I gathered they contained important papers. On the other hand time was passing, and the possibility of de Gaulle's departure from Bordeaux being detected was increasing. Somebody was sure to think of him in the course of the morning, then steps would be taken to locate him. If it occurred to anyone that he had gone, the aerodrome would be the natural place to look for him. Someone would remember having seen me in the car with him, that would be the clue. Then there would be a telephone call. Thank God the telephone service at Bordeaux was working incredibly badly. At last Courcel appeared, his stilt-like legs carrying him fast, though he appeared to be moving in slow motion. In his hand he carried a ball of string. I hope that never again will this commonplace article be so important to me. Our troubles were over. In a very short time the pilot announced that all was ready. The propellers started making their little private hurricanes. I bade my chauffeur a very sincere and affectionate farewell. He was only an ordinary French chap, but the salt of the earth like a few million others.

We had begun to move when with hooked hands I hoisted de Gaulle on board. Courcel, more nimble, was in in a trice. The door slammed. I just had time to see the gaping face of the chauffeur and one or two more beside him. Gingerly we taxied till the pilot found the space he had located, then with great skill, in a very short distance, he took off. I opened a local paper. It contained a eulogistic article concerning de Gaulle. The subject of the article, on the other side of the gangway, looked straight before him. Churchill, no bad judge in such matters, has written that he "carried with him, in this small aeroplane, the honour of France." I set to writing my notes.

In what seemed a matter of minutes we were flying over the sea

General Spears with General de Gaulle

The Vichy Government

between the island of Oléron and La Pallice. Having spent a pleasant month sailing on that coast two years earlier, I was busy locating the coves and landmarks I remembered when suddenly I beheld a terrible sight. A great ship was lying on her side, sinking. Hundreds of tiny figures could be seen in the water. It was the *Champlain*, with two thousand British troops on board.

We cut across Brittany. We were flying low and the entire country-side seemed to be on fire, for there was smoke everywhere. I thought it was the Germans burning villages, but was told later they were British Army dumps being destroyed. There must have been many of them.

Then we were over the sea. The short waves in long, disciplined rows were moving towards us; the sun set a spark on each and they became, as I watched, an immense army, a myriad riders with spears set and glinting, charging forward against any enemy who in his folly might dare to invade England. It was strangely comforting— too much so perhaps, for I found I was indulging in smug satisfaction, a rajah watching the defeat of an opposing army from the safety of his elephant.

The vision vanished, blotted out by a mist which rolled in from the sea as we touched down at Jersey for petrol. It was chilly. No one was about save a few mechanics. The place seemed abandoned, but there was a very pretty, unconcerned woman in charge of the canteen. I asked de Gaulle if he wanted anything, and he said he would like a cup of coffee. I handed it to him, whereupon, taking a sip, he said, in a voice which indicated that without implying criticism he must nevertheless proclaim the truth, that this was tea and he had asked for coffee. It was his first introduction to the tepid liquid which, in England, passes for either one or the other.

His martyrdom had begun.

I said this to myself as I watched him, interested and amused; then, with a sense of contrition deepening into one of intense self-reproach, I realised more vividly than before that there was nothing but this man's courage to kindle into flame the tiny spark of hope he had brought with him; all that was now left of the spirit of France.

We landed at Heston. The weather was beautiful again. I gave my French guests a late lunch at the R.A.C., and then took de Gaulle to Downing Street. Winston was sitting in the garden enjoying the sunshine. He got up to greet his guest, and his smile of welcome was very warm and friendly.

Index

GENERAL MAP OF
FRANCE & BELGIUM

St.
Tr
Diepp

Cherbourg

COTENTIN PENINSULA

le Havre

Rou

Elboeuf

Caen

NORMAN

Evre

D

Brest

St. Malo

BRITTANY

Rennes

le Mans

Concarneau

Lorient

Langeais

To

Saumur

Cang Ch

St. Nazaire

Nantes

F R

La Rochelle

La Pallice

Isle
d'Oléron

Limoge

Gironde

Beauvais

Compiègne

Soissons

Villers-
Cotterets

Bordeaux

Crépy

Senlis

Arcachon

Garonne

L'Isle Adam

Pontoise

Surésnes

PARIS

Meaux

Bayonne

Vincennes

St-Cloud

Versailles

MLS. O   10   20 MLS.

MLS.20   0   40